9/17/06

To Lew ...ister,

Best wishes,

*The Songs That Fought the War*

# THE SONGS THAT
# FOUGHT THE WAR

Popular Music and the Home Front, 1939–1945

John Bush Jones

*Brandeis University Press*   WALTHAM, MASSACHUSETTS

Published by University Press of New England : Hanover and London

BRANDEIS UNIVERSITY PRESS

Published by University Press of New England,

One Court Street, Lebanon, NH 03766

www.upne.com

© 2006 by Brandeis University Press

Printed in the United States of America

5   4   3   2   1

Library of Congress Cataloging-in-Publication Data

Jones, John Bush.

The songs that fought the war : popular music and the home front, 1939–1945 / John Bush Jones. — 1st ed.

    p.   cm.

Includes bibliographical references and index.

ISBN-13: 978–1–58465–443–8 (cloth : alk. paper)

ISBN-10: 1–58465–443–0 (cloth : alk. paper)

1. World War, 1939–1945—Music and the war.   2. Popular music—United States—1931–1940—History and criticism.   3. Popular music—United States—1941–1950—History and criticism.   I. Title.

ML3477.J68 2006

782.42'15990973—dc22    2006016247

*To Big Al Pavlow*
*for his infinite knowledge of the music business*
*and popular song, and for his generosity in sharing it*

# Contents

    Victory, Homecomings, the World after the War

    Bibliography                                                        295

    Index of Song Titles                                               301

    General Index                                                      315 brief section of *Our Musicals, Ourselves* about the media and entertainment industries vis-à-vis the war, I became aware that while there are good, comprehensive full-length books about war-related journalism, movies, and even cooking, there is no comparable comprehensive account of popular music related to the war. The few books that treat it at all are so narrow in their scope, and in some ways so unreliable, that they fail to present a broad as well as deep picture of the songs World War II inspired or occasioned. Accordingly, I decided to tackle the subject of what makes American popular music during World War II so singular—namely, the thousands of songs that touched on the war directly or by implication, and how those songs relate to the social history of the home front.

The basis of this book is the lyrics, and occasionally the music, of the songs themselves. For about a year, five days a week, I worked with the extensive sheet music collection in the John Hay Library at Brown University, either transcribing the lyrics or photocopying the sheet music of war-related songs in the library's special collection of World War II music, its 1,400 boxes of sheet music of American popular songs (arranged alphabetically by title), and about five hundred boxes of songs written for the musical stage or Hollywood musical films (not to mention the library's small but important collection of Yiddish-American songs). Even after a year spent collecting the lyrics of around 1,400 songs, I still came up empty for about three hundred other war-related titles I had gleaned from bibliographies and other finding-lists of American popular song, so I spent a month at the Library of Congress to supplement my findings at the John Hay. Curiously, while I in fact discovered there about three hundred new songs to add to my database (used in the informal, not technological, sense), most were different from the three hundred titles I had found in reference works. For many of those, there were not even copyright registrations in the U.S. Copyright Office. Others, quite frankly, the Performing Arts Division of the Library of Congress couldn't put its hands on. Still, overall I amassed a file of just about 1,700 songs by professional songwriters and a few other writers published by professional ASCAP, BMI, or SESAC-affiliated music publishers. (And new songs surface all the time, usually via wartime recordings reissued on CDs.) As detailed more fully in the first two chapters, I also began while still at Brown to transcribe pieces by amateur songwriters, but at the Library of Congress I discovered that the output of such songs was so vast, yet reached so few people, they were beyond the scope of this book except in a general way in chapter 2. With few exceptions, I further narrowed the field to exclude from my base of popular songs all concert pieces and other "art songs," choral works, and songs written for specific schools, churches, or civic organizations. So while this book is comprehensive in its coverage of professionally written war-related songs, I do not pretend that it's exhaustive of all World War II American songwriting. The body of songs remaining after these exclusions represents the songs that were heard, or had the best chance of being heard, by large segments of the American public, because they were published and promoted by professional publishing houses, recorded by major artists on major record labels, or, at the very least, performed in Hollywood films or on the radio. And I can say with complete confidence that thanks to the data provided by the various charts of song popularity and radio plays, I have overlooked virtually no war-related song that found a home front audience, however modestly or briefly.

For the most part I limited my reliance on secondary materials to those providing background information on the war and life on the home front, and to the invaluable retrospective charts of record popularity in the year-by-year volumes of *Hot Charts*. But between the songs themselves and the contemporary entertainment-industry trade journals *Billboard* and *Variety*, this account of war-related songs in the context of the home front's social history derives almost exclusively from primary sources.

There are some idiosyncrasies in my text. First, song titles are printed with every word capitalized, including prepositions and articles (for example, "With My Head In The Clouds"), which was the prevailing convention for titles in the sheet music of popular songs published during the 1930s and '40s. Similarly, when a song's title appears as a part of a lyric being quoted, the title is reproduced exactly as it was in the original sheet music—sometimes in ALL CAPITALS, sometimes With Every Word Capitalized, and, in a few instances, printed normally as part of the phrase or sentence containing the title. Also, the abbreviation of military ranks and titles follows the conventions of the war years. Rather than using footnotes, I cite within the text references to the secondary works listed in the bibliography according to the system of parenthetical documentation laid out in the *MLA Style Manual*. The exception to this is that no citation is given for sources of such factual information as biographical, recording, and motion picture data that can be readily found in standard discographies, filmographies, and other published reference works (for example, the *ASCAP Biographical Dictionary*) or online (for example, the "International Movie Database"). The sheet music itself does not appear in the bibliography, because the enormous number of songs mentioned or discussed would make the bibliography (and the whole book) unwieldy. Instead, at the first mention of a song (unless it first appears just as one title in an illustrative list of songs), parenthetical publishing information is provided following the song's title in the text. If the publishing house was in New York City, no city is named (for example, Chappell, 1944); if elsewhere, the city is identified (Hollywood: Saunders, 1943). The date on published sheet music is the copyright date of the song and not the date the song was published, which in some cases was a year or more after the piece was copyrighted. Also, publishing information is given only for the war-related songs that are the subject of this book, not for other songs incidentally referred to from time to time. Finally, when writing about America's young men and women during the war, whether in songs or in real life on the home front or overseas, most of the time I have used the common parlance of the day by referring to them as boy(s) and girl(s) rather than the more politically correct "men" and "women" by today's standards. To do otherwise would falsify the picture of the war years in America and, especially, the ways these boys and girls referred to themselves and were referred to by others.

The plan of the book is very straightforward. The first two chapters, respectively, deal with the state of the music business during the war and a sort of "demographic" overview of who wrote the thousands of war-related songs, professionals and amateurs alike. The remaining ten chapters deal with the songs themselves, according to the topics those songs treated. These chapters are also roughly chronological, according to either when a particular kind of song first began to appear or when a type of song reached the height of its popularity.

A lot of people helped in the making of this book. First, there is the institutional support (not in the financial sense) of two great research libraries. I am tremendously grateful to Henry Grossi, Head of Reader Services in the Performing Arts Reading Room of the Library of Congress, and his staff for helping me to navigate and negotiate the often arcane and labyrinthine system of sheet music cataloguing in our national library; they all helped make my month there both productive and pleasant. Because I worked in them for over a year, I owe an even greater debt of thanks to the libraries of Brown University and their staffs. While most of my work was in the John Hay Library with the sheet music itself, I also must acknowledge the helpfulness of Ned Quist, Music Librarian of the Orwig Music Library, and his staff, and Edwin Hayslip, Periodicals Specialist in the Rockefeller Library. But mostly it was the John Hay Library that was my "home away from home" (actually about seven minutes away by car) for my year of research there. And I mean that expression in more ways than one might at first imagine. I have worked in major research libraries from Los Angeles to London, but I have never done so in an atmosphere of greater helpfulness and congeniality—no, downright friendliness—and actual enthusiasm for my project than I encountered at the John Hay. Those who made my stay especially wonderful are Rosemary Cullen, Head Special Collections Librarian and Curator; Ann Patrick, Curatorial Assistant; Andy Moul, Pat Sirois, and Alison Bundy of Reader

Services; and Peter Harrington, Curator of the Anne S. K. Brown Military Collection, a definite asset to have around when you're writing a book about songs during World War II. Before leaving libraries, I must also acknowledge the great assistance I got from the Providence Public Library and the public libraries of Cranston and Pawtucket, Rhode Island, most specifically for having some books of a more "popular" nature that were important for my topic.

Quite at the opposite end of the spectrum from the tangible sheet music, books, records, periodicals, and microforms in the libraries where I did my research are the people who over the two and a half years of this project gave me that most intangible yet invaluable necessity for such an undertaking—moral support and encouragement. For this, and sometimes even more, I owe a lot to my son, Carson, and his wife, Dawn, and my friends Claudia Novack, Susan Ormont, Judy Stillman, Sarah Rachel Orleck, Tina Provencher, Bob and Elva Mathiesen, Lisa Long, attorney Jerry Cohen, and doctors Bruce Fischberg and Charles Sherman.

Finally there are those people, some already friends, others who have become friends during the course of my work, who in various ways directly helped in the research or writing of the book. Two former colleagues at Brandeis University gave me great assistance in putting together the section on war-related Yiddish-American songs—Professor Jonathan Sarna of the Department of Near Eastern and Judaic Studies for information on American Jewish demographics, and Professor Sylvia Fried, Executive Director of the Tauber Institute for the Study of European Jewry, for her expertise in Yiddish and for taking the time to read the songs I had photocopied and translating relevant portions for me. Equally invaluable was the readiness of Nick Marcovich, Executive Administrator and Archivist of The Yip Harburg Foundation, to provide me with copies of unpublished lyrics by E. Y. Harburg and a great deal of unpublished information about this singularly original lyricist. Since I am no musician myself, I owe much to the input of my two informal music consultants, long-time friend and Boston-area musical director Jonathan Goldberg, and a new friend I met when she was a student assistant in the John Hay Library, Michelle Menard, who—thanks to her double major in music and applied mathematics at Brown—was not only a music consultant but my computer consultant as well.

Like *Your Hit Parade* saving the top three songs till the end of the program each week, I have saved for the end three very special people without whom, quite literally, this book could not have taken the form that it has. It was quite by accident while working in the John Hay that I met a "regular" there named John "Mad" Peck, a man with considerable expertise in many things, from comic books to graphic design, and, of course, popular music. John first alerted me to the existence of the so-called lyric magazines, monthly pulp magazines published during the war years that reprinted the lyrics of popular (and not-so-popular) songs, of which the John Hay has random but extensive holdings. These turned out to be a valuable source of lyrics for which I could locate no available sheet music. John also told me about a series of retrospective charts of phonograph-record popularity compiled by popular music historian, record collector, and former music store owner Big Al Pavlow. I immediately purchased the volumes of *Hot Charts* for the war years, and they proved to be an indispensable source of information for this account of wartime songs. John Peck also, and perhaps even more importantly, gave me Big Al Pavlow's phone number, and in a series of lengthy phone calls throughout the writing of the book Big Al shared with me his encyclopedic knowledge of the music business and popular music, and especially phonograph records. Yet more significantly, he taught me how to think about the music business and the trade paper charts during the war years. In a very real way, then, though he is not often cited directly, Big Al's input and presence are at the very core of this book.

It's only fitting to conclude with the person who has become virtually my collaborator through the writing of two books published by Brandeis University Press/University Press of New England, its Editor-in-Chief and my editor for this book, as she was for *Our Musicals, Ourselves,* Phyllis Deutsch. Once again it was Phyllis who not only helped shape the book as a whole but also helped me shape and reshape much of my writing. As demanding and particular as before (but just as easy to negotiate with), Phyllis made the writing and revising of the book go not only smoothly but with a speed that surprised both of us. (Well, I guess I helped a little by not handing her a 750-page manuscript this time!) To Phyllis and all the rest mentioned above I give my sincerest thanks for helping bring to fruition what has been, in many ways, a labor of love.

J.B.J.
*Providence, Rhode Island*
*October 16, 2005*

*The Songs That Fought the War*

# "When This Crazy World Is Sane Again"

## The Setting for the Songs

Poet/singer/songwriter Rod McKuen once remarked that "1939–1945 was a terrible time for the world, but it was a glorious time for songs and fighter pilots" ("A Salute . . ."). He was right on both counts. World War II was the costliest war the world has ever known, one source reporting that *worldwide* it "took the lives of 40 million civilians and men in uniform" and cost in terms of property destroyed and "direct military expenditures" over four trillion dollars (*Life's* 361).

For the American home front, however, the war years comprised the longest sustained period of national unity in this country's history. Partly because the Axis Powers posed a threat to freedom globally (including in America) and partly because everyone in the United States had to cope with the same exigencies of home front conditions such as rationing, shortages, and the inconvenience of blackouts and air raid drills, support for the war was nearly unanimous (see Perrett 215, Bailey 23).

The war years were also one of the most fertile periods of songwriting, performance, and recording in the twentieth century. In the *New York Times* on May 17, 1942, Irving Berlin averred, "Songs make history. History makes songs." To confirm that they indeed make history, one need only look at the runaway popularity achieved by Berlin's own "White Christmas" (Irving Berlin Inc., 1942) during the war (and ever since). And history also helped "make" the song, since much of its popularity came from the way "White Christmas" appealed to both the home front and GIs abroad longing for simpler, more tranquil times. But World War II also "made" songs in a larger sense by inspiring or occasioning the writing, publishing, and recording of thousands of songs by thousands of composers and lyricists, both professional career songwriters and amateurs (see chapter 2).

Moreover, the war years were the years of the great "big bands"— Tommy and Jimmy Dorsey, Harry James, Duke Ellington, Artie Shaw, Kay Kyser, Glenn Miller, and many more. It was the time too of such distinctive vocalists as Bing Crosby, Frank Sinatra, Dick Haymes, Dinah Shore, Helen Forrest, and Kitty Kallen, not to mention those three ladies whose perky presence and close harmonies were in many ways the central icon of wartime music, the Andrews Sisters. Such popular bands, vocalists, and singing groups did not ignore war-related music but integrated it into the general fare of romantic ballads, rhythm numbers, dance tunes, and novelty songs. Numbers directly or obliquely associated with the war entered the repertoires of virtually all popular artists on recordings, on the radio, or in live concert or ballroom appearances, and many such songs that were popular then have remained standards— classics in the annals of American popular song—to the present day. The success of many such songs lies in their writers' wisely couching war-related subject matter in the familiar forms of the romantic ballads, rhythm numbers, dance tunes, and novelty numbers (rather than, say, militant marches or patriotic anthems). But to appreciate and understand the quantity and quality of the actual war-related songs themselves, it helps first to place them in the context of the internecine battles in the wartime music industry and similar skirmishes with Washington over what should be considered "appropriate" wartime songs. These bits of stateside World War II history comprise the remainder of this chapter.

### "S-N-A-F-U (Situation Normal All Fouled Up)": The Music Industry during the War

The title of this 1943 Redd Evans song about glitches in army life also encapsulates the problems within the American music business that began long before the United States entered the global conflict on December 7, 1941, following the Japanese attack on Pearl Harbor. In fact, ever since its founding in 1914, the American Society of Composers, Authors, and Publishers (ASCAP) had fought numerous legal battles and other challenges on its way to becoming the exclusive licensing agent and collector of royalties for the works of its member-songwriters and publishers. Restaurants, nightclubs, theatres, dance halls, and—eventually—radio stations and motion pictures that featured live musical performances had to pay ASCAP a monthly or yearly licensing fee. Since ASCAP controlled most of the music written and published in the United States after 1884 (Malone 178), it effectively licensed nearly any song performers wanted to perform and audiences wanted to hear. But less than a year before Pearl Harbor, in a classic instance of overreaching, ASCAP's attempt to further tighten its stranglehold backfired into a gradual but irreversible weakening of its virtual music licensing monopoly.

On December 31, 1940, ASCAP's five-year contract with radio broadcasters, under which networks and their local affiliates had been paying roughly $4.5 million annually for music licensing, expired. Now ASCAP was demanding about double their previous fees, or approximately $9 million. Needless to say, the radio executives balked. On January 1, 1941, the broadcasters pulled all ASCAP-controlled music from the airways, filling the void with tunes "in the public domain, . . . hillbilly [country] music, folk songs, and songs by young and inexperienced writers who had no ASCAP affiliation" (Ewen 303). By October 1941, ASCAP and the networks came to terms, but instead of increased fees ASCAP had to settle for even less than before, just $3 million annually. Previous to this trouble from ASCAP, on October 14, 1939, the National Association of Broadcasters had set up a rival licensing agency, Broadcast Music, Inc. (BMI), which, in the long run, seriously damaged ASCAP's tight control. BMI started small but gained strength during the war, signing on numerous songwriters and publishers, some defecting from ASCAP's ranks (see Ewen 300–304; Malone 178–79; Sanjek 184–211, 251–61).

With only a few small independent radio stations airing ASCAP songs for nearly ten months in 1941, it seems a minor miracle that the society's songwriters continued to write and its publishers to publish—and to make money doing so—during that time. But they did. Traditionally, new songs were "plugged" on the radio, not specifically by the recording artist but frequently by studio bands and vocalists, and this plugging was a tremendous source of free advertising for record companies and sheet music publishers. But for those ten months there was no such plugging of ASCAP songs. And yet the music industry survived, with sheet music and record sales managing fairly well. The months of the ASCAP ban still produced hit tunes like the Glenn Miller classics "A String Of Pearls" and "Chattanooga Choo Choo" and such enduring war-related hits as "Boogie Woogie Bugle Boy" (MCA Music, 1941) and "The White Cliffs Of Dover" (Shapiro, Bernstein, 1941). Still, the obstacles to both quality and quantity songwriting that the great ASCAP flap threw up were enormous.

Less than a year after ASCAP and the broadcasters came to terms, the autocratic president of the American Federation of Musicians (AFM) with the apt middle name, James Caesar Petrillo, grew concerned that more and more musicians were being put out of work by radio stations playing phonograph records rather than employing live musicians, and by the country's more than 400,000 jukeboxes. In his usual high-handed, tyrannical fashion, Petrillo declared a strike on August 1, 1942, barring all AFM musicians from making records, which, of course, also deprived them of considerable gainful employment. In the first year of the strike alone, union musicians lost about $4 million in wages from their former employers, the record companies (Sanjek 218). To end the strike, in February 1943 Petrillo demanded that every recording and radio transcription company make a direct payment into the AFM's "unemployment fund for every record and transcription made by its members" (*Billboard* 8 Nov. 1944: 13). At first, this was unanimously rejected, and some transcription companies took the issue to the U.S. Conciliation Service, which handed it over to the War Labor Board in July. By the time of the hearings in September and October, Columbia and Victor Records "became parties to [the] WLB proceedings" (13).

For quite some time, Petrillo's edict did less harm to the record companies than to his union members, since the recording interests had been forewarned and were prepared for such an eventuality. As early as May and certainly no later than July 25, 1942, Victor, Columbia, Decca, and some smaller record companies got word of Petrillo's banning AFM musicians from making records as of August 1. As a defense they began stockpiling their backlog of previously made but as yet unreleased records for release during the duration of the strike, and they even went as far as to schedule recording sessions with union musicians literally round-the-clock to build up an even larger supply of new releases prior to the ban going into effect. The result of this effort for just Victor, Decca, and Columbia was an unprecedented total of 130 million records sold during 1942 (see Malone 179; Sanjek 217).

But the good times couldn't spin forever. Stockpiles of "union-made" songs began to run low during 1943, and record companies couldn't meet consumers' demands for "new songs that caught the public's fancy in musicals and movies" (Malone 179); nor could they make records with instrumental accompaniment of the numerous war-related songs written and published during the ban, posing a real threat to the popular dissemination of songs touching on the war. Record companies found one limited solution—and not just for songs related to the war—by cutting strictly a capella (unaccompanied vocal) disks with no instrumental backup whatever. Today the notion of unaccompanied songs sounds strange in the field of popular music (with the exception of Gregorian chants and barbershop singing, I suppose), but a number of these were quite successful during the strike years. Just among war-related numbers, two by Frank Loesser had more than modest success—the Sportsmen's record of "What Do You Do In The Infantry?" (Hollywood: Saunders, 1943), and "First Class Private Mary Brown" (Frank Music, 1944), sung by then-rising star Perry Como with a mixed chorus. One a capella war song—the Song Spinners' Decca recording of Harold Adamson and Jimmy McHugh's

"Comin' In On A Wing And A Prayer" (Robbins, 1943)—was one of the biggest hits of 1943 (see chapter 8).

Yet again irony prevailed. In spite of that hit in the summer of '43, by early fall, Decca, whose "revenue came almost entirely from popular music," realized its rapidly depleting backlog of recordings would force it to capitulate to Petrillo if it wanted to record with union musicians again (Malone 179). On September 30, 1943, Decca and two transcription companies agreed to pay into the AFM's unemployment fund a set amount for each disk pressed (*Billboard* 8 Nov. 1944: 13), breaching a gaping hole in the hitherto impenetrable armor of the united and recalcitrant recording companies.

Between fall 1943 and fall 1944, more and more record and transcription companies (including Johnny Mercer's newly formed Capitol Records) gave in to Petrillo's demands. By October 1944 the only significant holdouts were Columbia, NBC, and its subsidiary Victor Records. But Petrillo held firm, refusing to grant concessions to the renegades despite entreaties from the War Labor Relations Board and President Roosevelt himself. And Petrillo's argument actually made some sense: if 105 companies had agreed to his terms, why should he concede to just three others, regardless of their size? Petrillo's standing pat worked; on November 11 (is Armistice Day symbolic of the companies' surrender?) NBC, Victor, and Columbia caved in—grudgingly and not without protest—and agreed to the per-disk contributions to the AFM unemployment fund. Within two days Victor and Columbia were recording with union musicians again (see Sanjek 217–20; Malone 179–80; *Billboard* 8 Nov. 1944:13).

The two years, three months, and ten days of the AFM recording ban coincided with the most prolific writing and publishing of war-related popular music during the war. With the ban in effect, however, how did the vast majority of such songs ever reach the public? A few significant war-inspired songs came out in December 1941, after the Pearl Harbor attack, and a fair number too in the first seven months of 1942, before Petrillo's decree. The ten months from the strike's settlement in November 1944 to the end of the war in August 1945 saw the production of relatively fewer war-related songs than had come before, even though some memorable and lasting pieces appeared at that late date. This leaves precisely the period of the strike as the time when the tunesmiths of Tin Pan Alley and their publishers produced the largest and most significant body of war-related songs. A number of explanations can be offered as to how they gained the public's ear. Two that can pretty much be discounted are stockpiling and a capella recording. It is inconceivable that America's popular songwriters had cranked out so many war-related songs between Pearl Harbor and the strike date about eight months later that record companies hastily called recording sessions to make masters of these tunes prior to the ban, squirreling them away until needed later on. A single fact argues against such a possibility. Some war-related songs mention or allude to events related to the war or the home front, while others clearly reflect the mood of the country or general home front conditions at a specific time; neither type of song could have been written in advance for commercial stockpiling. The easiest counter to the a capella argument is that, except in a very few cases, it simply didn't happen.

So how *could* war-related songs reach the public during the strike period? Precisely the same ways that other songs did. First and foremost, there was live radio performance; while almost unheard of today (except for symphony orchestras and the Metropolitan Opera), live music, much of it by bands and vocalists who had their own weekly programs, was very much the norm in radio programming of the 1940s. And, too, it was common for the big bands—both the top "name bands" and the relative unknowns—to tour nationwide, performing in ballrooms, theatres, and college gymnasiums, although gasoline and rubber (tire) rationing or shortages considerably curtailed touring as the war went on. Then there were songs in the movies; both musicals and non-musical films that contained an incidental song or two, like the revival of Herman Hupfeld's "As Time Goes By" (Harms, 1931) in the 1942 film *Casablanca*. And thanks to the recording ban, the records that made that number popular in 1942 were re-pressings of two 1931 originals (see chapter 11). And while radio, bandstand, or movie audiences may have heard a song (war-related or not) just once, often that was enough for them to buy the record (when available) or sheet music, and during the war sheet music sales were as big an industry as phonograph records. Finally, there was the nature of the strike itself, which saw more record companies agreeing to the new AFM contract as time went by. Most significantly, newcomer Capitol came to terms with Petrillo very early in the strike, and Decca—its roster of recording artists including big names like Jimmy Dorsey and his orchestra, Bing Crosby, and the Andrews Sisters—agreed to Petrillo's terms well over a year before Columbia and Victor, enabling Capitol and Decca to record and release new songs much earlier than their competitors. This explains why nearly all the recordings in *Hot Charts'* monthly listings during the recording ban were on Capitol, Decca, or, occasionally, a smaller label like Hit that had also settled early with the union.

Even before the outbreak of its twenty-seven-month battle with the musicians' union, the recording industry had another sticky mess on its hands (pun absolutely intended)—the shortage and imminent government rationing of shellac, a major component in the manufacture of the 78-r.p.m. phonograph records of the time. The reason for the shortage of shellac was its origin: it was derived only from a resinous substance deposited by a tiny beetle in Southeast Asia and India. By the spring of 1942 Japan had invaded and occupied Malaya, Thailand, what is now Vietnam, and Burma and was making incursions into India, effectively cutting off the supply area. At the same time, the ongoing fighting in the Pacific cut off shipping lanes. The most likely reason Washington decided to ration shellac is that it had a strategic purpose as a wood filler and finish for some boat decking and light wooden parts of aircraft wings, in addition to being a component of phonograph records.

The rationing began in April 1942, but some record manufacturers got early word of it and took proactive measures to ensure a continuing supply of shellac for their product. Victor launched a scrap shellac drive in January, with incentives to turn in old records, or even broken shards of records, for recycling: elementary and high school students could get a new RCA Victrola phonograph "for collecting a proportionate amount of old platters [records, in *Billboard*-speak]"; record buyers could receive one new record for "so many" old ones they exchanged; and charities could receive cash contributions from Victor for collecting and turning in old, used, and broken bits of records (*Billboard* 17 Jan. 1942: 9). Victor's effort, coming just a month or so after Pearl Harbor, was very likely the first of what would become a long succession of all sorts of scrap drives during the war. Confident that their present warehoused reserves of shellac would carry them for quite some time, Decca and Columbia didn't immediately follow Victor's lead in buying up scrap.

The shellac shortage was a game of percentages. Between early 1942 and September, the War Production Board (WPB) kept setting, then changing, then changing again, the amount of shellac record companies could use (including their own warehoused supplies) proportionate to what they had used the previous year. For example, initially the record companies were allowed to use 30 percent of the amount of shellac they had used the previous year (*Billboard* 14 Nov. 1942: 20), but for August 15 through September 30, the government reduced Decca, Columbia, and Victor's shellac equivalents to only 15 percent of their usage "of last year's consumption during the corresponding period" (*Billboard* 5 Sept. 1942: 19), and in November dropped it to a mere 5 percent of their shellac use in November 1941.

Recording firms put on a brave face, comforted by their stores of scrap shellac. Decca executive E. F. Stevens even proclaimed, "We are not going out of business and have every expectation of successfully overcoming the difficulty. Even if the difficulty works great hardship upon us, we are going to continue to do our utmost to keep going on an even keel. The value of records to civilian and service morale has been too well proven to admit the possibility of even a temporary end to the industry" (quoted in *Billboard* 14 Nov. 1942: 20; see below for more on music and morale).

By November 27, 1943, *Billboard* could report two bits of encouraging news. First, the Defense Supplies Corporation, "the government agency controlling such questions," confirmed that the "stockpile [of shellac] for war use is now enough to last four years at the current rate of distribution"; second, the amount of shellac available for both strategic and civilian uses was now dependent "entirely on the size of the spring crop of shellac in India and how much of it can be shipped here" (98). Consequently, the WPB was prepared for record makers in the first quarter of 1944 to use 100 percent of the shellac "quota they consumed in 1941" (*Billboard* 26 Feb. 1944: 16), and by September 23, 1944, *Billboard* could run a brief article with the headline (finally) "Shellac for All; Not Critical Now" (72).

Though the major record companies managed to withstand the shortage of materials, they could not combat the shortage of manpower as successfully. In addition to shellac and other substances vital to record pressing, it took highly skilled pressing-plant workers to operate the machines, along with maintenance and repair personnel to keep the machines running. As with skilled labor in other nonessential industries, many such employees of the diskers were, as the saying went, "gone with the draft," frequently to retool their skills for the maintenance and repair of tanks, ships, and planes. This reduced manpower, as much as the reduced shellac allocations, accounted for what drop-off there was in the manufacture and sales of records during the war. But the music industry coped with this as it coped with the ASCAP strike and the AFM's recording ban, the war years *still* producing an uncanny number of popular songs of the highest quality, including those directly or indirectly related to the war.

Totally different from strikes and shortages, conflicting attitudes about what constituted "proper" war music had nearly as much potential to severely curtail the writing and publishing of war-related music. But Tin Pan Alley rose above this often petty and ultimately pointless brouhaha as well.

### "I'll Be Marching To A Love Song": What Are War Songs Anyway?

The seeming oxymoron of marching and a romantic ballad in this Leo Robin/Ralph Rainger title (Twentieth Century Music, 1942) encapsulates the contradictions, confusion, and open dissension over just what a war song was—or should have been—during World War II. The war-long bickering began only a day after Pearl Harbor, with pundits trying to define a "proper" war song and decide what songs our armed services and Americans on the home front should be exposed to. On Monday, December 8, 1941, ASCAP president Gene Buck appealed to member-songwriters to "do their bit in the present crisis by writing 'fighting songs'"—this despite ASCAP publishers' doubts about "the American public's inclination for war songs" (*Variety* 10 Dec. 1941: 3). Because songs were their bread and butter, the music publishers clearly stayed on top of such matters. They recalled that right after Britain declared war on Germany on September 3, 1939, English tunesmiths rushed out a spate of fighting songs, but soon "the singing mood of the English changed and in the interim the more popular of British tunes have leaned toward themes of nostalgia and peace anticipation" (39). They also remembered American musical tastes during World War I, when some of the best-known songs were militant marching tunes—the most often cited being George M. Cohan's "Over There"—but when the dust of all those tramping feet had settled, most of that war's hits were "of a sentimental nature" (*Billboard* 3 Jan. 1942: 60).

At the outset, flag-wavers and rabble-rousers held sway. As early as December 17, 1941, *Variety* could report that Tin Pan Alley—roughly speaking, the professional songwriting and music publishing business—had begun churning out the kinds of "fighting songs" Gene Buck had pitched for. The trade paper published a list of such titles, followed by a sampling of comparable songs from the first year of America's involvement in World War I. But *Variety* failed to note that a good third of the World War I pieces were of the sentimental variety (2, 18).

On January 7, 1942, *Variety*'s editor Abel Green mentioned that the new crop of fighting songs emerged simultaneously with the *re*-emergence of somewhat older lyrical or sentimental numbers supportive of the Allies or looking forward to the world after the war (157; see chapters 4 and 12). Best known of the Allies-sympathizers is Oscar Hammerstein 2nd and Jerome Kern's "The Last Time I Saw Paris" (Chappell, 1940). Less well remembered but representative of the early "after the war" ballads is Irving Berlin's "When This Crazy World Is Sane Again" (Irving Berlin Inc., 1941), written and published before Pearl Harbor. Green concludes his piece by observing that the publishing firm of Shapiro, Bernstein had come up with another year-end hit, as they had done every year since 1934. The song that so eloquently combined positive sentiments for the British at war with a vision of future peace was, of course, Walter Kent and Nat Burton's "The White Cliffs Of Dover" (Shapiro, Bernstein, 1941). The significance of Green's article lies in his recognition that militant fighting songs and quieter lyrical pieces both played a role in conveying legitimate feelings about the war, without his getting judgmental about which kind of song was "better" or more needed.

In the early months of 1942 the trade papers were sounding the death knell for any popularity or commercial success of militant war songs. Coin-machine operators were banishing from their jukeboxes the poorly written "flood of war melodies" for being high risks as money-makers (*Variety* 25 Mar. 1942: 3). Publishers believed that "the public will not take to the fighting type of song until the United States has rung up a few resounding victories" (*Variety* 15 Apr. 1942: 1). And bandleader Paul Moorhead learned from his thirteen-week gig at the Paxton Hotel in Omaha, Nebraska—headquarter city of the Seventh Corps Area—that officers and enlisted men alike recoiled from the playing of "Remember Pearl Harbor" and other songs "with a martial or war flavor," clamoring instead for those "with a comedy angle, songs that will relax them" (*Variety* 6 May 1942: 2).

Despite such contrary evidence, the dual myth prevailed that the country craved *one* stirring war song to bring all Americans together and that during World War I "Over There" alone had been that song. Combined, these notions led to a three-year wild goose chase among interested parties—from professional and amateur songwriters to government bureaucrats—in an effort to write or discover *the* war song of World War II. It never happened. The notion of one unifying war song began spreading early, thanks to the article "Songs of the Times" in *Time* magazine on February 9, 1942, reporting that New Jersey Republican Congressman J. Parnell Thomas had exclaimed, rather hyperbolically, "What America needs today is a good 5¢ war song. The nation is literally crying for a good, peppy marching song, something with plenty of zip, ginger and fire. Something like *Over There, Keep the Home Fires Burning, Pack Up Your Troubles [In Your Old Kit Bag]* . . ." (41; ellipses in the article). One can't help wondering whether "superpatriot" Thomas (Lingeman 210) knew that two of the songs he cited were British. Even barring that, his nouns "zip, ginger, and fire"—archaic in this context even by 1942 standards—smacked of a sort of Kiplingesque jingoism perhaps explained by Thomas's having risen through the ranks from second lieutenant to captain overseas in the infantry during the previous world war.

Once Washington got into the act via the Office of War Information (OWI), the focus was on finding the "correct" song to pull both the home front and the military through the war. From the moment it began trying to drum up support for militant war songs, the OWI launched an equally noisy campaign against "slush," a term for romantic and other sentimental songs borrowed from our English allies. Of a July 1942 meeting with publishers, Abel Green reported that an OWI representative "stressed the OWI wants more 'fighting' songs and less boy-and-girl roseate stuff. It's part of the grim preparation for the glum long war ahead with plenty of deaths, disasters and doleful news generally expected" (*Variety* 22 July 1942: 1). While all agreed that no one could force a "spontaneous war hit" like "Over There" on the public, the OWI insisted that "the wrong kind of slushy stuff should be kept in the publisher's safe until after the war as a matter of patriotism." Seemingly agreeing, Abel Green characterized the collective OWI mentality as a desire "to at least check the kind of drivel that might handicap the fighting and winning of the war" until the "proper" kinds of war songs showed up. It is absolutely staggering that a government agency charged with effectively getting wartime messages out to the public could so little understand what truly touched that public's mind and heart. If songwriters could (and did) work war-related imagery into boy-girl songs about being apart, vowing eternal love, or being reunited, what better way to convey a personally meaningful war message to young lovers and married couples struggling with such feelings on a daily basis? But the government never got it.

In the same week's *Variety*, a brief opinion piece by a music publisher who chose to remain anonymous took a more balanced, if self-serving, view than the OWI. The writer admitted that many romantic ballads were formulaic love songs "re-staged in a war setting or re-hashed with a bit of military terminology" and defended these boy-girl songs as "desired and necessary" while conceding that they were "not enough": "If we song publishers are to make the contribution that we can and should make to the war effort, we ought to give our fighting boys, and the civilians behind them, songs which really express the spirit of the war," which the writer doesn't define (19).

Throughout the summer of 1942, William B. Lewis, radio chief of the OWI, crusaded to sell Washington on the importance of militant war songs as an "aspect of psychological warfare" (*Variety* 26 Aug. 1942: 3). By September, Lewis's strenuous campaign reached the floor of a U.S. Senate hearing on the activities of the American Federation of Musicians. During Senator Charles O. Andrews's questioning of FCC Chairman James L. Fly, both agreed on "the necessity of a fresh crop of stirring songs that would intensify the war effort" (*Variety* 23 Sept. 1942: 41). But senate hearings don't write songs any more than bureaucrats choreograph dances. About the time that *wacky* was becoming a favorite wartime adjective, one of the wackiest ideas emerging from the OWI called for the creation of energetic dances to get America on its feet to the "martial dance tunes" they expected to be produced. While Washington recognized that "it may be difficult to make over our listening and dancing habits," the government was still bent on coming up with "Victory Dances with spirited, military steps." Or, as one OWI spokesman put it in all seriousness, "If the dance idiom today differs from yesteryear we can get a Fred Astaire or Arthur Murray to make fashionable a new style of ripsnorting, patriotic stepping that will span the bridge from 1918 to 1942. We must become more oompah and militaristic" (*Variety* 7 Oct. 1942: 2, 70). Let's be thankful some wacky ideas never materialized.

Although the war-friendly dance craze didn't happen, the OWI's anti-slush/pro-militant song campaign had an impact in some rather unlikely places—the servicemen's homes-away-from-home run by the USO and the American Theatre Wing, such as the Stage Door Canteen, the Hollywood Canteen, and, for present purposes, the Philadelphia Stage Door Canteen. Early notice of canteen operators buying into the OWI's belief that slush softened America's fighting men appeared in the brief article "No Tear-Jerkers" in *Variety* on August 26, 1942. According to its stage director, Lincoln Wilmerton, the Philly canteen's rationale for consigning "tear-jerking ballads and sentimental sob-songs" to its "taboo list" was, "With most of the service men [*sic*] coming here from all parts of the country, they're bound to be a trifle homesick and we don't want them to be made worse by some teary tenor or soulful soprano singing about home and mother." The list of banned songs included "The White Cliffs Of Dover," "Remember Pearl Harbor" (which is a stirring march), "Dear Mom," and two revivals from decades past, "Miss You" and "My Buddy." At least borderline wacky was the canteen's inclusion of the national anthem on its "restricted list," since the men would have to stop dancing and stand to attention. Yet the club kept "The Star Spangled Banner" handy to stop brawls by eliciting just that response.

The next week's *Variety* for September 2, 1942, contained a letter to the editor from one Curt Weinberg, a show biz press agent turned soldier. Writing from Officers Candidate School at Fort Oglethorpe, Georgia, Weinberg rebutted what the Philly Canteen had decided were songs "bad for the morale of soldiers and sailors": "Funny thing about that is that these same songs [listed above] get, or got, the biggest play in Post Exchange jukeboxes when they were riding on the top of the Hit Parade, and the boys still seem to like them enough to drop a nickel in the slot and play them all night long. . . . You'll find slush tunes getting as big a play as the songs that Philly seems to think we soldiers should hear" (2). One couldn't ask for a more vivid depiction of the gulf between what so-called authorities thought our troops should listen to and what servicemen actually wanted.

From playing at the original and most famous Stage Door Canteen, in New York City, bandleader Woody Herman had a somewhat different take on what might be called the slush factor. Writing in the January 6, 1943, *Variety*, Herman concluded from his gig that the problem as perceived by the Canteen's operators had to do not with sentimentalism alone but with a wider variety of songs "which should not be played at all because they may arouse over-emotionalism in boys who are far from home." That such over-emotionalism was not the feared effect of slush alone is made clear by a sign Herman noticed asking performers to "please avoid war songs like 'White Cliffs of Dover,' 'My Buddy,' 'This Is Worth Fighting For,' 'When the Lights Go On Again,' and 'We Did It Before,'" the last-named as gung-ho a militant marching song as one could ask for (see chapter 6). Apparently, "over-emotionalism" took in songs that elicited all strong feelings, whether for home, mother, and sweetheart, or flag, God, and country. Herman observed that even "God Bless America" made the verboten list, and the national anthem was "played only on special occasions." Which seemingly left bands little to perform, other than popular and emotionally innocuous non-war-related novelty numbers of the day like "Mr. Five By Five," "Pennsylvania Polka," and "Cow-Cow Boogie!" With his band booked into the Stage Door in December, Herman was even personally asked not to play "White Christmas," because "it makes the boys too nostalgic" (188); despite this prohibition, it soon became one of the most requested songs by GIs worldwide. It can be argued—in fact *has* been argued by Jody Rosen, in his book on "White Christmas"—that although Berlin didn't originally intend any connections between his song and the war, the global conditions created them. The song's images of nostalgic longing for a more tranquil and simple place and time made it the one "war song" to universally capture the imagination of the home front and GIs abroad, although the tempo and tone differed greatly from anything the OWI deemed proper to unify wartime America.

In the same issue of *Variety* editor Abel Green wrote extensively, as he did every January, about the current state of the music biz, this time devoting much space to lamenting what was still the seeming lack of the kind of war songs the OWI hoped to see catch fire with the American public (187). About the only thing remotely accurate in Green's assessment was that more such songs were fizzling than sizzling. Indeed, just three pages before Green's editorial, his trade paper published a list headed "*WORLD WAR II SONGS (More or Less Complete).*" While the parenthetical is hopelessly short of the mark, in this list of 131 war-related songs published through the end of 1942 ninety-seven are of the blood-and-thunder militant marching variety sought by the OWI or, barring that, are equally peppy rabble-rousers designed to move folks on the home front to get behind the war effort, including Irving Berlin's "Any Bonds Today?" (copyright by Henry Morgenthau Jr., 1941) and Bud Green and Ray Henderson's "On The Old Assembly Line" (Green Bros. & Knight, 1942). In other words, even the numbers in *Variety*'s limited list show that the OWI's kinds of songs were in fact being written, published, played, and recorded; the problem was that the public wasn't paying much attention. The other thirty-four songs *Variety* saw fit to include in its war song list—many with much more widespread audience appeal—are a mixed bag of novelty numbers ("Little Bo-Peep Has Lost Her Jeep," "Gobs of Love"); homesickness, nostalgia, and "mother" songs ("Ma, I Miss Your Apple Pie," "She'll Always Remember"); songs in sympathy with the Allies ("The Last Time I Saw Paris," "The White Cliffs Of Dover"); visions of the world after the war ("When The Lights Go On Again (All Over The World)"); and romantic ballads of a serviceman's departure, separation, or longed-for return ("Just As Though You Were Here," "When The Roses Bloom Again"). What's important is *Variety*'s tacit concession that light or romantic musical treatments of war-related subjects deserved a place in a listing of World War II songs to date, however much its editor continued to side with the OWI's pro-militant, anti-slush stance.

Not only did this myopic focus on finding the "one" right war song prevail throughout the OWI's attempts to steer Tin Pan Alley toward that goal, but it continued even after May 24, 1943, when the songwriters took over from the bureaucrats to form the Music War Committee (MWC) of the American Theatre Wing, chaired by no less an eminence than Oscar Hammerstein 2nd. According to music critic and MWC song-judging panelist Mark Schubart, the committee's mission was to find a song "to do for this war what George M. Cohan's Over There did for the last one" (*PM* 7 July 1943: 26). After futilely seeking this song for more than a year and a half, the MWC finally had to set its sights lower, admitting that the failed mission had become at best a secondary concern for them (see Hammerstein's summary of the MWC's activities in the *Billboard 1944 Music Year Book,* October 1944: 49). As it turned out, the MWC was more productive in writing or commissioning, on request, musical tributes to the several branches of the armed forces and to specialized units within them (see chapter 8). But no service song stood a chance of becoming the one musical rallying cry for an entire nation at war.

The question remaining to be addressed is why no one militant war song ever fired up the public during World War II the way "Over There" supposedly did during World War I. (That itself, by the way, remains more myth than a matter of fact. World War I was not a one-song war. A lot of British as well as American marching tunes were popular with soldiers and civilians alike on both sides of the pond, including "It's A Long Way To Tipperary," "Pack Up Your Troubles In Your Old Kit Bag," "Mademoiselle From Armentieres," and more.) Writing from a vantage point fairly late in the war, in *Variety* for January 5, 1944, Oscar Hammerstein could base his assessment on more than just the hastily written war songs that surfaced in response to Pearl Harbor in late 1941 and early '42. Instead, Hammerstein looked at the continuing flow of militant flag-wavers produced during more than two years of America's involvement in the war, and his reason why the public "just didn't want" most of the war songs that kept coming along is about as sane as it gets: the songs were no damn good. "The important point about a war song," he wrote, risking infuriating the nation's thousands of amateur war-song writers, "is that there is no virtue in its high purpose or patriotic intent. To justify itself it must stand on its feet as a really good *song*. A fairly good war song is of no more use to the war effort than a fairly good egg is to a breakfast" (187). And, truth be told, taking the amateur and professional efforts together, there were a lot of rotten eggs in the national war-song basket.

In *Variety* for January 6, 1943, Sigmund Romberg, president of the Songwriters Protective Association and composer of hit operettas like *The Student Prince*, offered a simplistic explanation for the supposed dearth of war songs that, like most things simplistic, was simply wrong. "We've been asked to write marches," Romberg wrote, "but who besides civilians marches nowadays? Everything's on wheels—jeeps, trucks, planes, motorcycles, tanks. There's practically no trench warfare [though God knows what World War I's trenches had to do with marching!] and for some reason this combination of circumstances appears to stifle the composition of marching songs." Lyrics by a couple of army guys who were pretty fair songwriters dispel Romberg's notion that World War II wasn't a marching war. Best known for his lyrics to the 1945 Andrews Sisters hit "One Meat Ball" and the 1955 motion picture title song "Unchained Melody," Pvt. Hy Zaret spoke from experience when he revised World War I's "Mademoiselle From Armentieres" for his infantry buddies in World War II: "They say they've mechanized the war, / So what the Hell are we marching for" (*Hit Kit,* January 1944: #4). And if the war wasn't a marching war for countless infantrymen, why is the title question of Pfc. Frank Loesser's popular "What Do You Do In Infantry?" answered first by "You march, you march, you march," and in the second stanza by "You hike, you hike, you hike?" The only reply to there being no marching songs because it wasn't a marching war is that there were and it was.

Popular 1920s and '30s bandleader Isham Jones had a theory that had some validity for a brief time but held no water in the long run. Jones's thesis in the June 10, 1942, *Variety* was "America is too mad about this war to do much singing" (43), which, if he had stopped right there, is an interesting idea. But Jones tripped himself up while explaining it: "We never have known the taste of defeat until now. We don't like it and we don't feel like singing as long as that bad taste is still in our mouth." Had Jones said this a month or more earlier, it might have had validity, following the humiliating American debacles at Bataan and Corregidor and the surrender of all U.S. troops in the Philippines to the Japanese on May 6. But Jones spoke from Memphis on June 9, a month after the U.S. fleet seriously beat up on the Japanese navy in the Battle of the Coral Sea, and three days after its decisive victory in the Battle of Midway—all of which pretty much blows Jones's theory out of the water. By the time Jones spoke, Americans had a lot to sing about, though apparently they didn't.

Decades after the war, composer and music historian Alec Wilder claimed in *American Popular Song* that World War II produced no worthy war songs (or songs of any kind, according to him) because "The innocence, the slogans, the idealism [of World War I] had vanished. An *Over There* would have been jeered at this trip. . . . There was too much cynicism among the young. . . . There will be no mention in this study of the World War II songs" (502). The facts invalidate Wilder's claims of anti-idealism and cynicism. The enormous number of men who enlisted in the service after Pearl Harbor shows idealism in action. And how cynical could the country have been for the war years to be this nation's most sustained period of national unity? Nor could a country with a cynical mindset have produced and embraced romantic war-inspired ballads like "Long Ago And Far Away," "I'll Walk Alone," "It's Been A Long, Long Time," and many more. So far were the home front "young" from cynicism that it would have been unthinkable for a song like Tina Turner's 1984 number-one gold record and Grammy Award–winning hit "What's Love Got To Do With It?" to have been written and become popular.

Of course there were differences between the periods of World Wars I and II, but those that helped alter musical tastes from one war to the other had little to do with idealism or cynicism. To a great degree the altered tastes grew out of America's greater diversity—a growing and shifting social and cultural (not political) pluralism and a corresponding shift away from the relative homogeneity of America during World War I. Compared with 1914–18, by 1939–45 diverse ethnic and religious minorities were much larger. By winning the right to vote in 1920 women had become more empowered and, even before "Rosie the Riveter," had been entering the workforce in considerable numbers since the 1920s. The bifurcation of the United States into "urban" and "rural" was complicated in the 1940s by a growing suburban culture quite distinct from life in both the cities and the country. And migratory patterns of workers seeking employment in defense industries created pockets of once rural Americans (chiefly from the south and border states) in the large industrial cities of the north and the shipbuilding centers on both coasts. While Americans of diverse ethnic, religious, and geographic backgrounds— many displaced from their roots—agreed that it would take cooperation and national unity to win a war threatening the democracy that allowed for such diversity (Perrett 441, Bailey 23), it would have been all but impossible for them to agree on just one song to express those feelings.

Instead, the social and cultural pluralism of the war years helped create a pluralism of tastes in popular music. While a girl back home missing her GI overseas would find a sympathetic chord in "I'll Walk Alone" or "Wonder When My Baby's Coming Home," women defense workers knew their work was appreciated when hearing songs like "We're The

Janes That Make The Planes" or "Rosie The Riveter." Anyone from Boy Scout to housewife who was involved in scrap drives could relate to numbers like "(Get Some) Cash For Your Trash" and "Junk Ain't Junk No More," and coping with shortages and rationing was lightened up a bit by the hilarity of such songs as "Ration Blues" and "When The Nylons Bloom Again." Tin Pan Alley's professionals did a remarkable job of keeping jukeboxes, phonographs, parlor pianos, dance bands, and the airwaves supplied with war-related songs in sufficient quantity and variety that some were bound to appeal to one or another of the myriad tastes that made up their constituency. This time no one lone flag-waving successor to "Over There" was going to do the trick.

Writing in *Radio Hit Songs* for July 1942, bandleader Tommy Dorsey confirmed this pluralism of tastes by his own experiences with different kinds of people wanting different kinds of songs. By and large "the lads in khaki and blue want NO popular [militant] war music," he said, while the "general public—fond parents, former business associates and personal friends of the military men" wanted precisely that, and asked Dorsey to dedicate the songs "to this fellow or that one, to this outfit or the other, to demonstrate their appreciation for the boys" (9). Dorsey noticed that "many requests come to the bandstand for the more sentimental war numbers of the day": "The girls asked for the soft stuff," while their "soldier or sailor friends were responsible for the negative requests" not to play slush. (That would change, incidentally, as the war went on; song popularity polls of servicemen began only in 1944, but once they did, romantic ballads ranked right at the top.) Dorsey finally observed that businessmen and women and defense workers out for a night on the town wanted to hear "practically everything BUT [militant] war tunes," being "on the hunt for escapist entertainment." Again, different people, different tastes. Songwriters knew it; bandleaders knew it; the public knew it. But Washington never got it.

Washington also didn't get another key reason for differing musical tastes between the two world wars. World War II was a much more "personal" war than World War I. First, with the population of the United States at just over 130 million and about sixteen million men and women in the armed forces at one time or another during the war (a ratio of 8.125:1), the odds are that nearly every man, woman, and child in the United States was related to or knew someone in the service. Factor in the millions more Americans in defense work, and the odds shrink until just about everyone knew someone in the business of fighting the war. Small wonder, then, that professional Tin Pan Alley types and others published by major ASCAP and BMI publishing houses wrote over a hundred more songs about a GI away (or saying goodbye) and a girl (or mother, or child) back home than they did about the second largest category, home front conditions and support, which were also topics that brought the war down to a personal level for people. Second, since World War II's global enormity was beyond most people's grasp, even the best of the generic, militant songs almost never caught on. But numbers about personal heroism or sacrifice often found a large public, as with Frank Loesser's "Praise The Lord And Pass The Ammunition" (Famous Music, 1942) and Harold Adamson and Jimmy McHugh's "Comin' In On A Wing And A Prayer" (Robbins Music, 1943), two of the war years' biggest hits. It also didn't hurt that both are terrific pieces of songwriting, validating Oscar Hammerstein's contention that if a war song is good enough it will sell.

But what are war songs, anyway? Part of the answer came even as this question was raging during the war. It could be argued that this answer was just a self-serving plug for ASCAP's member songwriters and publishers, but even if it was, ASCAP's obviously paid-for full-page open letter on page 30 of *Billboard* for September 25, 1943, was the one clearheaded voice of reason during the whole war-long controversy over the nature of war songs. Headed "Where Are the War-Songs?" the letter begins by rebutting the charge that "this war isn't producing good music" by explaining that "good" is relative, and it's too early to make such a valuation because only the test of time finally decides which popular songs are good and which "great." The letter then proclaims, "American music and American musicians are having a profound effect on the war effort . . . both on the military front and at home" (ellipses in text throughout all the quotations). This leads to a definition of war-related music in the most generous sense: "songs the soldiers sing are not the only warsongs. The music that rings through our factories . . . that enlivens the tired workers . . . increases production so vigorously as to become beautiful, even to unmusical efficiency experts. Those are war-songs, too." The following section is, admittedly, a commercial pitch for more industries to buy music in order to increase defense production, employee morale, and, not incidentally, "the incomes of the men and women who produce it." But the conclusion returns to the earlier, more general theme: "It's no time to worry about war-songs . . . or American music. The people of this country want music today more than ever before in our history, and, as always, American writers will produce it and American musicians play it."

The ASCAP letter's implicit definition of war songs as *any* songs that made people feel good (and/or more productive) during the war covers the entire field of American popular music, war-related or not, a field much broader than just those songs related to the war directly or by association that are considered in the present study. And yet the ASCAP definition embraced a more capacious sense of "war song" than either Washington's OWI or Tin Pan Alley's MWC. The range of war-related songs here is narrower than ASCAP's inclusion of *all* wartime American popular music. Still, I include a broad range of songs that either make explicit references to the war or to life on the home front as well as those that allude to them.

I refer to the latter type of song as touching on the war "by association," and that associative process occurred in different ways. First, and most obviously, it happened through songs designed by skillful writers to deliberately evoke in the hearer an emotional response to something war-related, even though the song contains no concrete images of the war. By being at once so universal and yet so specific to wartime feelings, a good number of such songs became long-lasting standards, songs like "The Last Time I Saw Paris," "I'll Walk Alone," and "Long Ago And Far Away." The second type of war-related songs by association is comprised of numbers from earlier years or even decades that were revived because their writers or publishers realized that the lyrics had a greater chance for relevance and emotional clout during the war than when the songs were first released. In most cases they were absolutely right; only during the war did some songs that had their first life much earlier become major hits. Among these are Roy Turk and Fred E. Ahlert's "I'll Get By (As Long As I Have You)," Irving Kahal and Sammy Fain's "I'll Be Seeing You," and perhaps the most enduring revival of them all, Herman Hupfeld's immortal "As Time Goes By." The third kind of war song by association is comprised of those that became linked to the war in the minds and ears of listeners, even though such association was never the intention of the song or its writers. The example of two very similar songs will illustrate this associative process—one only presumed by its audience to have a war connection, the other intentionally war-related. Written in 1941 for the spring '42 release of Paramount's musical *Sweater Girl,* Frank Loesser and Jule Styne's "I Don't Want To Walk Without You" (Paramount Music, 1941) became an enormous hit starting in February 1942, even before the movie opened. It seems like a typical ballad of a girl back home separated from her lover because of the war. But lines like "I thought the day you left me behind, / I'd take a stroll and get you right off my mind" and "Why'd you have to turn off all that sunshine?" clearly don't reflect the loneliness and constancy of a girl waiting for her GI overseas to return but the unhappiness of a girl who's been dumped by her boyfriend. But sometimes audiences simply hear what they want to hear, and what they seemingly wanted to hear was a song about lovers separated by the war, even that early on. Conversely, though similar in appearance, Sammy Cahn and Jule Styne's "I'll Walk Alone" is deliberately filled with oblique yet unmistakable images of the war having parted two faithful sweethearts (see chapter 11).

In sum, whether they were militant or romantic, serious or humorous, direct or allusive, and by Tin Pan Alley pros or untried amateurs, *all* of the songs that kept the war before the public, boosted morale, or just touched people's feelings about the war and life on the home front were "the" World War II war song, *all* of them the songs that fought the war.

### *"Hip Hip Hooray": Song Popularity, War Messages, and Morale*

According to many people who were there, including some of those in charge, morale had a lot to do with winning the war, and popular songs played a central role in building it, on the home front and among GIs overseas. Yet early in her book on Tin Pan Alley and the government during the war, Kathleen E. R. Smith asserts that "music was of little or no consequence in the outcome of the war" (6), something she never proves. Good morale has always been deemed necessary for winning a war, but there is no objective, accurate methodology for measuring the impact of songs on morale, let alone their motivational capacity for getting the home front to buy War Bonds or participate in scrap drives. Throughout her book, Smith measures the "consequence" or importance of war songs by their commercial popularity, an unproductive criterion except for very commercial types such as war-related romantic ballads; songs about scrap drives and Victory Gardens were never big sellers, nor were they meant to be. Smith, for example, misreads the success of Sammy Kaye and Don Reid's "Remember Pearl Harbor," claiming it "was not a big hit (in terms of selling a million copies of sheet music or records) and did not last more than a few weeks on any of the popularity charts" (15). That's generally true, except that in the 1940s it was the rare song that became a million-seller; it took much less then to be a hit, and, more to the point, hit or no hit, the country needed to hear a rousing morale builder like Kaye and Reid's song just weeks after Pearl Harbor (see chapter 6). The place of war-related music vis-à-vis its home front audience can be measured only in part by the usual indices of song popularity—the trade paper charts and radio's weekly *Lucky Strike Hit Parade*. The range of popularity they charted was narrow, and far more songs had far wider audiences than ever appeared in their rankings.

But since the charts do have some value, especially for tracking the success of war-related songs of a commercial stamp, a brief description of what the charts were will render comprehensible and, hopefully, meaningful the frequent references to their data throughout the book. Since long before the war, *Variety* and *Billboard* (or *The Billboard*, as it called itself then) each ran weekly charts ranking the previous week's sales of sheet music, number of coin machine (jukebox) plays, and "radio plugs" (more about them in a moment), and *Billboard* also ran a chart ranking the sales of phonograph records. That *Variety* opted not to track record sales vividly shows how vital a place sheet music still held in the music biz.

The salient features of each chart reveal their basis for song popularity. Easiest to understand are the charts for sheet music sales in both *Variety* and *Billboard,* which were based on weekly reports from major music stores and other retailers of "sheets" nationwide. The same kind of reporting produced *Billboard*'s weekly chart of record sales. In this period *Billboard* consistently ranked the fifteen top-selling sheets, as did *Variety,* until March 5, 1944, when it dropped the number to ten with no explanation. *Billboard* limited its record sales rankings to the top ten throughout the war.

Both trade papers kept their rankings of most jukebox plays to the top ten songs (sometimes recorded by two or more different artists), followed by a supplementary list (normally unranked) of what *Variety* called "Other Favorites" and *Billboard* called "Coming Up." According to *Variety*'s weekly explanation of the chart, these songs were "grabbing most nickels this week in jukeboxes throughout the country, as reported by operators." Just how jukebox operators calculated the number of plays remains a mystery to me. It's hard to believe the jukes of those days were sophisticated enough to count and record each time a platter was played, but it's almost as hard to believe that the proprietors of every joint with a jukebox took the time to count every time a patron popped a nickel in to play a certain tune.

Grasping radio plug charts and how data for them was gathered is a bit more complicated. A song plug is the playing or singing of a recently published song on the radio, live or on transcription by band and/or singer(s), not on phonograph records (indeed, DJ shows barely existed in the '40s). Long before the war years, and even before radio, music publishers employed "song pluggers" to convince bands and singers to perform their songs, often with a (strictly speaking, illegal) monetary incentive to do so. The theory was that the more often people heard a song, the more likely they were to buy the sheet music or record. By the war years, this was pretty much standard operating procedure for song pluggers vis-à-vis the studio bands as well as the name (and not-so-name) bands and vocalists on the radio, many of whom had their own shows. Thus, what both trade papers were tracking in their "plug charts" was the number of times in a week that the radio broadcast newly published songs in live or transcribed performance. This data was tabulated at so-called "listening posts," sometimes by people employed by the papers, sometimes by employees of what we would now call market research firms, and, for a while, even by (presumably paid) students at Columbia and New York University who listened to earmarked stations for hours on end and noted each time every song was played. These lists in both *Variety* and *Billboard* were much longer than their charts of sheet music sales and jukebox plays, sometimes upward of fifty songs in a given week. And, given the charts' presumed audience, both papers named only the song titles and their *publishers*. For most of the war, each paper ranked the songs and gave the number of plugs each received during that week, but on May 19 and May 22, 1943, respectively (*Variety* was published on Wednesdays, *Billboard* on Saturdays) both switched to just an alphabetical listing of plugged songs.

Alike in these respects, the *Billboard* and *Variety* plug charts were very different in another way: their scope. *Variety* consistently limited what its inimitable jargon called the "totalization of the combined plugs of current tunes" strictly to network broadcasting. In 1939, that took in just NBC and CBS; later in the war years, Mutual and the "Blue" network were included as well. In addition to network broadcasting, *Billboard* included plugs on the New York City independent stations WOR, WNEW, WMCA, and WHN. During the years when *Variety* and *Billboard* both ranked songs by number of plugs, these differences, plus the four-day spread between their publication dates, help to explain why their charts sometimes differ for what seem to be plugs reported for almost the same week.

The charts for sheet music and record sales, and for jukebox plays, were direct indices of songs' actual popularity. The charts of radio plugs were not. As long as both trade journals published the number of plugs songs received and ranked them accordingly, the charts represented the extent of publishers' and entertainers' efforts to promote songs by repeatedly airing them on the radio. These charts are especially useful for seeing how often the public might have heard war-related songs with little commercial promise, such as patriotic numbers and pitches for War Bonds. Such songs didn't need to sell to have their effect; they just had to be heard, and the plug charts show that quite a few were—repeatedly. Millions of radio listeners heard these songs even if they weren't necessarily buying them, since during the war the average American listened to the radio about four and a half hours a day (Lingeman 224). Finally, because entertainment trade papers published all of the charts of song popularity and the radio song plug charts, their intended and actual readers were primarily entertainment professionals, not the nation's music listeners, who rarely dipped into *Billboard* or *Variety,* if ever.

But the *Lucky Strike Hit Parade* (a.k.a. *Your Hit Parade* or *The Hit Parade*) was the public's own weekly chart. Every Saturday night since 1935 CBS had aired it to bring listeners the week's top tunes (normally ten in number) plus a selection of other songs dubbed "Lucky Strike Extras." The popular program continued its mission throughout the war years plus fourteen, moving from radio to TV in 1950, where it remained until 1959. Whether with a giggle or a groan, those who remember the TV *Hit*

*Parade* do so for its singing icons Dorothy Collins and the dubiously talented Snooky Lanson. We often lose sight of the fact that during the war, one of the radio show's featured male crooners was the young and upcoming Frank Sinatra. Be that as it may, each week the *Hit Parade* announcer intoned, "Your Hit Parade survey checks the best sellers on sheet music and phonograph records—the songs most heard on the air and most played on the automatic coin machines—an accurate, authentic tabulation of America's taste in popular music" (qtd. in "YOUR HIT PARADE"). If the announcer's spiel is accurate, the *Hit Parade* rankings were an anomalous mishmash of actual popularity indices (sheet and record sales and juke plays) along with radio song plugs, which, as mentioned, didn't indicate a song's popularity.

The chief drawback with *Your Hit Parade* and the trade-paper song popularity charts is their limited scope. Weekly rankings of just the top fifteen pieces of sheet music sold, ten records sold, or ten songs most played on jukeboxes (in various recordings) represent just the tiny tip of the wartime popular music iceberg, under which lay a huge mass of other songs available to the music buying public. By contrast, and clearly in order to be more comprehensive, by the mid-1960s *Variety* ran a weekly chart called "*Variety* Single Record T.I.P.S. (Tune Index of Performance & Sales)" that ranked fifty records, and another list ranking fifty LP albums. In the same period, *Billboard* became even more comprehensive, with its "Hot 100" chart for singles and the 150 albums on its "Top LP's" chart.

Closest to such extensive rankings for the war years (indeed, for every year from 1940 through 1959 and counting) are the annual retrospective volumes of *Hot Charts,* produced and published by popular music historian and record collector Big Al Pavlow. Each volume contains month-by-month rankings of as many as sixty singles, though not necessarily sixty separate songs, because often two or more artists had success with the same number. The precise number of records on each month's chart depends on which ones achieved enough "points" in Pavlow's complex mathematical ranking formula to make that month's list. Along with the song title, each listing includes the name of the performer(s) and the record label and number. Following this chart is a separate monthly alphabetical list of records Pavlow labels "Extras" and describes as being "in action during the month," or, as Big Al explained to me in one of many telephone conversations, records selling well but not well enough to make the chart itself. Though he doesn't explain himself fully, in his introductory notes, Pavlow bases his "sophisticated system" of elaborate, weighted mathematical calculations on the same sources the trade papers used— "retail sales . . . jukebox spins . . . airplay," along with radio station surveys and other sources. *Hot Charts* tracks the popularity only of records, not sheet music.

The greatest value of Pavlow's volumes is their spectrum of popularity, which is far broader than the trade paper charts. For present purposes, this gives a clearer as well as broader view of how war-related songs of all varieties fared with America's music-buying and jukebox-playing public. The only occasional drawback of *Hot Charts* is its monthly, not weekly, format. But the *Billboard* and *Variety* charts contain enough fine-tuned data for anything one would want to see on a weekly basis, such as "Praise the Lord and Pass the Ammunition" and "White Christmas" (as different as two war-related songs could be) chasing each other for the charts' first-place slots during the late fall and winter of 1942. The weekly trade paper charts and monthly *Hot Charts* can be used together to demonstrate and evaluate the actual place of war-related songs during World War II. For example, the charts objectively dispel Isham Jones's previously noted contention that when the United States was losing a war Americans were in no mood to sing war-related songs. In fact, *Billboard*, *Variety*, and *Hot Charts* reveal precisely the opposite. During the home front's demoralizing days of U.S. troops in the Philippines losing and then surrendering to the Japanese at Bataan and Corregidor in April 1942, Pavlow's chart for that month includes among the big-selling records (with their rank) quite a few war-related and war-associated songs: "Don't Sit Under The Apple Tree," Glenn Miller, 9th; "Always In My Heart," Jimmy Dorsey/Bob Eberly, 34th; "We Must Be Vigilant," Phil Spitalny and His All Girl Orchestra, 40th; "Goodnight Captain Curlyhead," Dinah Shore, 43rd; "When The Roses Bloom Again," Jimmy Dorsey/Bob Eberly, 44th; and "Johnny Doughboy Found A Rose In Ireland," Kay Kyser, 48th; Guy Lombardo, 50th; Tommy Tucker, 52nd. Granted, "We Must Be Vigilant" is the only piece of the militant warhorse variety in Big Al's rankings, the others being more or less slush, but each of these tunes was still linked to the war directly or by association. The "Extra" list for April is even more telling. Just citing titles and not the multiple recordings of them (as many as five, in one case), the also-popular songs for that gloomy month included "The Army Air Corps," "Dear Mom," "Get Your Gun And Come Along (We're Fixin' To Kill A Skunk)," "I'll Pray For You," "I'll Wait For You," "Last Night I Said A Prayer," "The Marines' Hymn," "1942 Turkey In The Straw," "She'll Always Remember," "Three Little Sisters," and "You Can't Hold A Memory In Your Arms," *all* of them directly referring to the war or the armed services.

These recordings reveal Americans' readiness to listen to songs about the war, but were they reluctant, as Isham Jones contended, to *sing* about it in days of defeat and despair? Not at all, according to *Variety*'s sheet music charts. Songs with direct war referents in the latter half of April were "Don't Sit Under The Apple Tree," 3rd; "Johnny Doughboy Found A Rose In Ireland," 7th; "She'll Always Remember," 10th; and "I'll Pray

For You," 11th. *Billboard*'s list added in its own 9th place "The White Cliffs Of Dover," and in 13th the robustly martial "My Great Great Grandfather."

But rankings based on sales and jukebox plays alone are insufficient for showing the special place war-related music had in life on the home front. Here's where the plug charts are most revealing. For example, during the war paying one's income tax in full and on time was considered patriotic and a financial help for the war effort second only to buying War Bonds and Stamps. The income tax deadline was March 15, and *Variety*'s plug chart for March 18, 1942, reports that the networks had aired Irving Berlin's cheerfully patriotic ditty "I Paid My Income Tax Today" (copyright Henry Morgenthau Jr., 1942) seven times during the week preceding tax day. It's not on any previous week's charts, confirming that these airings were a plug for paying taxes, not for selling the song.

Berlin, who wrote numerous songs hyping the war effort, understood that their commercial popularity was less important than their intended effect. In a letter to the editor in *Variety* on June 23, 1943, Berlin proposed that Tin Pin Alley songwriters write morale-building and motivational songs with little expectation of profit: "The main object would be to get ideas across to the public through songs. Transcriptions could be made and sent to all the sustaining [radio] programs, as was done with the 'Bonds' song [Berlin's "Any Bonds Today?" in 1941]. And even if the song didn't become popular in the Tin Pan Alley sense, enough of people [*sic*] could hear it so that it could do the required amount of good. For example, when rationing comes along, we hear many spot announcements and broadcasts preparing the American people for that condition. A good song on the subject, not necessarily propaganda but an amusing idea, would do much more than reams of speeches" (31). As a seasoned songwriter, Berlin knew such songs could have their desired effect even if heard just once. Not only did he advocate the writing of war-supportive songs, Berlin literally put his money where his mouth was. Usually a commercially oriented songwriter to the nth degree, Berlin was more than generous when it came to helping his beloved adopted United States of America, always donating profits from his war-effort songs to war-related causes. His all-soldier show *This Is the Army* alone (including sale of the film rights) netted $10,000,000 for the Army Emergency Relief Fund (Lingeman 288).

In short, commercial success isn't always a good, or even valid, indicator of whether or not war-related songs got their messages out. Again, while there is no way to measure what precise *effects* such songs had on Americans in terms of boosting morale or motivating home front activities, it's a safe bet that the average citizen was hearing many more songs of this sort than the charts indicate. One bit of evidence for this comes from the movies, a wartime pastime that an "audience of roughly 90 million per week attended avidly" (Doherty 9). Between 1939 and 1945, 818 (or 53 percent) of the 1,540 feature-length films released by Hollywood studios were in one way or another "War Related," whether in their story or through just a scene, a line of dialogue, or a song that kept the war before America's moviegoers (Shull 84). In 1942 the Bureau of Motion Pictures (BMP) was established, nominally as a branch of the OWI. Shortly thereafter the BMP issued for Hollywood's guidance "a fifty-page loose-leaf brochure called 'Government Information for the Motion Picture Industry,'" which contained everything from encouragement for "the casual insertion of a constructive 'war message' in a picture whenever possible" to ideas for entire scripts dealing with the war (see Doherty 45–46; Lingeman 183).

Because most movie musicals, screwball comedies, westerns, and period or "costume" pieces had little or nothing to do with the war, their war messages were usually of the brief and "casual" variety. Because moviegoers usually saw a particular film only once (and we can presume that the government recognized this fact), the BMP and OWI were apparently satisfied with these messages reaching enormous numbers of people each week through a single viewing alone. By analogy, someone hearing a morale-building or motivational song *only once* may perhaps be presumed to have received that song's message as loud and clear as the moviegoer "got" the messages in films. Therefore, such songs heard just once or twice on the radio, in a dance hall, or in a Hollywood film would have kept the war before the public as surely as those that made the charts and *Hit Parade* for weeks on end.

Before leaving popularity in general for a look at some wartime attitudes about music and morale, a survey done well into the war tacitly related song popularity to military morale by tabulating the songs preferred by American servicemen and women "within the continental U.S.A." In 1944, after its annual survey of high school students and after "passing up its usual college survey because there weren't enough collegiates to be polled" (probably because so many were in the service), *Billboard* conducted "Hundreds of polls . . . in camps and naval installations to determine just what the gang [in all the armed forces stateside] wanted" (16 Sept. 1944: 12). *Billboard* published the results of the three-part survey in three installments on September 16, 23, and 30: part 1 asked service personnel to rank their favorite bands, solo vocalists, and vocal groups (not relevant here); parts 2 and 3 respectively asked for their favorite records and sheet music. Published on September 16 and 23, the results of those two parts vindicate the popularity of war-related songs (slush included) among America's military. Of the top thirteen records (not songs, remember), a full six of them (representing four different songs) were at least related to the war by association, with one very directly about army life: Bing Crosby's "I'll Be Seeing You" was 1st; the comic "G.I. Jive," sung by its creator, Johnny Mercer, 4th, Tommy Dorsey and Frank Sinatra's record of "I'll Be Seeing You," 6th; Harry James's revival of "I'll Get By," 7th; Bing crooning "Long Ago And Far Away," 8th; and Louis Jordan's own spin on "G.I. Jive," 10th. There's not a militant warhorse in the bunch, but neither did GIs shy away from sentimental treatments of emotions touching on the war or from spoofs of army routine.

In the following week's tally of sheet music preferences among service personnel, the same songs reappear in more or less the same rankings, plus another unabashedly sentimental one in 9th place: "I'll Be Seeing You," 1st; "Long Ago And Far Away," 2nd; "I'll Get By," 3rd; "G.I. Jive," 5th; and "I'll Walk Alone," 9th. Comparing the results of its high school and armed forces polls, *Billboard* concluded that "the disk tastes of the two groups don't differ too radically" (23 Sept. 1944:20).

Wanting to go beyond the tastes of only stateside servicemen and women but unable to survey GIs overseas, *Billboard* relied on anecdotal accounts from popular singer Dinah Shore, just back from entertaining troops abroad, to check its survey results "on behalf of the boys overseas." Shore's casual review revealed that nine of the eleven songs "tabbed in camps, stations and fields [stateside] were identical with what she had been asked for wherever she sang" (30 Sept. 1944: 11), and those nine included all the war-related numbers above.

In the absence of more objective measures of song popularity, anecdotal reportage (the stuff of oral history) such as Shore's is often all we have to go on, as can be seen in this brief personal account. Frank Loesser's "What Do You Do In The Infantry?" made no contemporary charts except *Variety*'s for radio plugs, and it is ranked 35th in *Hot Charts* for just a single month, October 1943. Yet the song still achieved a popularity greater than the numbers show both at home and with troops abroad, primarily those in the infantry. I remember humming or whistling Loesser's deliberately trudging melody as a four-year-old late in the war, so I must have heard the number repeatedly for it to stick with me. Further, while talking about my research for this book with my friend Professor Emeritus Robert Mathiesen of Brown University, I discovered the appeal of Loesser's song had long outlasted the war. At my mere mention of "What Do You Do In The Infantry?" Bob spontaneously began reciting the lyrics, afterward recounting that he knew the song from singing it in his eighth grade music classes in Berkeley, California, in 1955! Loesser's march clearly had caught the fancy of some music teacher during the war years and just never left the curriculum.

In addition to the songs GIs most requested during her performances, Dinah Shore also reported on those that the soldiers, sailors, and marines abroad sang themselves. In the top two slots were the lush and romantic war-related ballads "I'll Be Seeing You" and "Long Ago And Far Away," with the equally sentimental revival "I'll Get By" coming in 3rd, followed by the non-war-related stateside hit "Paper Doll" and Johnny Mercer's send-up of army life, "G.I. Jive." *Billboard* remarked that the lack of "marching songs in the G.I. preferences [for singing] is not surprising because [many of] the boys are just not marching to the wars—they're riding and when they ride they sing nostalgic and novelty songs—not marching or military slanted songs" (*Billboard* 30 Sept. 1944: 11). Or, as Dinah Shore put it, "You can sing anything you want to when you ride—and you probably do" (65). If Shore's reportage of what overseas troops liked to sing was accurate, her observation says a good deal about music and morale among the military. Romantic ballads were the clear singing choice among troops abroad, arguing strongly that they played a positive role in morale-building among GIs, rather than having the deleterious effects on fighting men the OWI expected.

Moreover, the music choices of GIs both stateside and overseas lend considerable credence to a thesis of mine that two primary ingredients of successful war-related songs (and of great songwriting) were sentiment and humor (though rarely together in the same song). These qualities had tremendous capacity for building morale and motivating war-related activities, because they both touched the hearer in a very personal way. As used here humor can be much more than just laugh-out-loud jokes; fun and playfulness play a part too, as being recreational without being comic, or, if you will, "fun" without being funny, such as watching or playing in a football game or other spectator sport (see Huizinga 2–3). Throughout the broad spectrum of war-related music, no category of songs escaped the humorous treatment, including patriotic anthems and militant war songs. Funny and lighthearted songs helped relieve tensions about everything from boot camp ("G.I. Jive") and the life of foot soldiers ("What Do You Do In The Infantry?") to working the defense plant swing shift ("Milkman Keep Those Bottles Quiet" [Leo Feist, 1944]) and gasoline rationing ("Let's Hitch A Horsie To The Automobile" [Leeds Music, 1942]). The first three songs became popular, and the last, from the 1942 Universal film *Get Hep To Love*, was a stand-out musical number that got out the gas rationing message by soft-pedaling it.

Primarily because the meaning of *sentiment* has collapsed into that of *sentimentality* in contemporary American culture, it's hard to appreciate that a much higher value was placed on sentiment during World War II than now. While *sentimentality* then as today carried the pejorative connotation of sentiment taken to mawkish or maudlin extremes, *sentiment* itself, simply as something based on feeling or emotion, was viewed positively. And its corresponding adjective *sentimental,* in its sense of appealing to tender feelings, often romantic ones, meant something equally positive. That songwriters of the time were well aware of the positive spin the public placed on all things sentimental is evidenced by such titles as "Sentimental Lady," "Something Sentimental" and the chart-busting hit for most of 1945, "Sentimental Journey." Charles Newman directly articulated the high value placed on sentiment in his lyric for "A Boy In Khaki, A Girl In Lace" (ABC Music, 1942) with music by Allie Wrubel. The verse asks the listener not to *neglect* it: "Tho' sentimental things are often forgotten / In a world so filled with care / Could you find some time to spare / For the story of a love affair?" For the most part, then, during World War II *sentimental* was almost synonymous with *romantic*.

Voices from within and without the music biz chimed in, supporting the positive effect of music on morale. *Variety* virtually defined the connection in an unsigned editorial on January 6, 1943: "'Morale' it is called from the front line to the home front. Morale means entertainment; entertainment means making a heavy heart lighter, a strained day of work or warfare just a shade brighter. The man at the front is sustained by a song on his lips; the men and women on the home front, ceaselessly twisting bolts and riveting steel, are bolstered by a laugh" (3). Earlier, just twenty days after Pearl Harbor, the first luminary to associate music and morale in the trades was the normally cantankerous musician's union boss James Caesar Petrillo in a full-page letter (paid for by the AFM, one presumes) "To The President And The People of The United States" (*Billboard* 27 Dec. 1941: 33). Petrillo acknowledges morale's importance for winning the war and declares that "in the building of morale the Federation and its members can and will do its share. For music has always been and is today one of the finest media for maintaining high public morale and the business, the profession, the very life work of the Federation and its members is Music." He concludes with a new union slogan—MUSIC FOR MORALE.

Agreeing with that sentiment was Dinah Shore in "Singing for Victory," an article she wrote for the May 1942 *Radio Hit Songs*, one of many pulp magazines during the 1940s that published the lyrics of new and recent popular songs. Shore recounts her struggle after graduating from Vanderbilt University between choosing a career in social service or becoming a professional singer. Even after she had "caught on," she says, "I'd find myself worrying whether I had done the right thing. December 7th, 1941, assured me that I had" (9). Before then she had never considered how singers "might prove of some national value," but thanks to the letters she started receiving from defense workers and "our lads in army corps, naval stations, aboard the battlewagons in the Pacific" who heard her on records or radio, she realized how she and other performers were improving the morale of both civilians and the military. Some of her own home front singing experiences helped raise not just morale but money, lots of it, for war-related causes. In her article Shore takes special delight in her appearance at a War Bond and Stamp rally in her home town of Nashville, Tennessee, where she helped raise $500,000 in a single day. Shore concludes with her thoughts on a "huge sign" at the corner of Broadway and Forty-seventh Street in New York City that read "Production Lines Are Battle Lines—What Have You Done Today?" "I never fail to read it without thinking that we in the entertainment field are on the production line. We're helping as best we can—in the only way we know how. I'm proud to have been given an opportunity to serve."

In a large patriotic ad in *Billboard* on October 10, 1942, the statements about morale are clearly sincere, though the ad is indirectly designed to sell a product. Seeburg, one of the country's top two or three manufacturers of jukeboxes, placed the ad. At the top is a large drawing of an "Uncle Sam" top hat decorated with the stars and stripes. Slightly behind the hat is a drawing of a jukebox, and both are surrounded by a ribbon with little stars in it and a sort of aura of musical notes. In large letters the ad reads "Let's Go America! / BUY MORE / U.S. DEFENSE BONDS / and STAMPS." But above that pitch for War Bonds, in slightly smaller letters, is the following: "MUSIC IS A MORALE BUILDER— / OVER 50,000,000 people a week listen / to Automatic Phonographs!"—Seeburg's pitch to have people keep popping nickels in its machines. But also, in and of itself, this is a dramatic statement of how widely music was listened to and connected with morale. At the bottom but equally impressive are the words "Keep 'em flying!" followed by "The J. P. Seeburg Corporation Is Making Gun Turret Assemblies For The U.S. Army Air Corps*Bomb Release Controls For The U.S. Army Air Corps*Signal Corps Radio Equipment." Like many other music biz businesses, Seeburg contributed to the war effort both by converting to war manufacturing and by helping boost morale.

As defense work continued, more and more manufacturers arranged for popular music to be played in their plants to lift the morale of workers at their monotonous tasks. Even whole traveling shows entertained people during breaks at industrial sites. Most famous was the *Lunch Time Follies* series produced by the American Theatre Wing, many editions of which featured dialogue material by Pulitzer Prize–winning playwright Maxwell Anderson and songs by Harold Rome, composer/lyricist of the long-running Garment Workers' Union revue *Pins and Needles* in the late 1930s (see Jones 116–19; Rome's individual songs for the *Follies* are taken up elsewhere in this book). The edition of *Lunch Time Follies* that played at the Revere Copper & Brass plant in Rome, New York, featured Vivienne Segal, the original Vera Simpson in Rodgers and Hart's recent *Pal Joey,* and other lesser-known Broadway performers doing songs and skits about defense work and the war in general, all of whom received for such an out-of-town gig just $10 per day, and for shows in the New York City area a mere $7.50. And at the Revere plant, at least, they performed at noon, 8 P.M., and 4 A.M. so workers from all shifts could attend a performance. For the performers, such morale-building efforts were a case of "what I did for love," with little thought of monetary gain. In the words of the plant's labor relations director, B. F. Dart, the "morale show," as *Billboard* dubbed it, was a "worth-while effort toward our defense program" (2 Jan. 1943: 4).

Also working for morale on the cheap, but by choice, was Phil Spitalny, leader of his famed (and very good) All Girl Orchestra, who "dedicated himself for the duration to entertaining the armed forces—and that also goes for all the girls." Spitalny's radio sponsor, General Electric, picked up the group's transportation expenses, but neither Spitalny nor the girls were "paid for army and naval encampment appearances" (*Variety* 25 Mar. 1942: 54). And Spitalny became an activist: "[Playing freebies] should also go for all the other name bands. . . . Making money nowadays should be the least important thing—'making victory possible is all-important. . . . What good will money do, anyhow, should the Axis triumph?' is a question Spitalny aims at bandleaders who are financially able to do what he's doing."

The most prominent public figure to recognize the contribution of entertainment—including popular music—to the war effort was also the most prominent public figure in the United States—President Franklin D. Roosevelt. In a congratulatory telegram to the National Conference of the Entertainment Industry for War Activities, which *Billboard* printed in full on June 12, 1943, FDR wrote, in part, "Entertainment is always a national asset. Invaluable in time of peace it is indispensable in wartime. . . . All those who are working in the entertainment industry . . . are building and maintaining national morale both on the battlefront and on the home front" (3). The need to maintain such morale among Americans who were becoming increasingly pluralistic, even in their musical tastes, resulted in the writing of literally thousands of war-related songs by professional and amateur songwriters who were in many ways as diverse and pluralistic as their intended audience.

# 2:

# *"I Hear America Singing"*

## But Who Wrote All Those Songs?

Walt Whitman first heard America singing back in the nineteenth century. By the time lyricist Mitchell Parish and composer Peter De Rose chose Whitman's words to title their national unity song (Robbins, 1940), they could have meant it literally, what with all of the patriotic and war-related pieces being written even by that early date. And thousands more would follow during the course of the war.

I've heard and read for years that World War I produced more songs than World War II or any other war, but I've never found proof of this assertion. In his 1972 *American Popular Song*, Alec Wilder asserted with no documentation that the "songs of the early forties didn't shift to war themes to the extent popular songs had during World War I" (502). And in an article on popular music and war, historian Jeffrey C. Livingston maintained that "Between April 1917 and November 1918, when the war ended, Tin Pan Alley produced more songs than any comparable period in its history" (33–34). While he may have meant popular songs generally, Livingston's context implies that he was specifically referring to war-related songs, which is clearly how Kathleen E. R. Smith took it when she repeated the statement when writing about war songs during both world wars (71). Finally, popular music historian David A. Jasen explicitly confines the songwriting and publishing he is talking about to that of Tin Pan Alley professionals: "World War I had the most songs published about and during it. This is not surprising, considering this was Tin Pan Alley's period of greatest dominance. . . . While the number of World War II songs was far fewer than those written for World War I, the quality was much better" (406–7).

Yet even Jasen's remark on Tin Pan Alley can be challenged, and indeed it *was* challenged long before he even wrote it, by an outfit with its finger surely on the pulse of American songwriting: ASCAP. In its open letter "Where Are the War-Songs?" ASCAP stated, "There have been more songs written in six months of this war than in ALL of World War Number One" (*Billboard* 25 Sept. 1943: 30). ASCAP would not have fabricated this comparison just to hype its member writers and publishers for fear of a public challenge from someone in the notoriously contentious (and litigious) music business at the time. One thus feels comfortable about the accuracy of ASCAP's comparison.

There is also strong documentary evidence that the output of American war-related songs during World War II was most probably unsurpassed in any other war as I found in my research described in the preface. Yet while the number of songs I counted is huge, the circumstances of many songs' publication and copyright registrations (or their absence) make it impossible to know for sure how many songs the war inspired. In assembling the "manageable" collection of about 1,700 songs upon which I based this book, literally thousands of others passed through my hands as sheet music or lyrics reprinted in the lyric magazines of the 1940s. These thousands mostly were written by America's wartime amateurs. Previously, I had no idea amateur songwriting during World War II was so vast a subject. And the more I read the songs, the more I realized that they would not be fruitful for my purposes, in part because of their limited exposure. But before deciding to treat them only peripherally, I had built up a tiny second database of 177 amateur song lyrics. Accordingly, amateur songwriters and their songs play only a marginal role in this book.

The reason we'll never come close to guessing the total number of war-related songs during World War II has largely to do with the amateur songwriters. Often these composers or lyricists privately published their songs, and despite a frequent claim of copyright on their title pages, many were never registered, according to my random spot check in the U.S. Copyright Office. Small regional presses published many other songs by amateurs, and it has been only a matter of chance—say, the gift to a library of someone's sheet music collection—that such material has found its way into repositories and archives. By their very nature, such collections are strictly hit or miss. Even more amateur war songs were published by so-called song poem publishers (more about them in the section following), who (for a fee) would have a person's lyrics set to music, printed, and even copyrighted, frequently in the lyricist's own name. I first became aware of this while at the John Hay Library, but I had my eyes truly opened at the Library of Congress, when I began turning up literally *hundreds* of songs from the same composer and publisher but each with a different lyricist. Just how many of these even the Library of Congress has retained for its collection is anybody's guess. Finally, there are the *unpublished* war-related songs. As I rifled through the Copyright Office card catalogues for the war years (the paper files a blessing for this project), I kept seeing song after song whose titles declared them to be war-related, most stamped "EU" for "entered unpublished," including many multiple songs with duplicate titles. As two preposterous examples, I decided to check out the titles "Over Here" and "Remember Pearl Harbor." My own files contain three published songs with the former title, four with the latter (one of which became a fleeting hit). But talk about the tip of an iceberg! The Copyright Office card files reveal that seventy different writers registered an "Over Here" and another sixty-eight a "Remember Pearl Harbor." Extrapolating from what I saw in the catalogues, in lyric magazines, and on the thousands of pieces of sheet music I examined, I feel confident that—professional and amateur songwriting taken together—there had to have been at least ten thousand if not literally tens of thousands of war-related songs written during World War II.

### *"From The Coast Of Maine To The Rockies": The Amateurs*

"From the Rockies all the way west" the lyric continues in Benny Davis, Russ Morgan, and Ted Murry's thoroughly professional song about men enlisting coast to coast (Santly-Joy, 1942). The lines also map the demographics of amateur war-song writers. After a few weeks at the Library of Congress reading the title pages of thousands of pieces of sheet music, it dawned on me that I had seen at least one song by an amateur published in each of the then forty-eight states—and Hawaii. In most cases it was clear that the songwriters themselves lived in these diverse locales, since small regional—virtually neighborhood—outfits published their songs, very few of which were affiliated with ASCAP or BMI. Another option for amateurs was to publish their songs themselves. Simply by way of illustration, Franklin Fillmore Lewis's "Good-Bye, Dear Homeland Goodbye," published in 1942 by Hunleth Music in St. Louis, is typical of regional publication, the copyright line noting that Lewis lived in Webster Grove, Missouri. Self-published sheet music presents its publishing information in one of two ways. Most forthright is a simple notice: "I Came To Say Goodbye Sweetheart" was "Published [or Copyright] by Felix Pisani, Cascade, New Hampshire, 1944." Other writers made their names (or another name) into a publishing company: "Copyright 1943 by Baxter Music, Roxbury, Mass." on Erna Baxter's "Keep A Star In The Window And A Prayer In Your Heart." Whether Baxter Music ever published another song is anybody's guess, but amateur songwriters like

Baxter most likely created publishing firms to give their work an aura of professionalism.

Other amateur songwriters, especially lyricists, sought a different route to professionalism, making them prey to "song sharks," the music-for-hire scam artists whose classified ads in pulp magazines offered the musical setting and publication of a person's lyrics for a fee, known to go as high as $125 during the war, a lot of money at the time. Magazines like *True Confessions, Photoplay,* and *Famous Fantastic Mysteries* ran numerous such ads:

> WANTED—Poems for musical setting. Submit for
> consideration. Phonograph transcriptions made.
> Rhyming Pamphlet FREE.
> Keenan's Studio, P. Box 2140, Bridgeport, Conn.
> (*Famous Fantastic Mysteries* March 1943: 144)

> ### POEMS WANTED
> **For Musical Setting**
> Mother, Home, Love, Sacred, Patriotic, Comic
> or any subject. Don't Delay–Send us your
> Original Poem at once–for immediate con-
> sideration and FREE Rhyming Dictionary
> RICHARD BROTHERS 27 WOODS BUILDING, CHICAGO, ILL.
> (*Fantastic Adventures* Jan. 1943: 232)

These were just two of literally dozens of such outfits. Song-poem publishing was no small-potatoes venture on the fringes of the music biz but a veritable industry unto itself. And like any industry, it had its giants. Keenan's Music Service was close to the top, though its namesake proprietor, Eddie Keenan, composed virtually all of its melodies. Way up there too were Leo and Hector Richard, who also banged out most of their own hack tunes but employed more freelance hired guns than Keenan. The Richard boys give an address in Chicago's Woods Building (albeit not always the *same* address), but their actual publishing firm, Success Music, was in Aurora, Illinois, a small city southwest of Chicago. Clearly, a Chicago address in an ad looked more "glamorous" to prospective clients. Seemingly, other song-poem publishers used not only "blind" addresses but company name aliases as well. While literally thousands of pieces of song-poem sheet music passed through my hands, I never saw any published over the names of the companies that advertised in the pulps. Equally interesting, and a bit disconcerting, is that five outfits that dealt at least partly in song-poem publishing were affiliated member-publishers with BMI—Success Music, Shelby Music in Detroit, Cine-Mart Music and

Claude Lapham Music, both in Hollywood, and Transradio Music in New York. Although BMI actively sought to increase its membership, it's doubtful the organization would have accepted firms known to be strictly rip-off artists in the song-poem publishing game. Those song-poem publishers that were BMI members also produced some legitimate material for publication and even potential recording.

Never affiliated with BMI, Nordyke was the Great White among the song-poem sharks. And for a monster, Nordyke was also something of a Johnny-come-lately, founded only in 1943 by thirty-two-year-old Mortimer Singer, who "capitalized on the glut of amateur lyricists whose patriotic sentiments burst forth during World War II" ("Nordyke"). Singer quickly assembled the largest stable of "top song-a-minute guys," who "worked on a freelance basis, literally mailing their music in from their respective spots on the national map." The output of some of these tunesmiths reached almost improbable figures, even if, in all likelihood, they recycled a single tune for one song-poet in Lafayette, Louisiana, and another in Lebanon, New Hampshire, banking on the odds the two wannabe lyricists would never hear each others' songs. My handling of prodigious quantities of their stuff tells me that the king of the "shirtsleeve songsmiths" working for Nordyke (and earlier Keenan's) had to be Bob Carleton, with the music for at least five hundred war-related songs to his dubious credit—each with its own lyricist. The Nordyke stable included other prolific hacks such as Cliff Dixon, Walter Samuels, M. C. Sax (who also punched out tunes for Superior Song Studios in Passaic, New Jersey), Lew Tobin, Rodney Van Tyle, David Hall, and Ray Hibbeler. Singer even got the Richard boys to write some tunes for him despite their own thriving racket. And some of the Nordyke team ran their own operations as well.

Song-poem firms didn't just reuse melodies and trade off melodists; they recycled and swapped their cover art. From a stock of perhaps eight to twelve designs Nordyke would select the appropriate one for the cover of a militant march, a patriotic anthem, or a romantic ballad. Whether song-poem companies employed artists to create such designs or merely cannibalized them from clip-art collections isn't clear, but, either way, identical cover art appears on the sheet music of different publishers, notably Keenan's and Shelby Music; some publishers even "borrowed" a few Nordyke designs.

What kinds of songs did wartime amateurs write? The thousands of song titles I looked at revealed that amateurs were writing the same kinds of songs as professionals—either directly war-oriented songs or sentimental songs on war-associated themes, amateurs writing far more of the former than the latter. My modest data base of around 180 amateur songs includes 117 in the war-song categories of militant and Axis-bashing, national unity and home front support, patriotism, and service tributes. Sentimental song titles number just thirty-six, or about 20 percent. By comparison, professional and other songwriters published by ASCAP and BMI publishers wrote 834 in the war-song group (or nearly 50 percent) and 544 (or 32 percent) in the sentimental or romantic class. The remaining three hundred or so professional songs were about our allies, army life, the world after the war, and other subjects. The "other" professionally published songwriters include amateur war-song contest winners, non-professional songwriting servicemen and women, and writers of amateur songs deemed worthy of publication by an ASCAP or BMI publisher. Factoring in the thousands of other amateur titles I read, it's clear that there were far and away more songs of the martial war-song variety by amateurs and professionals alike than there were songs of wartime romance and sentiment. These figures should dispel the cognate war-song myth that "Only in World War I did the number of war songs approximate those about love" (Livingston 33), embellished by Smith as "No American war, with the possible exception of the Civil War, yielded as many martial tunes as did the Great War, nor has any war added such numbers of sentimental songs to the permanent repertory of American popular songs" (71). To the contrary, the numbers show that World War II produced both the most war-related songs overall and the most specifically militant war songs.

So much for the quantity of amateur songs. What about their quality? The kindest thing to say is that most of the lyrics and music just wasn't very good. Regardless of the subject matter, amateur songs suffered from banal sentiments, unimaginative and clichéd language, and "rhymes" that didn't. Moreover, most also lacked drama, logic, and emotional progression, not to mention the playfulness and skillful manipulation of language found in songs by professionals. For example, in Hy Zaret and Alex Kramer's "Counting The Days" (Santly-Joy, 1945), a lovely ballad of a girl waiting for her guy's imminent return, the girl plays on different meanings of "count" in a natural and easy manner, with no forced artifice in the writing: "Counting the stars I hear you whisper / 'Darling, count on my love to see you through.'" The absence of such playfulness, coupled with the almost reverent seriousness of most amateur writers' approaches to their subject, results in their lyrics' pervasive, unsmiling solemnity.

The starched-collar formality of their writing is mirrored in the way many amateurs identified themselves on the sheet music. Rarely did they use the familiar first names or nicknames that were so common among professionals: Johnny Mercer, Sammy Cahn, Hoagy Carmichael, Jimmy McHugh, Pee Wee King, Fats Waller, and so on. Of the nearly seven hundred Tin Pan Alley writers of war-related songs, only two always used their formal three full names—John Jacob Loeb (best known for "Seems

Like Old Times") and John Benson Brooks ("You Came A Long Way From Missouri"). But many amateur songsmiths used both their first and middle names, as, for example, Louisa May Muffly, May Fiske Hoffman, Albert Thatcher Yarna, and Harold Webster Cate, New Hampshire's self-styled George M. Cohan, who churned out over a half-dozen patriotic flag-wavers, militant rabble-rousers, and other assorted war-songs. Some amateurs included a title as well (for example, Mrs. G. C. Kimberlin, Dr. Lorin F. Wheelwright). Both practices seem to be attempts to dignify the fact that these people were writing popular songs.

Three-name songwriter Grace Warner Gulesian (1884–1984) was a Boston-area pianist, piano teacher, and minor composer of songs, choral pieces, and operettas (Cohen 1:292). But in the realm of writing lyrics and popular war songs she certainly qualifies as a novice. Fortuitously, one of her songs has the same title, source, and year of publication (1943) as another by three seasoned Tin Pan Alleymen, lyricists Henry Myers and Edward ("Flying Down To Rio") Eliscu and composer Jay ("Brother, Can You Spare A Dime") Gorney. Both called "Damn The Torpedoes Full Speed Ahead," the two songs conveniently illustrate salient differences between most professional and amateur war-song writing. The starting point of each was Admiral David Farragut's exclamation of defiance at the Battle of Mobile Bay during the Civil War. But the sheet music cover of Gulesian's song also notes that Farragut's words were "Quoted by President Franklin Delano Roosevelt in his Navy Day Radio Address on October 27, 1941," suggesting that Gulesian was also inspired by FDR's war-preparedness speech.

How the two songs' lyricists make use of Farragut's familiar phrase is markedly different. Myers and Eliscu's lyric takes the form of a folk ballad (with music to match by Gorney). In just eight lines of tight, economical writing, each verse vividly recounts the exploits of a war hero who showed courage under fire and pressed on despite overwhelming odds. After treating Farragut himself in the first verse, Myers and Eliscu follow with the heroics of three very different men in World War II itself. The second verse summarizes in few and witty words James H. "Jimmy" Doolittle's desire to "nip at the Nipponese," climaxing in his audacious bombing raid on Tokyo on April 18, 1942; the writers play the pilot's name against a current colloquialism in telling how Doolittle "dooed his duty and he dooed it good!" The third verse pays tribute to Dorie Miller, a black mess attendant in the navy at Pearl Harbor. When the attack began, he dropped his kitchen chores, grabbed an anti-aircraft machine gun he had never been trained to operate, and scored a number of hits on Japanese planes, for which Admiral Nimitz decorated him with the Navy Cross. The fourth verse recounts Dr. Corydon Wassell's heroics under fire as the Japanese were advancing on Java early in 1942; the fifty-eight-year-old doctor singlehandedly evacuated twelve men supposedly too badly wounded to be moved and got them to safety and medical help (by himself) on a ship bound for Australia. The chorus following each verse says that each hero figuratively if not literally echoed Farragut's "Damn the torpedoes. Full speed ahead" by their actions in seemingly impossible situations. A final fifth stanza admonishes not just servicemen but all Americans to be "up and on our toes" in order to win the war, concluding with the outrageous but appropriate pun, "The cowards have their 'ifs' and 'buts' but we've got plenty of Farra*guts!*" (italics supplied). All of which illustrates well how playfulness (not humor) can serve an altogether serious subject.

Gulesian, on the other hand, doesn't repeat Farragut's battle cry thematically throughout, as do Myers and Eliscu; she quotes it only once at the very end of her song, which is intended to be a general tribute to the U.S. Navy. The song's first verse begins with two familiar nautical expressions back-to-back—"Clear the decks! Anchors aweigh!"—which make little or no sense in this order, since the first means to prepare for battle action and the second simply that the anchors have been hoisted up so the ship can start sailing. The rest of the brief verse has the ship predictably speeding "through wind and wave," the U.S. flag guarding the "Freedom of the seas." The second verse starts as if battle will be engaged, justifying the song's title. "On they come! / There are millions on the way" sounds like the enemy is coming, but the third line identifies the "millions" as the young American sailors who are prepared to fight for "the Grand old U.S.A." These little verses are murky enough, but the song's considerably longer chorus (it's a march, by the way) confuses things more, starting off with the U.S. fleet "Ploughing along, / Singing a song" and "Bound to conquer ever more." "Conquer" is a word the Office of War Information chastised songwriters for using. A long OWI directive to radio writers and songwriters stated that the armed forces should never be depicted as out to "conquer" (that's what the enemy did) but to "liberate" (see Smith 66 and 186 n. 1). From the lyrics I've read, those guidelines for professional writers never reached the likes of Gulesian and her amateur peers, who continued to project the "conquering hero" image of the American soldier or sailor in their songs. Gulesian finally wraps up with "Our commander in chief," that is, FDR, saying "Damn the torpedoes! Full speed ahead!"—a reference to his Navy Day Address mentioned on the song's title page—despite the fact that the song contains not one image of courage under fire to properly elicit that expression.

Among the general run of amateur lyric writing during World War II, Gulesian's piece is pretty average and therefore a useful illustration of some songwriting pitfalls of amateurs. Despite their poor quality, though, these songs are of historical importance in demonstrating the widespread patriotism of ordinary people. Most amateur songwriters didn't expect fame or fortune, except perhaps those who became marks for the song-poem sharks. In addition to expressing patriotism, such songs served as an important catharsis for their writers. For example, quite a number of amateur war songs by men as well as women pay tribute to a son or other relative in the service, pray for his safety or speedy return, or memorialize his death in combat. The act of writing such songs becomes an emotional, even spiritual, release for the writer. For amateurs and professionals alike, writing militant war songs and Axis-bashers also provided a catharsis of hate, in which writers could vent in a public medium their feelings about the Axis Powers generally, or specific events (Pearl Harbor, Bataan) or in-dividuals (Hitler, Tojo, Mussolini). (For more on this, see chapter 6.)

Finally, for many amateur composers and lyricists, writing war songs provided a feeling of inclusiveness, of direct involvement in the war ef-fort. The vast outpouring of amateur war songs was a major expression of popular participation, especially because the United States of World War II was more textually and aurally oriented (thanks to radio) than the later visually oriented eras of TV and computers. Songs' words and music were more central in the consciousness of all Americans than of mainly younger ones as in the post-fifties decades of the rock/pop culture, so even amateur songwriters could view what they were doing as an active, par-ticipatory contribution to home front support for the war.

### *"Little Americans": The Youngest Amateurs of All*

Dick Sanford, Jack Betzner, and Irv Carroll's song of that name (Mills Music, 1942) praises the unselfconscious displays of patriotism by Amer-ica's children, some of whom turned their patriotic fervor into songs sup-porting the war effort. So before we leave amateur songwriters entirely, the few known wartime songs by children deserve some mention, though more for their interest as documents of home front social history than as songwriting.

In 1942, Hall & McCreary, a Chicago publisher affiliated with SESAC (the Society of European Stage Authors and Composers, a licensing agency similar to ASCAP and BMI), brought out a song called "Mow The Japs Down!" that took for its melody the traditional sea chanty "Blow The Man Down," arranged by one John Royce but with lyrics collectively by "The students of FORT VANNOY SCHOOL," an elementary school in Grants Pass, Oregon. The song's first four stanzas vigorously assault the Japanese, the fifth shifts to complying with rationing ("We'll give up our sugar, we'll give up our tires"), and the sixth, as is almost inevitable in such songs, pro-motes buying War Bonds and Stamps. There's nothing remarkable about the song itself. But that someone, presumably one of the kids' teachers, took the trouble to find a professional publisher for it, and that it got published, shows that some adults took seriously children's desire to participate in the war effort.

*Songs for Schools at War* was a twelve-page booklet containing, among other pieces, some war songs by children; it was published by the Education Section of the War Savings Staff of the Treasury Department in 1942 for the Music Educators National Conference. The contents of this curiosity are a mixed bag: two pages of lyrics by Earl T. Ross of the War Savings Staff Field Division about (what else?) buying War Bonds and Stamps, set to familiar tunes like "Take Me Out To The Ball Game" and "It's A Long Way To Tipperary"; two more pages of War Bond lyrics to equally familiar melodies submitted by the Pittsburgh Public Schools, with no indication of whether students or teachers wrote them; and a song about wartime thrift called "It's The Little Things That Count" by two professionals serving in the army at the time, composer Dick Uhl and lyricist Tom Adair, the latter best known for his clever lyrics to Matt Dennis's "Let's Get Away From It All" and "Will You Still Be Mine?" In the midst of this grown-up writing are three songs by schoolchildren, each with an informational headnote by their proud teachers.

Like "Mow The Japs Down!" the first, "Friends of Uncle Sam," was a group effort, but this time the music as well as the lyrics were written by the Junior Boys Glee Club of Beaumont High School in St. Louis. The song is a standard bond-buying pitch, but the kids' energy and desire to get it into its final form, written down by their teacher, Else Brix, is worth recounting: "Line-by-line they put together the first stanza with many suggestions, arguments, erasures and much rewriting. Then, came attempts at setting these words to music. They sang them or worked them out at the piano and told me quite definitely when they liked a chord or disliked one." Clearly this was serious business for the glee club. The remaining two songs by kids were solo efforts by pupils at West Hill School in Ilion, New York. "Buy A Bond," another conventional fundraising spiel, was by ten-year-old Bobby Clark of the fourth grade, newly arrived in Ilion from "a one-room school in New Hampshire." Fifth-grader Shirley Swarthout wrote the words and music of "Take It On The Chin, America." Its general theme—rare for any war songs in 1942—was that America had to take its recent setbacks "on the chin" and persevere if it was to win the war. The song's final phrases are quite striking, especially for a fifth-grader's composition: "As MacArthur on Bataan / Took it like a man, / Take it on the chin, America, do!" Like home front adults, kids clearly found that writing songs to boost morale or encourage home front support offered a meaningful, significant sense of public participation in the war effort.

Songs by amateurs, whether children or adult, civilian or military, benefited song publishers in terms of public relations, if not financially. No sooner did the United States enter the war than publishers had to answer the charge that they were "still inclined to steer away from war-inspired numbers unless the latter have a novelty or romantic twist" (*Variety* 15 Apr. 1942: 1). One way for publishers to counter this perception and at the same time display their non-commercial patriotism and support for the war was to publish occasional militant war songs by amateurs and war-related songs of all kinds by the men and women of the U.S. armed forces. Accordingly, the names of songwriting GIs and occasional home front amateurs appear on the sheet music of such prestigious firms as Leeds, Carl Fischer, Witmark, Irving Berlin Inc., Robbins, and Shapiro, Bernstein.

### "Jumping To The Jukebox": The Tin Pan Alley Professionals

But let's face it, war or no war, music publishing *is* a commercial enterprise, and while some bigtime publishers showed support for the war by promoting songs by amateur civilians or service personnel, nearly all the war-related songs with wide distribution came from Tin Pan Alley. Despite its name, Tin Pan Alley has never been so much a place as a profession, or, more accurately, the related professions of songwriters, arrangers, publishers, pluggers, and the like. "According to legend," around the turn of the century, composer/lyricist Monroe Rosenfeld gave the name Tin Pan Alley to the cacophony of tinny upright pianos banging out tunes in dozens of publishers' offices on West Twenty-eighth Street between Broadway and Sixth Avenue in New York City (Jasen ix). By the war, Tin Pan Alley's epicenter had moved midtown to the Brill Building at 1619 Broadway, home to at least forty ASCAP publishers and others.

Historically, Tin Pan Alley was "the branch of the music publishing business that hired composers and lyricists on a permanent basis to create popular songs" (Jasen ix). This definition, mostly known only by people in the music biz, is far too narrow for the war years. By the 1940s songwriters in the permanent employ of publishers were pretty much a thing of the past, so in talking about Tin Pan Alley during the war it would be an absurdity to exclude the majority who were *not* thus employed but nevertheless central to American popular music (the names Jerome Kern and Hoagy Carmichael come immediately to mind). The general public more broadly sees "Tin Pan Alley" as the "generic term for all publishers of popular American sheet music, regardless of their geographic location" (ix). This book embraces something like this looser connotation of Tin Pan Alley, the population of which includes all publishers affiliated with ASCAP, BMI, or SESAC and all professional song-writers similarly affiliated, whether they wrote primarily for Hollywood, Broadway, or Tin Pan Alley's world of popular music.

During the war years there was much crossover of songwriters for stage, screen, and the popular song outlets of sheet music, records, radio, and dance bands. In the aggregate, about seven hundred Tin Pan Alley writers wrote a huge number of war songs—1,700 or more. That figure, plus the fact that Tin Pan Alley publishers published those tunes, should dispel the myth that professional songwriters balked at writing war songs as much as professional publishers allegedly balked at publishing them. In fact, there's solid evidence that songsmiths sometimes went out of their way to include a war reference even in songs that didn't need one, much as Hollywood inserted war messages in movies just to keep the war before the public. Albert De Brue, Irving Taylor, and Vic Mizzy's "Take It Easy" (Santly-Joy, 1943) is a comic number in which a girl is admonishing her dancing partner not to dance so athletically and, hence, unromantically. The song was interpolated into the MGM musical *Two Girls and a Sailor,* released in April 1944, and Guy Lombardo's recording was a modest hit in the first five months of that year. The song's only glance at the war occurs when the girl offers her guy a practical reason to tone down his dancing style—"TAKE IT EASY—TAKE IT EASY, / Don't you know you only get three pairs of shoes a year?"—a direct reference to shoe rationing, which had begun in February 1943. In 1945, Al Hoffman, Jerry Livingston, and Milton Drake, the team that created the inimitable nonsense of "Mairzy Doats," came up with the equally silly saga of the de-furred polar bear "Fuzzy Wuzzy," which was published by its authors' own firm in late 1944 and had strong record sales by both Al Trace and the Jesters from March through August 1945. The familiar chorus about a bear who got too close a shave at the North Pole barbershop is as remote from the war as possible, but the verse setting up poor Fuzzy's tale begins "Private Elmer Johnson, stationed up Alaska way / Saw the strangest animal walk through the woods one day," about which he then wrote the folks back home. What he wrote, of course, is the chorus of "Fuzzy Wuzzy," which stands alone perfectly well without this set-up glancing at the war, and yet that glance is only one of two in popular songs that took notice of our Alaska campaign.

An informal "census" of the race, ethnicity, and religion of war-song writers—professional and amateur together—broadly parallels the demographic distribution of the wartime population of the United States as a whole. In the absence of biographical data, it can only be inferred from the names and geographic locations of amateur songwriters (gleaned from self-published songs and copyright notices) that their many thousands comprised the majority of war-song writers and were proportionally representative of the majority of the actual population—primarily Caucasian and Christian (Catholic and Protestant together). But nearly all of the ethnically diverse (or, more traditionally, "minority") writers of war-related songs were squarely in the ranks of the Tin Pan Alley professionals. During the twentieth century and beyond, these "minorities" of African Americans, Hispanics, and Jews have made far more extensive contributions to American songwriting, including war-related songs during World War II, than their numbers represent in relation to the total population. Since their wartime songs are generally indistinguishable in style and content from those of other professional songsmiths, they are treated together in the appropriate theme-based chapters, but some of their songs mirror issues of specific concern to each diverse group of war-song writing professionals.

### *"We Are Americans Too": Black Songwriters, Black Pride*

When the previous decade's depression economy shifted almost overnight to a defense economy even before Pearl Harbor, most of America's nearly thirteen million blacks were not as prosperous as whites. Segregation prevailed in the south and discrimination in the north, race riots flared up in Detroit and Harlem in 1942 and 1943, and the doors to economic upward mobility were closed practically everywhere. But as the war went on, the economic status of many African Americans improved. On June 27, 1941, President Roosevelt issued Executive Order 8802, which "forbade racial discrimination in defense industries and established the Fair Employment Practices Commission to enforce the ban" (Bailey 150). Partly because of this, black employment in manufacturing rose from about 500,000 in 1941 to over 1,200,000 in 1944 (see Perrett 321). Correspondingly, 961,000 blacks had entered the military by 1944. Some were drafted, but most enlisted out of a genuine desire to serve, despite the indignities of segregated units in the army, the navy accepting blacks only as mess attendants, and the marines not accepting them at all (Bailey 55). Yet eventually many African American soldiers and sailors saw combat duty, with some, like Dorie Miller, distinguishing themselves for personal heroism. Only in 1948 did an executive order from President Harry S. Truman desegregate the armed services.

With difficult to intolerable social conditions for blacks in both the service and civilian life, one might expect songs by those who wrote about the war or the home front to be filled with protest. But that wasn't the case. Like the thousands who enlisted, the songwriting blacks of World War II were patriotic, fighting mad, and racially proud. A case in point: blues aficionados will know the name Son House (born Eddie James

House Jr.). Ann Patrick of the John Hay Library introduced me to a CD reissue of a war-related song by this early bluesman of the Delta School, who recorded commercially only in 1930 and 1965 but whom Alan Lomax made a field recording of for the Library of Congress in 1942. It's doubtful anyone in the 1940s heard House's "American Defense," except for folks at local bars and town socials in his rural Mississippi. House wrote for them, not to conform to Tin Pan Alley's expectations. Even so, he proposes a very mainstream answer to low home front morale: "No use to sheddin' no tears, / No use to havin' no cares, / This war may last two more years" (House), his advice predating by longer than that Johnny Mercer and Harold Arlen's hit similarly urging people to "AC-CENT-TCHU-ATE THE POSITIVE, / E-limynate the negative" (Edwin H. Morris, 1944).

Of the forty or so war-related songs by black professionals, most were the same kinds of militant war songs, spoofs of rationing and shortages, and sentimental ballads of soldiers away and girls back home that white Tin Pan Alley wrote. Some scored big, like Phil Moore's "Shoo-Shoo Baby" (Leeds, 1943), a huge hit for both the Andrews Sisters and Ella Mae Morse in 1944 (see chapter 11). But wartime black songwriters also dealt with specifically black matters, as in two lyrics by prolific and talented Andy Razaf and another by the country's premier black poet of the time, Langston Hughes.

Best known for collaborating with Fats Waller on such classics as "Ain't Misbehavin'" and "Honeysuckle Rose," Andy Razaf (born Andreamentania Paul Razafkeriefo) is the only American songwriter who could say he was related to royalty; Razaf's mother was American, the daughter of the first black U.S. ambassador to Madagascar, but his father was a nephew of Madagascar's Queen Ranavalona II. Razaf attributed his fierce black pride in part to his connection with black African nobility. Razaf's militant songs as well as those advocating War Bond drives also proclaim him to be a fiercely loyal and devoted American. Both of his war-related lyrics dealing with African Americans reflect Razaf's dual pride as an American and a black. Written before Pearl Harbor and with music by prominent black Broadway composer Eubie Blake with Charles L. Cooke, Razaf's lyric for "We Are Americans Too" (Handy Brothers, 1941) only tacitly suggests that black Americans deserve the same treatment, respect, and status as whites. In fact, the entire song makes no mention of color. All that indicates that blacks are the "We" of the title and of lines like "We have given up our blood and bone" is a single mention of "Twelve Million strong," the approximate black population in 1941. My guess is that the racial identity of the song's singer would have made the referent of "we" perfectly clear. With music by J. C. Johnson, Razaf's "A Yankee Doodle Tan (The Double 'V' Song)" (Broadway Music, 1942) is as explicitly about blacks as "We Are Americans Too" is oblique. The *Pittsburgh Courier,* considered the nation's most powerful black newspaper at the time (Burroughs), created the Double V campaign and its logo: one V within another, surmounted by the American eagle, with "DEMOCRACY" above and "AT HOME — ABROAD" below. This was to serve as a rallying point for blacks' civil rights at home while the United States was fighting a war for democracy abroad. Razaf's song praises the "tan" fighting man and his loyalty to the United States in the wonderfully playful pun "His color doesn't run."

Langston Hughes's lyric and Emerson Harper's music for "Freedom Road" (Musette, 1942) are in the style of a spiritual. The gist of the lyric is that "Hitler he may rant / Mussolini he may rave / I'm going after freedom if it leads me to my grave," each chorus repeatedly declaring that the singer is "marching down FREEDOM ROAD." Only once, still in the context of fighting the Axis, does Hughes even imply that his song is about equal rights for American blacks in addition to freedom for other oppressed peoples, when he writes, "Room in this world / For ev'ry race," but given Hughes's views on racial equality, the implication was most likely deliberate.

A black-white collaboration unusual on a song specifically about blacks occurred when Gene Krupa's all-white band, with vocal by equally white Anita O'Day, on January 23, 1942, recorded a tribute to blacks in the military, "Harlem On Parade," by white Redd Evans and black Benny Carter.

### "Hands Across the Border": The Hispanics

Not surprisingly, there weren't many Hispanic songwriters writing war-related songs—or popular songs in general—during the war, since the United States had a Latino population of only about 1,861,000 in 1940. Some who did write war-related numbers weren't Hispanic Americans but nationals of Latin American countries. For the Warner Brothers film of the same name released in March 1942, Cuban composer Ernesto ("Malagueña") Lecuona and American lyricist Kim Gannon wrote "Always In My Heart" (Remick, 1942); the title and Gannon's lyric expressed war-related feelings about separation and constancy ("I don't know exactly when dear / But I'm sure we'll meet again dear"). Lecuona and Gannon got an Academy Award nomination, close to half a year on the popularity charts, and lots of sales of sheet music and records by Glenn Miller and Jimmy Dorsey.

With the threat of war looming since the late 1930s, the government began taking a more visibly proactive approach to strengthening Pan-

American solidarity than just President Roosevelt's 1933 "Good Neighbor" pledge of non-intervention in Central and South American affairs. Americans' greater awareness of Latin American and Caribbean culture during the war years spurred a fad for all things South and Central American, notably a flood of Latin-inspired dance numbers from Tin Pan Alley, Hollywood, and Broadway (see Jones 133–34). Some Alleymen like Mort Greene and Harry Revel in "Hands Across The Border" (Greene-Revel, 1942) made Pan-American solidarity itself the subject of a song. Americans William B. Friedlander and Stanley Melba and Hispanic Guy Bagar even managed to squeeze Latin American relations and the Brazilian dance of its punning title into one song, "Uncle Sam-Ba (Tio Sam-Ba)" (Edward B. Marks, 1943). To return the compliment, Latino songwriter Sergio De Karlo and popular Cuban-American bandleader Xavier Cugat (with Spanish lyrics by Emilio De Torre and English by Al Stillman) each wrote a song praising and thanking FDR in "Mister Franklin D." (Latin American Publishing, 1942) and "Viva Roosevelt!" (Edward B. Marks, 1942).

### *"Koift War Bonds Un Stamps": Yiddish-American Songs and Their Audience*

Of all America's so-called minority songwriters, only Jewish composers and lyricists produced numbers of war-related songs way out of proportion to the country's comparatively small Jewish population, which, according to the *American Jewish Desk Reference,* was estimated at between 4,770,000 and 4,975,000 in 1940 (35). This abundance of songs is perfectly understandable, as Jews had been a dominant force in American popular music for decades prior to World War II, and, except for Cole Porter and a few less eminent figures, by the 1940s had a virtual monopoly on writing scores for Broadway musicals. Jewish studio songwriters flourished in Hollywood during the heyday of movie musicals in the 1930s and '40s, and while the position of Jews was not quite so dominant in Tin Pan Alley (except as publishers), by my own rough calculations professional Jewish composers and lyricists account for just over two hundred (or about 30 percent) of the seven hundred or so Alleymen and women who wrote war-related songs between 1939 and 1945. But like Broadway numbers by Jewish writers at the time, there was nothing particularly "Jewish" about their popular songwriting in general or their war-related songs in particular; accordingly, the huge output of war-related songs by Jewish songwriters will be dealt with alongside those by other professionals in the thematic chapters to follow. Just one commercial novelty number about the war was explicitly Jewish—Frank Davis, Win Brookhouse, Sam Braverman, and Charles Cody's "Make With The

Bullets, Benny" (Cherio Music, 1942). In the song, "Missus Goldberg" writes her darling soldier-boy son overseas, "Don't waste time in retail shots; Mow 'em down in wholesale lots," and other motherly advice.

But Jewish identity permeated another group of songs by Jewish composers and lyricists clustered farther downtown, in the vicinity of Second Avenue. These were the writers of Yiddish-American war-related songs, most written for the still-thriving Yiddish theatre and films. Their audience was primarily Yiddish-speaking (or at least comprehending) Jews in New York's Lower East Side, Brooklyn, Philadelphia, Baltimore, Detroit, and Chicago. Broadly speaking, the Yiddish songs were on the same war-related topics as those pouring out of Tin Pan Alley, from the pitch to buy War Bonds—Louis Stein and Sidney S. Cahan's "Koift War Bonds Un Stamps" (Metro Music, 1942)—to the love song of a girl back home to her sweetheart overseas—Louis Markowitz and Ilia Triling's "Got Hit Op Mein Bashertn" (Metro Music, 1944). One song even plays out like a Russian-Jewish cousin to Mack David and Vee Lawnhurst's popular "Johnny Zero" (see chapter 8), both about a hometown schlemiel who becomes a hero. In Herman Yablokoff's Yiddish "Berele Gorille," (J. & J. Kammen, 1943), the people of his village laughed at the fictional Berele as a kid, because, like his American counterpart Johnny, he was a real dummy. But in the Red Army at the Battle of Stalingrad he becomes a "gorilla," taking revenge on the Germans for shedding Jewish blood, and Stalin awards him a medal.

While such songs parallel types of mainstream war-related songs from Tin Pan Alley, others have some singular characteristics found only in Yiddish-American songwriting, according to Sylvia Fried, Yiddish language and literature authority at Brandeis University. They are often bi- or tri-lingual (a holdover from European Yiddish folksong tradition), with occasional passages in Hebrew and even English within the predominantly Yiddish text. Also, even essentially secular songs often incorporate such religious material as biblical references and passages from the liturgy in Hebrew. But above all, a small group of these songs is unique because even early in the war they were far more cognizant of and vocal about the suffering of European Jewry than other American songwriting, often including an explicit Zionistic appeal for a return to "Eretz Yisroel" as the solution.

Most of these war-related songs were written by distinguished composers and lyricists for the Yiddish theatre and Yiddish-language film in America—many of whom, incidentally, were also ASCAP members. Three songs typical of those empathetic with European Jews all appeared in 1940: "A Refuo Sheleimo," with lyrics by Isador Lillian and music by Joseph Rumshinsky (Metro Music, 1940); David Meyerowitz's "Es Is Doch A Gott ('There Is A God In Heaven')" (Brooklyn: J. & J. Kammen,

1940); and "Halt Eich Alle Tsu Samen," with words by Sam Lowenwirth and music by Jack and Joseph Kammen, who also published it. "A Refuo" appeals to God directly to relieve the suffering of European Jews who "live in fear and trembling," explicitly asking God to "free us from the anti-Semites, save us from Jew-hatred." "Es Is Doch" picks up the same themes just about as graphically, declaring that the Nazis "have no fear of God; they have killed thousands already. Our people are burning." "Halt Eich Doch" departs from such relentless lamentation by contrasting the suffering of European Jews with the good fortune of those in the United States, praising American Christians for helping the Jewish people here, while in Europe the antisemites persecute them. The song's second verse is upbeat and rather charming in its exaggeration, as it harkens back to the older Jewish immigrant myth of the United States as the "golden land" and boasts that here the Jew lives like a millionaire with "Radio a Telefon un a frigider" in his house "in Park Avenue, mit a busness in Broadway" (translation hardly necessary). Later in the war, lyricist Jacob J. Heller and composer Sholom Secunda's "Yid, Fihl Sich Nit Mied" (Metro Music, 1943) invoked both God and the United States to help save European Jewry, but the song's most striking feature is its direct equation of Hitler with Haman, the villainous adviser to King Ahasuerus in the Book of Esther who plotted the genocidal extermination of the Jews.

### "Hey! Zeke Your Country's Callin'": Hillbilly Music Goes to War

Today we call it "country" (or "country and western"), a multi-billion-dollar industry with Nashville as its publishing and recording epicenter, millions of followers, both urban and rural, nationwide, and its own annual music awards ceremony on TV. But through the 1930s it was "hillbilly," and it remained "still basically regional at the end of the decade" (Malone 178). Anathema to many publishers and record companies, most of hillbilly's national radio exposure came only on *Grand Ole Opry* out of Nashville's WSM and *National Barn Dance* from WLS in Chicago. But it became "a national phenomenon during the war" (178) and all that changed except its name—it would be hillbilly music for years to come.

From the build-up of defense industries in 1939 until the end of the war in 1945, the United States experienced its largest and most prolonged population shift. In those six years about 15,300,000 people moved across county lines, 7,700,000 of them to a different though nearby state and another 3,600,000 to a different region of the country entirely (see Bailey 143). Overall, these migrants cut across all economic, ethnic, and racial lines, but the vast majority was rural, from the deep south, the border states, and the vast reaches of the Depression era's midwestern Dust Bowl.

Their common destination was a better job with better pay in the defense plants of northern cities like Chicago and Detroit, in shipbuilding centers on the East, West, and Gulf Coasts, and in the huge aircraft plants of California. Still other hillbillies enlisted or were drafted into the service. And, whether from Nebraska, West Virginia, or North Dakota, these rural people took their music with them as they mingled with urban Americans from equally disparate parts of the country. And their music began to catch on.

But not without a struggle. During the war "virtually every cowboy or hillbilly record in the hit class would sell . . . 100,000 copies with little or no effort" (*Billboard 1944 Music Year Book* 353), but such songs rarely appeared on *Billboard* or *Variety* charts. Only three ever made the top three spots in Lucky Strike's popular *Your Hit Parade*. One was country singer Al Dexter's "Pistol Packin' Mama," probably more because of mainstream Bing Crosby and Andrews Sisters' hit record than Dexter's own. The other two were faux-hillbilly tunes, so to speak, by very un-country Tin Pan Alley types jumping on the hay wagon of hillbilly success—Frank Loesser and Joseph J. Lilley's "Jingle, Jangle, Jingle" and Cole Porter's "Don't Fence Me In." But the *Hit Parade* consistently closed its doors to even million-sellers whose singers and writers were squarely in the country camp, including even Tex Ritter's 1940 record of Jimmie Davis and Charles Mitchell's classic "You Are My Sunshine" and, among war-related songs, Paul Roberts and Shelby Darnell's "There's A Star Spangled Banner Waving Somewhere" (Bob Miller, 1942), one of the biggest-selling songs of the war (see chapter 6).

In 1943, *Billboard* tried to rectify its neglect of hillbilly and other music but just made things worse with a new chart for "MOST PLAYED JUKEBOX FOLK RECORDS (Hillbilly, Race, Cowboy Songs, Spirituals)," as if any such commercially written and marketed songs had anything to do with the spontaneous, often topical, and frequently uncommercial thing we call folk music. "Race music" was the music biz term then for all African American music aimed primarily at black audiences—especially blues, rhythm and blues, and black jazz. But when performers like Nat "King" Cole, the Mills Brothers, Ella Fitzgerald, and Duke Ellington had a hit with white audiences, the same record of theirs sometimes wound up on both the Tin Pan Alley chart and the "race" chart. Lumping black music together with hillbilly and cowboy songs (both actually branches of country and western) as "folk music" was ludicrous, and, to *Billboard,* patently embarrassing. In 1945 it replaced that catch-all chart with separate ones for "Most-Played Juke Box Race Records" (black) and "Most-Played Juke Box Folk Records" (hillbilly of all types)—still separate and not very equal, but at least acknowledged.

A small body of war-related songs from the actual folk tradition did emerge just before and during the war. Like twentieth-century American folk music generally, the songs were often improvised or hastily written reactions to current events or social conditions. The writers and performers of this special breed of war-related songs were often one and the same, people like Woodie Guthrie, Pete Seeger, Josh White, Lead Belly, and Tom Glazer. And like some Tin Pan Alley writers, most of this decidedly left-of-center gang swung from pre–Pearl Harbor anti-interventionism to flag-waving advocacy of the war and home front support once the United States was in the fight (see chapter 3). The Almanac Singers' notorious pre-Pearl album *Songs for John Doe* (Almanac Records album no. 102) received enough play and sold enough records for Carl Frederick to label it "subversive and illegal" in the *Atlantic Monthly* for June 1941. Most other left-wing war-related folk songs were commercially recorded only after the war. Still, between radio, union meetings, and other public gatherings, these folk voices were heard and deserve their place alongside the Tin Pan Alley regulars in the ensuing chapters.

In the metropolitan destinations of migrants seeking defense work, not just in "hillbilly bars" but in almost any place with a jukebox, from the corner malt shop to the neighborhood tavern, "city folk . . . [were] manifesting an almost enthusiastic preference for . . . hillbilly and cowboy recordings." In three related articles in 1944—"Hillbillies Win in New York: Much Mazuma Found in Mountain-Music Making" (*Billboard* 22 July:16, 64–65), and "Folk Music Takes Hold on the Jukes" and "Folk Music Finds Its Way to the City," both in the *Billboard 1944 Music Yearbook* (343, 353)—the common thread is that hillbilly songs on jukeboxes were uncommonly popular not only during the "influx of workers" but even after they began "to trickle back to the plains and the mountains as shifts in war production come" (343). This suggests that their urban neighbors had caught hillbilly fever and had no intention of recovering. Statistically, half the places with jukes in such war plant centers as Detroit found hillbilly songs profitable, and nearly 70 percent in St. Louis and adjacent blue-collar East St. Louis, Illinois. Correspondingly, hillbilly record and sheet music sales continued to move upward during the war.

With the popularity of hillbilly music rising, country singers and songwriters great and small wrote and performed numerous war-related songs (110 in my files alone, and I suspect there were many more). Some Tin Pan Alley regulars joined in with quite a few faux-hillbilly war songs of their own, including the one that titles this section, by Al Hoffman, Mann Curtis, and Jerry Livingston (Hoffman and Livingston being two-thirds of the very un-hillbilly "Mairzy Doats" and "Fuzzy Wuzzy" bunch).

The salient feature of hillbilly war-song lyrics, serious or humorous, is their forthrightness. Typical of their often atypical subject matter is Dave McEnery's "We Turned Our Darling's Picture To The Wall" (Bob Miller,

1943), which is the only song about a family's shame over a draft-dodging son, their pain cutting so deep that he has become symbolically dead to them. Another, from a common store of songs written and sung from the perspective of a child missing daddy overseas, is equally singular. Bill Nettles's "I Wonder Why Daddy Don't Write" (Peer International, 1944) focuses on a young child's incomprehension that his or her father has been killed in action, and it does so in simple and heart-wrenching language. In Frank Loesser's estimation, the reason for hillbilly music's popularity was that "because of the war we instinctively turn to simpler and more fundamental things," (*Billboard* 23 Oct. 1943: 66), to which I would add simpler, more fundamental emotions as well, which is what so much country music expresses. The best songs are so simple and sincere, written with so little artifice and affectation, that the effect is of complete genuineness (or even ingenuousness) and honesty, qualities that put some hillbilly numbers among the most effective and popular war-related songs of the war.

### *"The Lady's On The Job": Women at War, at Work, and Writing Songs*

Literally engraved in stone on the World War II Memorial in Washington, D.C., are these words of Colonel Oveta Culp Hobby, first Director of the Women's Army Corps (WAC): "Women who stepped up were measured as citizens of the nation, not as women . . . This was a people's war, and everyone was in it." While explicitly referring to the more than 200,000 women who between 1942 and 1945 wore the uniforms of the WACS, WAVES, SPARS, WASPS (Army Air Force Women's Auxiliary Service Pilots) and women marines (who never got an acronym!), Colonel Hobby's remark encompasses also civilian women whose uniforms ranged from those of defense workers to bank tellers, each of whom freed a man to fight (see chapter 9). Or, as Harold Rome's "The Lady's On the Job" put it in *Lunchtime Follies* (Leeds Music, 1943), "Uncle Sammy's got a niece with elbow grease, the lady's on the job! / Putting by her fancy clothes, rolling up her these and those, / hard at work and pitching in to help us win."

Comprehensive figures for women at work for the duration are hard to come by, but some partial ones are revelatory. Between 1941 and 1945, 6.5 million women went to work for the first time, "most of them middle-aged and married" (Blum 94), and over half the female work force "were full-time housewives" also (Bailey 86). Millions of women who didn't or couldn't work, whether by choice or necessity, participated in such volunteer efforts as crop harvesting, civil defense plane spotting, or Red Cross activities. Still others wrote songs to entertain both servicemen and civilians, including a staggering number of war-related songs. This doesn't mean that amateur (or even professional) female songwriters didn't also volunteer or work for a wage, but the huge output of war-related songs by women suggests that they viewed their creative work as their special contribution to the war effort.

The total number of women—mostly amateurs—who wrote war songs will never be known, the circumstances of their songs' publication and/or copyright registry making the numbers uncountable. But until the advent and proliferation of female pop and rock singer-songwriters like Tori Amos in the late decades of the twentieth century, women wrote more popular songs during World War II than in any other comparable period in the country's history, the vast majority of them war-related. One or more women had a hand in writing 199, or roughly 12 percent, of the nearly 1,700 songs in my main collection of those by professional song-writers. In the amateur ranks, the number and percentage are even more dramatic. A woman composer, lyricist, or both wrote fully fifty-seven, or 33 percent, of the 177 songs in my sample of amateur war songs. With-out formally extrapolating from those figures to the thousands of ama-teur war-related songs I casually examined during my research, I would still have to say, based just on the names that caught my eye, that it would not be surprising if even *more* than one-third of just the *published* ama-teur war songs had one or more female collaborators. Examining copy-right registrations of unpublished songs would most likely make the number and percentage of women war-song writers rise even higher.

With this demographic overview of war-related songwriters behind us, we can finally answer the chapter title's question "Who wrote all those songs?" with "Practically everybody."

# "Over Here"

## Prewar Isolationism, Patriotism, and Preparedness

Throughout this book, "prewar" refers to the period before the United States entered the war on December 8, 1941, while the combatants in Europe, Asia, and Africa were already fighting (roughly 1938–41). In the late 1930s and early '40s, America inherited an isolationist mindset from the post–World War I disillusionment of the early 1920s, aggravated by the country being understandably self-absorbed during the Great Depression of the 1930s. By the immediate prewar years, the roots of isolationism (and its bedfellows—pacifism, non-interventionism, and "America First" patriotism) ran deep and spread wide. Its adherents included conservative Republicans, liberal Democrats, socialists, and such polar opposites as so-called "native [that is, American-born] Fascists" and Communists. It's not surprising, then, that isolationism was a small but significant theme in popular songwriting, starting in the late 1930s. In the view of historian William E. Leuchtenburg, World War I "left a determination in millions of Americans never to fight again; at no time in our history has the hold of pacifism been stronger than in the interlude between the first and second world wars" (104). In *Only Yesterday,* Frederick Lewis Allen's perspective on the 1920s confirms this: as early as 1921, "The nation was spiritually tired. . . . Sick of Wilson and his talk of America's duty to humanity, callous to political idealism, they hoped for a chance . . . to forget about public affairs" (94). And international affairs as well: "The country was hostile to everything foreign; isolation in foreign affairs had its counterpart in a determination to curb immigration, to avoid foreign contamination, and to preserve the old America ethnically before it was too late" (Leuchtenburg 205).

The aftermath of World War I in the 1920s was conducive to an isolationism that would grow in strength and outspokenness in the '30s. Not long after Roosevelt's first inauguration in 1933, nearly 75 percent of 20,000 surveyed male college students "declared they would not willingly serve in the armed forces in time of war; almost half of them further stated they would not fight even if this country were invaded" (Stillman 377). In April 1937—after Mussolini's 1935 invasion of Ethiopia, after Hitler's unchallenged 1936 incursion into the Rhineland, even after the outbreak of the Spanish Revolution and Japan's 1937 invasion of China— a Gallup poll asked people if they thought "it was a mistake for the United States to enter the World War," to which 71 percent replied with a resounding "Yes" (Allen, *Since* 321–22). Such was the nation's mood just prior to Britain and France declaring war on Germany in the fall of 1939.

Nor did it change much after that. On September 21, 1939, FDR called a special session of Congress "to consider repealing the arms embargo provision of the 1935 Neutrality Act and applying a cash-and-carry formula to munitions—in short, giving England and France immediate access to materials of war they desperately needed" (Stillman 389). A chorus of isolationist protest went up from the far right, led by notorious "radio priest" and proto-Nazi Father Charles Coughlin and automobile magnate Henry Ford (both also avowed antisemites). Interestingly, the attack was mostly Anglophobic, portraying Britain as a greater threat to the United States than Hitler, with Ford (clearly *not* making munitions then) arguing that the repeal was only "to enable munitions makers to profit financially through what is nothing less than mass murder" (389). But by that point in time public opinion had swayed, if not directly into interventionism then at least toward aiding the Allies materially, and on November 4 Congress repealed the embargo and approved arms sale to the Allies for ready money.

Yet throughout the autumn of 1939, "the majority of Americans still had no heart for intervention in the war" (Stillman 390), many believing that selling arms to the Allies would help keep the United States out of the hostilities by allowing Britain and France to go it alone. But then America witnessed German troops overrunning Denmark, Norway, Holland, and Luxembourg, Germany and Italy's invasions of France, and the British evacuation of Dunkirk "during the nightmare spring of 1940" (Blum 7). On June 14 came the ignominious fall of Paris, and on June 22 the equally demoralizing French armistice with the Axis Powers. Yet here in the states, in historian Geoffrey Perrett's words, "As soon as the shock over the Nazi conquest of France had passed, the debate on isolation resumed, more vehement than ever" (54). To steer the country from such ostrich-like attitudes, in the summer of 1940 Roosevelt appointed two Republicans to his cabinet—Henry L. Stimson as secretary of war and Frank Knox as secretary of the navy. FDR's aim wasn't just to achieve a more bipartisan balance in the executive branch; he made the moves as a way of "offsetting the isolationist bloc in Congress" (Stillman 391), a bloc as vociferous as it was strong, epitomized by "Mr. Republican," Ohio's Senator Robert A. Taft.

In the summer of 1940, the most well-known isolationist organization was created by Yale law student R. Douglas Stuart and editor of the student newspaper Kingman Brewster Jr. They convinced the likes of Sears Roebuck president General Robert Wood, former head of the NRA General Hugh S. Johnson, and Teddy Roosevelt's daughter Alice Roosevelt Longworth to serve on the board of their new America First Committee. "America First" has passed into the language (and song titles and lyrics) as a synonym for chauvinistic, isolationist super-patriotism. But the committee itself never had more than 850,000 members among its 450 chapters, with "the vast majority of members and chapters . . . within 300 miles of Chicago," which is probably why isolationism is often thought of as a mostly Midwestern phenomenon. America First was more diverse in its membership than its geography: "anxious parents of healthy young men; Europaphobes; Anglophobes; German-Americans; Roosevelt haters; native Fascists; Communists; pacifists; liberals apprehensive that entry into the war would end the social gains of recent years; and conservatives who feared that exactly the opposite would occur" (Perrett 61).

Historians of the prewar years generally agree that as 1941 went on the dominant mood in the United States was starting to swing from isolationism to interventionism. One influence may have been the general worsening of the war for the Allies and a widening of the grip of the Axis Powers, which culminated, on June 22, 1941, in Germany's invasion of the Soviet Union. That event brought far-left American isolationists around to interventionism, including even folksinger Pete Seeger. Also, it was becoming ever clearer that, despite the strong isolationist bloc still in Congress, official Washington was moving closer to an internationalist, interventionist position. On January 6, 1941, in his annual address to Congress, FDR first uttered the now famous Four Freedoms—"freedom of speech and worship and freedom from want and fear"—in an internationalist setting, by saying we "must give unlimited support to people everywhere who were defending those freedoms at such great sacrifice" (Wecter 314; Stillman 392–93). On March 11 Congress passed the Lend-Lease Act, empowering the president "to provide arms and other supplies by sale, transfer, exchange, or lease," "to foes of the Axis according to their need rather than ability to pay" (Stillman 393; Wecter 311). In support of Lend-Lease, during the spring months the United States began seizing "all Axis shipping tied up in domestic ports" (Wecter 314), and on May 27 FDR "proclaimed an unlimited national emergency" (Stillman

393). By midsummer, American eyes were looking more to Asia than Europe, when on July 24 Japan occupied French Indochina. Two days later, Roosevelt froze all Japanese assets in this country and put a complete halt to trade with Japan (Stillman 395). In his October 27 Navy Day address, alluded to in Gulesian's "Damn The Torpedoes Full Speed Ahead," FDR made clear noises about preparedness, even saying "We do not propose to take this lying down" (qtd. in Stillman 394). The country's mood was shifting, but it hadn't shifted enough for Congress to declare war in the absence of direct provocation.

Historians don't agree about when isolationism finally took a back seat to interventionism in the months before Pearl Harbor, but if we throw the history of popular songwriting into the mix, it shows that some isolationist songs and a huge quantity of patriotic ones continued to be written, published, and recorded right up until the first bombs fell on Honolulu that quiet Sunday morning in December.

### "The Yanks Aren't Coming!": Anti-War Voices Before the War

The year 1935 was a banner one for isolationism, very visible in the mood of the country and likewise reflected in a popular song. That year Congress passed the Neutrality Act, which the nation in its mid-Depression frame of mind enthusiastically applauded. The act "decreed that when war broke out *anywhere* [italics supplied], Americans must not sell munitions to either of the belligerents" (Allen, *Since* 323). That same year, quite appropriately, the firm of Shapiro, Bernstein brought out "If They Feel Like Having A War Let Them Keep It Over There." The title alone just about defines non-interventionism, as do lines like "But if they try to drag us in we'll holler 'On your way / We're having lovely weather over here.'" (To help keep these songs' sentiments straight, non-interventionism is opposition to entering a present and specific war; pacifism is the philosophical opposition to all war; and isolationism is the opposition to involvement in *all* international affairs, including trade agreements and treaties.) The song illustrates the shifting politics of its writers, Howard (no relation to the motel and restaurant man) Johnson and Willie Raskin. Johnson wrote several war songs during World War I, including the popular and very militant "Just Like Washington Crossed The Delaware, General Pershing Will Cross the Rhine" (Leo Feist, 1918). Johnson is a one-man illustration of the country's shift from interventionism to isolationism during the 1920s and '30s. Even before Pearl Harbor, Raskin collaborated on "Ev'ryone's A Fighting Son Of That Old Gang Of Mine" (Irving Caesar, 1940), praising men who enlisted or were drafted. This clearly indicates that between the mid-'30s and the early '40s Raskin, like most Americans, had made the mental and emotional move from isolationism to interventionism.

For the three years just before Pearl Harbor, I've acquired lyrics to just twenty-two isolationist, pacifistic, or non-interventionist songs either published by ASCAP or BMI publishers, performed in Broadway shows, or recorded by New York recording companies. This isn't too surprising considering the limited appeal of such a genre of popular music, regardless of the country's mood. Yet for professional songwriters to turn out even twenty-two such numbers in under three years argues that they believed the American public would be receptive to such viewpoints in song. They were wrong. None of these pieces achieved anything like hit status, though a couple were well received on Broadway and some others found a following for a time among the radical left.

Seven of the isolationist songs were published in 1939, nine in 1940—the year the America First Committee was formed—and only six in 1941, as the country was turning perceptibly if slowly toward more interventionist sympathies. Mainstream ASCAP publishers published thirteen of these, including three by Mills, two by Chappell, and a single song each by such firms as Carl Fischer, Santly-Joy-Select, Robbins, Schirmer, and Belwin. Since isolationist music wasn't a big moneymaker, some song publishers must have published them because they supported the songs' messages.

Those messages were pretty consistent throughout the nearly three years such songs were written, the main differences being their tone, their degree of vehemence in stating their position, and—it almost goes without saying—the quality of the writing. Only one early song stood for total, unequivocal pacifism. In 1939 Tin Pan Alley and Broadway old-timer Malvin Franklin, who wrote "Let's Get Behind The Man Behind The Gun" during World War I, shifted to an anti-war philosophy in his collaboration with Bill Gaston, "(If They'd Only Fight Their Battles With) Little Toy Men" (Mills Music, 1939). The title, like that of many isolationist pieces, says everything you need to know about the content; this one just went farther than the rest in abjuring war entirely because it kills people.

Of the other songs of 1939, only Allan Flynn and Frank Madden's "I'm The Son of a Legionnaire" (Nattrass-Schenck, 1939) is explicitly non-interventionist. It takes the position—one repeated in later songs—that America should have learned from the last world war: "My daddy was Over There / That's why this guy is gonna stay over here," yet with the proviso that if the United States is invaded, "This son of a gun will grab a gun and do his very best." The other songs of that ilk in '39 were just generically isolationist. Larry Conley's lyrics and J. Russel Robinson's music told us to shout "Hooray for Our Side Of The Ocean" (Atlas Music,

1939). Chicago bandleader and songwriter Frank Westphal went farther in "My Own U.S.A." (Gamble Hinged Music, 1939), declaring, "Let's stay at home, / Why should we roam . . . Let us say, U.S.A. / You're good enough for me." Al Maister and Chick Floyd capped "Over Here" (Chappell, 1939) by telling us to "be thankful we're living OVER HERE."

Also of interest is one song that espoused diplomatic as well as military isolationism. By two nonprofessional women but published by Carl Fischer, one of the most prestigious New York music publishers, Ethel Wall and Edythe Vell's "Stand By America!" asserts that we'll always be "the greatest of nations" because "With no entangling relations, / We will be happy and free." The remaining song of this type in 1939 was isolationist comfort food. From the Broadway musical *Yokel Boy*, "Uncle Sam's Lullaby" (Chappell, 1939) was written by Lew Brown, Charlie Tobias, and Sam H. Stept, three seasoned Broadway and Tin Pan Alley types whose songs just a few years down the road would vigorously support the war. But in 1939 Brown, Tobias, and Stept had our country's avuncular icon crooning, "Sleep tight, my babies, / . . . There'll be no fight, my babies, / That's Uncle Sam's lullaby." These three wouldn't be the only songwriters to do a one-hundred-and-eighty-degree turnaround after Pearl Harbor.

Fred Fisher was another one. A name not as familiar as some of his standards, such as "Peg O' My Heart" and "Chicago (that toddlin' town)," Fisher wrote some rather quirky war-related songs, discussed in later chapters, at the time the nation was preparing itself with the draft and defense production in 1940 and '41 (Fisher died in January 1942). But earlier in 1940 he penned and published "Go Back Over There," a xenophobic bit of isolationism attacking seemingly disloyal "hyphenated-Americans" (Italian-Americans, German-Americans, Russian-Americans, and so on): "If you don't like the way our country is run . . . / Go back over there." Fisher had been born in Germany but clearly liked it over here. More musically soothing, "Good Night, Mother" (Santly-Joy-Select, 1940) reassures women that "America has answered ev'ry mother's prayer, / You won't have the heartaches they have 'over there.'" But in almost no time, the song's top-notch ASCAP collaborators Al Bryan, Mack David, and Vee Lawnhurst (the last two already mentioned for "Johnny Zero") would be on the pro-war bandwagon.

As would a famous name in Broadway songwriting. That the tone of his songs was never extremist helped Harold Rome's success as one of the most committed Depression-era left-wing composer/lyricists. However left-of-center his points of view, Rome's good sense, judgment, and taste made his songs attractive to general audiences by couching pro-union (sometimes almost pro-Communist), anti-establishment, and anti-Fascist sentiments in clever topical lyrics set to catchy tunes. Because of this quality and Rome's continual updating of the revue's material to keep abreast of current events, *Pins and Needles* went from being an amateur show by and for members of the International Ladies' Garment Workers Union on November 27, 1937, to becoming the second-longest-running show of the 1930s, closing on Broadway on June 22, 1940, at 1,108 performances (see Jones 116–19).

Two songs Rome added late in the show's run were explicitly antiinterventionist, although dramatically different in their final statements. When the third edition of *Pins and Needles* premiered on November 29, 1939, the new song "Stay Out, Sammy!" (Mills, 1940) had a mother trying to keep her kid out of a brawl on the other side of the street, Rome's metaphor for Uncle Sam not scrapping with the European belligerents. But the number ends aggressively, with the mother telling Sammy, "If they try to cross the street / Then we'll all give them 'what for!'"—in case of invasion, all non-interventionist bets are off. Even later Rome added "The Yanks Aren't Coming!" in which his non-interventionism is unequivocal. While "Stay Out Sammy!" remained in the show through June 17, 1940 (see Goldstein 212), it's almost impossible to ascertain when "The Yanks" entered the revue. The unpublished song's copyright deposit date of May 3, 1940, suggests that it may have been some time around then, but if both songs were in the show concurrently, they would have sent mixed messages. "The Yanks Aren't Coming!" repeats the idea that America should have learned from the last war not to get suckered into another one: "Don't let propaganda pull the wool / Remember that England is called John Bull." Left-winger that he was, Rome maintains that the only war we should fight is a war on "unemployment and poverty." Unlike "Stay Out Sammy!" "The Yanks" makes no concessions, ending, "Uncle Sam sits this one out." By early 1942, however, Rome was writing pro-war songs for both commercial audiences and military and defense plant personnel in shows like *Stars and Gripes* and *Lunch Time Follies*.

By the early war years, Hy Zaret would be Pvt. Hy Zaret, an ASCAP member as of 1942, and the lyricist for some very successful war-related songs. But in 1940, he teamed with Bernie Wayne and Nat Gardner on a song whose title and sentiment are remarkably similar to Rome's "The Yanks Aren't Coming," called "The Yanks Are Not Coming!" (Trio Music, 1940): "They fooled us back in seventeen but now we know the gag / . . . THE YANKS ARE NOT COMING a hundred million strong / We're staying in our own backyard 'cause that's where we belong."

The year 1941 brought the publication of three rabidly isolationist songs that were mediocre or worse as songwriting; the brief record release of three others of an equally passionate anti-interventionist stamp that were witty, incisive, and bitingly satiric in their writing; and one more that was uncharacteristically oblique for songs of this genre that showed up in a seemingly unlikely show for such a song. This last oddity was written by two of the most gifted songwriters of the period, lyricist Mitchell ("Stardust") Parish and composer Vernon ("Autumn In New York") Duke, rather improbably for *Ice-Capades of 1941*. Purportedly about the new dance that lends its name to the title, "The Yankee Doodle Polka" (Robbins, 1941) glides into a metaphoric isolationist note at the end with "We don't wanna learn a new step like the ones from oversea / The Yankee Doodle Polka is good enough for me."

Their titles define the stridently isolationist songs of 1941: "America First (Last And Always)," "Who Wants War?" and "America! Love It, Or Leave It." The first, with words and music by Reidy Reid and published by Dixie Music, a BMI affiliate, was the only excursion of hillbilly songwriting into isolationism and, quite literally, says little more than what's in its title; within a few years Reid, like others, would be singing a different tune. H. E. Moynihan and R. Martino's "Who Wants War?" (Boston: Eastern Music) is almost hysterical in its emotionalism, scattering ten exclamation points over its four stanzas and capitalizing words like Ships, Guns, Planes, and "the old Sword of Might." "America! Love It, Or Leave It" came from the hands of three seasoned ASCAP professionals, lyricist John W. Bratton, whose best-known song is "The Teddy Bear's Picnic," and composers Harold Levey and Geoffrey O'Hara, whose "K-K-K-Katy" was enormously popular with the troops in World War I, when O'Hara himself was an armed forces song leader. Their "Love It, Or Leave It" shouts its xenophobic message to all hyphenated-Americans: "Pack up your bag, if you can't brag, over the flag."

Three non-interventionist songs from 1941 weren't published then, just recorded on a minor label and released for less than two months. Still, these songs, written and sung by members of the radical-left folk group the Almanac Singers, said more and said it better than any of the published isolationist songs. Dedicated to performing and writing "folksong-based labor and anti-war songs," the Almanacs formed early in 1941 with a nucleus of Pete Seeger and Lee Hays and soon included Millard Lampell, Woody Guthrie, and, at various times, Josh White, Arthur Stern, Cisco Huston, John "Peter" Hawes, his brother Baldwin "Butch" Hawes, and others (Logsdon 2, 3). Between March and April of 1941 the Almanacs recorded the proletarian album *Songs for John Doe,* issued in May by Eric Bernay's Keynote Records but under the Almanac label— Bernay wanting to distance himself and his company from such potentially inflammatory material (Klein 191). And it was! Reviews damned the Almanacs as dangerous Communists, *Time* even saying the songs "echoed the mendacious Moscow tune" (qtd. in Klein 191). Once Germany invaded the Soviet Union in June, the album was dead in the water.

Bernay pulled the songs from distribution and destroyed his remaining inventory ("Songs for John Doe").

Three of the numbers on *Songs for John Doe* are scathingly non-interventionist but with a deep undercurrent of fundamental pacifism in their simple statement that, at bottom, war destroys human lives, especially those of young men. Lee Hays and Pete Seeger's words for "Billy Boy" are also rich in black humor and satire, the song being based on the familiar "Oh where have you been, Billy Boy, Billy Boy." At one point Billy explains his reluctance to fight: "No desire do I feel / To defend Republic Steel." Of all the steel companies, the Almanacs did not choose anti-union Republic randomly. On Memorial Day 1937 at the Republic plant in South Chicago, Illinois, police and the company management's thugs routed workers peacefully demonstrating for unionization, wounding ninety and killing another ten, seven of those shot in the back while trying to flee (see Allen *Since* 291–93). Hays and Seeger's "Plow Under" draws an analogy between war and the New Deal's Agricultural Adjustment Act (AAA), which paid farmers to destroy animals and plow surplus crops under: going to war would "plow under every fourth American boy."

What raised the most public ire, however, was "Ballad of October 16," its music adapted from "Jesse James." The song is a darkly humorous condemnation of that date in 1940 by which men had to register for the draft, according to the Draft Act Congress passed on September 16; and, indeed, 16,316,908 did (Bailey 43). The refrain to the song's four verses has President Roosevelt saying "I hate war and so does Eleanor / But we won't be safe till everybody's dead." The Almanac Singers' album died young, but its singers continued singing their left-wing sentiments, usually to factory and agricultural workers and other left-thinking citizens; accordingly, the Almanacs were usually preaching to the choir. Once the country was in the war, Seeger and Hays went into the service, Woody Guthrie, Cisco Huston, and Pete Hawes into the Merchant Marine, and Baldwin Hawes into defense work. And they all changed to a pro-war and pro–defense industry stance, still largely preaching to the choir, but now a different-thinking choir and their song a different song.

### "We Have Sandwiches": A Glut of Musical Patriotism

Irving Berlin's "God Bless America" (Irving Berlin Inc., 1939) was copyrighted as an unpublished song on October 27, 1938, its final published version copyrighted on February 20, 1939. America first heard it when Kate Smith—with whom it would be indelibly linked—sang it on the Armistice Day edition of her CBS radio show *The Kate Smith Hour* on November 10, 1938. America has been singing it ever since, with Berlin's heartfelt paean to America achieving its greatest popularity since the war in the days and months following the events of September 11, 2001.

No song from the huge patriotic outpouring published by ASCAP, BMI, and SESAC affiliates beginning in 1939 even came close. But they continued unabated through the attack on Pearl Harbor and on into 1942, only slowing to a trickle when a flood of more militant tunes swamped them for the rest of the war. Reading through this generally mediocre plethora of patriotic devotion, I began to wish that Congress had passed a law barring the publishing, recording, and performance of all such numbers after "God Bless America." And I'm not alone. Late in 1940 some respected Alleymen humorously vented their distaste for the glut of patriotic tunes gushing from the pens of fellow writers.

Lyricist Albert (Al) Stillman, whose career stretched from the early 1930s to his death in 1979, in effect cried, "Enough already!" not in a song but in a rhymed fifty-three-line free-form poem called "Of Thee They Sing" on *Variety*'s equivalent of an op-ed page (page 2) on December 4, 1940. Stillman's name isn't exactly a household word, though he worked with major composers from George Gershwin to Henry Mancini. He wrote a few war-related numbers, but his biggest wartime hit was "Juke Box Saturday Night," with music by Paul McGrane, recorded by the Glenn Miller Orchestra. Most of Stillman's major successes came after the war with songs like "I Believe," " It's Not For Me To Say," "Moments To Remember," and the Johnny Mathis blockbuster "Chances Are." But in 1940, this literate, intelligent lyricist was fed up with patriotic songs that were neither. Selected lines from his poem will make his points clear. Stillman declares that he loves his country just as much as the next guy but has thought since he was kid that "The Star Spangled Banner" was enough to express such feelings:

> Until about six months ago,
> At which time every songwriter in the country simultaneously got the
>   brilliant notion
> That this was the Land of his Devotion,
> From ocean to ocean;
> That this country was really terrific,
> From the Atlantic to the Pacific;
> Or, to make it plain,
> From California to Maine.

He blasts writers of such hackneyed stuff who express their "Undivided Loyalty . . . in return for the usual royalty— / So much per record, so much per sheet— / And some of the take was pretty sweet." "I hate Hitler, and when they flash him on the screen, I'm the loudest hisser," but, Stillman gripes, "I object to having the American Flag waved right in my kisser." Before listing some of the offending songs, the poet remarks on their questionable merit: "Mine ears have heard and have been badly bent / By patriotic compositions of indubitably meritorious intent." A native New Yorker, Stillman concludes with a wacky rhyme that works only with a New York (or maybe Rhode Island) accent: "And I still like— so help me Hannah— / America and The Star Spangled Banner." More remarkable even than Stillman writing and *Variety* publishing this broadside is that no one replied with an angry letter to the editor.

A Broadway musical revue for general audiences is far better than a trade journal as a public forum for songwriters' ideas. Such was *Meet the People,* with Jay Gorney's music, a book by Edward Eliscu and Henry Meyers, and lyrics by Eliscu, Myers, or the two together. The show opened on December 25, 1940, ran for 160 performances, and might have run longer if it didn't have to compete for opening-night reviewers' attention with Rodgers and Hart's monumental *Pal Joey* (Bordman 522). One lyric by Myers comprised a gentle but pointed spoof of the heavily clichéd patriotic songwriting in the prewar period. Echoing many of its serious counterparts, the verse extols "our mountains, . . . our valleys . . . our fountains" and the like. But after that set-up, the chorus deliciously proclaims with the song's title that the real reason America is great is because "We Have Sandwiches" (Mills Music 1940): "To heck with living high . . . / When we can have a ham on rye." The rest of this wacky satire is an impassioned paean to delicatessen: "We got baloney We got salami We got liver sausage We got pastrami / We got 'em with slaw, We got 'em with pickle, We got 'em on toast And on pumpernickel."

The trite texts of the patriotic songs resoundingly demonstrate that Stillman and Meyers had good reason to carp about them. Their frequency of readymade words and phrases makes it look as if lyricists could dip into a great public vat of such stuff, like clip-art for songwriters. Counting just one appearance of any particular phrase or image per song, so as not to skew the statistics by tallying multiple occurrences of them in a single number, I spent two days reading all the patriotic pieces written and published both before and after Pearl Harbor, categorizing and tabulating their inclusion of national emblems and icons (the flag, Uncle Sam, Yankee Doodle, the Statue of Liberty), catchphrases (land of the free, let freedom ring), and more. The results were either pretty impressive or terribly disheartening, depending on one's point of view and sense of humor. In the aggregate, 132 instances of such hackneyed writing appear in the seventy-one professional patriotic lyrics before the United States entered the war, and 113 in the fifty-eight that followed, averaging just under two per song. Of course, some songs have more, and, mercifully, a few songs both before and after Pearl Harbor have none.

Stillman was understandably irked at having the American Flag "waved right in [his] kisser." Of all the overused imagery and emblems, the hands-

*Clichéd Phrases and Images in Patriotic Songs*

| Image, Emblem, Icon, or Catchphrase | Prewar | Wartime | Total |
|---|---|---|---|
| Red, white, and blue | 24 | 9 | 33 |
| [Flag, banner] wave high, flying high, ever wave | 11 | 12 | 23 |
| Old Glory | 9 | 9 | 18 |
| Land of the free, home of the brave (with variants) | 6 | 12 | 18 |
| Statue of Liberty, Lady Liberty, torch of liberty | 7 | 10 | 17 |
| ["Topography"]: mountains, valleys, prairies, plains | 9 | 6 | 15 |
| Uncle Sam, Uncle Sammy | 8 | 7 | 15 |
| Land of Liberty | 9 | 5 | 14 |
| On land and sea; land, sea, and air (with variants) | 4 | 10 | 14 |
| Stars and Stripes | 8 | 5 | 13 |
| Let freedom ring | 10 | 2 | 12 |
| ["Geography"]: east and west, north or south (and variants) | 8 | 3 | 11 |
| So true, loyal and true, brave and true | 3 | 7 | 10 |
| The American way | 3 | 3 | 6 |
| Yankee Doodle | 2 | 4 | 6 |
| Flag unfurled (with variants) | 2 | 4 | 6 |
| Land of my (our) birth | 3 | 2 | 5 |

down winner (or loser) was our flag in various guises (Stars and Stripes, Old Glory), with "red, white, and blue" topping everything with a total of thirty-three appearances, partly because the phrase is so familiar and partly because "blue" is so easy to rhyme. The table shows the frequency, in descending order, of ready-to-hand images and language appearing five or more times in both prewar and wartime patriotic songs by professional songwriters.

While the post-Pearl patriotic anthems are slightly more varied, the sameness in the bulk of the prewar songs is numbing. Their titles alone become a repetitive blur. Taking just those with "America" in the title, there's "A-M-E-R-I-C-A (We All Love You)," "We Sing America," "America, My Own," "My Own America," "Faithful To America," "My Heart's In America," "My Heart Is In America, "On Guard, America," "America, Forever Free," "America, My Wondrous Land," "America Of Thee I Sing," "America! To Thee My Land," "Beloved America," "Hail To America," "I Hear America Calling," "Keep Your Head Up, America," "Ode To America," and "Thank You America." Most of the lyrics are as homogeneous as the titles—at best, flat, uninspired, and repetitive, at worst, filled with pretentious and archaic diction and syntax that sometimes degenerate into non-sequiturs or ungrammatical writing. But one positive thing *can* be said for nearly all of the patriotic songs: their evident sincerity makes up in some small way for their almost universal lack of creativity.

Fortunately, there were a few islands of real originality in this otherwise dank sea of banality, some songs of purely historical interest, others that enjoyed some popularity in their day, and two that continue to endure. To begin with those enduring, Irving Berlin's classic "God Bless America" opens with a verse that no one knows because nobody sings it anymore. The reason is simple: it's topically tied to contemporary world events. Like literally hundreds of later war-related songs, Berlin's verse starts with an image of some kind of lousy weather—storms, gray skies, dark clouds, rain—as a metaphor for the war: "While the storm clouds gather / Far across the sea." But once this song, which is arguably a hymn, moves into its chorus, three salient qualities of Berlin's songwriting are responsible for its success and durability—the eminently singable melody, the utter simplicity and clarity of the text's through-line, and, not least of all, the song's brevity. Laid out on paper as a poem, the chorus is only eight lines long, and it conveys its single focus through just three verbs. All in the imperative mood, these verbs implore the divinity to "bless" Berlin's adopted homeland, and to "stand beside her and guide her / Thru the night." Night was another wartime metaphor for the darkening world of global conflict, yet one that has universal application, as does the entire chorus, which in part explains the song's lasting place in American music.

Even shorter and as durable, though never as popular, is lyricist Don Raye and composer Al Jacobs's "This Is My Country"—"land of my birth," and so forth (Words and Music, 1940)—still a staple of music classes in the nation's public schools, if not as well-known among the public at large. I sang it from elementary through high school in suburban Chicago from the mid-1940s through the late '50s, just as my friend and computer consultant Michelle Menard, a student assistant in Brown's John Hay Library, sang it in elementary school in Houston in the early 1990s. Like "God Bless America," "This Is My Country" owes much of its endurance to a simple, straightforward lyric, a memorable melody, and its brevity, while other less successful patriotic songs ramble on through multiple and tedious stanzas.

Not that brevity is always an element of fine songwriting. One of the most historically significant and powerful patriotic pieces of the prewar years runs in performance between ten and thirteen minutes—John Latouche and Earl Robinson's "Ballad For Americans" (Robbins, 1940). Called by its authors "A Narrative Solo for Baritone," the piece is in fact a cantata for solo voice, orchestra, and chorus. But this does not consign "Ballad" to the ranks of concert works or art songs; the colloquial quality of Latouche's lyrics and Robinson's music makes it accessible to any audience. The writers' "Suggestions for Production" in the Robbins edition warns, "An operatic or false dramatic approach can destroy the conception on which it is built." Latouche's lyric details what makes the United States a democracy for everyone—the little guy as well as the big shot—but even more, it extols America for its racial, ethnic, and religious diversity. The song lists among the heroes of the Revolution "Washington, Tom Paine, Benjamin Franklin, Chiam Solomon [Jewish], Crispus Attucks [black], Lafayette [French]." The number's modernity is obvious when it asks who the Declaration of Independence intended to be created equal: "Farmer? Office clerk? Housewife? Fact'ry worker? Stenographer? Beauty specialist? Bartender? Truck Driver?" The answer to all: "*Definitely.*" In even longer lists, Latouche strings out some of America's ethnicities and diverse religions. The breadth and scope of "Ballad" are enormous, but its core message is plain: the strength of the United States lies in its people.

But even a display of patriotism can get you into trouble. "Ballad For Americans" first appeared as "The Ballad Of Uncle Sam" on April 29, 1939, in the revue *Sing for Your Supper* under the aegis of the Federal Theatre Project. Though the show wasn't very incendiary, it still ran afoul of notorious Commie-hunting Congressman Martin Dies and his House Un-American Activities Committee in June. According to Federal Theatre national director Hallie Flanagan, "The Ballad Of Uncle Sam" became the "object of some of the most violent attacks before the Committee, and later on the floor of Congress" (Flanagan 366), probably more because of Robinson's well-known leftist leanings than the song's actual content. But soon the song, its composer, and its lyricist would be more than vindicated. With its new title, "Ballad For Americans" first reached a wide public on November 5, 1939, on CBS radio's *Pursuit of Happiness*. With chorus and orchestra, the great African American singer-actor Paul Robeson, himself a frequent object of un-American witch-hunts, sang the solo part. A note in the Robbins edition mentions that *Time* magazine reported, "the studio audience of six hundred bravoed for fifteen minutes at its conclusion." Robeson subsequently made a successful recording of the piece, but the final slap in the face to Congressman Dies came in 1940, when millions heard "Ballad For Americans" broadcast as the theme of the *Republican* National Convention in Philadelphia (see Jones 122).

Concert pieces per se are beyond the scope of this account since they are not, strictly speaking, popular music, but two prewar patriotic concert pieces deserve mention as much for who wrote them as for the unusual aspects of their content. African American Jules Bledsoe is less remembered as a composer than as an actor, creating the role of Joe and first singing "Old Man River" in the original 1927 production of *Show Boat*, though the role (and the song) are more usually associated with Paul

Robeson. In addition to performing, Bledsoe wrote several concert works and the patriotic hymn "Ode To America" (Broadcast Music, 1941), a long song that's as much a hymn as an ode, asking for God's guidance and for the protection of the United States; it concludes with a section that begins "Guide the hand that leads this land. / Keep him well and safe from harm"—a prayer for the wellbeing of President Roosevelt.

Written by two seemingly unlikely collaborators, "Plain-Chant For America" (J. Fischer, 1941) is a more intricate art song. The music is by eminent black composer of genres from jazz to symphonic works and opera, William Grant Still, who was working, not for the first time, with poet Katherine Garrison Chapin, "in private life," as the sheet music notes, "the wife of Francis Biddle, United States Attorney General." Together they created a stunningly specific account of what makes America the bastion of democracy, but the song's special interest lies in a section in which Chapin emerges as just about the only prewar or wartime lyricist to recount any of the nation's shortcomings: "If we have failed— / Lynchings in Georgia, / Justice in Massachusetts undone [alluding to the Sacco-Vanzetti trial], / The bloody fields of South Chicago." Chapin evidently was a woman who spoke from a strong, independent mind, which, with Still's music, makes the piece powerful stuff indeed. Its premiere by John Barbirolli and the New York Philharmonic Orchestra at its centennial on October 23, 1941, was as distinguished as the song.

Popular songwriter and 1947 Academy Award–winner for "Zip-A-Dee-Doo-Dah" from Walt Disney's *Song of the South,* Allie Wrubel wrote a patriotic song called "My Own America" (Robbins 1941) that was remarkable at the time for its music: instead of a march or a stately anthem, Wrubel composed it as a love ballad. As he explained in *Song Hits* for June 1942, "It was always a puzzle to me that America's patriotic songs were either in a martial or a hymnal vein. There never seemed to be a real 'love song'—love for one's country—about our wonderful Nation" (29). So Wrubel wrote one.

Wrubel was correct: no other lyrical patriotic ballads preceded his song. But a few Tin Pan Alley types did write national pride numbers couched in one or another idiom of the novelty songs so popular in the 1940s. In their fun with language, their overall conception, and/or their music, most of these display how playfulness in songwriting can make even serious subject matter entertaining. Putting a new spin on an overworked patriotic image or phrase is inherently playful, as is illustrated by the titles alone of three such songs: David Gregory and Al Moss's "The Rhythm Is Red An' White An' Blue" (Broadcast Music, 1940) from the RKO picture *They Meet Again;* James S. Donohue and Renee Dietrich Wright's "That Star-Spangled Baby Of Mine" (Edward B. Marks, 1941); and, from the RKO-Radio film *Playmates,* "Thank Your Lucky Stars And Stripes"

(Southern Music, 1941), by Johnny Burke and Jimmy Van Heusen, writers of "Swinging On A Star." Eons away from the archaic diction of many a patriotic anthem, the first of these numbers declares, "you better get hep and jivin' to / RHYTHM THAT'S RED AN' WHITE AN' BLUE," but most of the song's fun is in its music; as the title fairly proclaims, it's a swing tune. In the second of the three songs, a guy extols his girlfriend, his "Star-Spangled Baby," in terms that make her sound like the epitome of everything American. The Burke–Van Heusen piece is playful in its up-to-date catalogue of many reasons to "thank our lucky stars and stripes" that we live in the U.S.A., including "Steam heat and ham and eggs and hay rides and cider kegs."

Other than "God Bless America," the only prewar patriotic song to make any of the trade papers' popularity charts was "Shout! Wherever You May Be I Am An American" (Mercer and Morris, 1940). This proclamation of national pride by Ira Schuster, Paul Cunningham, and Leonard Whitcup—three men who would go on to write a number of significant war-related songs—stayed on *Variety*'s top-selling sheet-music chart for an impressive twenty-one weeks between August 28 and December 18, 1940. Though not playful as such, the song's strong melody and almost total absence of clichés helped account for the longevity of this vigorously personal expression of pride in one's "American-ness." Personal in a different way is the approach to patriotism in the longish but entertaining "Uncle Sam Gets Around," from the 20th Century-Fox movie *Cadet Girl,* by lyricist Leo Robin and composer Ralph Rainger, whose strikingly original work together was cut off all too soon when Rainger died in a civilian airplane crash near Palm Springs, California, on October 23, 1942; he had just turned just 42. Robin and Rainger portray Uncle Sam as the personification of the United States as he helps people around the country up close and personal in the ways that various New Deal agencies and progressive legislation had been helping people for nearly a decade. For instance, Robin's lyric alludes to the Tennessee Valley Authority when it describes seeing Uncle Sam "turn a river to an artificial flood / That gave people cheap electric light." The government's agricultural price controls here become Uncle Sam "in a wheat-field sizin' up the crop / When prices get too high or too low," and lofty industrial legislation and court decisions come down to the level of the blue-collar worker seeing Uncle Sam "in a fact'ry where he gave the men the right / To kick against conditions that were wrong." And so on throughout the song, which vividly depicts in human terms anti–child labor laws, assistance for the elderly, urban renewal, and, generally, Uncle Sam giving a hand anyplace "where people have a hard row to hoe." At the end of nearly nine full pages of sheet music, "Uncle Sam Gets Around" segues into a two-page number called "It Won't Be Fun But It's Gotta Be Done," which proclaims, "We'll defend to the end ev'ry acre of the land that we love," a nice segue into the final section of this chapter.

### "We Must Be Ready": The Not So Still, Small Voice of Preparedness

Despite increased defense production, the draft, Lend-Lease, and Roosevelt's frequent speeches on the subject, most Americans, many still in an isolationist frame of mind, didn't want to hear about military preparedness in the prewar years. I've unearthed just six songs about preparedness, four by minor writers, the other two by a titan of Broadway and Tin Pan Alley for close to half a century.

Not unexpectedly, three of the songs by the minor songwriters were also pretty minor songs: "Defend Your Country," by John W. Bratton and Leo Edwards (Paull-Pioneer Music, 1940), "Wake Up! America," by George O. Perry, Bob Shoemaker, Tony Fillie, and Armond Fiore (Ideal Music, 1941), and George McKinnon and Ray Perkins's "Uncle Sam, Here I Am" (Kanner Music, 1941). All say little more than, in the words of the first, "Stand by and be ready," and in those of the second, "we must not be caught without defense." The fourth song is a bit more interesting, because it won a patriotic song contest, was published by a major publisher, and, according to the photo caption on the sheet music, was "Featured by Dinah Shore." "Me And My Uncle Sam" (Robbins Music, 1941) was written by William A. Dillon, whose only major hit came way back in 1911, when, with prolific composer Harry Von Tilzer, he wrote the words to "I Want A Girl Just Like The Girl That Married Dear Old Dad." Basically just saying things like "when freedom is in danger we prepare," and not saying them very imaginatively, "Me And My Uncle Sam" met with no such success and was quickly forgotten.

Perhaps because of their still unpopular message of preparedness, such would also be the fate of two songs on this theme by none other than America's unofficial flag-waving grand marshal of patriotic popular song since 1901, George M. Cohan. Cohan himself premiered "We Must Be Ready," the earliest of all the preparedness songs, at a national press dinner in New York on April 27, 1939, and Jerry Vogel, Cohan's long-standing publisher, quickly published it. An article in the *New York Herald Tribune* on April 28, partly reprinted on the sheet music, reported that the song "lit the fuse for the evening's explosion of enthusiasm" and "stirred the audience" of publishers, editors, and their families "to enthusiastic applause." But the fuse fizzled with the public; although newspapermen and women would have been pretty savvy to the need for preparedness even in 1939, most average citizens were not. The song's premise is that because "something might explode" in Europe, "It's well to be ready / You never can tell." While the old flag-waver's final statement may be seen as slightly isolationist (and also typically self-referential), it doesn't lose sight of the need to prepare: "The way to keep out of it / Is just stand steady / But let 'em know we're ready / To go marching to the tune of Over There." The following year Cohan repeated this theme in "This Is Our Side Of The Ocean" (Jerry Vogel, 1940). The title smacks of isolationism, but the text makes it clear that the song is a warning (or threat) to anyone "over there" who might want to violate our nation's sovereignty. Claiming that "ev'ryone is doing his share / To prepare," Cohan concludes with some of his familiar sabre-rattling: "We will fight for the right to declare: / That This Is Our Side Of The Ocean / So beware." But for all its vigor, like "We Must Be Ready" the song had little public success. Shortly after Pearl Harbor Cohan would have one more war song left in him, and a rousingly good one at that (see chapter 6), but nothing patriotic or militant that he wrote in the prewar and early war years of World War II ever achieved the stupendous success of "Yankee Doodle Boy," "You're A Grand Old Flag," or "Over There" earlier in the century.

Overall, with the exception of "God Bless America" and the handful of shorter-lived successes, prewar isolationist, patriotic, and preparedness songs mostly fell on deaf ears. But this doesn't mean the public ignored all songs touching on the "European War." American songs showing support for the overrun nations of Europe or our soon-to-be Allies, as well as some songs they sent to us, often were very well received, a few becoming major hits just prior to the United States entering the war.

# 4:

# "Chin Up! Cheerio! Carry On!"

## The Allies and Us

Other than "God Bless America" and "This Is My Country," almost the only war-related American songs to succeed prior to Pearl Harbor and also achieve lasting popularity were a handful that expressed sympathy or support for the European Allies. Yet even before Tin Pan Alleymen and women began writing such songs, as early as 1939 English songsmiths and their publishers were exporting to the United States their own war-related pieces, many meeting with considerable success over here. This exchange of war-related numbers between England and the United States continued to the war's end and beyond.

### "London Pride": British War Songs in America

Because Great Britain entered the war more than two years before the United States, British songwriters began writing war songs considerably earlier than their American counterparts. Most of their songs remained within the British Isles, but some crossed the Atlantic to the United States and Canada. English songs that reached American ears can be roughly divided into two groups: romantic or sentimental slush focusing on personal relationships, and more public, even national, "stiff upper lip" or "muddling through" pieces (to keep with the British idiom), including one militant war song of sorts.

A few English songs of both types became popular in the United States, and some of the most memorable came early. The first stiff upper lip arrival on our shores was a song whose words and music sound as venerable as "God Save The King" or "Rule Britannia," yet "There'll Always Be An England" (London: Irwin Dash, 1939) was written by two contemporary British songwriters, Ross Parker and Hughie (a.k.a. Hugh) Charles, in the year England declared war on Germany. While this paean to Britain's durability never became "Hit Parade" material, millions of Americans came to know it not just from radio, concerts, and recordings but because it was interpolated into the 1941 Universal film *Nice Girl?* in which it was sung by the picture's young and very popular Canadian-born star, Deanna Durbin. In Britain, "There'll Always Be An England" became something of a second, unofficial national anthem, very much as "God Bless America" did here.

Two other English songs from 1939 of the chin up variety also arrived in the United States—one promoting national unity, the other a militant war song in the British tradition of humor and whimsy. Written by Ralph Butler and Raymond Wallace, the jaunty "We Must All Stick Together" was published in London by Noel Gay Music in 1939. The date of its American publication is uncertain, but its lyrics show up in the November 1941 *Song Hits Magazine,* one of the lyric magazines of the 1940s. Lyric magazines tried to include only currently popular songs, suggesting that "We Must All Stick Together" was first heard in this country earlier in 1941. With its infectious melody, it's a happy song about national unity having to take precedence over issues of social class. The listener is admonished to "Never mind the old school tie" and reminded that "The richest in the land, the poorest of us all" must stick together.

Cocky about swiftly defeating the Germans, "We're Gonna Hang Out Our Washing On The Siegfried Line" (London: Peter Maurice, 1939), by Jimmy Kennedy and Michael Carr (born Maurice Cohen), was recorded by the popular music hall and variety team of Flanagan and Allen. So certain that the British Expeditionary Force (BEF) in France would swiftly smash through Germany's legendary western line of defense, a young soldier writes to his mother with waggish humor, asking, "Have you any dirty washing, mother dear?"—punning on *line,* as in what the British troops will hang their laundry on, "If the Siegfried Line's still there." Of course Allied troops didn't actually smash the line and cross into Germany until the spring of 1945. Such English bravado was soon squelched by the heroic but demoralizing evacuation of the BEF from Dunkirk between May 26 and June 4, 1940, and the ensuing Battle of Britain, which began with aerial combat over the English Channel in July and climaxed with the Germans' blitz of London in September, helping to explain the absence of such confident tunes in 1940. It wasn't until 1941, following some British victories in North Africa and the Middle East and the sinking of the *Bismarck,* that English songs of this kind made their way to America again.

Two such 1941 arrivals were tributes to England's endurance in adversity. With words and music by Roma Campbell Hunter and the seemingly ubiquitous Hugh Charles, "The King Is Still In London" was published there by Irwin Dash and in New York by the firm's American branch, Dash Connelly, both in 1941. The song's simple statement is that "THE KING IS STILL IN LONDON . . . / Like Mister Jones and Mister Brown," ready to tough it out with the city's commoners despite the Blitz. "London Pride" (Chappell, 1941), a charming song detailing the life of Londoners during the Blitz, from the Cockneys of Covent Garden Market in the first verse to Mayfair's aristocracy in the second, has words and music by the equally charming multitalented Noel Coward. Coward's title is the popular name for an urban wildflower that blooms all over London "ev'ry spring unfailing / Growing in the crevices"—a splendid image of survival in impossible conditions. Putting metaphors aside, Coward ends the third stanza by declaring that all of London will do the same, "Ev'ry Blitz [our] resistance toughening / From the Ritz to the Anchor and Crown"—or from the elegant haunts of the titled and/or wealthy to neighborhood working-class pubs. A third English song that came here in 1941 is a curiosity, notable mostly because its composer/lyricist was Tommie Connor, much better known for his English version of "Lili Marlene," and for "I Saw Mommy Kissing Santa Claus." But in 1941 Connor set England's appreciation for Lend-Lease to music in "Thank You Mister Roosevelt" (London: B. Feldman, 1941), thanking FDR and the American people for the material aid that was "helping us to carry on." A few English songs about army life arrived after Pearl Harbor, some revised by American lyricists for American listeners (see chapter 5), but most other wartime English imports were of a different sort indeed.

### "He Wears A Pair Of Silver Wings": English Slush, American Success

They were few but triumphant, some for the moment, others forever. Of the nine war-related romantic ballads by English songwriters in my files, five had some success in the United States, two becoming classics of English-language popular music even though poor timing accounted for the very cool reception of the earliest when it first came to America. Ross Parker and Hughie Charles's "We'll Meet Again" (London: Irwin Dash, 1939) today is best remembered as the darkly ironic musical background for the finale of Stanley Kubrick's 1964 film *Dr. Strangelove*. When the song came here in 1941, it made none of the trade papers' charts, let alone the *Hit Parade*. Even in the more extensive retrospective *Hot Charts,* its best and only showings are Guy Lombardo's record at 69th in January 1941 and Kay Kyser's at 56th that April. But when it was revived in the early spring of 1942, "We'll Meet Again" made the sheet music charts of both trade papers, and the Benny Goodman/Peggy Lee recording did well on *Billboard*'s record sales chart. The reason for the difference a year made is pretty obvious. The song is a typical one of a soldier's parting words to his sweetheart as he is about to leave for war, in many ways a precursor of the numerous songs of parting by American songsmiths yet to come. When it was first released in the United States, we weren't even at war. But with vast numbers of American servicemen being shipped out overseas early in 1942, the song verbalized what many of them must have been thinking or saying to wives or girlfriends back home. The departing serviceman tells his girl to keep her chin up "Till the blue skies drive the dark clouds far away," when they will meet again "some sunny day," images of war and peace that would recur in countless American and English songs.

The other romantic war-associated English import destined for immortality was a blockbuster from the moment it arrived, and the huge success of "A Nightingale Sang In Berkeley Square" (Peter Maurice, 1940) had little to do with the war. The American public bought up records and sheet music of Eric Maschwitz and Manning Sherwin's masterpiece simply because it was a wonderful song. When Maschwitz and Sherwin wrote "Nightingale" for the London revue *New Faces / An Eric Maschwitz Revue,* which opened on April 11, 1940, they didn't intend for it to relate to the war. Who knew then that the Dunkirk debacle was less than two months away, or that by the time most Londoners would first hear Vera Lynn's exceptional recording of "Nightingale," cut on June 5, German bombs would be falling on their beloved city? Here was another case of war by association in the minds of listeners. Americans may have missed allusions to Mayfair and "angels dining at the Ritz," but Londoners surely saw in the song's brilliant imagery a picture of two people so in love that for them Berkeley Square still radiated with its pre-Blitz charm and elegance. Reg Connelly, writing from London in *Variety* on January 5, 1944, observed: "Why was the sophisticated 'Nightingale Sang In Berkeley Square' so popular? Perhaps because it brought a touch of light, warmth, and charm into blacked-out homes" (189). Unintentionally a war song, "A Nightingale Sang in Berkeley Square" was very much the British "White Christmas."

The first radio song plugs for "Nightingale" appeared on *Billboard*'s chart for October 16, 1940, with *Variety* starting to track it a week later. Records by Gene Krupa and Ray Noble first appear in *Hot Charts* as Extras in October 1940, and the sheet music first shows up on the *Variety* charts on November 27, where it stayed for ten weeks, including four in the top spot. Guy Lombardo, Sammy Kaye, and Glenn Miller also recorded "Nightingale," but only the Glenn Miller disk hit the *Billboard* chart, for six weeks, placing 2nd for one of them and 3rd for three more. "Nightingale" stayed on the jukebox-play charts for eleven solid weeks, and in the memories of many of us who first heard it during the war or even later for much longer than that. But it never made the top three on *Your Hit Parade.*

A wartime English export that was an even bigger hit is a song barely remembered today, probably because the lyric is so closely tied to the war and because Michael Carr's music falls just short of memorable. The lyric, too, is pleasant but conventional, with a girl expressing how much she adores her "crazy guy" and how proud she is that "He Wears A Pair Of Silver Wings" (Peter Maurice, 1941) as a flier with the RAF. And yet, two lines soar above the ordinary in their succinct juxtaposition of the literal and the metaphoric; the girl describes going out walking with her boyfriend in his uniform, "He with those wings on his tunic / Me with my heart on my sleeve." There jolly well *should* be a stroke of brilliance in the lyric since it's another by Eric Maschwitz, responsible for the consistent brilliance of "A Nightingale Sang In Berkeley Square." By the time "He Wears A Pair Of Silver Wings" reached this country in the summer of 1942, many young men here were wearing the silver wings of the U.S. Army Air Force. Since Maschwitz's lyric refers only to the wings and not the RAF specifically, it's easy to see why the song hit so big. In fact, I wouldn't be surprised if most American listeners thought it was an American song. Kay Kyser with Harry Babbitt's vocal, Dinah Shore, Abe Lyman, Alvino Rey, and Connie Haynes all recorded the number here. Kyser's disk came up the winner, with ten weeks on *Billboard*'s record sales charts, placing 2nd for four of them. "Silver Wings" outstripped "Nightingale" in sheet music sales, remaining on *Billboard* and *Variety*'s charts for an impressive eighteen weeks, three times in 1st on *Billboard*'s and four times on *Variety*'s during late August and early September 1942. It was on the *Hit Parade* for fifteen weeks, as number one for four.

A quite lovely ballad with both music and lyrics by Michael Carr had its chance for popularity in Britain and America cut short by the terrible events of the war. The song must have been written, published, and recorded before the Dunkirk evacuation in 1940, since a girl back home declares to her absent soldier that "every beat of her heart will always be" "Somewhere In France With You" (Peter Maurice, 1939; U.S. selling agents Shapiro, Bernstein). After Dunkirk British troops would not be anywhere in France again until D-Day in 1944. Two other English war-related ballads from 1939 fared a bit better in America. The singer, clearly female, in Roy King and Stanley Hill's "I'll Pray For You" (London: Noel Gay, 1939; New York: Mills, 1939) lets her soldier-lover know that she will pray for him "Till troubles cease / Then you and I will live in peace." The song met with a modest reception here in 1940 recordings by Mildred

Bailey and by Blue Barron and Woody Herman's orchestras, but, as with "We'll Meet Again," it was too early for real success in America. One other ballad popular in England was a victim of bad timing here. Hugh Charles and Lewis Elton's "When They Sound The Last All Clear" (London: Irwin Dash, 1941) was popularized in Britain by Vera Lynn, who was to English musical morale-building what the Andrews Sisters and Kate Smith were to American. The number fuses a standard love refrain of the girl back home to her soldier abroad with what the OWI disparaged as a "peace and ease" description of a world after the war. By the time the song reached America, however, Eddie Seiler, Sol Marcus, and Bennie Benjamin's "When The Lights Go On Again (All Over The World)" (Campbell, Loft and Porgie, 1942), which also depicted the world after the war but more inventively (see chapter 12), was a major hit, especially in Vaughn Monroe's recording. With some slight irony, Vera Lynn had the hit record of this American song in England.

The last war-related English love song to have even a short life over here came and went between the late months of 1943 and early 1944. Hugh Charles (yet again!), Leo Towers, and Sonny Miller's "Silver Wings In The Moonlight" (London: Irwin Dash, 1943; New York: Miller Music, 1943) was recorded here by Freddie Slack's orchestra with vocal by Margaret Whiting and is a *Hot Charts* Extra for April and May of 1944. It's unusual in that the girl isn't singing to her flier-lover but, depending on one's reading of the song, either to his airplane or to the whole RAF as symbolized by the silver wings on the guy's uniform. She refers to either the plane or the RAF as "his other love" but swears she's not jealous and asks the silver wings to "take him safely and then . . . / Bring him homeward again." After this song, no more war-related romantic ballads came here from England till just after the war was over.

### "Lili Marlene": Appropriated Enemy Property

One imported song transcended the hostilities between the Allies and the Axis during World War II. At bottom nothing more or less than the simple ballad of a soldier's and girl's fidelity while he's away at war set to a hauntingly beautiful and memorable melody, "Lili Marlene" was the subject of legends even during the war, some that make sifting fact from fancy difficult. But at least the song's genesis in Germany is clear. In 1915, prior to his assignment to the Russian front in World War I, Hans Leip (1893–1983), a young soldier and minor German poet, wrote a poem called "Das Leid eines jungen Soldaten auf der Wacht" (The Song of a Young Sentry). Twenty-four years later it became the basis for the lyrics of "Mädchens under der Laterne" (The Girl under the Lantern), better known, in its German spelling, as "Lili Marleen." Leip's original 1915 poem questioned the madness of World War I, but that's absent from both the German and the English versions of the song (see "Norbert" for Leip's original and a literal English translation). The girl's name is a composite of Leip's girlfriend (Lili) and either another girlfriend, a friend's girlfriend, or a young nurse who waved to Leip while he was on sentry duty (Marleen). The poem first appeared in 1937 in a collection of Leip's verse, where Norbert Schultze (1911–2002), already a successful composer, saw it and set it to music. No published or Internet account mentions who altered the lyrics from an antiwar plea to a romantic ballad of love's travails in wartime, although the British sheet music credits Leip with the German lyric.

"Lili Marlene" was first performed in 1935, with music not by Schultze but by one Rudolf Zink, the accompanist and arranger for a singer at the Munich restaurant Simplizissimus who called herself Liselott Wilke. Coincidentally, four years later Fraulein "Wilke" made the first recording of "Lili Marlene" with Norbert Schultze's now familiar melody under her later stage name, Lale Andersen, launching the song toward international fame. Some sources try to make Andersen either Danish or Swedish, but she was solidly German, born Liselotte Helene Berta Eulalia Bunnenberg in Bremerhaven, either in 1905 or 1910. Andersen recorded "Lili Marlene" at least once again in German in 1942, and in an English-language version in 1943. The 1939 record flopped, selling only about seven hundred copies. It took the fortunes of war to make "Lili Marlene" a global success. On April 18, 1941, only days after the German occupation of Yugoslavia and a week after the siege of Tobruk began, the director of the German-run *Soldatensender Belgrad* (Radio Belgrade) aired the song for a friend in the Afrika Korps. The "Desert Fox" himself, General Field Marshal Erwin Rommel, so liked "Lili Marlene" that he requested it be played nightly on Radio Belgrade's broadcasts to the German troops. The song became the station's sign-off tune. Not only did the Afrika Korps hear those nightly airings of "Lili," but so did soldiers of the British 8th Army, who tried to memorize the German words or improvised English ones.

Back in Germany, "Lili Marlene" and Lale Andersen were in trouble. Over the course of two years or so, the song's popularity among the German armed forces reached the German home front as well. But Joseph Goebbels, Propaganda Minister of the Nazi Party, hated the song and tried to have it banned early in 1943, but his attempt to squelch the recording proved futile (Lotz). Because he objected to the song's "unheilvollen Charakters" (pernicious or harmful character), Goebbels wanted it set to martial music since he believed its current setting as a romantic ballad would "sap fighting morale" (Boyes). Andersen's recording was already nearly in march tempo, backed by a lusty male chorus, and punctuated with little trumpet calls and drum beats that give this "Lili Marlene" a military air absent from any English-language rendition except Andersen's own. How much more did Herr Goebbels want? In fact, he probably disliked Andersen as much as the song. By all accounts, she was a free spirit and outspoken independent thinker, known to "associate with Jews and other subversive types when this was expressly forbidden" (Panse). What must have rankled Goebbels even more was her open criticism of the Nazis and her intention to defect, which was expressed in a letter to a Swiss friend that the Gestapo intercepted (Boyes). When Goebbels banned her from performing in public, Andersen allegedly took an overdose of sleeping pills but survived, as did her singing career. Public demand for her and "Lili Marlene" became so great that Goebbels had to back down and rescind his order later in 1943.

Around this time Andersen recorded a quite lovely "Lili Marlene" in English, backed by the German swing band known as Charlie and His Orchestra, which recorded for propaganda broadcasts mostly American swing tunes in English with their lyrics partly altered to inject a pro-Nazi, anti-Allies, and/or antisemitic message. Andersen's English "Lili Marlene" isn't typical of Charlie, since it's a straightforward rendering of the German with no air of propaganda about it. Yet the fact that Andersen recorded with Charlie at all seems to have been her trade-off for her liberty since Charlie and His Orchestra was Herr Goebbels's propaganda brainchild. Andersen made other recordings with Charlie but "always stubbornly refused to sing propaganda texts," which Goebbels apparently accepted, since he allowed her to perform and record for the remainder of the war (Lotz). Her career flourished almost until her death in 1972, yet Lale Andersen remains most closely identified with "Lili Marlene."

The chance meeting of a London publisher and a British army officer moved "Lilli Marlene" from the improvisations of the British troops to a published version for the home front that ultimately reached the United States. At an inn in Stoke Poges, England, J. J. Phillips, managing director of Peter Maurice, Ltd., met a major in the British 8th Army who had recently returned from the North Africa campaign. The major told Phillips how popular "Lili" was among British troops; the 8th Army had even adopted it as their unofficial song. But he also asked Phillips if an English lyric might be written to keep the boys from singing the German! Learning that the BBC and the Ministry of Information wanted "Lili" broadcast in English, Phillips recruited songwriter Tommie Connor to write a commercial English-language lyric.

Thus the British "Lilli [with two l's] Marlene" was born. Unlike the "American version" below, the British one published in this country by Marks Music credits Hans Leip and Norbert Schultze and, in addition to "Lyric Copyright 1944 by Peter Maurice Music Co. Ltd.," also includes the information "Copyright 1941 by Apollo Music Co." Apollo Music turns out to be Apollo-Verlag, the song's original German publisher; by not printing where "Apollo Music" was located, Peter Maurice and Marks avoided any direct references to the song's German origins. In Britain, Vera Lynn and Anne Shelton's immensely successful recordings popularized the Tommie Connor "Lilli Marlene" in 1944.

Around the same time, "Lili" got a boost when documentary film director Humphrey Jennings made the twenty-two minute short *The Story of Lilli Marlene,* a.k.a *The True Story of Lili Marlene.* Produced by the British Crown Film Unit as a Ministry of Information Film, it was released in both Britain and the United States in late 1943 or early 1944, here by Universal Studios. It contains striking historical footage of British troops in Africa, a mass rally for Hitler, and the Battle of Stalingrad, but in other ways this "documentary" about "Lili Marlene" is pure fabrication and possibly even the source of some of the legends. For instance, the film claims that the lyrics were written in Hamburg in 1923, that Lale Andersen was Swedish and sang in a Berlin café, and that the German public went wild for "Lili" with no condemnation by Goebbels. Other than the news footage, the most authentic sequence is the recreation of former German actress Lucie Mannheim singing an anti-Hitler rewrite of "Lili Marlene" on a BBC program broadcast into Germany. Mannheim fled Germany in 1933; before she was in the film she had married British actor Marius Goring, its narrator. The English lyrics of "Lili" are uncredited in the short, but the lyric magazine *Song Parade* for November 1944 reprints them and the anti-Hitler parody, crediting Goring with both. Their mere appearance there suggests that Americans were seeing the film.

Performed by the March of Time Orchestra and Chorus with a soloist conjecturally identified as Jack Smith, "Lili Marlene" was first broadcast in the states on April 29, 1943, on *The March of Time,* sponsored by *Time* magazine (Weiner). Announcer Westbrook Van Voorhis's introduction described the song's German origins, how it became a favorite of both Axis and Allied soldiers, and how an English version aired on the BBC had taken Britain by storm. The translator of the program's "Lili" remains unknown, but of the six or more English-language versions, it's most faithful to the German lyric sung by Lale Andersen. With a self-congratulatory pat on the back for premiering "Lili Marlene" in the United States, *Time* issued a complimentary record inscribed, as reproduced in the booklet for the CD *Something for the Boys,* as follows:

With the Compliments of

**TIME**

THE WEEKLY NEWS MAGAZINE

A Special Recording of

LILI MARLENE

*The soldiers' song of both the Axis*
*and the Allies overseas*
BROADCAST IN AMERICA FOR THE FIRST TIME BY
THE MARCH OF TIME
*April 29, 1943*

On May 3, 1943, an article in the music section of *Time* made Americans yet more familiar with "Lili Marlene." Among other things, the article treats the song's global success. Evidently its German popularity was officially sanctioned by then, since actress Emmy Sonnemann sang "Lili" to an audience of "Nazi bigwigs" in Berlin's Kroll Opera House (40). Offstage, Sonnemann was Frau Hermann Göring! The article's opening was astute and accepting: "A great war song has come out of Germany."

It's unclear why more than a year elapsed before Perry Como, Hildegarde, Martha Tilton, Connie Boswell (who sang the British version), and others recorded "Lili Marlene" at various times in 1944. But in the interim another dynamic and influential voice sang it to Americans in radio broadcasts, concerts, and other public appearances both stateside and on USO tours "for three long years in North Africa, Sicily, Italy, in Alaska, Greenland, Iceland, in England," as she later recalled (qtd. in Brock). German by birth and a naturalized American citizen, singer/actress Marlene Dietrich was fiercely anti-Nazi. During the war she familiarized U.S. troops abroad and civilians at home with "Lili Marlene" entirely through personal appearances and radio. She didn't record the song until after the war, in September 1945, and then at least six more times in the '50s and '60s ("Newsletter"). Dietrich's USO performances of "Lili" began before any records by American singers appeared. Like all others, Dietrich's version tells of the soldier away and the patient, faithful girl back home, but the text of the lyric is uncredited and markedly different from any other; perhaps Dietrich wrote it herself.

The "Battle of the Publishers" is central to the story of "Lili" in the United States. Evidence suggests that the sheet music and recordings of the "American version" of "Lili Marlene" were on sale here prior to the arrival of Tommie Connor's British version. Published by the major ASCAP affiliate Chappell & Co., early issues of the sheet music have under the title "by PHIL PARK / American version by / MACK DAVID," with no mention of the writers of the German song, Hans Leip and Norbert Schultze. Park appears to have been fictitious, perhaps a stand-in to indicate that the song existed before Mack David's version without disclosing its German origin. Evidence for Park's nonexistence is that later covers read just "by / MACK DAVID." Phil Park was expunged. On the other hand, Mack David was the very real writer of songs like "La Vie En Rose," "Walk On The Wild Side," and, for Walt Disney animated feature films, "A Dream Is A Wish Your Heart Makes" and "Bibbidi-Bobbidi-Boo."

The Chappell edition of Mack David's "Lili" is copyright 1943, so it's possible that Hildegarde began performing it in her usual venues of supper clubs and cabarets late that year, before both she and Perry Como recorded it in 1944. The date of Hildegarde's recording session isn't clear, but since Decca had already settled with the musicians' union, she recorded it with a full orchestra and a small singing ensemble. Como recorded "Lili" on June 27, 1944. Since Victor was still holding out against the AFM, Como's disk is a capella, with an unnamed mixed chorus. Both singers sing the first, second, and fourth stanzas of Mack David's American version, omitting the third probably just for the sake of brevity.

With Marks's sheet music of "Lilli Marlene" flaunting its English authenticity, on the sheet music cover with Perry Como's picture Chappell tried to hype its version by making it appear it had been featured in the "Lili Marlene" documentary film, which, of course, was patently untrue. Marks fired back with a couple of rounds of its own. Already featuring on the back J. J. Phillips's letter about how the "authentic" British version of the song came to be, the sheet music now added on the front in boldface letters *above* the song's title, and very visible to music buyers, "THE ONLY AUTHENTIC PETER MAURICE VERSION OF THE FAMOUS INTERNATIONAL HIT." Of the two issues of the Marks edition I've seen, presumably the earlier is graced by a photo captioned "Sung Exquisitely by JOAN BROOKS," a fairly popular singer of the day now largely forgotten. The later cover contains a photo captioned "Sung in inimitable style by Connie Boswell on Decca Record #3858."

Except for different licensing numbers, the one constant among all variant issues of both the Chappell and Marks editions of "Lili Marlene" is an extraordinary legal notice: "Published & distributed in the public interest with the consent of the Alien Property Custodian under License No. 00." This declaration on their sheet music suggests that the publishers legally circumvented crediting or paying royalties or other fees to the original writers or publisher of "Lili Marlene" since they were citizens of a country at war with the United States. As appropriated enemy property, in a sense, the English-language versions of the song did not have to abide by the regulations of international copyright.

Both Hildegarde and Perry Como's records were released between late June and early August 1944. "Lili Marlene" never made the top ten or fifteen in sheet music or record sales, but *Billboard*'s weekly chart of jukebox plays first listed the Perry Como record as 2nd in its "Coming Up" group on August 26, and on September 9 Hildegarde's was 16th under "Going Strong," then overtaken in the next two weeks by Como at 13th and 15th, respectively. *Hot Charts* lists both records as tied at 37th during August 1944, with Como's alone at 33rd in September. One reason for the greater success of Como's "Lili Marlene" may have been that its flip side was Frank Loesser's delightfully offbeat take on wartime romance, "First Class Private Mary Brown" (Frank Music, 1944; see chapter 11). Connie Boswell's disk of the British "Lilli Marlene" never made the charts.

The short duration of only modest chart rankings suggests that "Lili Marlene" was never very popular in America, but that was not the case. In addition to strong if not spectacular record and sheet music sales, the song was widely heard thanks to Marlene Dietrich's many radio and live performances, plus performances by other singers on the air or on the country's bandstands. And American GIs were singing it as their British Allies had been doing for years. The song's simple sentiments, beautifully articulated in its words and unforgettable melody, deeply touched the wartime American consciousness, even if it was never a runaway hit or an enormous moneymaker. And that was possibly because of timing. Just when the sheet music and records of "Lili Marlene" were released, another fine song of a girl back home and a soldier away was skyrocketing to the top of all the charts, where it remained till the end of 1944— Sammy Cahn and Jule Styne's "I'll Walk Alone." Similar in sentiment to "Lili" and also American born and bred, "I'll Walk Alone" won out.

Despite its popularity in the United States, "Lili Marlene" still encountered the occasional flap over its German origin. *Variety* reported a humorous one as late as May 16, 1945. Some days earlier, in the Cotillion Room of the Hotel Pierre—New York home to the rich and sometimes famous—a singer named Margaret Scott was performing "Lili Marlene" when one Lady Doverdale and her companion, Mary Hoyt Wiborg, began heckling the songstress because of the song's "Nazi origin." A U.S. Army major present rose to explain how the song had long since been adopted by the Allied forces, but nothing placated the two women and "their dudgeon resulted in the titled widow moving out of the hotel" (41). Ruffled feathers of English dowagers aside, the popularity of "Lili Marlene" continued. In fact, based on the song's success among the military and civilians in both Axis and Allied countries, nearly everyone who writes about "Lili Marlene" claims it was in all probability the single most popular war-related song *worldwide* during World War II. And while a case could also perhaps be made for "White Christmas" giving it a good run for the money, I am personally inclined to accept that claim as true.

### "The Last Time I Saw Paris": American Songwriters Reach Out

Until Congress passed the Lend-Lease Act on March 11, 1941, the official position of the United States vis-à-vis the combatants in the "European War" had been one of neutrality. But long before then, most Americans' sentiments were far from neutral; they were sympathetic to countries overrun by the Nazis and solidly behind the Allies from Britain to the Soviet Union that were fighting against the Axis Powers. The same held true for the nation's professional songwriters. Before Pearl Harbor, Tin Pan Alley, Broadway, and Hollywood songsmiths wrote at least twenty-seven songs supportive of the Allies and the Western European countries under Nazi domination, and twenty more once the United States was in the war, plus fourteen others paying tribute to the USSR. Because of their temporal nature, most were songs of the moment, but some became songs for the ages. While lesser lights in America's galaxy of songwriters wrote many of these songs, quite a few were by more distinguished names in the Alley.

The earliest written, if not perhaps the earliest released, was a distinguished song by distinguished writers. On June 14, 1940, Paris fell to the German troops. Oscar Hammerstein 2nd almost never wrote a stand-alone song, only songs for specific contexts in musicals, and until he began collaborating with Richard Rodgers a few years later, he nearly always wrote lyrics to his composer's melodies. But so moved was he upon learning of this crushing blow to one of his favorite cities that Hammerstein immediately sat down and wrote the lyric for "The Last Time I Saw Paris." As Hammerstein tells it, at first he "started to think of Paris rather superficially; what it had been before the Germans had come in . . . I thought of Mistinguette . . . and Chevalier in his straw hat" (qtd. in Citron 126). But in his final draft, Hammerstein opted for the little things that made Paris unique—its taxi cab horns and street cafés, children laughing at a Punch and Judy show, lovers walking on the city's tree-lined boulevards—wrapping it all up with his famous "No matter how they change her I'll remember her that way." The lyric finished, Hammerstein phoned Jerome Kern, his friend and frequent collaborator ever since their *Show Boat* in 1927, and Kern promptly wrote the song's music. If there was ever a successful song touching on the war entirely by association, "The Last Time I Saw Paris" is it.

Yet the song was not a smash when it first appeared on the trade paper charts for sheet music sales and juke box plays between January and March 1941, climbing no higher than 4th for sheet music and 3rd for coin machines. It never showed up on *Billboard*'s chart of top-selling records or in the three top slots on the *Hit Parade*. Even *Hot Charts* places the favored Kate Smith recording at only 62nd in January, 47th in February, and 56th in March; records by Hildegarde and others didn't make the charts at all. Still, millions of Americans heard "The Last Time I Saw Paris" interpolated into the MGM picture *Lady, Be Good!* (1941), in which Ann Sothern sang the song that netted Hammerstein and Kern the Academy Award. While flattered to have won, they felt they had no right to the Oscar since their song was an interpolation and argued with the

Academy that the award should rightly go to Harold Arlen and Johnny Mercer's "Blues In The Night," written for the MGM film of the same name. Thanks to Kern and Hammerstein's advocacy, the Motion Picture Academy of Arts and Sciences henceforth allowed only songs specifically written for films to be eligible for Academy Award nominations.

Of the remaining songs written in sympathy with France—four before Pearl, four after—only one caught on briefly with the public, but some others are of historical interest. Written by Lew Brown and Ray Henderson, two-thirds of De Sylva, Brown, and Henderson, whose Broadway songs virtually defined the roar of the Roaring Twenties, "Don't Cry, Cherie" (Shapiro, Bernstein, 1941) is a little ballad in which a Frenchman tries to console his wife or lover that better days will come and "Our garden will bloom once more." It was noted as "Gaining" on *Variety*'s jukebox chart on July 2, 1941, and *Hot Charts* lists the records by Glenn Miller, Sammy Kaye, Harry James, Gene Krupa, and Woody Herman as Extras for July and August. After that the song and its recordings disappear from the charts.

Two songs supportive of France written after the United States entered the war are interesting for being written from a French perspective, even though neither gained much of an audience. In 1942, Al Lewis, Larry Stock, and Vincent Rose—the team that gave the world "Blueberry Hill" and many other songs—wrote "The Cross Of Lorraine" (Triangle Music, 1942), the substance of which is the familiar soldier away promising his girl back home that he'll return when the war is over. But in this song the soldier is in the Free French Army, fighting alongside the British in the Middle East and elsewhere, and the song's title page proclaims it was "Dedicated to General De Gaulle and the Free French Forces." Similarly, the singer in Lou Leaman and Lou Dahlman's "I'm A Soldier of De Gaulle" (Mills Music, 1943) sings of his pride as a Free French soldier who intends to liberate his country from the Germans. Not only textually but rhythmically, the line "The next time I see Paris, her heart will beat anew" is a deliberate spin-off of Hammerstein's "The last time I saw Paris / Her heart was warm and gay."

Historically, America's ties to Britain have always been stronger than those to France, so it's easy to see why far more songs supportive of the British rolled off Tin Pan Alley sheet music and record presses, especially before Pearl Harbor. Fifteen bear a copyright date of 1941, three times the number of those in sympathy with France during our entire prewar period; four others of little consequence followed in 1943, with none, inexplicably, in 1942. With only copyright dates to go by, it's almost impossible to ascertain the order in which songs were written or went on sale to the public, but the content of some American songs intended to cheer on or cheer up the English allows for at least a rough chronology to be established. As with the songs about France, almost all those about England are of interest as historical documents, with only one enormous hit, late in 1941, the success of which can perhaps be attributed as much to the unintentional timing of the song's release as to its inherent brilliance. But first, a look at some with only temporal significance.

Probably dating from the winter or early spring of 1941 was one of several songs urging Americans to participate in Bundles for Britain. Mrs. Wales Latham, a socially conscious "young New York society matron" founded that private, non-governmental relief agency in December 1939 to knit caps, sweaters, and the like for British sailors in the North Atlantic ("Collecting"). According to an article in *Look* the following December, the enterprising Mrs. Latham "got a license from the State Department, wheedled an empty store rent-free from a Park Avenue landlord, [and] persuaded Mrs. Winston Churchill to become a sponsor" (qtd. in "Collecting"). By that time the women of Bundles for Britain were not just knitting but sewing garments, collecting and repairing cast-off clothing, and, ultimately, taking in cash contributions of whatever amount, whether "$1.15, the profit from two sisters' Kool Aid stand" or $30,000 from a radio appeal by actors Ronald Coleman and Charles Boyer ("Collecting"). From its storefront beginnings, Bundles for Britain quickly grew to be the largest war relief agency in the country, with over one thousand chapters and half a million members (Perrett 77).

The title of Dick Sanford, Jack Millrich, and Harry Jentes's "Knittin' For Britain" (Bob Miller, 1941) makes it clear the song appeared relatively early, in the primarily knitting days of Bundles for Britain. Even though Bundles began as a women's organization, the song's opening line, "There's an army of busy people," seems to be not gender-specific by design. Abner Silver and Mann Curtis's "Let's Stand Behind Great Britain" (Lincoln Music, 1941) is more expansive, even including Lend-Lease, with the verse beginning, "Not so long ago on the radio / Pres'dent Roosevelt made a stirring speech" and the chorus mentioning "our factories" aiding overseas. Yet the song was specifically intended to support Bundles for Britain. A full-page article and fundraising pitch in the sheet music is headed "Abner Silver and Mann Curtis Have Donated All Their Royalties Of This Song to Bundles for Britain." The article stresses the ever-greater need: "As the horrors of war reach the very shores of England, . . . we must also be prepared to help the civilian population." James E. Donahue and Renee Dietrich Wright allude to Lend-Lease in the second chorus of their "Tell All Our Friends In America" (Edward B. Marks, 1941). The first stanza is a letter from England to the United States telling America that the English are carrying on and will defend their country to the end; America replies in the second stanza that it will stand behind Great Britain with "guns and fighting planes, ammunition, ships, and grains," a catalogue of war matériel that would have been impossible in a song prior to the passage of Lend-Lease.

As with all wartime motivational songs, it's difficult to gauge the actual impact of these, but by the usual indices of popularity none had much commercial success. Nor, interestingly, did songs in sympathy with the English written by some of the foremost Broadway writers of the day. Evidently trying to capitalize on even the modest success of "The Last Time I Saw Paris," Kern and Hammerstein wrote a piece praising England's fight to stay free and its endurance in adversity. But this time the lyric is too abstract and lacks the specificity, warmth, and personal feeling Hammerstein put into the earlier song. It's no surprise, then, that Hammerstein and Kern's "Forever And A Day" (Chappell, 1941) lasted for neither. Similarly, Irving Berlin's "A Little Old Church in England" (Irving Berlin Inc., 1941) is a short song telling how a bombed-out church somewhere in London will someday be replaced where it once stood. Fred Waring, his chorus, and orchestra's premiere of the number at New York's Vanderbilt Theatre on January 30, 1941, was transcribed for broadcast on radio's *ASCAP on Parade* on February 1, but the song wasn't heard much after that. E. Y. Harburg and Burton Lane's "Chin Up! Cheerio! Carry On!" (Leo Feist, 1941) had no better luck on records or sheet music, but millions of Americans still heard—and probably remembered—the upbeat little tune thanks to its placement in a movie. The song simply encourages the English not to give up, to "be a stout fella," and, showing Harburg's marvelous ear for wacky rhymes, to "hang on to your wits and you'll turn the blitz on Fritz." But the song's context in MGM's *Babes on Broadway* (1941) was as emotionally charged as the song was brightly uplifting. In the film, Judy Garland sings the number at a rally for war orphans from Britain as scenes of "war-torn London accompany Judy's song. The empty streets and bombed buildings are superimposed over" the faces of the orphans, who begin to cry at thoughts of home (Woll 159).

One song in support of the English was a runaway hit in both Britain and the United States. It was also the epitome of the "peace-and-ease" slush that was anathema to the OWI, which often cited the song's vision of a tranquil postwar world as an example of what undermines military and civilian morale. Working together or with others, composer Walter Kent and lyricist Nat Burton wrote a number of hits, even though Burton died in 1945 at only forty-three. But nothing else they wrote ever came close to the contemporary popularity or the ongoing longevity of—to give the song its true and proper title—"(There'll Be Blue Birds Over) The White Cliffs Of Dover." So British was it in its diction, imagery, and tone, most Americans thought the song was written by an Englishman, not a couple of native New Yorkers. Yet the first of two rarely heard verses suggests the song's American origins: "I'll never forget the people I met / Braving those angry skies . . . though I'm far away."

In tandem with Kent's elegantly singable melody, Burton's lyrics for the chorus are simple, vivid in their imagery, and even a bit sentimental in the best sense of the word. Yet the lines "And Jimmy will go to sleep / In his own little room again." seem deliberately ambiguous. They are usually thought to refer to the homecoming of the combat-weary English soldier, but they could also allude to the return to London of a child who'd been sent for the duration to the comparative safety of the north of England. Either way, that image, at once concrete and ambiguous, is the core of the song's emotional wallop.

Kate Smith introduced "The White Cliffs of Dover" on her radio show, and recordings and sheet music of it began appearing in late November 1941. On November 26, *Variety* reported in its chart of radio song plugs that the piece had been played twelve times the previous week; by December 24, thirty-two; and on January 14, 1942, a high of thirty-five (which was repeated a few weeks later). It seems as if everyone who was anyone (and others who were not) performed and/or recorded the song; variant issues of the Shapiro, Bernstein sheet music bear the photos and names of Abe Lyman, Russ Morgan, Kate Smith, Shep Fields, Glenn Miller, Boyd Raeburn, Bing Crosby, Kay Kyser, Guy Lombardo, Dick Robertson, Roy Shield, Harold Stokes, Tommy Tucker, and Blue Barron— possibly a record for the most singers and bandleaders identified with a single song during the war years. Glenn Miller, Kay Kyser, and Kate Smith had the biggest-selling records. On *Billboard*'s weekly chart of record sales, Glenn Miller's reached a high of 6th the week before Christmas 1941, but the monthly lists in *Hot Charts* ranking *all* charted records of a song in the aggregate provide a better view of the big picture, putting "White Cliffs" at 8th for December 1941, 1st for January 1942, 2nd for February, and 9th for March. The sheet music stayed on both *Billboard* and *Variety*'s charts for nineteen weeks, and it was the number-one seller for eight consecutive weeks in the former, eleven in the latter. And beyond the arcane precincts of trade journals, "The White Cliffs of Dover" made *Your Hit Parade* for seventeen weeks, in 1st place for six. It is entirely possible that the extraordinary success of "The White Cliffs of Dover" was aided by its release shortly before the Japanese attack on Pearl Harbor, an event no one could have anticipated in advance. Sales began to escalate soon after December 7, 1941; despite its single English reference to Dover, "White Cliffs" most likely took on new meaning for Americans with the United States now in the war.

Besides France and Great Britain, Holland, Scandinavia, and Austria also became the subjects of a few wartime songs by American songwriters, two of which had considerable popularity then, though neither is much remembered today. German forces invaded the Netherlands on May 10, 1940, and the Dutch army surrendered on May 14. Though their song alluded to the German invasion of Holland, the reason Hy Zaret and the husband-and-wife team of Joan Whitney and Alex Kramer didn't write "My Sister And I" (Broadcast Music, 1941) until nearly a year later is because the song was not so much based on the event as "Inspired by The Current Best Seller 'MY SISTER AND I' by Dirk Van Der Heide," according to the sheet music. That book is something of a Protestant *Diary of Anne Frank* with a happy ending, written by a twelve-year-old Dutch boy who, with his nine-year-old sister, survived the bombings (though their mother did not) and, through the efforts of an uncle, made their way first to England and then to the United States. Writing under the pseudonym Dirk Van Der Heide to protect his father, a veterinarian who was still in the Netherlands, the boy recounts with touchingly childlike naiveté and pathos what his life in Holland was like before, during, and after the Nazi invasion. Translated into English by Mrs. Antoon Deventer and published in 1941, *My Sister and I* was in fact a bestseller in this country. Each stanza of Zaret, Whitney, and Kramer's lyric strikingly juxtaposes a warm recollection of the past with a repeated tag phrase literally expressing the unspeakable horror of what followed; in the second stanza the boy recalls "the fishing schooners pulling into shore / And the dog-cart we drove in the days before . . . but we don't talk about that" (ellipses in text). Repeated in every stanza, that tag line exponentially intensifies what the boy and his sister must have felt upon seeing their homeland all but destroyed. Released in April 1941, "My Sister And I" was plugged heavily on radio, *Variety* reporting it on the air between fourteen and thirty-eight times a week from April to mid-May. It rode high on all the trade journal charts from April through mid-July, though only rarely in the number-one position, and it made *Your Hit Parade* for fourteen weeks, twice in 1st place. The King Sisters, Bea Wain, Bob Chester's orchestra, Benny Goodman with Helen Forrest's vocal, Eddie Howard, Jack Leonard, Dick Jurgens, and Jimmy Dorsey with vocal by Bob Eberly— the biggest seller—all recorded it. Looked at objectively, "My Sister And I" was just about as popular for just about as long a time as "The White Cliffs of Dover," but all before the United States entered the war. Once we joined the conflict, Tin Pan Alley produced three more songs in sympathy with Holland—Bobby Worth's "Dear Home in Holland" (Southern Music, 1942), Herb Magidson and Jimmy McHugh's "The Tulips Are Talking Tonight" (ABC Music, 1942), and Lily Blake and Vic Mizzy's "The Old Dutch Mill Will Turn Again" (Santly-Joy, 1943)—but none of these came close to the popularity of "My Sister and I."

Moving from the Netherlands to Scandinavia, the Andrews Sisters scored something of a major triumph with "The Shrine of St. Cecilia"

(Chicago: Braun, 1941; Swedish copyright 1940), a song with music by Jokern, the pseudonym of Swedish composer Nils Johan Perne, and English words by Carroll Loveday (no Swedish lyricist is named). And the sisters scored it in precisely the same months that "The White Cliffs Of Dover" was hitting the top of all the charts—December 1941 through April '42. The cover art of the American sheet music is a drawing of a church spire on a hill above the ruins of a small bombed-out village, which is precisely what the song's lyrics are about, in quite specific and affecting detail. Because Sweden had declared its neutrality and remained neutral throughout the war, it was never invaded by Germany. It's possible, then, that the song was written in sympathy with Norway, Sweden's neighbor to the west, which German forces invaded on April 9, 1940, and which signed an armistice with Germany on June 9. But, according to Peter Harrington, military historian and curator of the Anne S. K. Brown Military Collection in Brown University's John Hay Library, the subject of the song may indeed be Swedish after all. It is altogether possible that when German troops overran the very narrow northern part of Norway, they mistakenly decimated some small Swedish border towns as well. Whatever the case, the plaintive yet hopeful lyric laments how a "storm came from up above" to destroy the town, yet miraculously "somehow it missed / THE SHRINE OF ST. CECILIA," where the singer hopes to meet his/her beloved again someday. With its ten weeks on the trade papers' jukebox charts and seventeen on *Billboard*'s record sales charts, Americans clearly found something to relate to in the song in the aftermath of Pearl Harbor. Recordings by Sammy Kaye and Vaughn Monroe also sold well, and according to *Variety* the public bought a lot of the sheet music for seventeen weeks.

"Violins Were Playing" (Lincoln Music, 1943), by brothers Nick and Charles "Gone Fishin'" Kenny and Abner Silver, was just too late. Touching on war-related events wholly by association, the song is a reminiscence of a romantic "little café" in "Old Vienna" where the singer and his or her lover used to waltz and have their fortunes told while the violins of the title were playing. Then the violins "faded away," but, the singer reassures, "we'll meet again some day / When the violins play." The song is lovely, but Germany's virtually bloodless *Anschluss* (annexation) of Austria on March 12, 1938, was much too old news by 1943 for the song to have much impact, though according to the sheet music it was "Successfully introduced by KATE SMITH," presumably on her weekly radio show.

In addition to songs about a single country there were a dozen others that reached out to more than one—anywhere from two to all the Allied fighting forces. Two had some popular success. Charlie Spivak and his orchestra made a recording of Sam M. Lewis and Joe Burke's "A Tale Of Two Cities" (Remick, 1941) that is a *Hot Charts* Extra from May through

July 1941, as are disks by Harry James, Sammy Kaye, and Vaughn Monroe of Jack Fulton, Lee Erwin, and Paul De Fur's "Last Night I Said A Prayer" (Martin Block, 1941) for March and April 1942. Both songs are about London and Paris, the earlier lamenting how the war interrupted the cities' traditional friendship, the later praying for the prewar charm and splendor of the two capitals to be restored once the war is over. Of interest for who wrote it is "If That's Propaganda" (Chappell, 1941), Ira Gershwin's short lyric managing to cram nine nationalities or countries into Harold Arlen's tune. More about Lend-Lease and Bundles for Britain than propaganda, the number says that material aid from the United States will help the Allies "Take the chains off the Danes, Clutch off the Dutch, The curbs off the Serbs! . . . And the legions of Norwegians," and so forth. Once the United States entered the war, songs about groups of countries shifted from sympathy and optimism for the future to rallying cries for the Allies (or United Nations) to stick together and defeat the Axis. The only one of lasting interest, mostly because of its "collaborators," is "United Nations March" (a.k.a., "United Nations On The March"; Am-Rus Music, 1942). The musical arrangement and stately lyric promising a "new day for mankind" with the "United Nations on the march" is the work of Harold Rome, the music itself from a previously written piece by Russian composer Dmitri Shostakovich—another convenient segue to a chapter's final section.

### *"And Russia Is Her Name"*: Songs for the Soviets

It's not at all surprising that composer/lyricist Harold Rome had a hand in one-fourth of the sixteen songs written after the United States entered the war that dealt in whole or in part with the Soviet Union. While never a member of the Communist Party, Rome in the 1930s was, like other noted left-leaning songwriters such as Marc Blitzstein, Earl Robinson, and E. Y. Harburg, generally sympathetic to the Soviet Union as the "ideal society" of proletarian values and workers' rights (Goldstein 209). And, like Blitzstein in his monumental *The Cradle Will Rock,* Rome openly aired his left-wing viewpoints in *Pins and Needles* and other revues. Rome, like virtually all such American writers allied with the so-called "Popular Front," backed off their pro-Soviet leanings when, on August 23, 1939, Russia signed its non-aggression pact with Germany. But once Germany violated the pact and invaded the Soviet Union on June 22, 1941, numbering Russia now among the Allies, pro-Russian sympathy returned to left-leaning songwriters once again, with Harold Rome very much in the forefront.

In addition to his "United Nations March" using Shostakovich's music, three of Rome's four songs honoring the Soviets have lyrics he translated or adapted from existing Russian songs, including the "Anthem Of The Union Of Soviet Socialist Republics" (Am-Rus Music, 1944); Rome's lyric was based on the Russian of Sergei Mihalkov and El-Registan, set to the original music by A. V. Alexandrov. "Forward (Song Of The Red Army Tank Brigade)" (copyright unpublished, June 9, 1943), with music by Dan and Dimitri Pokrass, and "Meadowland (Cavalry Of The Steppes)" (Leeds Music, 1943), with music by Lev Knipper, both pay tribute to the seeming invincibility of Russian armies on the move, a theme picked up by other American songwriters. Rome's one wholly original song about Russia as an ally of Britain and the United States was actually a spin-off of two of his songs for revues—the hit "Franklin D. Roosevelt Jones" from *Sing Out the News* (1938) and "Little Miss Liberty Jones" from *Let Freedom Sing* (1942). With the Russians in the war on our side, Rome transformed the number into "Franklin D.—Winston C.—Joseph V. [for Stalin's given middle name, Vissarionovich] Victory Jones" (Leeds, 1942), the premise simply being that the Allies were an unbeatable team.

Praise for the indomitable will and inevitable triumph of the Russian forces came from very varied songwriters. Meredith Willson—not known for left-wing leanings and best-known years later for his hit 1957 musical *The Music Man*—contributed "And Still The Volga Flows" (Witmark, 1942), writing the lyrics and part of the music, the rest borrowed from Rachmaninoff's Second Piano Concerto. The text bemoans the fact that Russia's "fields are silent and bare" thanks to the advancing German troops, but "Her star will rise again . . . / And never fall / While the Volga flows." The sheet music of Willson's song includes the note "GROSS RE-CEIPTS, without deduction, Donated to RUSSIAN WAR RELIEF, INC." Laden with outrageous puns and rhymes, starting with its title, Clarence Gaskill's "The Russians Go Rushin' Along" (Mills, 1943) is thoroughly upbeat in tone, depicting Russian armies as an unstoppable juggernaut. In his all-soldier show *This Is The Army* (1942), Irving Berlin added his voice to this theme in an amusing song that factors the elements into the Red Army's success. As had happened to other would-be invaders in the past, the German armies were halted on their drive toward Moscow on December 5, 1941, by "That Russian Winter" (This Is The Army Inc., 1942), as was all neatly summed up at the end: "When Hitler cried 'This cannot be,' Napoleon's ghost beneath a tree / Looked up and yelled 'You're telling me!' THAT RUSSIAN WINTER." African American lyricist Andy Razaf chimed in on the inevitability of Russia's success and survival in a song that has a Russian soldier saying goodbye to his girl. With music by Teri Josefovitz (who was born in Hartford, Connecticut, despite his Slavic name), "When The River Don Runs Dry" (Carl Fischer, 1945) concludes with Razaf's reassuring words, "Sweetheart, *then* and *only then,* will mighty Russia die."

Folksinger Woody Guthrie addressed not the might of the Red Army en masse but instead individual valor in the person of "Miss Pavlachenko," a heroine of the Battle of Stalingrad. Although he didn't record the number until 1946, late in 1942 Guthrie wrote and began performing his tribute to Lyudmilla Pavlachenko, a lieutenant in the Soviet Army cited by the Southern Red Army Council for killing 257 German soldiers (Logsdon). Guthrie's refrain of "More than three hundred Nazis fell by your gun" exaggerated Pavlachenko's heroics a bit but still effectively made its point.

The most poetic and affecting of all the songs about Russia written during the war was, in a very real sense, a love song. With music by Jerome Kern and lyrics by E. Y. Harburg, a writer nearly as left as Harold Rome, "And Russia Is Her Name" (Chappell, 1943) is apolitical and has none of the satirical touches that are the hallmarks of much of Harburg's writing. Rather, in this first-person song, the singer personifies Russia as a woman, and not just any woman, but the singer's own beloved: "She stood beside my plow, she kissed away my tears / And warmed my empty hands through all the empty years / . . . And she is still my own and Russia is her name." Tenor Allan Jones premiered the song at a gala for Russian War Relief at the Hollywood Bowl in 1943 (Meyerson 173).

If American songs about Russia weren't commercially successful, at least they were sincere about having the Soviet Union as an ally. But like all American numbers about the other Allies, songs about Russia slowed to just a few insignificant pieces in the last two years of the war. By then—and, of course, even long before then—Tin Pan Alley was devoting most of its war-related songwriting efforts to matters American, whether civilian or military.

# *"G.I. Jive"*

## The Draft, Enlistment, and Army Life

As of May 1940, the United States Army was underfunded, under-equipped, and, worst of all, undermanned. With roughly 260,000 troops, 6,000 pilots, and 5,000 planes (Perrett 194), the military was unprepared for an enemy attack upon the country, let alone capable of mounting a foreign invasion in the war already raging in Europe and elsewhere. Increased government spending and stepped-up defense production rapidly improved the shortage of war matériel. Whereas up to July 1940 Washington had been laying out only $165 million for defense per month, by January 1941 the figure had increased to $500 million, by July 1941 to $900 million, and by December 1, 1941 (still before Pearl Harbor), to nearly two billion dollars a month (Perrett 257). Money and manufacturing could shore up the shortage of everything from tanks to canteens, warships to M.P.'s whistles, but increasing the military's manpower demanded a different solution. That solution, initially less popular in Congress than among Americans at large, was military conscription, even though this would be the first time such a measure was instituted when the United States wasn't actually at war. The Burke-Wadsworth Bill (formally the Selective Service Act and, more casually, the Draft Act) began working its tortuous way through the House and Senate in early August 1940, to the accompaniment of vocal protests in the galleries from anti-draft groups as diverse as mothers of young men, unionists, isolationists, college boys, and Communists; at one point a fistfight even broke out on the floor of the House (see Perrett 30–32). But ultimately the worsening conditions worldwide won out over the objections of folks at home who would later be called peaceniks, and the Selective Service Act became law on September 16, 1940.

No sooner did Secretary of War Henry L. Stimson draw the number of this nation's first peacetime draftee on October 29, 1940, than Tin Pan Alley's sheet music presses began rolling out a spate of songs about conscription, enlistment, and recruitment, and they continued to do so almost until the end of the war. Even more songs about life in the service followed in hot pursuit. Like the songs about home front conditions that began to appear about two years later, most numbers dealing with the draft and military life were designed to help make the best of a bad situation. And like most songs about shortages, rationing, and blackouts, the majority of those about conscription and the drudgery of military training camps tried to make such situations bearable through lightheartedness or humor. Of the 132 professionally written songs about conscription, enlistment, and military life, ninety-five have fun with the lives of soldiers and sailors, especially rookie recruits in all branches of the service. The rest were serious pieces written to build morale or express pride over being in the military. With few exceptions, whether humorous or serious, songs about the draft and army life didn't become popular during the war in the commercial sense, let alone have much longevity after the war, chiefly because of their topical, transitory nature. But because they were written to help lighten the load, if such a song amused a civilian or GI who heard it even once from a bandstand, in a film, or on the radio, it had served its purpose.

### *"Is It Love, Or Is It Conscription": The Draft, Enlistment, and Recruiting*

In the race to write timely songs about the draft, veteran Alleyman Fred Fisher was first off the starting block with not just one but a booklet of fourteen little ditties collectively called *Selective Service Songs* (Fred Fisher, 1940), the hot pink cover featuring a drawing of a scantily clad and seductive young lady wearing a navy hat. But even titillating cover art couldn't seduce the public, with the single fleeting exception of "Blitzkrieg Baby." That number and a few others such as "Parachute Papa, Drop Down And See Me Sometime" are ribald songs of seduction having little or nothing to do with the Selective Service. Others like "I Can't Dance In Those Sailor Pants," "Bullets And Beans," and "What'll We Have For Chow?" have more to do with service life than the draft per se. But a few numbers scored direct hits on their draft-related targets. The singer of "I Claim Exemption" contrives numerous excuses for not being drafted: "Got a wife and seven kids, got a mother-in-law / Captain don't you really think I've got enough of war?" The flip side of this sentiment is the comic thrust of "Why Should We Marry?": "Girls all like the uniform, there's no need for a wife / We can sign up for a year, why should we sign for life?" Sticking with marriage, or at least engagement, is Fisher's most outrageous song. A guy's difficult girlfriend actually laughs at him when he's drafted, but he still tries to propose before being shipped off to boot camp. The title of this little gem—and yes, the expression meant then precisely what it means now—is "I Gave Her The Ring (She Gave Me The Finger)."

The draft's impact on countless Americans makes it understandable that between 1940 and 1942 conscription intersected with romantic and marital life in quite a few songs. Although the Selective Service Act didn't defer men from serving because they were married, so many young men *assumed* it would that "one of the nation's manufacturers of wedding rings, J. R. Woods & Sons, reported a 250 percent increase in sales" after the Draft Act was signed into law in the fall of 1940 (Bailey 44). And that was still during peacetime. Once we were actually at war, in "the first five months after Pearl Harbor an estimated 1,000 women a day married servicemen" or men called up in the draft (Bailey 55). Such post-Pearl marriages of men already serving or about to serve obviously weren't about avoiding the draft but "for many, [were] the search for an emotional anchor among the new uncertainties of war" (55).

Some Alleymen were quick to turn these motives for marriage into song. Just after Selective Service went into effect and young men were dashing to the altar in the false hope of a marriage deferment, Walter Bishop and Lou Singer asked the musical questions "Is It Love, Or Is It Conscription" (Leeds, 1940) and "What is it that drives 'em romantic? Is it fear of what goes on 'cross the Atlantic?" Vaughn Monroe's recording caught on enough to rank 60th in *Hot Charts* for November 1940, the first full month after the draft lottery began. Despite its playful title, Lyle Moraine (soon to be Pvt. Lyle Moraine) and Chuck Foster's "I've Been Drafted (Now I'm Drafting You)" (Hollywood: Vanguard, 1941) is a romantic ballad in which a draftee is seeking the kind of emotional grounding historian Ronald Bailey wrote of: "I want someone whose heart will volunteer / To wait for me at least another year." Two more or less humorous love songs had almost identical titles—"I Feel A Draft Coming On," by Clarence Kulseth and J. Fred "Santa Claus Is Coming To Town" Coots (Santly-Joy, 1941), and Bill Nettles's hillbilly number "I Can Feel The Draft Coming On" (Dixie Music, 1942). The draftee in each song proposes to his sweetheart, but the public didn't accept their proposals. The only fairly sustained minor hit to combine romance with military induction was Redd Evans's "He's 1-A In The Army And He's A-1 In My Heart" (Valiant Music, 1941). In this upbeat swing or jump tune, a girl confesses, "I love him so because I know he wants to do his part," and because he "rates so high on Uncle Sammy's chart." Records by Harry James, the King Sisters, Johnny Long, and Les Brown kept young Americans jitterbugging to this outpouring of passion and patriotic pride between November 1941 and February 1942. After that, no more songs appeared linking the draft with engagements or marriage.

But what did appear was the first significant emergence of hillbilly songs on any war-related subject. This makes sense, of course, since most hillbilly and country music has always been on very personal subjects, and though Selective Service was a national institution, when that infamous "Greetings" letter from Uncle Sam arrived, it became a very personal thing indeed for a man. Between 1942 and 1944 no fewer than fourteen hillbilly songs (including four faux-hillbilly ones) concerning the draft or enlistment were published and recorded, only four of them humorous or lighthearted, the rest patriotic, sentimental, or both. For the reasons described in chapter 2, it's impossible to measure how successful these songs were. But it may be assumed that country and western audiences received some of the early ones well enough for hillbilly songsmiths to keep writing such numbers for the duration.

Briefly, and without getting musically technical, hillbilly songs often consist of several stanzas comprised of a verse followed by a repeated refrain, and they employ musical styles associated with country or square dances and the sorts of lyrical ballads traditional among rural Americans; many, interestingly, are also in ¾ or waltz time. The lyrics of such songs are characterized by the appearance of rural characters or images of rural life, whether western or that of the hill country. The genuine articles were almost invariably written by songwriters whose own roots were in one of the rural cultures embraced by hillbilly music, many of whom performed their songs themselves. Faux-hillbilly songs employed the same musical styles and conventions but were written by mainstream, non-country, Tin Pan Alley songwriters.

Late in 1941 a very urban (and urbane) team wrote a song about enlistment that's as faux as a faux-hillbilly number could get. For "Time's A-Waistin'" (Broadcast Music, 1941), the comic duo of Olsen and Johnson teamed with hit-makers Jay Livingston (then still Levison) and Ray Evans, who after the war turned out the Academy Award–winners "Mona Lisa," "Buttons and Bows," and "Que Sera Sera," the million-selling urban Christmas classic "Silver Bells," and much more, mostly for the movies. But in 1941 these Eastern city boys wrote a song based on the popular syndicated hillbilly comic strip "Barney Google and Snuffy Smith" with permission of its creator, Billy De Beck. In the song Barney is proud that Snuffy left his home in Punkin Holler to join the army, where "Thutty bucks is riches jest fer wearin' cacky britches, / Even though the varmints make you wear a collar." Early in 1942 the faux-hillbilly "Hey!

Zeke (Your Country's Callin')" (Santly-Joy-Select, 1942) took a light-hearted approach to its serious goal of persuading rural Americans to enlist. Alleymen Al Hoffman, Mann Curtis, and Jerry Livingston encouraged "Zeke" and other country boys to "Leave the farm to maw and paw / We gotta win this gosh-darn war!" And as the guys who wrote "Mairzy Doats," they just had to throw in a pretty silly multiple rhyme: "And, by cracky, the boys in khaki will drive 'em wacky in Nagasaki."

The six draft-related hillbilly numbers in 1942 were the most during any year of the war. One was an altogether serious faux-hillbilly song with words and music by comedian (and occasional songwriter) Milton Berle and Brooklyn-born composer and lyricist Leon Navara. In "We're Ridin' For Uncle Sammy Now" (Greene-Revel, 1942), a cowboy is proud that he and his horse have been called to serve in the Texas Cavalry (yes, horses were still in the military in World War II). Other than the previously mentioned "I Can Feel The Draft Coming On," all but one of the other hillbilly draft or enlistment songs of 1942 are straightforward expressions of pride about serving in the armed forces and, frankly, not terribly interesting. Only Polly Jenkins's "They Drafted Zeke From The Mountains" (Dixie Music, 1942) is fun in a quirky way because of its mixture of pride with humor. Though seven-foot Zeke is proud to serve his country, "they couldn't fit him good, The pants were short, the coat was tight, / They did the best they could." Also in 1942 actual folk musician Woody Guthrie rewrote his Depression-era Dust Bowl song "So Long, It's Been Good To Know You," punctuating a young's man's pride in enlisting with a few comic touches. The song takes the young man from the proud sendoff given him by his country town through his days of basic training, where he "learned how to fight Fascists in daytime, 'skeeters at night," to actual combat.

Humor prevailed in only one more hillbilly draft or enlistment song after 1942, and then only in the number's final line. In "She's In The Army Now" (Southern Music, 1943) by the King's Jesters and Jack Foy, Cindy's boyfriend has enlisted in the army, so she joins the "doub-ya A. A. C. [WAAC, later WAC]" hoping to be near him. Her hill-country kinfolk are mighty proud of her in her snappy uniform, and the number seems to be a plug for women to enlist in the Women's Auxiliary Army Corp—until the final hilarious kicker. Cindy's enlisting was "A noble deed and how! / But rust is on her pappy's still, SHE'S IN THE ARMY NOW!" (The 1940s catchphrase "And how!" used frequently in songs during the war, was roughly equivalent to "Yes, indeed" or "You bet!")

During 1943 and '44 hillbilly draft and enlistment songs shifted from humor to sentiment, accompanying a musical shift in all country music from the earlier predominance of "mountain music" (for example, "Wabash Cannonball") to western or cowboy songs (for example, "You Are

My Sunshine," "Tumbling Tumbleweeds"). Throughout Eddie Stone, Berkeley Graham, and Dewey Bergman's "A New Trail In The Sky" (Shapiro, Bernstein, 1943), Porter Johns's "Gonna Hang Up My Saddle And Go" (Hollywood: Cine-Mart, 1944), and Margaret Acker and cowboy star Gene Autry's "Spurs And Wings" (Westr'n Music, 1944) runs the common thread of a cowhand's melancholy at having to leave the wide open spaces, his cowpuncher pals, and his horse, even as he's proud to go serve his country. But the most emotionally charged of the country songs is the earlier mentioned "We Turned Our Darling's Picture To The Wall." A World War I veteran's son turns draft dodger, and his family feels such shame that "one loving face today we forever turned away / When we turned our Darling's picture to the wall."

This heart-tugging approach to the draft wasn't the private property of hillbilly songwriters, but such numbers from mainstream Tin Pan Alley were few and far between. The earliest was Jack Scholl and M. K. "My Wild Irish Rose" Jerome's "They've Broken Up Our Glee Club" (Remick, 1940), in which the four remaining members of a twenty-man glee club sadly watch as the others get drafted one by one. In a similar vein, "I'm Mighty Proud Of That Old Gang Of Mine" (Warock Music, 1942), by two old pros, lyricist Ted Koehler and composer Sam H. Stept, is a wistful tribute to so many guys from the old hometown who enlisted or were drafted that "There's no one on the corner of Main and Second Street, / The loneliest guy in town is the cop on the beat." In Paul Cunningham and Leonard Whitcup's "Four Buddies" (Broadway Music, 1943), four inseparable pals all enlist, breaking up their foursome for the duration, but the song ends confidently that they'll be back together again after the war. That same year Kay and Sue Werner—in all probability the only twin-sister professional songwriting team in history—wrote the thoroughly delightful "Mama, Where Did Papa Go?" (Mills, 1943). The singer is an inquisitive, slightly bratty child who keeps asking her mother the title question, even though "For a nickel I can tell you where he really went." The kid sleuths her daddy's routine every day of the week and eavesdrops on his phone calls. The song ends with the child proudly concluding from her amassed evidence (as if her mother didn't know already), "Did you notice he was wearing a peculiar shirt? / What a funny color brown and it wasn't dirt. / Oh! Mama, he's in the army now!"

Tin Pan Alley fared no better than hillbilly writers with songs expressing pride over enlistment or being drafted, even though some of Broadway's best tried their hand at them. For example, "There Are Yanks From The Banks Of The Wabash" (Harms, 1944), from Howard Dietz and Vernon Duke's sixty-nine-performance Broadway flop *Jackpot,* and Cole Porter's "Shootin' The Works For Uncle Sam" (Chappell, 1941) are at best fairly uninspired rosters of the kinds of men who had enlisted, Porter's by occupation, Dietz and Duke's by geographic origins. This pattern of mediocrity from Broadway writers continued throughout the war no matter what the specific topic or subject of the war-related song. With very few exceptions, such as "The Last Time I Saw Paris" and some, though not all, of Irving Berlin's many war-connected numbers, virtually all the war songs by established Broadway writers of the day are more pedestrian than those by the men and women who primarily wrote popular songs or songs for the movies. It was only a few, like Frank Loesser and Jule Styne, who established themselves as musical theatre writers *after* the war that wrote outstanding and successful war-related numbers during it.

Broadway and Tin Pan Alley songwriters were far more successful writing of the draft and enlistment in a comic or lighthearted mode, not commercially perhaps, but in the sense that these songs were definitely more entertaining. In 1944 Broadway regulars (though usually with other collaborators) lyricist Howard Dietz and composer Vernon Duke wrote a United States Coast Guard show called *Tars and Spars: A Recruiting Revue,* the latter billed as "Lieut. Vernon Duke U. S. C. G. R. (T)," which he was at the time. The "Spars" of the title refers to the Women's Reserve of the United States Coast Guard. Spars isn't an acronym but a collapsing of the letters in the Coast Guard motto "Semper Paratus" (Taylor 184). In a hilarious number called "Civilian" (Carl Fischer, 1944), Dietz rolls out a litany of preposterous excuses people gave recruiting officers to keep their civilian status, none of which was a good enough reason not to sign up, and that went for women as well as men: "You gotta have a reason to be a civilian / That goes for May or Elsie or Lillian. / This war's inclusive from Maine down to Texas / They ain't partic'lar what your angle on sex is." Alleymen Don Raye and Gene De Paul, writers of several wartime hits jointly and with others, wrote a draft song that wasn't one in "Short, Fat and 4F" (Leeds, 1943). It's an amusing tale of a guy so fat his "One A rating ended way out where the waist begins," so the navy rejected him because "he took up too much space." But here was a rare case where a song's humor successfully shifted to a patriotic and participatory note at the end: "He's trying hard to lose that lard, so he can do his part, / "He's short, fat and four F, with a great big One A heart." Donald Kahn's "Sam's Got Him" (Robbins, 1944), which Johnny Mercer recorded on his own new Capitol label, uses something of the same approach in reverse. The verse and most of the chorus describe how, since he's been drafted, the army's made quite a guy out of a once square, unassuming schlemiel, to the point that, in the comic and slightly suggestive kicker, "In his khaki suit he looks so cute that the chicks all yell with delight / 'Mister Sam release that man for active duty tonight.'"

Most such comic pieces fall into the broad classification of novelty songs that takes in, among other things, nonsense songs, songs "inventing" and naming a new dance, and songs with titles, lyrics, and music that reference a current popular musical style. From beginning to end, war year ears were filled with every imaginable sort of novelty song, war-related or not, although the draft inspired no nonsense songs that I know of (though army life did, as we shall see). But conscription occasioned three numbers of the other types; two fell flat while the third became the most popular song about the draft during the war. In the very first year of Selective Service, J. P. Fox and Maurice Roffman wrote two tunes "inventing" new dances based on the draft—"Conscription Swing" and "Conscription Waltz" (both A-1 Music, 1940). Neither got America dancing, even though the title page of each declares that the piece was "Endorsed by Arthur Murray," the nation's guru of ballroom dance instruction.

On the other hand, on January 2, 1941, the Andrews Sisters recorded an early draft number capitalizing on a current musical craze that was destined for immediate popularity then and immortality afterward—with a little help from Bette Midler's very '40s-sounding revival in 1973. Prior to the draft, on August 28, 1940, the Andrews Sisters recorded what became one of their hit boogie woogie numbers, totally unrelated to the war, "Beat Me, Daddy, Eight To The Bar," by Don Raye, Hughie Prince, and Eleanor Sheehy (boogie woogie generally characterized by a hard-driving, repetitive rhythm with eight beats to the measure). With conscription in full swing, Raye and Prince wrote another boogie woogie tune for the three singing sisters' appearance as themselves in the Universal comedy *Buck Privates,* starring Abbott and Costello. This number is about a "famous trumpet man from out Chicago way . . . [whose] number came up / And he was gone with the draft" to become "The Boogie Woogie Bugle Boy (Of Company B)" (MCA Music, 1941). It's a good thing the movie and record were both released in January 1941, and that the film was a major box office hit for Universal, giving wide exposure to "Bugle Boy" in the Andrews Sisters' inimitable rendition. Without millions of Americans hearing the song in *Buck Privates,* it may not have sold as well as it did, since that same January ASCAP pulled all its songs from the airways, which meant no network radio plugs for "Boogie Woogie Bugle Boy." As it was, the record never did make *Billboard's* top-ten bestselling record chart, though it was strong on its jukebox charts between March 29 and May 3, 1941. In *Hot Charts* it ranks very respectably between 26th and 34th from February through May—not bad considering the ASCAP ban. The song's success can be attributed not just to the Andrews Sisters' unique close-harmony styling but to Raye and Prince's memorable and danceable music, and the clever lyrics through which they paint a fanciful comic picture of the army: a drafted jazzman turned bugler claimed he "couldn't jam" without back-up musicians, so his captain drafts a band he can play reveille with "eight to the bar." Whether or not wartime songwriters saw in "Boogie Woogie Bugle Boy" a prototype for their own work, it was the same combination of topnotch music with a lighthearted look at training camp routine that produced the best of the numerous songs about life in the service that would follow.

### "It's Great To Be In A Uniform": Taking Army Life Seriously

Between 1940 and 1945, making the best of things through humor was the hallmark of at least seventy-four songs about life in the military, their quality ranging from masterful to awful. Along with these comic or light-hearted numbers were another thirteen entirely serious songs about service life, most of which fall into the awful category. This can be explained partly by the fact that something as serious as military training is infi-nitely more entertaining (at least in song) when *not* taken seriously. Also, with few exceptions, no especially skilled songwriters wrote any of the se-rious songs about service life. As might be expected, none of these songs achieved anything close to widespread or long-term popularity, though the content of some is worth a brief look.

Whether they depict a new recruit's feelings of displacement or the ge-ographic diversity of American troops, at bottom nearly all the serious songs about service life reflect one's happiness and pride about being a soldier, which means, in a very real sense, that they're all the same. A few will illustrate the point. Charles Newman and Allie Wrubel's "Private Buckaroo" (Southern Music, 1942) appeared in the Universal musical of the same name, starring the Andrews Sisters and Harry James and his or-chestra. The song is about a young recruit missing the "Corrals, / And all the pals he knew" at home on the range, yet the lyric is quick to point out that, lonesomeness aside, as a soldier "there's nothing he's afraid of / Got the stuff a cowboy's made of / True blue PRIVATE BUCKAROO." The songs of the army's geographic diversity fall into the loose category of "list songs." "Buck Private Jones," by Ed Womack, Will E. Dulmage, and Eddie Dorr (Detroit: Mackley Music, 1941), mostly checks off the com-pass points from which the boys have joined the army, with additional lists of typical American first names and nicknames. Lou Lawrence and Michael Field's "Hi' Ya Chum (Where' Ya From?)" (Parade Music, 1943) is even more numbing as it rattles off dozens and dozens of states where the soldiers have come from. The guys in both songs are really proud to be there and really happy with life in the army. Not surprisingly, serious morale-boosting and marching songs convey the same sort of message, although some—by some of the better writers of such stuff—do so in rather inventive ways. Ralph Blane and Huge Martin, whose "The Trolley Song" is their best-remembered number, rewrote their own football fight song, "Buckle Down, Winsocki" from the musical *Best Foot Forward* (1941), to become in the same year a rousing pep talk for raw recruits stressing pride of service, "Buckle Down Buck Private" (Crawford Music, 1941). Duke Leonard, Jimmy DuPre, and Curly Mahr's "With A Pack On His Back (And A Girl On His Mind)" (Harry Tenney, 1942) united drilling with a heavy pack and thinking of his girl back home as the two things that keep the American soldier "fit to fight for love and liberty."

A few songs were written to raise the spirits of men in combat. One had lyrics by a man who knew about such things firsthand, Lieut. Gen. George S. Patton Jr. Patton's poem "God Of Battles" (Robbins, 1943)— a pious if bloodthirsty appeal to the divinity for combat victory—was set to music by Peter "Deep Purple" De Rose. With a title more like a love song than a morale booster for troops in combat, "Tonight And Every Night" (Chicago: Bourne, 1945) was written late in the war by the highly successful duo of Sammy Cahn and Jule Styne, the team behind such war-related hits as "I'll Walk Alone" and "It's Been A Long, Long Time." Beginning "If you've a faith like mine," yet in no way denominational, the lyric is, if you will, something of a faith-based inspirational number addressed to troops under fire that even asks one despondent soldier, "How can we go forward when you're in reverse?" The thrust of the song is that with faith, courage, and pride in country, army, and uniform, "We'll go on and on and on / TONIGHT AND EV'RY NIGHT." Even though Sammy Cahn never served in the military, this lyric's eloquence, depth, and sincerity far surpass any serious songs of army life written by servicemen—and there were several, one ranking officer included.

Tom B. Woodburn (1893–1980) was an established artist/illustrator and a career soldier who by 1941 was a lieutenant colonel in the U.S. Army. Throughout the war, his military and recruiting paintings and posters graced the sheet music covers of songs by various writers, but "Soldier's Life" (Famous Music, 1941), with music by Ethel Bridges, had Lt. Colonel Woodburn not just as cover artist but as lyricist. Yet as devoted as Woodburn was to both soldiering and art (some of his military paintings are equally beautiful and powerful), when trying to express in song how great army life is, his words ring hollow. With a blind eye to the drudgery of training camp, Woodburn—who was heavily involved with recruiting—writes, "A soldier's life is the life for me / Swinging along as happy as can be." The best part of the song is the reproduction of Woodburn's recruiting poster *Soldier Life* on the cover.

When it came to writing songs about how great army life was and how great it felt to be in uniform, the privates did no better than the brass— except for two who wrote a song about the navy! Professional songsmiths Don Raye and Gene De Paul served in the U.S. Army during the war and also wrote a number of songs for Universal's Abbott and Costello comedy (once again with the Andrews Sisters on board) *In the Navy,* released in May 1941. Most of Raye and De Paul's numbers are in their usual lighthearted mode, but "Off To See The World" (Leeds, 1941) is a straight-faced account of how happy sailors on active duty should be because of all the places they'll get to see—up until the last two lines. Here the song turns sardonic, telling sailors to be glad for the chance to see the world "while there's still a world left to see." Being happy about serving in the army isn't nearly as convincing in "You First Get Your Spirit In The Army" (Leeds, 1943) by Privates Alan Wilson, Nicholas Conte, and Buddy Kosse, none of whom were or would become professional songwriters. Their Pollyanna vision of this undefined "spirit" making everything in training camp seem fine to rookies even extends to the unlikelihood that "You take your discipline with a shrug and happy grin." Pvt. J. C. Lewis Jr. wasn't a songwriting professional either, although some of his songs for the all-soldier musical revue *Hey, Rookie!* first performed at Fort Mac-Arthur in 1942, later appeared in the Columbia picture of the same name in 1944; Pvt. Lewis's only other claim to fame is that he was the brother-in-law of actor William Powell. One of Lewis's least successful songs for the revue was a pride of service number called "It's Great To Be In A Uniform" (Hollywood: Lewcon Music, 1943). While the sentiment rings truer than in some other songs of this type, its lyric merely reiterates in various ways what the title says. But another song, called "It's a Helluva Swelluva Helluva Life In The Army" (Lewcon, 1942), reveals Pvt. Lewis to be a clever and witty lyricist when *comically* extolling the joys of army life at the expense of civilians suffering the indignities of the rationing that had just begun: "We get all the sugar and we get all the gas / Best of all we even get the girls with all the class . . . Gee you poor civilians, the things you must go thru / When we're drinkin' coffee we will always think of you"— a much more entertaining approach to what makes army life bearable than straitlaced solemnity.

### *"The Military Polka": Novelty Dance Numbers and Nonsense Songs*

Undoubtedly anticipating a higher success rate than for songs taking army life seriously, Tin Pan Alley turned out many more that were humorous or lighthearted, including some downright silly nonsense songs and novelty dance tunes. Among the numbers that tried to move soldiers' and civilians' feet off the parade ground and onto the dance floor were such inanities as Kim Gannon and Josef Myrow's "Yankee Bugle Conga" (North & South American Music, 1941), John Redmond, James Cavanaugh, and Nat Simon's "The Parachute Jump" (Melo-Art Music, 1943), Bob Hamilton and Addy Amor's "The Military Polka" (Jewel Music, 1943), George

E. Banbury's "The Regimental Polka" (George F. Briegel, 1943), and Max Spickol and Johnny Fortis's "The Canteen Bounce" (Edward B. Marks, 1943). Though the sheet music says "Canteen Bounce" was featured by popular trumpeter Charlie Spivak and *Variety*'s charts show it was heavily plugged between January and May of 1943, with eighteen to twenty-five airplays in some weeks, it doesn't appear even as an Extra in the wide-ranging *Hot Charts*, suggesting that this service-inspired dance tune didn't get many people on their feet to buy records, let alone dance.

The out-and-out novelty and nonsense songs with roots in army life were cleverer. Clarence Stout's "Machine Gun Butch" (Bob Miller, 1943) is much like the Boogie Woogie Bugle Boy of Company B, who's mentioned in the verse. Hip machine gunner Butch McGee can make his gun go "Rat-tat-tat-tat-tat-tat Eight beats to the bar" in a boogie beat, but Stout's music never gets the requisite eight beats of "rat-tat" into a single measure. Jimmy Eaton and Grady Watts's "Esmerelda, The Soprano Of Guadalcanal" (Bob Miller, 1944) is a wonderfully funny piece about a soldier there who didn't have the heart to swat a mosquito, because her buzzing "Ziggy zing, ziggy ziggy zing" melody made him dream all night of "a maiden, so fair." When the GI returns to New Jersey, he's rewarded for his mercy by Esmerelda the "skeeter" waiting there to meet him, having followed him back from the Solomon Islands.

The cleverest and most intricate of the pure nonsense songs about army life found its way from an all-soldier revue into the screen musical *Private Buckaroo,* performed there by the inimitable Andrews Sisters. According to the sheet music, soldier-songwriter Pvt. Sid Robin originally wrote "Six Jerks In A Jeep" (Leeds, 1942) for the 2nd Corps area theatre Section A-11 Soldier Show. The song is about absolutely nothing except six guys (or gals) riding in that icon of clunky army transport, a jeep. That premise is an excuse for Robin's seemingly endless inventiveness with intricate rhyme schemes that alternate singulars and plurals in a very catchy swing tune—"We're six wacks in a hack / Six quacks here to send you, Jack / Now look here, Max, No Cracks / Six wacks in a hack"—with similar stuff in interminable stanzas, each sillier than the last. ("Wacks," incidentally, simply means "wackos" or "goofs" and is not a misprint for WAACS). The Andrews Sisters put their trademark close harmony to the service of the song, creating screechy dissonances that would do any jeep (and its horn) proud as it bumped over rough terrain. Pvt. Robin's number held its own in the movie against others by some Tin Pan Alley pros, and the Andrews Sisters' performance is almost always looked upon favorably by film historians. Yet while they recorded "Six Jerks In A Jeep" on April 23, 1942, their record label, Decca, rejected it. The sisters' biographer, John Sforza, in what is clearly just his opinion, asserts this was because the number "was a poor endeavor and probably should have been cut [from the film]" (95). I would suggest instead that Decca chose not to release what was in fact a fine number to keep it from competing with another Andrews Sisters song from the same film that was recorded a few weeks earlier, on April 4, and already had "hit" written all over it— "Don't Sit Under The Apple Tree" (see chapter 10). Still, millions of movie-goers got to hear Robin's and the Andrews Sisters' wacky jeep go "Beep beep," even if they couldn't buy the record.

### "The Little Brown Suit My Uncle Bought Me": A Potpourri of Pleasant Service Songs

Between the handful of novelty dance and nonsense songs and a large group of numbers that comically gripe about life in the military is a group of just over twenty miscellaneous songs that have only one thing in common: they find service life amusing without bitching about it. Harold Rome's song that titles this section (Leeds, 1944) is a good illustration. Prior to Pearl Harbor, Rome had been an ardent left-wing anti-interventionist, but once the United States was in the war, he became as supportive of our troops and defense industries as any one else in Tin Pan Alley. He often wrote songs without expectation of compensation, and even was Pvt. Harold Rome from 1943 to 1945. "The Little Brown Suit My Uncle Bought Me" is typical of such songs by Rome, as are the rest in his 1943 all-soldier show *Stars and Gripes,* which premiered at the base theatre at Fort Hamilton in Brooklyn and toured other army bases and servicemen's canteens. The August 14, 1943, issue of *Variety* touted Rome's score as "Equal" to his smash Depression-era hit *Pins and Needles* (3). In the same vein as J. C. Lewis's "It's a Helluva Swelluva," "The Little Brown Suit" has fun comparing the positives of army life with the negatives of being a civilian: "Got no doc or dentist bills to pay, no straw hats or fancy head of hair, / Moth'r-in-law cannot come here to stay, never worry over what tie I should wear!" Also for *Stars and Gripes* Rome wrote an army-life song that exudes a spirit of fun without being funny. In "Jumping To The Jukebox" (Leeds, 1943), he pays tribute to juke joints like "Joe's" where rookies go to unwind from the drudgery of their daily routine with a Coke, a chocolate malted, or some dancing "with a county cutie jitterbug."

A less familiar name than Harold Rome is that of Lt. (later Capt.) Ruby Jane Douglass, 2nd Officer, WAAC (later WAC), a young woman with undergraduate and graduate degrees in music who wrote some significant war-related songs of various kinds before pursuing a postwar civilian career as Jane Douglass White, composer, singer, pianist, and producer of TV's *Name That Tune.* Among Lt. Douglass's wartime songs were two lighthearted though not comic pieces that fall into this catchall bunch, each happily pointing out, as one of their titles proclaims, "Something New Has Been Added To The Army" (Leeds, 1943), that something neatly summed up in the single line "Right along with khaki shirts comes the sight of khaki skirts." Lt. Douglass expands upon her theme to cover all the women's service branches in "There'll Be A New Style Bonnet In The Easter Parade" (Leeds, 1943), declaring "the WACS will wear a hat that is smart and new, the WAVES wear a bonnet of Navy blue, / And the SPARS come out in a hat that's O.K., there's no original by Lily Daché." The previous year, Irving Berlin was also fashion conscious when he wrote for *This Is The Army* "That's What The Well-Dressed Man In Harlem Will Wear" (This Is The Army Inc., 1942), wherein Lenox Avenue's enlisted or drafted "Mister Dude" retires his "flashy tie" to sport "an olive drab color scheme" for the duration.

The subject of women in the army was also material for outright humor, actual or attempted, in three other "non-griping" songs about service life. Fortunately, the earliest had its pitiful little life cut short by the formation of the Women's Auxiliary Army Corps in 1942. Douglas D. Ballin and Bob Byron's "We Oughta Have The Girls (In The Army)" (Paull-Pioneer, 1941) conjectures in what today would be considered egregious gender stereotypes what roles women could play in combat. The slightly suggestive sheet music cover drawing of very cute girls in army blouses, caps, and *shorts* descending in parachutes is perfect preparation for the song to follow. The gist of the tasteless lyric is that these "bathing beauties . . . in parachuties" would unexpectedly drop down on the enemy "Amid a flash of lipstick and powder" and with "A kiss or two, [and] a little bit of lovin'" physically seduce the Axis troops to come over to our side. By comparison, Sunny Skylar and Vincent Lopez's "Tillie The Toiler (The WAAC)" (Marchant Music, 1942) and Kay Twomey and Al Goodhart's "Wait Till The Girls Get In The Army, Boys" (Advanced Music, 1942) look like a couple of masterpieces. To the credit of both, neither song's humor is at the expense of women or the Women's Army Corps, which was up and running by the time these numbers were written. For those who don't remember her, Tillie the Toiler had already been the "working-girl" heroine of the hugely popular comic strip and comic books bearing her name for two decades by the time the United States entered the war. In Skylar and Lopez's song, when Tillie quit her office job and enlisted as a WAAC, she "left her heart at her boy friend's door, but saved a part for the Army Corps." "Wait Till The Girls Get In The Army" had the good fortune to have a more than competent female lyricist with some hits to her credit in the person of Kay Twomey, a name that will appear here with some regularity. Like the offending pre-WAAC number, Twomey's lyric trades on feminine charms, but without the smarmy physicality; here the Axis troops simply have to *see* our girls in uniform to capitulate: "Imagine what the enemy will do when they appear, / They'll throw away their arms and holler 'I surrender, dear'"—Twomey here having fun with the title of the 1931 hit song "I Surrender, Dear," which remained popular during the war years.

But, predictably, lyricists who were most consistently clever whenever they wrote humorous numbers of *any* kind wrote the funniest "non-gripe" comic songs about service life. Milton "Mairzy Doats" and Erwin "I Wuv A Wabbit" Drake fall into that class of writers. While the Drakes almost never collaborated with each other, when they combined to write "They Can't Do That To Me" (American Theatre Wing Music War Committee, 1944) they produced a very funny mock complaint from a soldier who's unhappy because he never gets to see combat duty: "[When I] landed in Salerno I thought 'I'm in it now.' / But I was sent behind the lines to guard the army chow!" The final stanza is oddly prophetic, as the soldier dreams that Hitler "bumped himself off just before we got our hands on him!" Although fun, this piece produced under the aegis of Hammerstein's Music War Committee was a far cry from the ideal unifying war song the MWC had charged itself with finding or writing. Harold Adamson could swing easily from the lyrically sentimental to the outrageously funny with the most versatile of Tin Pan Alley's better-known lyricists. For the RKO Radio movie musical *Around the World*, he and composer Jimmy McHugh wrote "The Seasick Sailor" (Robbins, 1943) for the film's star, bandleader Kay Kyser. Kyser played himself as he and his orchestra entertained our troops around the globe, something Kyser did in real life in over fifteen hundred camp shows for American GIs during the war (Shull 337). The song recounts the troubles of a guy who was in all ways a model navy man, except that "he couldn't stand the motion of the ocean." The song's three long, wacky choruses gave Adamson ample opportunity to create some preposterously comic scenarios and just the right offbeat rhymes to go with them: "Just to see the Hudson River, that did something to his liver, / The result of which was water on the knee," and "On his chest he had a tattoo of a stormy day at Attu, / So he had to keep his shirt on constantly." The result was a hilarious musical moment in a movie rich in musical moments, but the number had no commercial success on its own. Similarly, three years earlier Frank Loesser and Frederick Hollander's "The Man's In The Navy" (Universal Music, 1940) from the Universal film *Seven Sinners* had just as little luck outside of movie theatres, despite a Decca recording by Marlene Dietrich, who performed the song in the film. Loesser's characteristically clever lyric describes how to tell if a man is a sailor by his on-shore behavior: "when ten thousand gorgeous women'll / Chase him like some hunted criminal, / You can bet your life the man's in the navy!" Fun as this lyric is, Pfc. Loesser saved the best of his humor about service life for numbers that griped about it, as did quite a few other songwriters, with the result that of all the songs about army life, the hits came from those that bitched about it.

### "Why Do They Call A Private A Private?": Is Army Life An Oxymoron?

From before Pearl Harbor until the end of the war, rookie draftees and enlistees in all the armed forces found a lot to gripe about in the daily grind of basic training. These gripes were an almost endless source of humor for Tin Pan Alley songsmiths and some songwriting servicemen. A few songs concerned a single gripe, such as two that focused entirely on the notoriously bad army food—Fred Fisher's "What'll We Have For Chow?" (Fred Fisher, 1940) and Sam M. Lewis and Abel Baer's "The Cook Of Company B" (copyright unpublished, July 8, 1943)—and another two bewailing the private's loathsome "kitchen police" or K.P. detail—Kay Twomey and Al Goodhart's "The K.P. Serenade" (Gordon, Kaufman, and Real, 1942) and Sid Robin's hands-down winner for the longest war-related title, "I've Got Those Peelin' Those Potatoes, Slicin' Those Tomatoes, Liftin' Up Those Garbage Can Blues" (Leeds, 1944), which the sheet music states was "Introduced and Featured" by the Andrews Sisters, probably on the radio, since it isn't in Sforza's Andrews Sisters discography or filmography.

But usually songs complained about the sorry lot of privates by stringing out many brief gripes in a single song or lumping together just a few. The targets of comic complaint in between ten and twelve different songs each were sergeants and their famously foul dispositions, endless marching and hiking, and lack of sleep. Along with chow and K.P., other popular complaints were ugly or ill-fitting uniforms, ranking officers' privileges, and unpleasant routines for navy, coast guard, or marine recruits.

Not all forty-three griping songs were uniformly funny—or terribly well-written—but the theme, and the comic approach to it, seemed to bring out the best in lyricists of all degrees of talent and experience, sparking flashes of brilliance, or at least genuinely clever writing, in even the most pedestrian of songs. Every year of the war had its standouts, and in each year but 1940 and '45 at least one such song found favor with the public. Because conscription began only in October 1940 and none of the services had swelled its ranks much by the end of the year, it's not surprising that the public took little notice of that year's crop of just four army or navy gripe songs, including Fred Fisher's "I Can't Dance In Those Sailor Pants" (Fred Fisher, 1940), in which a sailor complains his trousers are so tight, "I can hardly catch my breath / Some day I'll choke to death," and Fisher's aforementioned "What'll We Have For Chow?" with its vivid lines like "They cleaned up ev'rything in sight / I guess that we'll have hash tonight." In 1940, too, appeared the first of many songs focusing in whole or part on the aching body and soul of the weary foot soldier, even though Ira Schuster, Paul Cunningham, and Leonard Whitcup's "Oh! They're Makin' Me All Over In The Army" (Mercer and Morris, 1940) kept the griping fairly mild: "'Forward march,' / It's getting in my hair, / We're marching here and marching there, / And marching ev'rywhere." Such beefs became increasingly vocal and energetic as the war went on.

Comic griping about service life escalated exponentially in 1941, both in quality and quantity, with twelve such songs written and published, and some of them recorded as well. And the objects of the gripes began to expand. In J. Swanson's "Another Day, Another Dollar" (Mills, 1941), those hapless graduates of Officers Candidate School, called formally second lieutenants and not so formally shavetails, first began to be ribbed: "The shavetail is an officer, and he's nobody's fool; / He learned to run the army / After ninety days at school." The song also succinctly defined the private's place in the military: "The colonel gives the orders, and the captain tells the clerk; / The sergeant tells the corp'ral and the privates do the work." Succinctness also made for some striking moments in Raymond B. "Sleepy Time Gal" Egan's lyric to "Here I Am In The Army (And I Don't Look Good In Brown)" (Chappell, 1941), with music by long-timer J. Fred Coots. Egan's mostly prosaic lyric bursts with a few flashes of scathing humor packed into the fewest possible words: "The bugler gets me up at dawn, but the sergeant gets me down," and "An officer stole my girl from me, / But I've got to call him 'Sir.'" Similarly, old pro L. Wolfe Gilbert's ironies are pretty conventional when an office clerk turned soldier describes army life as "A Grand Vacation With Pay" (Hollywood: L. Wolfe Gilbert Music, 1941), with music by Jimmy McHugh, except for one hilariously off-the-wall crack about his hideous uniform: "Had my picture took in my outfit, / That should keep the Nazis away." Frank Luther's "I'm In The Army Now" (Broadcast Music, 1941) continued the gripes about clothing and battle gear, an especially common theme in 1941; the singer says his "uniform is a masterpiece, the seat of my pants looks like a valise" and his helmet is as "hard as a rock and as big as a boat, . . . / If my ears give way it'll cut my throat." The titles alone identify the object of complaint in Hy Heath and Fred Rose's "When Johnny Toots His Horn" (Irving Berlin Inc., 1941) and Morty Jacobs and Ed Nulty's "Who Wakes the Bugler In The Morning" (Doraine Music, 1941). Moviegoers got an earful of gripes about basic training in *Buck Privates* when Lou Costello rattled off a litany of grievances in Don Raye and Hughie Prince's "When Private Brown Becomes a Captain" (Leeds, 1941). Among Costello's endless beefs were "too much water in the soup; too many pairs of pants that droop; too many orders, too many drills, iodine and c c pills; too much mud, and too much rain; too many aches, and too much pain" (c. c. pills were the army's all-purpose stomach remedy and laxative). The navy shared in the griping, as in Don Raye and Gene De Paul's "A Sailor's Life For Me" (Leeds, 1941) in the Universal film *In The Navy:* "Oh, join the navy and see the world is what they said to me. / And they stuck me down in the engine room and I've never seen the sea."

The two griping numbers with any commercial success in 1941 had rather offbeat origins. Felix Bernard and Ray Klages's "$21 A Day—Once A Month" (Leeds, 1941)—later changed to "$50 A Day"—catalogues all a rookie must put up with for very little pay and was written for a Walter Lantz animated cartoon of that title released by Universal. It evidently had enough audience appeal in the short that popular bandleader Tony Pastor recorded it, his disk selling well enough to be a *Hot Charts* Extra for August and rank 44th in September. And according to *Variety,* Pastor's record and another by Dick Robertson did well in jukebox plays between August and October. The origin of the other gripe song popular in 1941 was more remote than a Hollywood cartoon—it was England. "Bless 'Em All," by Jimmy Hughes and Frank Lake (London: Keith Prowse, 1940), naturally griped about the *British* army. Subsequently, Al Stillman rewrote the lyrics for more relevance (and comprehensibility) to Americans (Cleveland: Sam Fox, 1941). Its eight long stanzas are devoted to comic gripes about the navy and marines as well as the army, all set to a rollicking, hummable tune. For American recruits, Stillman changed each stanza's refrain from "You'll get no promotion this side of the ocean" to "No ice cream and cookies for flat footed rookies." A typical army gripe is "Bless all the sergeants we have to obey, / Bless all the corp'rals who drill us all day," while the navy gripes include "Bless the instructors who teach us to dive, / Bless all our stars that we still are alive," and, in a rare glance at the marines in song, griping or otherwise, "Bless all the posters with beautiful scenes / We were to see if we join the marines; / Well, we've seen no scenery at all, / Except what they scrawl on the wall." The Jesters recorded it, as did Barry Wood with the King Sisters. By June 1941 Wood's disk ranked 53rd in *Hot Charts.* New life was breathed into "Bless 'Em All" when it was interpolated into the Warner Brothers picture *Captains of the Clouds,* starring James Cagney, released in February 1942, and in May and June 1944 Bing Crosby featured the song on his radio show, adding a chorus plugging War Bonds.

In 1942, humorous griping tailed off from the twelve songs of 1941 to only seven. One reason may have been that the United States, now in the war, suffered more defeats than it celebrated victories in the first half of 1942. Complaining about military life, even comically, seemed inappropriate, if not disloyal. Some evidence for this is suggested by the fate of

Frank Loesser's "In The Army," written for the Paramount picture *True to the Army*, released in late March 1942, just when U.S. forces began taking a terrible beating in the Pacific. Never published (or, seemingly, copyrighted separately from the film), the song had opening and closing sections expressing pride over being in the army, while in between were eight very funny stanzas complaining about army life. All that remained in the movie were the serious first and last verses, all the comic stuff cut or perhaps not even filmed (see Kimball and Nelson, 82). Most of the remaining musical gripes of 1942 appeared later in the year.

One came from Pvt. Lyle Moraine, who knew whereof he wrote in one of the cleverest of the few but especially well-written gripe songs of 1942. Moraine's number recites how the gruff, bullying sergeant's father calls him "sonny," his mother calls him "dear," his grandma calls him "snookie," and his sweetheart calls him "sugar pie," but "That Ain't What We Call Him In The Army" (Leeds, 1942), leaving unspoken what rookies *did* call sergeants as unprintable in sheet music and unsingable on radio at the time. Sunny Skylar also took an indirect, ironic approach to sergeants in "Move It Over" (Santly-Joy, 1942), written and published late in the year; by February 1943 Ethel Merman's recording ranks 24th in *Hot Charts*. In thirteen stanzas that relentlessly repeat the formula "Said the private to the sergeant . . . Said the sergeant to the private" with only slight variation, Skylar paints ludicrous pictures of sweet, lovable sergeants who never existed in this man's army—or any other: for example, "Said the private to the sergeant, 'I need a week to see my gal.' / Said the sergeant to the private, 'Take a month, old pal.'"

In *This Is the Army*, which opened on Broadway on July 4, 1942, Irving Berlin tried something similar in "My Sergeant And I Are Buddies" (This Is the Army Inc., 1942), but, by comparison, Berlin's humor here feels forced and uncomfortable. If I may interject a personal sidebar, it's my feeling that whether he was writing war-related numbers, songs for Broadway shows and Hollywood films, or just popular songs, Irving Berlin wrote far more songs than he should have. When he took time and care with lyrics, as with, say, "Let's Face The Music And Dance," "You're Just In Love," and the best songs in *Annie Get Your Gun*, the rhymes are ingenious, the language witty, and the ideas or sentiments pointed and original. Some Berlin material achieves true brilliance. But far too many of his songs have a slapdash quality that suggests they were written hastily and without much thought or detailed attention to what goes into quality lyric writing, something Berlin was certainly capable of achieving when he took care to do so. A case in point is another number of the gripe type from *This Is the Army*, one that deservedly remains among the best-known war-related numbers of World War II—"This Is The Army, Mr. Jones" (This Is the Army Inc., 1942). Reading or hearing the verse that is almost never performed any more reveals that Berlin's conceit for the song is wholly original: a "sergeant [is] laying down the law" to a bunch of rookies about what to expect from army life precisely to forestall any subsequent griping. This is why the chorus consists not of gripes per se but of explanations of how army and civilian life differ: "You had a housemaid to clean your floor / But she won't help you out anymore." Berlin's concise, clever lyric and simple, memorable melody netted "This Is The Army, Mr. Jones" a healthy life outside the theatre; in the September 1942 *Hot Charts,* Hal McIntyre's record ranks 48th, and in December Horace Heidt's claims the 36th slot, continuing to sell well through May 1943.

Like Irving Berlin, lyricist Kay Twomey also tended to run hot and cold, but sometimes in a single song. Most of "The K. P. Serenade" is a monotonous list of everything a new recruit's parents used to ask him to do that he didn't (peel potatoes, etc.), but now that the sergeant yells at him to do the same things, he does so with alacrity. Yet in the midst of the first of three choruses of such stuff, Twomey is suddenly at her best in a bit of inspired nonsense: "My uniform is an apron, I'm learning to cook and bake, / When I get out of the army, / What a wonderful wife I'll make." Similar in tone and wonderfully silly is "Buttons For The Major" (Remick, 1942) by Carter Allen, an ingenious songwriter about whom I have discovered absolutely nothing. The gripe in this number is entirely different from the rest—that packages arrive for the brass and the sergeants but none for the privates. Allen even manages to tie the major who is receiving boxes of medals, buttons, and other decorations to problems stateside: "Another box of MEDALS FOR THE MAJOR, / That's why there's a copper shortage in the land." And what does the lowly private get? Nothing: "Oh, his uniform is bare and they've chopped away his scalp, / He's just about as worthless as a snowball on an alp, / Another box of nothing for the private, / as private as a goldfish in a bowl"—a sentiment Frank Loesser would have great success with in 1944.

In 1943, the number of griping songs increased by one, but the lyrics in all but two were markedly inferior to the wit and humor pervading the 1942 numbers. Those two deservedly became hits to one or another degree: Frank Loesser's "What Do You Do In The Infantry?" and Johnny Mercer's "G.I. Jive" (Capitol Songs, 1943), the latter published and recorded so late in '43 that most of its success came in 1944. Loesser begins "What Do You Do" with more than two stanzas of amusing grumblings of foot soldiers like "The son-of-a-gun in the Signal Corps is traveling on a bike." The number seamlessly segues into a declaration that in the end it's the infantry that wins wars, brilliantly becoming a comedy song and pride in the service number all in one. Bing Crosby introduced it on radio's *Kraft Music Hall* on August 5, 1943, encoring it on August 19 and September 23, and again on January 20, 1944 (Morgereth). Loesser was rewarded for his efforts by the song getting numerous radio plays between mid-October and late December, and *Hot Charts* ranks the Sportsmen's recording at 35th in October. Recorded during the musicians' union strike, this was an a capella arrangement that served a song especially well; with no instrumental backing, the Sportsmen sound like a bunch of infantrymen trudging and singing to the accompaniment of only marching feet.

If "What Do You Do In The Infantry?" was a short-term mini-hit, "G.I. Jive" was a maxi-hit of epic proportions among both civilians and servicemen. It first shows up as an Extra in *Hot Charts* in December 1943, after which it ranks among the top records every month between January and October 1944, from a low of 37th to a high of 7th, variously in the recordings by Louis Jordan and Johnny Mercer, who wrote it as well. The *Billboard* chart of top-selling records put "G.I. Jive" even higher between June and September 1944, averaging between 6th and 9th weekly, once hitting 3rd. This coincided with *Billboard*'s survey of record preferences among stateside GIs that put Mercer's version at 4th and Jordan's 10th, and the song was also service personnel's 5th choice in sheet music. Much of its success came from the "jive" not just in its title but throughout the number's groovy music, rhythm, and language that describe some of the vicissitudes of basic training, such as meals in a "beautiful little café they call the mess. / Jack, when you convalesce, / Out of your seat, into the street, make with the feet! *Reet!*" Of all the songs griping about army life, "G.I. Jive" was the biggest hit.

The number of griping songs rose to ten in 1944, the last year for any significant output of them during the war. The year produced just one outstanding song of this type, a truly well-crafted piece, rich in original humor, by Pfc. Frank Loesser, this time teaming up with Technical Sgt. Peter Lind Hayes on "Why Do They Call A Private A Private?" (Famous Music, 1944). It was written for the Army Special Services Revue *About Face,* first presented on May 26 at Camp Shanks of the New York Port of Embarkation; Ethel Merman later performed it on radio and recorded it as a V-Disc for our GIs. Though its sheet music was published, "Private" didn't find much of a civilian audience. Still, it was a huge hit among servicemen at home and abroad for its graphic portrayal of the embarrassingly public life of privates. Of necessity, Loesser and Hayes cleaned up some lines between the camp show lyric and that for the sheet music and radio, but both versions are equally funny. For example, the camp show lyric "And when a fellow's gotta go / A fellow's gotta go, you know / With seven other fellows sitting there. (Who's got my *Colliers?*)" becomes in the sheet music "And in the morning when he wakes, / With ev'ry shower that he takes / There's seven other fellows standing there. (I'm so embarrassed!)" Both versions humorously make Loesser and Hayes's point that a private's life was anything but.

What's different about the griping songs in 1944 is that most were written by men in the service. It's difficult to say whether this was because they had more to gripe about as the war went on or because they felt more comfortable griping in '44 with the war going pretty much the Allies' way. Whatever the reason, alongside professionals like Pfc. Frank Loesser of the Army Air Force and Lieut. Vernon Duke of the Coast Guard were more occasional songwriters in various branches of the service, even including a marine. Sgt. Al Carbuto, U.S.M.C., had a gripe endemic among marines that was pretty much contained in the title of his "Get Your Gear On (We're Moving Out Again)" (Broadcast Music, 1945), words marines hated hearing when they thought they had settled down someplace for a while. Coastguardsman Chris Yacich, Sp. 2c had a more encompassing beef in "I'd Like To Find The Guy That Named The Coast Guard" (Mills, 1944), since he never can "find that bit of coast he had in mind" while in the middle of the Atlantic dodging torpedoes and sinking submarines.

Also in 1944 appeared the only hillbilly song about army life I'm aware of, even though fourteen hillbilly tunes about the draft and enlistment were published during the course of the war. "G.I. Blues" (Southern Music, 1944), written, performed, and recorded by Floyd Tillman, doesn't look like much on paper, but according to popular music encyclopedist Colin Larkin it was among the top ten hillbilly tunes of 1944 (3:2,496). The brief lyric gripes about some things rarely touched on by mainstream Alleymen or even servicemen: "G.I. Gals, G.I. pals, / Thousand guys and a dozen gals, / Most of them too darn fat; / How we gonna win a war like that?"—not terribly diplomatic, but typical of so much hillbilly music that tells it exactly as the writer/singer sees it. If Tillman's song is unique as the only country griping song, hillbilly songwriters were anything but silent when it came to other kinds of songs about the armed forces. In fact, the hillbilly voice was especially strong among the post-Pearl patriotic, militant, and Axis-bashing numbers that are the subject of the following chapter.

# *"Johnny Get Your Gun Again"*

## From National Pride to Axis-Bashing

Nothing else in the twentieth century coalesced the American people to full engagement in a single cause for so long a time as the Japanese sneak attack on December 7, 1941. Except for a handful of pacifists and conscientious objectors and approximately 15,000 so-called native Fascists, about 130 million Americans of all political and philosophical persuasions ceased debating whether to enter the war. Pearl Harbor provided a clear answer.

It is also true that even as catastrophic events bond people in a united effort, they also engender a wide range of emotional reactions. In the case of Pearl Harbor, most Americans' initial reactions were shock, horror, and anger. These feelings were soon joined by the desire to get even, fear over more invasions, dismay that young men would have to go to war again, and, above all, hatred—hatred for Hirohito and the Japanese Empire, Hitler and Nazi Germany, and, to a lesser degree, Mussolini and Fascist Italy. Undoubtedly, such powerful feelings are what got Americans behind the war effort almost before FDR famously labeled December 7, 1941, "a date that will live in infamy" in his address to Congress on December 8. Almost at once, people began to respond any way they knew how, illustrated by George M. Cohan's archetypal American family in the verse of "For The Flag, For The Home, For The Family" (Jerry Vogel, 1942), one of the first songs written after the Pearl Harbor attack: "Johnny's in the Army / Tommy's in the Navy / Father's buying Savings Bonds and Stamps. / Mother's knitting sweaters / Sister's writing letters, / And sending cigarettes to all the camps."

Like other Americans, professional songwriters responded in various ways to the United States being at war. Some Alleymen like Frank Loesser, Tom Adair, Vernon Duke, Hy Zaret, John Latouche, and Harold Rome entered one or another branch of the service at some point during the war, as did some folksinger/songwriters, as was noted in chapter 3. Yet most songwriters, including all of these men, chiefly participated by doing what they did best. Their songs about America at war were of three distinct and different kinds—patriotic, militant, and Axis-bashing. (I've given the name "Axis-bashing" songs, or Axis-bashers to those directly attacking any or all of the Axis powers. They range from genuinely clever and often outrageously funny satire to vicious, vitriolic, and totally unsmiling denigration and name-calling.) Just from the end of 1941 through the end of 1942, songwriters published by ASCAP, BMI, and SESAC music publishers wrote no fewer than thirty-three purely patriotic pieces, seventy militant war songs cheering on America's fighting forces, and thirty Axis-bashers. Year by year the numbers diminished for some types of songs, especially the purely patriotic, which were mostly subsumed by the militant war songs. Still, by the time the war ended, Tin Pan Alley and hillbilly writers had written a total of fifty-eight patriotic, 119 militant, and fifty-six Axis-bashing songs. The number of such songs by amateurs was likely somewhere in the thousands, most written as a catharsis for the kinds of emotions just described. Yet despite the large output of songs by professionals, few caught fire with the public, the hillbilly numbers among them scoring the biggest hits in all three categories.

### *"There's A Star Spangled Banner Waving Somewhere":* *Patriotism, Post–Pearl Harbor Style*

The traditional and conventional sentiments and rhetoric in over half of the professional patriotic songs written after Pearl Harbor form an unbroken continuum with those written before the war. Filled with the same formulaic expressions of love of country and national pride, they are the least interesting and had little success during the war. As songwriters looked for more original and effective ways to express their support of the war, the number of such conventionally written songs tailed off rapidly.

Traditional patriotic lyrics by the few major professionals who wrote such things were not much different from or better than those by the virtual unknowns who penned most of the post-Pearl patriotic anthems. The handful of Tin Pan Alley types whose gifts and talents failed them when writing such patriotic songs includes some already mentioned, like J. Fred Coots, Nick Kenny, and Al Stillman, as well as Clarence "I Can't Believe That You're In Love With Me" Gaskill and Sammy "Elmer's Tune" Gallop. Even Johnny Mercer and Harold Arlen, the two most prominent

Alleymen to tackle conventional patriotic expression, didn't pull it off very well in "Old Glory" (Famous Music, 1942), which Bing Crosby sang in the splashy finale of Paramount's musical *Star Spangled Rhythm*. All the glitz in Hollywood couldn't disguise a lyric benefit of Mercer's wit ("G.I. Jive") or lyricism ("Moon River"), containing instead flat, predictable phrases like "Old Glory, Old Glory, / Our dreams are all in you."

The sameness of the conventional post-Pearl patriotic songs is suggested just by a selection of their titles: "America Calling" (by Meredith Willson, incidentally), "America For Me," "America, My Own, My Native Land," "American Anthem," "Long Live America," "A Real American," "Wave That Flag, America," "America, I Pray For You," "America, My Home," "Love America (Or Leave It Alone)," "Rise Up And Shine! America," "March On, America," and "This, Our Land (A Prayer For America)." With the nation already taking "God Bless America" to heart as its favored patriotic song next to our national anthem, it remains unclear why so many songwriters wrote so many songs with similar titles expressing similar sentiments in similar language, and why both major and minor music publishers incurred the expense of publishing them. Did any of them believe they could come close to unseating Irving Berlin's popular favorite? Evidently not. Song pluggers made little effort to get these pieces on the radio, evidence that publishers had little hope for their success. Only one of these numbers ever had the five or more airplays in a single week required for listing on *Billboard* and *Variety*'s plug charts. For the week prior to June 17, 1942, *Variety* noted that Phelps H. Adams and Howard Acton's "Wave That Flag, America" (Broadway Music, 1942) was played eight times.

Only four of the conventional patriotic songs acknowledged directly or allusively that the United States was at war—Lawrence Welk, Leonard Hagel, and Frances Emmerich's "Every State Has Answered The Call" (Chicago: Chart House Music, 1942); Albert Stillman, Lawrence Stock, and Vincent Rose's "The Flame of Freedom" (Mutual Music Society, 1943); Joe Davis's "I Have Only One Life (But I'd Gladly Give It Up For My Country)" (Beacon Music, 1943); and Charles H. and Marjorie Elliot's "March On, America" (Chicago: Raymond A. Hoffman, 1944). The war's absence from the rest is explained by the rush of militant war songs that started just days after Pearl Harbor. They were implicitly patriotic as rallying cries for the country to get behind our armed forces, making purely patriotic numbers seem obsolete. Indeed, some people who wrote both kinds of songs kept the war out of their purely patriotic ones but featured it in their militant or marching numbers.

Colloquial, contemporary, and often playful qualities characterize not just the titles but the lyrics (and some of the music) of a smaller but more entertaining group of post-Pearl patriotic songs; four even succeeded commercially to some degree. Their patriotic conviction is as sincere as the conventionally written songs, but these eighteen numbers are as informal as the titles of a few: "The Flag's Still There, Mr. Key," "Fun To Be Free," "Hip Hip Hooray," "Gee, Isn't It Great To Be An American," and "Thank You, Columbus." Put another way, what distinguishes these songs from the traditional patriotic anthems is that while their texts still express national pride, they do so without the pious solemnity that's seemingly obligatory in the conventional songs, and their lyrics are in the breezy conversational style of the 1940s. Some of these songs also include references or allusions to current events or situations. For example, "The Flag's Still There, Mr. Key" (Leo Feist, 1942), with lyrics by George Jessel, who was better known as a stand-up comic than songwriter, and music by Ben Oakland, is directly addressed to the spirit of Francis Scott Key, presumably hovering over America. The song is serious in its playfulness, assuring the writer of "The Star Spangled Banner" that, despite the war, "Oh, say, you can see, / That the Flag's still there, Mister Key." Lyricist Edward "Body and Soul" Heyman also has fun with the stock-in-trade language of patriotic songs in "Fun To Be Free" (Hollywood: Saunders, 1942), with music by Louis Alter, when he writes that we'll "always think that Yankee Doodle's dandy!" In these songs and a few others, vivid language expressing feelings about America is much more entertaining than the stodgy, canned "land of Liberty" lyrics in far too many patriotic anthems before and after Pearl Harbor.

Four colloquial, sometimes playful patriotic songs had some luck with the public, but in different ways for different lengths of time. The earliest, Edna Fischer and Al Garman's "My Great, Great, Great, Great Grandfather" (Edwin H. Morris, 1942) is one of several robust songs during the war years consisting of a litany of all the singer's male ancestors who ever served in any war fought by Americans (including the Confederacy), back to and including the Revolution. Unlike the other songs' dignified language, Fischer and Garman's fighting genealogy is perfectly comfortable using phrases like "Ready to dish out the works" and "What a fool some guy would be / To try to take this land away from me." No recording caught on, but *Billboard*'s sheet music sales chart gave Fischer and Garman's song its one brief shining hour (or week, actually) as 13th out of the chart's fifteen sheets for April 25, 1942.

"Hip Hip Hooray" (Robbins, 1942), by Henry Nemo and Milt Ebbins, was a patriotic swing tune! How much more contemporary could you get in 1942? The song's tight, brief lyric simply proclaims how great it is to live here and how grateful people should be that they do: "Hip Hip Hooray / We're living in the U. S. A. / Come on, you Yanks, holler thanks, / Hip Hip Hooray." I own reissued radio transcriptions of the song by Bing Crosby and the Nat "King" Cole Trio, but the top-selling record was by Vaughn Monroe's orchestra with vocal by the Four V's, whose name, if not the group itself, was obviously created to trade on the war's "V for Victory" slogan. And, incidentally, the song was on the Victor label. In *Hot Charts,* Monroe's "Hip Hip Hooray" shows up at 51st in September 1942 and then is an Extra for every month through January 1943, showing that it sold reasonably well for nearly six months. Yet this was partly because the song was riding the coattails of a hit. Despite the OWI's objections to "peace and ease" songs, the flip side of the record was Vaughn Monroe's hugely popular rendition of Eddie Seiler, Sol Marcus, and Bennie Benjamin's vision of the world after the war, "When The Lights Go On Again (All Over The World)" (see chapter 12). In addition to Monroe's recording, *Hot Charts* lists records of "Hip Hip Hooray" by Scat Davis and Dick Jurgens as Extras between August of '42 and January of '43, and Lissauer mentions another by Andy Kirk with vocal by June Richmond (301).

Also in 1942 composer Earl Robinson, who before the war had written the monumental and controversial "Ballad For Americans" with John Latouche, now teamed up with lyricist Lewis Allan (born Abel Meeropol) to write the similar but shorter "The House I Live In" (Chappell, 1942). In reply to the question "What is America to me?" this song, like its predecessor, answers that, among other things, it is mostly its religious, ethnic, and racial diversity. Allan's lyric also displays its contemporary relevance in a list of other things that define America. He cites Midway right after Gettysburg and even includes "the story of Bataan"—one of this country's worst setbacks early in the war—as a part of the American experience. Paul Robeson, who first recorded "Ballad For Americans," was also the first to record "The House I Live In," but the song didn't receive too much attention until about three years later, when Frank Sinatra, playing himself, sang it in an eleven-minute RKO Radio short subject released in July 1945 that had the same title as the song. Sinatra comes across a bunch of street punks harassing another kid about his religion, whereupon "in song and talk, he voices the evils of anti-Semitism to [the] back-alley boys in need of a dulcet lesson in religious tolerance" (Doherty 194). The film, its producer, its director, and its writers, including Allan and Robinson, received a Special Achievement Academy Award for a "tolerance short subject," and Sinatra's recording of "The House I Live In" ranked among the top forty records for 1945 (Lissauer 310).

The other commercially successful colloquial and contemporary patriotic song actually met with the approval of the Office of War Information, even though "This Is Worth Fighting For" (Harms, 1942), with words by Edgar (Eddie) De Lange and music by Sam H. Stept, sounds like lyrical slush, not a patriotic anthem. Harms got it heavily plugged on radio between late May and late October 1942, especially during July and August, when *Variety*'s charts note that it was aired anywhere from seventeen to twenty-eight times a week. The plugs apparently paid off. *Hot Charts* ranks the Jimmy Dorsey/Bob Eberly record 17th in July and 19th in August, and the sheet music charted between 11th and 15th in late July and August in *Billboard*. Both Jimmy Dorsey's record and Kate Smith's also got a fair number of jukebox spins in July. Allan Jones sang the song (with its writers left uncredited) in the Universal musical *When Johnny Comes Marching Home*, released on Christmas Eve 1942, so a lot of people heard the number, whether they bought it or not. The song's appeal lies not only in Stept's lyrical and lilting music but in the personal kind of patriotism the words express. A man looks out over his family homestead and sings, "I saw a little old cabin and the river that flowed by the door / And I heard a voice within me whisper / THIS IS WORTH FIGHTING FOR." In the final stanza, he repeats the title's words with all his "loved ones" around him, clearly implying that he's telling them he plans to enlist. De Lange's lyric brings the lofty abstractions of generic patriotic songs—democracy, freedom, liberty, "the American way of life"—down to a very immediate level in the tangible manifestations of what a man and his family had worked hard to achieve for themselves. The number successfully connected patriotism and national pride to one's personal reasons for fighting in the war.

The smallest group of post-Pearl patriotic songs was also the most commercially successful. Of five patriotic numbers written by hillbilly songwriters and sung by hillbilly performers, three had at least limited public popularity and one other was a hit of blockbuster proportions, the only million-plus seller among all of the patriotic numbers written once we were at war. With trade papers in the 1940s ambivalent at best about tracking the popularity of hillbilly songs, *Hot Charts* is especially useful here for casting its retrospective net wider to include more kinds of songs than did *Billboard, Variety,* or, especially, "The Hit Parade," thus offering a broad-spectrum indicator of hillbilly song popularity.

Like "This Is Worth Fighting For," the successful hillbilly songs brought patriotism down to a personal level, three going even beyond the personal to the absolutely idiosyncratic in portraying the patriotic desire of people with physical or other disabilities to participate in the war effort. The earliest of such hillbilly tunes, Gene Autry and Fred Rose's "God Must Have Loved America" (West'rn Music, 1942), came out just after the United States entered the war, since "singing cowboy" Autry's own recording is listed as a *Hot Charts* Extra already for January 1942, and subsequently for every month through May—a good run for an also-ran record that didn't quite make the ranked listings. The idea of this brief song is that God must have loved America to make it as wonderful as it is, but it takes an odd personal turn at the end with "GOD MUST HAVE LOVED AMERICA /

So I love America too," which basically suggests something like if America's good enough for God, it's good enough for me.

About six months after Autry's record came out, Elton Britt's recording of Paul Roberts and Shelby Darnell's "There's A Star Spangled Banner Waving Somewhere" (Bob Miller, 1942) quietly (in retrospect) appears as a *Hot Charts* Extra for June 1942 and stays one through August, moving into the ranked listings from September 1942 through March 1943, as high as 19th and usually in the twenties, respectable numbers for a hillbilly song with literally *no* network plugs. By fall 1942 the sheet music was on the charts of the fifteen best sellers in both *Billboard* and *Variety,* where it stayed every week through late summer 1943. An article about hillbilly music in *Billboard* on June 22, 1944, reported that "Miller sold 1,400,000 copies of sheet music of *There's a Star-Spangled Banner Waving Somewhere.* The Victor (Bluebird) waxing [recording] by Elton Britt sold over 1,250,00 disks" (65), and country singer Jimmy Wakely made yet another strong-selling record of the song. When all the numbers were in, this patriotic hillbilly song about a "crippled" boy who wishes he could fight for Uncle Sam was arguably the biggest-selling war-related song next to "White Christmas," and "White Christmas" wasn't even meant to be one. A "mountain boy" with a "twisted leg" sings to a recruiting officer of his desire to go to that "Somewhere" where American heroes like Custer and Washington go after they die. While the singer's wish to fight for his country seems sincere, the lyric reveals that his motives are more purely personal (I sometimes wonder if people *really* listen to the words of songs). The boy's brand of patriotism turns out to be narcissistic and selfish, not altruistic: "If I do some great deed I will be a hero / And a hero brave is what I want to be / [then] In that heaven there should be a place for me." Rather than helping for the sake of his country, the boy's motive is personal glory as compensation for his physical disability. Nonetheless, people grabbed up the disks and sheets like those proverbial hotcakes.

In "I'd Like To Give My Dog To Uncle Sam" (Shapiro, Bernstein, 1944), by Dave McEnery (a.k.a. Red River Dave), the singer's expectations are more realistic, his patriotism and motives entirely unselfish. In the time-honored tradition of country music that tugs hard at the heartstrings, this song is even more sentimental than "There's A Star Spangled Banner." A "blind boy," knowing he can't enlist, offers to give his guide dog to the K-9 Corps and claims, "I'll get along somehow / If my country needs him now," ending with an eloquent personal statement of his patriotism and sacrifice: "I've never seen Old Glory wave above / But still I know she's there for me to love / I've told my dog 'good-bye' / I don't mean it if I cry / I'D LIKE TO GIVE MY DOG TO UNCLE SAM." The absolute simplicity and sincerity of McEnery's lyric—as in the best of country music—make the number not just sentimental but genuinely affecting (especially to devoted dog owners like me). Under his performing name of Red River Dave, the song's writer had the best-selling record—a *Hot Charts* Extra for April and May 1944. The final patriotic hillbilly song to make any kind of splash also did so in 1944. Rather than a physical disability, the singer here has a legal infirmity, so to speak, that prevents him from joining the armed forces. "I'm A Convict With Old Glory In My Heart" (Bob Miller, 1944), with words by Dave McEnery and music by songwriter/publisher Miller, depicts a patriotic American who wants to fight for his country but can't because "Those foolish things I did" still have him serving time in prison. The song is filled with noble sentiments about how even a convict can be a loyal American who wants to enlist, but unless the singer's crime was a capital offense, the song's entire premise rings false. The truth of the matter is that "special draft boards were set up in most state and federal prisons, and more than 100,000 convicted felons were taken into the armed forces" (Bailey 44). Despite misrepresenting historical reality, Elton Britt's and Red River Dave's records both did well enough to be *Hot Charts* Extras for December 1944 and January 1945. Just as the hillbilly voice proved strong and popular among wartime patriotic numbers, it resonated significantly among militant war songs and, especially, Axis-bashers.

### "We Did It Before And We Can Do It Again": But We're Not Buying Many War Songs

On December 20, 1941, just thirteen days after Pearl Harbor, *Billboard* prophesied with confident, professional certainty, "There can be no doubt that the next months will see another *Over There* take the country by storm" (11). But none did, then or at any other time during the war. If the American public had wanted one supercharged militant war song to be *the* musical rallying cry for World War II, the few weeks after Pearl Harbor gave them two perfectly splendid ones to choose from. One—ironically, by Mr. *Over There* himself, George M. Cohan—they overlooked completely, while the other caught on for just a veritable nanosecond in the timeline of World War II. If the *Billboard* article wasn't very adept at prophesy on December 20, 1941, it reported on the present war-song situation with lucidity and acumen, writing of the "unbelievable number of war ditties which appeared like so many mushrooms within 24 hours after Nippon attacked us. Reliable estimates place the number of tunes at over 1,000. Many of them have found publishers, but it is conceded by the street's best minds that if 10 of the songs ever get anywhere, a high average will be struck." Not even ten made it. As for Axis-bashers that specifically lambasted Japan, Germany, and/or Italy, *Billboard* predicted that "99.9 per cent . . . will never be heard outside of publishers' offices" (11). This time *Billboard* was right.

On December 17 *Variety* published "Inevitably, the War Songs," a piece just laying out the facts about the war song business at the time and listing nineteen song titles, each with a publisher's name in parentheses, that were "now in the Tin Pan Alley mill," which didn't mean the mill finally published them all. This list is the likely source of some "phantom titles" of supposed war songs that never actually existed but that later writers have cited as real. Reliable sources indicate that eleven of the nineteen songs on the *Variety* list never got published, so such writers as Mohrmann and Scott, Lingeman, and Kathleen E. R. Smith most likely presumed their existence from the *Variety* article or a later work citing it. That none of these writers saw actual sheet music for these titles is suggested by the fact that they never quote from any of the songs or even name a composer or lyricist. About a year later *Variety* itself provided the earliest evidence that none of the eleven was published; all are absent from the paper's "More Or Less Complete" list of war songs published since Pearl Harbor (6 Jan. 1943: 184). My searches of World War II sheet music in the extensive John Hay and Library of Congress collections turned up none of them. But the most convincing evidence that none of these songs ever made it into print, or maybe even got written, is that not one was registered with the U.S. Copyright Office. Some of the most notorious, and most often mentioned, of these phantom titles are "When The Little Yellow Bellies Meet The Cohens and the Kelleys," "We're Going To Find A Fellow Who Is Yellow And Beat Him Red White and Blue," "Put The Heat On Hitler, Muss Up Mussolini And Tie A Can To Japan," "Oh, You Little Son Of An Oriental," and "To Be Specific, It's Our Pacific."

To return to the militant war songs that *did* exist, those two perfectly splendid ones—and a couple of others—were written almost before the smoke had cleared in Honolulu. One of those "others," according to an undocumented anecdote in Lingeman's *Don't You Know There's a War On,* was the earliest public performance of a professionally written war song. Bert Wheeler sang Ned Washington and Lew Pollack's "We'll Knock The Japs Right Into The Laps Of The Nazis" (Mills, 1942) in a nightclub on the very night of Sunday, December 7 (Lingeman 211). The nightclub was most probably in Los Angeles, since Wheeler was doing a lot of films then and Washington and Pollack were writing prolifically for Hollywood. Given the time differences, they could have easily heard the news and gotten together to write, rehearse, and perform the song in one afternoon and evening. Despite its title, the song isn't an Axis-basher. Rather, in the spirit of most militant war songs it just says we're going to thrash the enemy in short order: "Chins up, Yankees, let's see it thru, / And we'll show them there's no yellow in the red, white, and blue." "Yellow" in this context (unlike in the Axis-bashers) seems meant only as the color of cowardice and not as a dig at the "yellow race."

A song as topically titled as "We'll Knock The Japs Right Into The Laps Of The Nazis" had little chance of becoming a long-term, unifying rallying cry. In its war song article on December 20, *Billboard* observed, "Smart songwriters and pubs [publishers] are concentrating their patriotic efforts on tunes of a less specific nature" (11). Indeed they were, as when Charlie Tobias and Cliff Friend wrote "We Did It Before And We Can Do It Again" (Witmark, 1941), the first of the few truly outstanding militant war songs to come out of World War II and the earliest to reach a wide national audience. There is plenty of documentary evidence, including *Variety*'s war song article on December 17, that Eddie Cantor premiered "We Did It Before" on the Wednesday, December 10, broadcast of his weekly network radio show—just three days after Pearl Harbor—and that on Sunday, December 14, Dinah Shore featured it on her show as well (2). Beside the fact that Charlie Tobias was Cantor's brother-in-law (Ewen 427), Cantor so took to the rousing tune that he had it interpolated into the musical *Banjo Eyes* that he was starring in, currently in its out-of-town tryout in Philadelphia. It opened in New York on December 25 and the song stayed in the show throughout its sixteen-week run (Bordman 527).

What makes "We Did It Before" stand out among over one hundred professionally written militant war songs is its direct yet clever lyric set to a catchy, singable tune in march tempo; it avoids the usual clichés of expression in such songs while retaining the message that with the United States in the war, the Allies will quickly defeat the Axis: "We'll knock them over and then we'll get the guy in back of them." The Music Publishers Holding Corporation, an umbrella company for Witmark, Harms, and Remick, must have anticipated good things right from the start since they took out a full-page ad in the December 17 *Variety* that reproduced the music and lyrics of the verse and both choruses, flagged "HERE'S YOUR PROFESSIONAL COPY." This effectively gave singers, musical arrangers, and bandleaders all they needed for arranging and performing the song on radio or in live performance just days after Tobias and Friend wrote it. Witmark's hunch and the song's quality paid off—at least in the short run. According to *Variety*, "We Did It Before" got between eleven and eighteen network airplays weekly during January and February 1942 and still six or seven a week in March. Both *Variety* and *Billboard* ranked the weekly sheet music sales between 7th and 4th during those same months. Only record sales lagged; recorded as early as December 23, 1941, by Carl Hoff's orchestra, and also by Eddie Howard and Dick Robertson's bands, Robertson's disk alone reached 45th in *Hot Charts*, and only for February 1942. The discrepancy between sheet music and record sales may be because "We Did It Before" was the kind of song people wanted to sing, not just listen to. This should have been a good omen for its becoming *the* militant war song the pundits were seeking, but I suspect it never achieved that status because of its length—much longer than the short, tight "Over There"—and its melody, which, though singable, is tricky in spots. Or maybe Americans just weren't in the market for a war song.

Like "We Did It Before," George M. Cohan's sole foray into the World War II war song field, "For The Flag, For The Home, For The Family" had just about everything going for it—except public interest. Its rousing martial melody is short, eminently singable, and deliberately evocative of "Columbia The Gem Of The Ocean" and Cohan's own "Over There." The lyric is a sharp and witty expression of militant patriotism, as when Cohan playfully hails America's entry into the war: "Tell the world / That the Yankees are at bat." But the song never got to first base. Jerry Vogel, Cohan's publisher since 1934, copyrighted and published "For The Flag" in January 1942, so Cohan had to have written it earlier that month, or in December 1941. Other than its publication as sheet music, not much happened; this stirring and playful piece of militant songwriting never made the trade paper charts or even the retrospective *Hot Charts*. Since Vogel pretty aggressively marketed Cohan's material, it's even more baffling that it appears not once on *Variety* or *Billboard*'s radio plug charts, meaning that no network stations ever aired the piece more than four times a week, if at all. It's equally mysterious that the earliest record I've heard or found a reference to was cut by Johnny Long's orchestra with Bob Houston's vocal as late as April 3, 1942. That America's public, broadcasters, and record companies really didn't want an all-purpose universal war song is confirmed by their dismissal of "For The Flag." And in retrospect that's really a shame, not only because Cohan had written "the" war song of World War I but because this would turn out to be his last militant/patriotic number. The man who had been penning flag-wavers and morale boosters since 1901 died on November 5, 1942.

Amidst a flurry of songs with identical or similar titles published in the few weeks following December 7, 1941, Don Reid and Sammy Kaye's "Remember Pearl Harbor" (Republic Music—Kaye's own publishing house—1941) came up the winner. It looked for a time as if this might be the war song some people were waiting for. Though not quality song-writing like "We Did It Before" and "For The Flag," "Remember Pearl Harbor" is very singable and very short—so short that Sammy Kaye's recording gets through the two-line verse once and the six-line chorus *four times*—twice by a male chorus and twice as an instrumental—in just two minutes and twenty-five seconds. That's not just short, it's a brilliant marketing strategy for beating a song into listeners' heads so they'll run out and buy it. It also didn't hurt that on the flip side was Maury Coleman

Harris's "Dear Mom" (Republic, 1941), one of the earliest sentimental "mother songs" of the war. With militancy on one side and sentimentality on the other, how could the disk go wrong? In *Hot Charts* for January and February 1942 Kaye's record ranks 11th and 7th, and the song made both trade papers' charts of best-selling sheet music every week through early April, ranking as high as 5th. But the song's strengths are also its weaknesses. Its lyric isn't just brief but banal, with lines like "Let's RE-MEMBER PEARL HARBOR / As we go to meet the foe," and Sammy Kaye's music sounds less like a militant war song than a football fight song. In fact it's very similar to Blane and Martin's concurrently popular college pep song "Buckle Down, Winsocki," making Reid and Kaye's number sound like it's about scoring touchdowns, not winning a war, and its rousing "rah rah" rhythm cloys very quickly.

The other "Remember Pearl Harbor" songs that Reid and Kaye's left behind in the dust were inconsequential, uninteresting, and commercially unsuccessful, which pretty much describes all but a few of the other hundred-plus militant war songs to come out of Tin Pan Alley between Pearl Harbor and the Japanese surrender. As with conventional patriotic numbers, their chief problem is lyrics that rely on a convenient stockpile of formulaic phrases, clichéd imagery, and repetitive vocabulary, which quickly accumulated and were repeated by lyricists from one end of the war to the other. A sampling of these songs' numbingly similar titles (grouped by similarities) suggests something of the redundancy of their familiar-sounding lyrics: "We're In It," "We're In To Win," "We're In It! Let's Win It!"; "Let's Get Over And Get It Over," "Wait 'Till We Get Over There," "We're Coming Back Again," "We're Coming Over," "We'll Be There And Don't Forget"; "Fighting Men Of Uncle Sam," "Follow Your Uncle Sam," "Uncle Sam Goes To Town," "Uncle Sam's Boys," "Uncle Sammie's Boys"; "The Yanks Are Coming" (twice), "The Yanks Are On The March Again," "The Yanks Will Do It Again," "The Yanks Are Comin' Again"; "We're On Our Way To Tokyo," "All The Way to Tokio!" and "I Want To Go To Tokio"—"Tokio" still a common variant spelling in the 1940s. Only one of these songs is of even historical interest. Lew Pollack and Tony Stern's "The Yanks Are Coming" (Southern Music, 1942) is the only Tin Pan Alley militant song to acknowledge America's early setbacks in the war: "Times have been tough, and this war has been rough / But we will see it through."

Because war songs with more original titles generally had more original content, they often did better with the public. One of the earliest, Leo Corday, Paul Mann, and Stephan Weiss's "Let's Put The Axe To The Axis" (Paramount Music, 1941) had an offbeat but rousing tune and was apparently the first militant number to use its title phrase, one that became the stock-in-trade of many other war songs. The publisher took out an ad for the song in *Variety* on December 17, 1941 (the same week Witmark's ad for "We Did It Before" ran), containing the line "WATCH FOR ABE LYMAN BLUEBIRD RECORD" (53). Paramount was evidently optimistic about the recording in advance, since Abe Lyman and His Californians didn't even record the number until December 18. It's a *Hot Charts* Extra for January 1942. Almost as early was J. Fred Coots's "Goodbye Mama (I'm Off To Yokohama)" (Chappell, 1941), which, despite its title, is not an Axis-basher but a straightforward militant war song and the possible origin of a groaner of a pun that other lyricists quickly overworked, when it declares we'll "soon have all those Japs right down on their 'Jap-a-knees.'" Art Jarrett's recording is a *Hot Charts* Extra for January and February 1942, and in the latter month Teddy Powell's record ranks 43rd. During those same two months, Kate Smith brought momentary popularity and record sales to one of the many "don't get mad, get even"– themed war songs, Robert Sour, Don McCray, and Ernest Gold's "They Started Somethin' (But We're Gonna End It!)" (Broadcast Music, 1942). Also, on her February 13 radio program, Smith premiered "This Time" (Irving Berlin Inc., 1942), one of Irving Berlin's two militant war songs. The terse lyric pointedly looks back to issues left unfinished by World War I and to a future in which "we won't have to do it again." Berlin's other war song was a novelty piece called "A Kick In The Pants" (This Is The Army Inc., 1943), added to his all-soldier show in London on November 10, 1943, during its overseas tour. The number has the Allies and overrun countries rehearsing a new dance aimed at the behinds of the Axis Powers. And, yes, even Berlin succumbed to that tired pun: "Mister Tojo, if you please / . . . Bend down on your Japan knees / That's our target for tonight."

Neither song had much success. In fact, only one other mainstream Tin Pan Alley war song did. For "We Must Be Vigilant" (Bregman, Vocco, and Conn, 1942), Edgar "For Me And My Gal" Leslie wrote lyrics to F. W. Meacham's 1880 march "American Patrol." Together the familiar march tune and Leslie's muscular lyrics made for quite a rousing war song. Phil Spitalny and His All-Girl Orchestra featured it on their *Hour of Charm* radio broadcasts and also recorded it, their disk ranking 40th in *Hot Charts* for April 1942. Still, Glenn Miller's swing instrumental of "American Patrol" itself was a much bigger hit. In 1942 a militant number by two of Tin Pan Alley's best saw active duty only in a movie—Don Raye and Gene De Paul's "Johnny Get Your Gun Again" in the Universal picture *Private Buckaroo*. The number plays Raye's often slangy lyrics ("Mister Whiskers needs each mother's son again") off De Paul's march music, but audiences took more notice of the film's splashier war-related non-militant numbers, like "Don't Sit Under The Apple Tree" and "Six Jerks in a Jeep."

In 1943 Oscar Hammerstein's Music War Committee first attempted to fulfill its charge of finding, commissioning, or writing the great all-purpose war song, but the results of its quest were pretty pathetic. Al Barry's cliché-ridden "Rainbow 'Round The World" won the MWC's first war-song contest; for a prize Barry saw his song published by American Music in 1943 and then vanish from view. The MWC itself published "One More Mile And We're There," with lyrics by solidly professional Bob "Don't Get Around Much Any More" Russell and music by Charles Hathaway. More lively and original than "Rainbow," it still faded into oblivion just as quickly.

But in 1943 Tin Pan Alley also produced two militant numbers the public heard loud and clear—one on the radio, the other in a movie, though neither made any of the charts. On his January 19 CBS radio show, Al Jolson sang the ripsnorting "(We're Gonna Make Sure) There'll Never Be Another War!" (Paull-Pioneer, 1942), by Nelson Cogane, Ira Schuster, and Joseph Meyer. Jolson's performance of the song is so electrifying (preserved on a reissued transcription) because the number was tailor-made for him by composer Joseph Meyer, who had written "California, Here I Come" for (and with) Jolson almost twenty years earlier. The song's militancy extends to home front support for our troops: "Why are we working and fighting / Like we never did before? / Why, we wanna make sure, / We're gonna make sure THERE'LL NEVER BE ANOTHER WAR!" Jolson's idiosyncratic styling of this vigorous song is riveting; to me the mystery is that he didn't record it. Ted Koehler and Harold Arlen's standard "Stormy Weather" is far better known than their militant war number "All Out For Freedom (The Yankee Doodle Battle Cry)" (Harms, 1943), from the 1943 RKO musical *Up in Arms*. Still, this exuberant though obscure flag-waver has considerable merit, not only in Arlen's always tuneful and original music but also in Koehler's laid back, slangy approach to war-song writing, in lines like "Ten million Yankees are standing pat / Any rat knows that isn't hay" and "So, so long for a while till those heels forget to heil." Such colloquial diction in militant war songs is as refreshing as it is rare.

Equally rare are Tin Pan Alley militant war songs whose music breaks out of the conventional mold of military airs. "All America Swings" (Melo-Art, 1943), by Claude Reese, Al J. Neiburg, Ray Bloch, and Claude Garreau, was obviously a swing tune. Buck Ram and Clarence Stout's "Hey Tojo! Count Yo' Men (Hallelujah! 8–9–10)" (Noble Music, 1944), with its jive repetitions of the title phrases, is a rhythm number. Paul J. Winkopp styled the lyrics and music of his five-stanza "Hallelu! (Judgment Day Is Comin')" (Broadcast Music, 1942) as a good ol' fashioned stompin' and shoutin' spiritual: "Uncle Sam has strapped his wings on! HALLELU! / Uncle Sam has strapped his wings on! HALLELU! / See him soar above the crowd as he hollers from a cloud that the JUDGMENT DAY IS COMIN'! HALLELU!" Two giants in their fields combined to write a militant blues, of all things, and a very authentic blues at that. Legendary black cornetist and writer of "St. Louis Blues," W. C. Handy, wrote the music for "Go And Get The Enemy Blues" (Handy Brothers, 1942)—with an assist from Clarence M. Jones. By the war, Handy was blind and primarily a music publisher, but he could still turn out blues riffs with the best of them. With lyrics by formidable African American poet Langston Hughes, the song is a fascinating specimen of militant sentiments in a vastly different musical idiom: "We're fighting a war and we're fighting this war to win— / I'm fighting this war and I'm fighting this war to win— / If we don't win now we'll have to start all over again."

The militant war songs of America's folksingers were even farther from mainstream martial music, largely because they took or adapted many of their melodies from traditional folk music, which, almost by definition, doesn't feature many marches. About the closest any folksinger's contribution came to martial-sounding music was Woody Guthrie's collaboration with Earl Robinson on "When The Yanks Go Marching In," their adaptation of the traditional Dixieland march "When The Saints Go Marching In." Unusual for a war-related song by a folksinger, it was published contemporaneously with its writing: Robbins Music brought out the sheet music in 1943, and it was printed in a U.S. Army *Hit Kit* of songs for soldiers. Guthrie's lyric is a no-frills list of America's fighting superiority, couched in the familiar repetitions of "The Saints": "Oh when our guns and cannon roar, Oh when our guns and cannon roar, / Oh boys, I want to be in that number, When our guns and cannon roar."

Guthrie was more original and personal in a song wholly his own called variously "Talking Sailor" and "Talking Merchant Marine," which he recorded for Asch Records on April 19, 1944 (Logsdon 10). The song is a "talking blues"; rather than singing, Guthrie recites a rhythmic, sometimes rhymed, text to his own guitar accompaniment—think of it as "folk rap." In casual, fragmented language, he speaks of his pride as both a C.I.O. union man and a member of the Merchant Marine—by being both, he helps to win the war: "Win some freedom. Liberty. Stuff like that. " In 1942, Guthrie adapted the melody of the folk classic "John Henry" for "What Are We Waitin' On," a vigorous defense of America's entry into the war: "You can have ten million Yanks, if it takes them to tear the Fascists down." Also in 1942, some of the Almanac Singers humorously deconstructed for wartime the eternal feud between those legendary mountain boys known variously as the Hatfields/Martins and the Coys/McCoys. The song was published as "The New Hatfields And The Coys" in *Songs Of The Almanac Singers* (Bob Miller, 1942) and performed on the radio by Pete Seeger, Burl Ives, and others as "The Martins And The Coys." (Logsdon 16). Whatever the title, this hilarious song is also seriously militant. The feuding clans put aside their internecine skirmishes—"now for the duration they have changed their occupation"— to fight side by side for Uncle Sam. At an unspecified time during the war, Huddie Ledbetter (Lead Belly) wrote and performed "Mr. Hitler." With the exception of some songs in Yiddish written for Yiddish-speaking audiences, this folksong is the only militant song of any kind to address directly the Nazi regime's persecution of European Jewry. To justify his refrain of "we're gonna tear Hitler down," Lead Belly sings, earlier in the song, "When Hitler started out he took the Jews from their homes." Can't get much more direct than that.

Almost as direct was the first of two militant hillbilly war songs that had major success. In 1942 Bill Boyd and Earl Nunn based their "Modern Cannonball" (Southern Music, 1942) on "Wabash Cannonball," which is usually attributed to A. P. Carter, though this has been questioned (Malone 67). Boyd and Nunn's hard-hitting militant piece is aimed mostly at Japan. It borders on Axis-bashing but is neither satiric nor foaming with racial slurs as it proclaims how the United States will annihilate Japan in retaliation for "Pearl Harbor and Luzon": "We'll blast this little island from the ocean mighty soon; / We'll blow them up so doggone high, they'll splatter on the moon." These musical sentiments must have touched the right chords with Americans who were feeling the sting of those defeats, since country singer Denver Darling's record of "Modern Cannonball" is a *Hot Charts* Extra from October 1942 through January 1943. Earl Nunn and Zeke Clements's "Smoke On The Water" (Chicago: Adams, Vee & Abbott, 1943) was a flat-out hit later in the war. More allusive than "Modern Cannonball," "Smoke On The Water" sings of the might of America smiting the Axis Powers: "For there is a great destroyer made of fire and flesh and steel / Rolling towards the foes of freedom, they'll go down beneath its wheels." In the absence of network plugs, national awareness of this song began slowly. But in August 1944, Red Foley's record of "Smoke On The Water" is a *Hot Charts* Extra, in September it ranks 38th, rises to 25th in October, and then slides back to 30th and 41st in November and December. That it is once again an Extra for January through June 1945 doesn't mean it was no longer popular; instead, it received stiff competition from recordings by Bob Wills and Boyd Heath, whose disks appear along with Foley's as Extras between March and June. With strong sales for the eleven months from August 1944 through June 1945, "Smoke On The Water" had a longer run of popularity than any militant war song by a mainstream Tin Pan Alley writer.

## *"Der Fuehrer's Face": The Several Complexions of Axis-Bashing*

The musical attacks began almost a year before Pearl Harbor, and kicking off Tin Pan Alley's perennial wartime sport of Axis-bashing was none other than Irving Berlin. Originally registered for copyright as an unpublished song on January 14, 1941, Berlin's "When That Man Is Dead And Gone" (Irving Berlin Inc., 1941) was the first of several Tin Pan Alley and hillbilly Axis-bashers to equate Hitler with the devil: "Some fine day the news will flash / Satan with a small moustache / Is asleep beneath the lawn / WHEN THAT MAN IS DEAD AND GONE." On February 1, the number was introduced on radio's *ASCAP on Parade* (Kimball and Emmet 371), and in *Hot Charts* the Glenn Miller record with vocal by Tex Beneke ranks 54th in April. These signs point to things to come for Axis-bashing and its public reception. Despite Japan's attack on Pearl Harbor, Hitler was the man Americans loved to hate. Of the combined fifty-six Tin Pan Alley and hillbilly Axis-bashers, twenty-three dealt just with Nazi Germany, often with Hitler as the personal embodiment of the Third Reich, and thirteen of those focused specifically on the prospect of Hitler's death or funeral, or on thoughts about hanging Der Fuehrer (almost invariably from a "sour apple tree"). Twenty other Tin Pan Alley and hillbilly numbers bashed all three Axis Powers, but, by contrast, only thirteen bashed Japan exclusively. Some lambasted Emperor Hirohito or General and Prime Minister Hideki Tojo, but none depicted either as evil incarnate, the way Hitler often was; instead, the object of these musical assaults was usually the Japanese Empire as a whole.

Moreover, not one Axis-basher targeted just Benito Mussolini or his Fascist Italy, suggesting the relative insignificance of "Il Duce" in the imaginations of American songwriters and most of the public. Even Lew Brown's "Bye, Bye Benito" (Shapiro, Bernstein, 1942) got in a few whacks at Hitler and the Japanese as well; and here, as in other songs where he appears, Mussolini comes off pretty much as a bit player in the drama of the war, usually one who's a dupe, a dope, or a puffed-up pompous ass. Typical of the Mussolini jokes in Axis-bashing songs are three in numbers by hillbilly songwriter/singer Carson J. Robison (much more of him soon), Meredith Willson, and Irving Berlin. Robison's "1942 Turkey in the Straw" (Robbins, 1942), an update of the traditional tune, briefly pokes at Il Duce's well-known inflated self-importance: "Oh I saw Mussolini settin' on a log all puffed up like a great big frog / I sneaked up close and stuck him with a wire and he just went 'Poof' like an old flat tire." Meredith Willson did some updating of his own to make jokes at the expense of the Axis in "Three Blind Mice" (Irving Berlin Inc., 1942, 1943), singling out Mussolini for his ineptitude and constant whining for help: "While Adolph's yelling for Tojo's gun, Tojo yells for the Rising Sun,

Benito's yelling for anyone." One of Irving Berlin's few wholly successful excursions into satire is "Ve Don't Like It" (This Is The Army Inc., 1943), first added to *This Is The Army* for radio broadcast on ABC's *Lux Radio Theater* in February 1943. The song is a mock radio address by "Herr Doktor Goebbels" about everything that "ve don't like" now that the war wasn't going Germany's way. Among Goebbels's many hilarious complaints is Mussolini being a less than useful ally: "In Japan our hands are tied; Ve don't like it. / Mussolini's on our side; / Ve don't like it." For both hillbilly and Tin Pan Alley songwriters, Mussolini was the comic relief among the Axis leaders.

The better Axis-bashing songs didn't need comic relief. All but three that achieved any kind of popularity were successful because of their humor, an entertaining and effective device for belittling an object of contempt and fear. The best of them were satiric as well. But one can also disparage an enemy in singularly unfunny ways. This was the approach of the first wave of Axis-bashing songs immediately after Pearl Harbor, their sole target understandably being Japan. The OWI's guidelines cautioned songwriters against downplaying the size and strength of the enemy, name-calling, and derogatory language (see *Variety* 15 July 1942: 3), but these things were the lifeblood of Japan-bashers, with the result that most are just ugly without being clever or funny. Their titles alone display their vituperative tone: "You're A Sap, Mister Jap," "We're Gonna Have To Slap The Dirty Little Jap," "I've Got A Scrap With A Jap," "We're Gonna Stop Your Yappin', Mister Jap," and "Japs Haven't Got A Chinaman's Chance," a title also so offensive to our Chinese allies that it was changed to "Japs Haven't Got A Ghost Of A Chance" before publication. In denigrating the Japanese, some songs equate or associate them with the Chinese through stereotypes of each nationality. Country songwriter Bobby Gregory's "The Hillbilly Recruit" (American Music, 1942) declares, "I'm gonna make those squint eyed Japs wash out my laundry," trading on the very real presence of numerous Chinese-run laundries across the United States in the 1940s but confusing them with things Japanese. Similarly, in his "We're Gonna Have To Slap The Dirty Little Jap" (Bob Miller, 1941) hillbilly songwriter and publisher Miller wrote, "The Japs and all their hooey will be changed into chop suey." A general anti-Asian bias was prevalent among white Americans for decades before World War II, but scrambling an ally with one of the Axis Powers seems particularly offensive. Even some songs that specifically mention the Chinese as our ally also denigrate them, usually by calling them "Chinks." The writer of the stylish "As Time Goes By," Herman Hupfeld, was guilty of this in his Axis-basher "When Uncle Sammy Tiddly-Winks In Tokio" (Shapiro, Bernstein, 1942). The American forces plan a party for the Allies after they defeat Japan: "Oh! we'll invite the Chinks to have a smokio." The second verse is even less kind to the Japanese: "Those sneaky little ginks we've gotta croakio." (This is not a great song.)

Other slurs in Japan-bashing songs include unflattering parodies of how Japanese people supposedly speak English: "Sorry please, we fooling you, I thinking," in Lee Ryer and Noel Marchant's "I've Got A Scrap With A Jap" (Berkeley: Melody Moderne, 1942), and "Me velly velly sorry, excuse please," in "The Hillbilly Recruit." Even more frequent are disparaging remarks about the physical characteristics of Japanese, whether the shape of their eyes ("squint eyed Japs") or their generally short stature and skin color, both of which Bob Miller worked into "We'll skin the streak of yellow from this sneaky little fellow," in "We're Gonna Have To Slap The Dirty Little Jap." There are also numerous put-downs of Japanese national symbols and cultural norms. Nearly every Japan-basher gets in some kind of crack about "The Land of the Rising Sun" setting or being extinguished by the Allies, and a few numbers belittle the Japanese idea of saving (or losing) face. And, of course, the Japanese themselves are just about universally called "Japs," "Jappies," or "Nips." These songs' common denominator is their hostile, angry, vengeful, and almost entirely humorless tone. Two had some success shortly after Pearl Harbor, according to *Hot Charts*. Carl Hoff's recording of James Cavanaugh, John Redmond, and Nat Simon's "You're A Sap, Mister Jap" (Mills, 1941) with the Murphy Sisters' vocal ranks 47th in February 1942, and Carson Robison's disk of Bob Miller's "We're Gonna Have To Slap The Dirty Little Jap" is an Extra from January through March of that year.

One Japan-basher, subtitled "America's Hymn Of Hate," from as late as 1944 deserves mention as the most unremittingly hostile and hate-filled of the group. The opening lines say it all: "We'll kill the lousy bastards and we'll knife them with a yell! / For there is only one good Japanese and he is dead as hell!" The writer of those words in "Kill The Bastards! (America's Hymn Of Hate)" (copyrighted unpublished, September 2, 1944) was Captain Robert M. Crawford, the man who five years earlier wrote the more famous opening words "Off we go into the wild blue yonder" for "The Army Air Corps" (Carl Fischer, 1939, 1942), the most popular armed forces musical tribute during the war (see chapter 8).

Songs lambasting just the Nazis or the combined Axis Powers were for the most part more varied and entertaining in their methods than the Japan-bashers. The playful tone of their titles reveals much about their content, which, more often than not, is ironic, satiric, or comic, although some of that comedy gets pretty dark. To fully grasp the fun, it helps to bear in mind that Hitler's family name was Shickelgruber and by trade he was a wallpaper hanger before becoming a dictator. Among the many playful titles are "Who's Gonna Bury Hitler (When The Onery [sic] Cuss

Is Dead?), "The Fuehrer's Got The Jitters," "Der Fuehrer Isn't Feeling Very Well," "The Russians Are Crushing The Prussians (Und Der Fuehrer Is Having The Fits)," "Judgment Day's A-Comin' (For That Shickelgruber Man)," and "Who Swiped Adolph's Paste Pot?"

The most prevalent mode of attack in Nazi-bashing songs is derisive humor, the lyrics usually firing salvos of often clever and always caustic jokes directly at Hitler and sometimes at Goebbels, Goering, and other cronies of Der Fuehrer. Some numbers employ outrageous puns, as in one of two Axis-bashers published by the Music War Committee in 1943, Milton Drake's "Der Fuehrer Isn't Feeling Very Well." Playing medical jargon off of military jargon, the song explains that Hitler's indigestion is from "something that he Soviet, no doubt! / Der Fuehrer has a pain in both his flanks / His underbelly's getting full of Yanks." Gags without puns in songs about Hitler's projected death, burial, and/or funeral include such lines about disposing of his body as "They placed him in a pig pen but the pigs all ran away, / Yes the pigs, the pigs refused to stay," in Abner Silver and Nick and Charles Kenny's "Hitler's Funeral March" (Lincoln Music, 1943), and "Dig his grave much deeper, / So he'll be near to where he's goin'," from Carson Robison's "Who's Gonna Bury Hitler" (Bob Miller, 1944). Don Baxter's record of the "Funeral March" is a *Hot Charts* Extra for December 1943.

But in nationwide popularity, one of the earliest of the Nazi-bashers chased circles around all the rest for the duration. Oliver Wallace, a Walt Disney studio songwriter, wrote his magnum opus "Der Fuehrer's Face" (Southern Music, 1942) for an animated propaganda short featuring Disney's irrepressible fowl that was originally titled *Donald Duck in Nutzi Land*. But with the enormous success of Spike Jones's record of "Der Fuehrer's Face" within weeks after its release, Disney changed the cartoon's title to that of Wallace's song ("Disney Song"). A front-page article in *Variety* on September 30, 1942, reported that Victor Records was caught off guard by the instant success of the Spike Jones disk and had to rush-order more pressings to fill the demands from distributors. New York's WNEW disk jockey Martin Block gave away free copies of the scarce "Der Fuehrer's Face" to anyone buying $50 or more worth of War Bonds. While not stating when Block began his offer, the article says that by September 28, his giveaway had raised $60,000 in bond sales, *Life* magazine adding that Block had sold $30,000 worth of bonds in just one evening with his "Der Fuehrer's Face" gimmick. *Billboard*'s record charts ranked the disk between 5th and 7th in national sales every week between October 24 and December 12, 1942, and in early January 1943 it still showed up at 9th. Because the number's fun lies almost as much in Spike Jones's wacky rendition as in Wallace's hilariously vulgar song, it's not surprising that sheet music sales did not fare quite as well, although

*Variety* charted "Der Fuehrer's Face" between 10th and 15th in weekly sales from November 11 to December 9, 1942, and noted that jukebox plays between October and November were strong, especially for a song that was almost impossible to dance to. When all was said and done, for Spike Jones and His City Slickers—at the time not yet well-known entertainers—"Der Fuehrer's Face" became a million-seller before 1942 was over (Visser).

Even without factoring in the Spike Jones performance, a number of elements in Wallace's writing account for the song's phenomenal success: its fun, infectious melody; its total and totally rude trashing of everything the Third Reich believed in; and its mix of fairly sophisticated satire with crude comedy, in which every "Heil!" is followed by that noise known variously as a Bronx cheer or the razzberries. Wallace wrote the lyric as if from the German point of view, and in Carl Grayson's vocal the "German" singing is a heavily accented and thoroughly outrageous parody. Typical of the song's numerous put-downs are "Ven Der Fuehrer says, 'Ve iss der Master Race,' / Ve Heil! (*Razz*) Heil! (*Razz*) Right in Der Fuehrer's Face," and "Ven Herr Goehring says: 'Dey'll neffer bomb dis place,' / Ve Heil! (*Razz*) Heil! (*Razz*) Right in Herr Goehring's face." Even the sheet music cover art embraces the tone of the song inside: a drawing of Donald Duck hurling a rotten tomato into Der Fuehrer's eye.

If indeed imitation is the sincerest form of flattery, other songwriters paid Oliver Wallace a high compliment by echoing his words and noises in their own Axis-bashers. Lee Pearl and Lou Shelley did it in "Now that I'm no Superman dey (*Razz*) right in my face" from "The Russians Are Crushing the Prussians (Und Der Fuehrer Is Having The Fits)" (Original Music, 1944), and the notable E. Y. Harburg and Sammy Fain did it in "But I get (shrug) and you get (pfft) right in the Fuehrer's Face" from "Shickelgruber" (copyrighted unpublished, June 16, 1943) in the MGM 1944 musical *Meet the People*. Performed in the film by Spike Jones and his wacky entourage, Harburg and Fain's piece was a long satiric production number in which a singer playing Mussolini aired his gripes to Hitler, as portrayed by a costumed and moustached chimpanzee (Shull 384). Amidst a field of Tin Pan Alley Axis-bashers consisting mostly of wisecracking humor, the only two to engage in more intricate and sophisticated satire were Irving Berlin's previously mentioned "Ve Don't Like It" and a song of mostly British origin in which the witty Axis-bashing is so subtle that many Americans may have missed it entirely. The ostensible thrust of Noel Coward's "Don't Let's Be Beastly To The Germans" (Chappell, 1943), with an additional verse for American audiences by Ira Gershwin, is that the Allies should treat the Germans kindly once we have won the war. But after each few lines of this seeming generosity, Coward hands the Germans a mighty slap in the face, usually via derogatory name-calling: "It was just those nasty Nazis who persuaded them to fight / And their Beethoven and Bach are really far worse than their bite / . . . Let's give them full air parity and treat the rats with charity, / But don't let's be beastly to the Hun." Rarely as subtle but far more popular were the satiric Axis-bashers not from Tin Pan Alley or London but from the almost unlikely realm of hillbilly music—and all one man's creation.

### "Get Your Gun And Come Along": Carson J. Robison, Grand Champion Axis-Basher

While Oliver Wallace's "Der Fuehrer's Face" was the single biggest-selling Axis-basher, noted hillbilly singer/songwriter Carson J. Robison wrote and recorded more, and more successful ones than any other professional songwriter. His method in over half of them is quite urbane satire, seemingly remarkable since Robison "may have had only a grade school education"; yet since the 1920s he had developed a well-deserved reputation as a "master at writing topical songs about natural disasters and news events," such as his 1925 "The John T. Scopes Trial (The Old Religion's Better After All)" (Birchfield 682). Robison wrote ten published Axis-bashers, of which six had some success with the public and also represent almost half of the thirteen Axis-bashers by *all* professional songsmiths to attain any popularity. Adding in Robison's wartime songs about national unity and home front support, his work, in terms of both quantity and popularity, is nearly equal to that of such mainstream Tin Pan Alleymen as Irving Berlin and Frank Loesser.

A rough chronology of Robison's ten Axis-bashers reveals his varied writing methods and the success of his work. The earliest, and one of the most popular, was "1942 Turkey In The Straw," already cited for deflating Mussolini's ego. In *Hot Charts* it ranks 46th in March 1942 and is an Extra from April through August. Robison alternates jokes at the expense of Hitler and the Japanese with outright name-calling, all styled like the square dance calls in the original "Turkey In The Straw": "Four hands round and ev'rybody shout / Skunk in the woodpile—gotta chase him out / Adolf Hitler bit off a chaw / Jam it down his throat with Turkey In The Straw." The skunk in a woodpile metaphor is what Robison used next for the Japanese, with glances at the other Axis Powers, in "Get Your Gun And Come Along (We're Fixin' To Kill A Skunk)" (Robbins, 1942). The song is a kind of "folk allegory" in which a grim-faced "Ol' Uncle Sam" is rounding up the neighbors to help him exterminate a skunk on his property: "A varmint's hangin' 'round my house a sneaky dirty feller / And the stripes that's runnin' down his back ain't white, in fact they're yeller." The number is clever but not at all funny as it makes its case for getting the skunk out of the woodpile and the Axis off the face of the earth. Both Robison's own recording and one by country singer Denver Darling are *Hot Charts* Extras for April 1942.

Also in 1942 Robison wrote the first two of several Axis-bashers in the form of ingenious and sophisticated "epistolary satires"—letters ostensibly written from one major player in the war to another and set to music, of course. These early ones were the matched set "Mussolini's Letter To Hitler" and "Hitler's Reply To Mussolini" (both Robbins, 1942). In addition to content both sharp and silly, what makes these and Robison's other epistolary satires so funny is that, musically, the letters are all in the frothy three-quarter rhythm of waltz time, which, along with hilarious orchestrations on his recordings, has the comic effect of trivializing the letter writers and what they are writing about. In his letter to Hitler, Mussolini is typically griping about everything from the lack of respect he's getting—"And I liked the old salute better— / Without their thumb to their nose"—to having nothing to wear—"P.S. Don't think I'm complaining / But my wardrobe is looking quite sad. / Can you spare me an old suit of Goering's / Maybe it won't smell too bad." Hitler, backed by the sounds of a typical Bavarian "oompah" band, in turn tells Mussolini that his letter gave him "the first laugh I've had in a year" and tries to make light of the Germans' rout by the Russians. Mussolini had asked Hitler for Great Britain, and Robison is incisively topical in Hitler's reply when he brings up Rudolf Hess's ill-fated solo flight to Scotland. Hess flew there supposedly to cut a deal with the British, but the trip netted Hess a crash landing, an arrest, and incarceration in Britain for the remainder of the war. Hitler writes Mussolini, "My promise to give you Great Britain / Is a promise I'll never forget / I've sent Rudolf Hess to get it / But I just haven't heard from him yet." (Robison would be back at Hess again in 1945.) Robison's own record of "Hitler's Reply" is a *Hot Charts* Extra for March 1942. His other 1942 Axis-basher was the derogatory, humorless, and unsuccessful "It's Just A Matter Of Time" (Bob Miller, 1942).

Robison took a break from Axis-bashing during 1943, returning to the task in 1944 with mixed results. Written in the manner of a traditional folk tune, the previously mentioned "Who's Gonna Bury Hitler" is a string of unkind and fairly predictable jokes about his grave, his burial clothes, and his tombstone. The only thing that distinguishes Robison's from other songs about Hitler's funeral is that none of the lines rhyme! That same year Robison wrote an uncharacteristic epistolary satire without a reply. Written by an unnamed American (or perhaps by "America") to General Tojo, "In Answer To Yours Of December Seventh" (Bob Miller, 1944) is a verbal reply to Tojo's calling on America by way of Pearl Harbor years earlier. The satire in this song is strident and filled with veiled threats to Tojo and Japan. The writer even says it's just a prefatory note letting Tojo know that the real reply "to be sent by air mail . . . may prove quite explosive." The tenor of the satire is especially mordant: "You really don't need to remember Pearl Harbor, / We will remember it for you, and how!" Despite the song's dark tone, Robison couldn't resist a purely comic crack at the butt of everyone's humor. The letter writer says he sent a copy to Hitler and "also sent one to your pal Mussolini, / But when it arrived he had changed his address"—Mussolini had been overthrown and arrested in July 1943. Whether too dark or not funny enough, "In Answer To Yours Of December Seventh" was not one of Robison's popular Axis-bashers.

But 1945 was a banner year for Robison. One of his funniest songs, "1945 Nursery Rhymes" (Bob Miller, 1944), combines parody with satire by stringing together familiar nursery melodies (plus "Yankee Doodle" and "Jingle Bells") with new lyrics appropriate to the Allies' clear superiority at the time. "Pop Goes The Weasel" becomes "From Newfoundland to Guadalcanal / The Yankees chase the Axis, / Root-i-toot-toot, they give 'em the boot, / (*pft!*) Goes the Axis!" Instead of "Oh Where, Oh Where, Has My Little Dog Gone," Hitler sings forlornly, "Oh, vere, oh, vere iss dot Rudolf Hess? Oh, vere, oh, vere can he be? / I sent him to England a long time ago, I vonder if he stayed for tea." Carson's recording had strong sales early in the year and is a *Hot Charts* Extra for March. For his Axis-bashing finale, Robison went out with a flourish and a double-whammy in another set of paired epistolary satires, "Hirohito's Letter To Hitler" and "Hitler's Last Letter To Hirohito," published together in the same sheet music by Bob Miller and sung by Robison back to back on the same Bluebird record. With Mussolini out of the picture, in the first song Japan's Emperor Hirohito is now cast in the role of the perpetual whiner and complainer, griping to Hitler about Eisenhower, MacArthur, the B-29, and Hitler's miscalculation when he told Hirohito that Americans "are all too complacent to fight": "But Yankees are very queer people / And we don't know just what to do. / My soldiers call out, 'Yanks, surrender!' / And they yell right back, 'Nuts to you!' In his reply, Hitler, faced with enough problems of his own, has neither patience nor sympathy for the embattled Hirohito, and his replies are viciously caustic. Hirohito had voiced his fear that because of recent reverses his ancestors were laughing at him, at which Hitler fairly sneers, "You say you hear ancestors laughing / But I think you hear the Chinese." And with the cruelest irony of all, Hitler offers Hirohito a way to feel better: "Why don't you review your great navy? / 'Twill boost your morale I am sure, / Just borrow a suit from a diver, / And you should have an int'resting tour." As for himself, Hitler tells Hirohito he's expecting the worst, in which case, "I'll hike to my fort in the mountains, / If Himmler don't bump me off first." These two numbers resonate with some of the darkest and clever-est humor and satire in all of Robison's Axis-bashers, and both are *Hot Charts* Extras for May and June 1945.

A fair question about not just Carson Robison's but all Axis-bashers is why were they written and who was their intended audience? They weren't propaganda. The United States did not broadcast Axis-bashers to demoralize the Axis countries the way Germany's Charlie and His Or-chestra blared Nazi messages in "propaganda swing" to the Allies. I would suggest that these comic, satiric, and sometimes simply scurrilous songs were meant, in a topsy-turvy way, to build morale for the home front by tearing down the Axis. Americans laughing at their jokes and sneering with their sneers could vicariously share in bashing the Axis, and, with Donald Duck, hurl some rotten tomatoes of their own.

# "There's An F. D. R. In Freedom"

## The War's Faces and Places

Throughout the American twentieth century, popular songs about celebrities and current events are pretty rare and very scattered, so don't be surprised if no familiar bells are rung by titles like "Teddy Da Roose" (praising Theodore Roosevelt), "Lucky Lindy" (the most popular of several salutes to Charles Lindbergh's solo flight from Long Island to France), "Joltin' Joe DiMaggio," "Elvis For President," or "Hoppy, Gene, and Me" (about cowboy stars William "Hopalong Cassidy" Boyd, Gene Autry, and Roy Rogers, the "Me" who recorded the song). Celebrating famous people in song sometimes has caught the public's fleeting fancy, but no such pieces, by their very nature, ever had much chance of lingering on in the collective musical memory. Between 1941 and 1945 Tin Pan Alley produced thirty-eight songs treating personalities and events of World War II, more celebrity songs than in any other comparable period during the twentieth century, including World War I and its handful of songs about General John "Fighting Jack" Pershing. No numbers about prominent figures during World War II became widely popular. One number about an event had success, as did two about war heroes unknown to most people until they were celebrated in songs—one of these becoming one of the biggest hits of the war.

The primary impetus to write celebrity songs at any time appears to be the awe public figures inspire in songwriters and the public. For the most part, the lyrics extolling public figures during World War II implicitly hint at the songwriters' motive for writing and the intention of their songs. The motive often seems to be a desire to show their personal participation in the war effort through songs telling the world that they stand behind the president or admire and support the deeds of military men. The chief intention of celebrity songs vis-à-vis the public was to build morale in a totally different way from Axis-bashers. While Axis-bashing made the public feel positive about America by putting down the enemy, celebrity songs were designed to express for Americans their good feelings about the country's strong and capable civilian and military leaders in the war years.

### "Hats Off To MacArthur!": Military Celebrities, and Civilian

Despite their best intentions, some songs in praise of famous men became the embarrassing victims of bad timing, the fortunes of war, or, in one case, tasteless writing. To take that misguided piece first, a songwriter named Edward P. Carter sometime late in 1942 wrote a piece paying tribute not to the usual subjects (FDR, Churchill) but to "Gen'ralissimo Chiang Kai-Shek" (George Lomas, 1942), president of the Republic of China and supreme commander of the forces in the Chinese theatre of war. Unfortunately, the lyric of this unusual tribute was filled with offensive imitations of Chinese-American speech that serve more to denigrate the man (and all Chinese) than to extol his role in the war: "He no foolee around / . . . Him the little man Japs respect / He now goee to town, He Yokohama bound."

Some songs about General of the Army Douglas MacArthur became victims of the accident of when they were written, published, and recorded vis-à-vis actual events in MacArthur's career and the war in the Pacific. Lee Wilson's "There Stands A Man!" (Modern Music, 1942) was tripped up by the specificity of its lyrics relative to the date it was published. Monthly issues of lyric magazines hit the newsstands during the last week or two of the previous month. "There Stands a Man!" was reprinted in the April 1942 issue of *Radio Song Hits,* so it had to have been written and published, at the latest, by February or early March. Events made success impossible for this song, which calls MacArthur "The hero of Corregidor and Bataan" and declares, "we know in our hearts he will never give in." The regrettable fact was that the Japanese assault on Luzon drove MacArthur to declare Manila an "open city" on December 26, 1941, at which point his troops, both Philippine and American, began withdrawing to Bataan Peninsula and Corregidor Island. On April 9, 1942, the American forces on Bataan surrendered to the Japanese, and on May 6 Corregidor fell and General Jonathan Wainwright—MacArthur's replacement—surrendered all Americans in the Philippines to Japan. Well before then, on March 17, MacArthur reached Australia to take command of the Allied forces there (*Life's* 99, 100).

Bad timing put on hold for a few months another MacArthur song, the number's infectiously jaunty tune and upbeat, sanguine lyrics coming along at an inappropriate time. *Variety* reported on its chart of radio plugs on March 25, 1942, that Ira Schuster, Paul Cunningham, and Leonard Whitcup's "Hats Off To MacArthur! (And Our Boys Down There)" (Paull-Pioneer, 1942) was broadcast eight times on network-affiliated stations between Monday, March 16, and Sunday, March 22. But by then MacArthur, ordered to Australia by President Roosevelt, had already turned over the Filipino command to Wainwright with his famous parting "I shall return" and was in charge of the Allied troops in Melbourne (Calvocoressi and Wint 718; *Life's* 99). On Tuesday, March 24, Dick Robertson's orchestra, with himself on vocal, recorded "Hats Off To MacArthur!" for Decca. The ASCAP flap stopped radio plugs the following week and Robertson's record didn't sell well enough to make any contemporary or retrospective charts. With MacArthur not looking terribly heroic while sitting fairly idly in Australia as the Philippines situation worsened, the public had little interest in the song. But on June 17, *Variety* noted that "Hats Off To MacArthur!" had resurfaced, airing eight times on network radio during the previous week, which was the week following America's decisive naval victory at the Battle of Midway. Once again ground troops of the United States and other Allies were preparing to mount new offensives in the Pacific—in a word, a far more opportune time for a number about MacArthur. Not that it became a genuine hit, though its words and music by three long-time Alleymen have the earmarks of one, and Robertson's recording is quite splendid, notable for an intricate clarinet obbligato soaring above and behind both the vocal and instrumental sections of the disk. The tune of the very brief number is original yet singable, and its lyrics vivid and direct, as in the rhyming nouns that other writers would later use often to characterize the unity and unanimity of Americans: "From the stoker to the broker, they are shouting ev'rywhere: / HATS OFF TO MACARTHUR and our boys down there."

Even earlier than these two songs, another musical tribute to the general got nowhere just about as fast, despite some high-powered national hype and recordings by two major bands. Early in 1942 Buck Ram wrote "Fightin' Doug MacArthur" (Harms, 1942), a swing tune for MacArthur with words like a football pep song: "He's the one who slapped the Japs right down to their size (Hit 'em, hit 'em, hit 'em, hit 'em)," which MacArthur had *not* done by the time Ram wrote that. Still, it caught the eye of black bandleader Lucky Millinder, who, it's said, played no instrument and didn't read music. (Neither did Kay Kyser.) With Trevor Bacon on vocal, Millinder recorded "Fightin' Doug MacArthur" on February 18, 1942, with Bob Miller's "Were Gonna Have To Slap The Dirty Little Jap" on the flip side. On February 28, drummer Gene Krupa's orchestra with

Anita O'Day singing cut a very different but equally supercharged disk of Ram's celebratory jump tune. According to an ad in *Variety* on March 11, 1942, syndicated columnist Walter Winchell hyped Millinder's disk "in 800 Newspapers" on February 16, *before it had even been recorded*, saying "Get a recording called '*FIGHTIN' DOUG MACARTHUR*' as done by Lucky Millinder's crew" (42). *Variety*'s chart for April 1 notes six plugs for "Fightin' Doug" the previous week, but the plugs, Winchell's column, and records by two top bands amounted to a mere blip on the radar screen of public song awareness.

No greater success came to the remaining two songs about MacArthur in 1942, after which, incidentally, there were no more. Nat Burton and Walter Kent, writers of the mega-hit "The White Cliffs Of Dover," wrote "Here's To You, MacArthur" (Shapiro, Bernstein, 1942). One honest glance at current events suggests Burton wrote the lyric after MacArthur left the Philippines. The song says the country is behind the general in good fortune and bad, since he's made of the same mettle as his father, a hero of the Spanish-American War: "Rise or fall, we'll sing your praises throughout our history / For it's men like you that make us great / You've got the stuff and you're just as tough as your dad in Ninety Eight." Weekly NBC radio entertainers Gene Carroll and Glenn Rowell wrote a song collection published by Paull-Pioneer in 1942 as *Gene and Glenn's "Morale Songs,"* a group of little numbers mostly encouraging home front support (see chapter 9) but also including the song "Stonewall MacArthur." Lines like "There's a man of fighting stock / . . . Who doesn't know what surrender means" suggest that the song was written before MacArthur shipped out of Luzon and left Wainwright to do the surrendering. But the rest of the song would have had relevance throughout the war, depicting the general as "A fighting man who'll teach Japan / To stay in its own back yard." The public didn't buy this song any more than the other MacArthur tributes, but its lyric contains a rare pun in militant or patriotic writing to elicit more smiles than groans: "Stonewall MacArthur, you'll show 'em what a Yankee dude'll do."

Tin Pan Alley songs about General Dwight David Eisenhower fared no better, and as far as I can ascertain there were only two. Before Eisenhower's most famous command of the Allied landings at Normandy on D-Day, June 6, 1944, "Ike" commanded the successful invasion of French North Africa on November 8, 1942 (Ambrose 374). For this James Cavanaugh, John Redmond, and Nat Simon called him "The Man Of The Hour, General Eisenhower" (Joe Davis, 1942), praising Ike's dogged determination: "He's on the move now and really in the groove now, / . . . He'll never stop until he's in Berlin!" The only other Eisenhower song came late in the war and isn't a celebration but, as its title makes explicit, "A Prayer For General Eisenhower And His Men" (Mutual Music Society,

1945). During the war Tin Pan Alley composers occasionally teamed with amateur lyricists on war-related songs. Some may have been friends of the composers, but more often publishers engaged composers to write music for lyrics the publishing house received and thought worthy of becoming songs. It's not clear which scenario this was, but Lawrence Stock, composer of the standards "Blueberry Hill" and "You're Nobody Till Somebody Loves You," set one Alice Menaker's lyric to music, a lyric part prayer and part visual gimmick. The sheet music cover is a photo of Ike talking to combat troops, but the lyric, a heartfelt prayer for victory, never mentions him by name. Instead, in the sheet music a box encloses the first letter of each line in a sequence spelling E-I-S-E-N-H-O-W-E-R. The question is "Why?" Hearing the song one couldn't even perceive this; only looking at the lyrics as printed in the Mutual Music edition makes this obvious. Menaker's gimmick had nothing to do with a song for singing. Her poem's visual element would have been more effective published in a magazine.

America's two most prominent career soldiers weren't the only ranking officers in the armed forces celebrated in popular song. Two of the navy's most acclaimed admirals also had their musical moment in the sun, but in an amusing and roundabout way—and both in a single song by another naval officer who was also an ASCAP songwriter. Gordon Beecher (born William Gordon Beecher Jr.), a graduate of the U.S. Naval Academy and the National War College, was a captain by the time he wrote the lyrics to "Nimitz And Halsey And Me" (Robbins, 1945), with music by Ralph Barnhart. During the war Beecher commanded a destroyer squadron, fought at Pearl Harbor, Iwo Jima, and Okinawa, was awarded the Legion of Merit, and wrote songs. After thirty-four years in the navy he retired in 1955 at the rank of vice admiral. "Nimitz And Halsey And Me" was the last of several patriotic, militant, and Axis-bashing songs Beecher wrote, its late date confirmed by the line "We hear that the fightin' is finished." The number is a kind of offhand compliment to Admirals Chester Nimitz and William F. Halsey, whose photos figure prominently on the sheet music's cover, along with a drawing of an enlisted sailor. The song is primarily comic Axis-bashing. The lyric makes it plain that Captain Beecher had neither the arrogance nor the disrespect for his superior officers to have the "Me" in the title refer to himself. Rather, the premise is that Patsy McCoy, a cocky Irish-American sailor from New York, is bragging "In a well-censored note" to the folks at home how the war in the Pacific "is under control" thanks to "Nimitz and Halsey And Me," and there's a lot of truth in his crediting much of that situation to the first two gentlemen at least. In a sense the number is a celebrity song praising the two admirals' achievements, but the stuff of most lines is militant Japan-bashing: "Me and Halsey and Nimitz / Are havin' a wonderful time /

What we ain't uprootin' by bombin' and shootin' / Would fit on the face of a dime." However roundabout the compliment to the admirals, "Nimitz And Halsey And Me" is the most entertaining song about any ranking members of the armed forces.

It's only natural that when celebrating wartime civilians, most of Tin Pan Alley's efforts were reserved for the public figure most loved by Americans, President Franklin Delano Roosevelt. But the Alley had enough love left over to salute two other men equally cherished by the home front and our fighting forces overseas. These men's occupations were peripheral to the business of fighting the war, but they brought to what they did a dedication and charisma that made them central to the morale of soldiers and civilians alike: singer Bing Crosby and war correspondent Ernie Pyle. Bing's hits during the war ranged from feel-good novelties like "Deep in the Heart of Texas" through romantic ballads such as "Sunday, Monday, Or Always" to that perennial piece of seasonal nostalgia, "White Christmas." His warm, mellow bass-baritone and effortless, casual delivery made Crosby the war years' vocal equivalent of comfort food for countless Americans at home and millions of GIs abroad. Gene Vincent, a minor songwriter of the time (and not the same Gene Vincent who wrote and recorded the rockabilly hit "Be-Bop-A-Lula" in 1956), captured the effect Crosby's singing had on servicemen in "Bing In A Blackout" (A-1 Music, 1943). The set-up is that on a stormy night in the mid-Atlantic, a sailor relieved from duty on a cruiser protecting a convoy goes below. He has a cup of coffee and turns on the radio. In the chorus the sailor reacts and ruminates as he listens to Crosby sing: "It was Bing in a Blackout, / That brought me peace of mind, / . . . My heart was warm / Although outside the sting of the cold was strong," ending with "When he begins to croon, / It's like Christmas in June."

Newspaperman Ernie Pyle endeared himself both to stateside Americans and to mud-caked, combat-weary foot-soldiers by bringing the war down to a personal level from the lofty heights of international politics and battle strategies that were incomprehensible to the average layman (and most soldiers too). Instead, Pyle wrote about the day-to-day routines of America's infantrymen from what he called his "worm's eye view." He "admired combat pilots but positively revered long-suffering infantrymen; they were cold, dirty, apprehensive, lonely, understanding, funny— and routinely brave" (Gale 18). Through his idiosyncratically terse, vivid prose, Pyle for nearly all of the war gave the world his very personal picture of "GI Joe," the U.S. infantryman. So much a part of the war was this newspaperman that in July 1945 United Artists released the film variously known as *Ernie Pyle's The Story of G.I. Joe* or simply *The Story of GI Joe,* in which Pyle, played by Burgess Meredith, figured as a central character as well as the narrator. In a very real way, the motion picture was a posthumous tribute to the man, since Ernie Pyle had been killed by a Japanese sniper's bullet on April 18 while covering the Okinawa and Iwo Jima invasions. (The film is about earlier events and does not include Pyle's death.) Like all Hollywood films, this one needed a musical score, and perhaps even a song. Stepping up to do double duty by writing both was the first woman to compose and conduct for films, Ann Ronell, one of the better women songwriters of the time. Her two best-known songs tell a lot about Ronell's versatility: "Who's Afraid Of The Big Bad Wolf" from the Walt Disney cartoon *The Three Little Pigs* and the enduring popular and jazz classic originally recorded by Paul Whiteman in 1932, "Willow Weep For Me." For the Ernie Pyle movie, Ronell wrote a musical tribute, "The Ernie Pyle Infantry March" (Picture Music, 1945). The song is unusual on two counts; it celebrates the U.S. Infantry at the same time it celebrates Pyle; and it's the only celebrity song of the war years to memorialize a public figure after his death. Ronell's clipped and succinct summation of Pyle's reportage is a perfectly apt tribute to this singular journalist: "Not for glory, / Ernie Pyle told the story, / Told how the Infantry goes in there / Brave men crawling, where steel rain is falling."

At least eight songs celebrating President Roosevelt came out of Tin Pan Alley during the war years, most of them in 1942. The two compliments to FDR by Hispanic writers briefly mentioned in chapter 2 naturally took a Pan-American or Good Neighbor Policy approach. Sergio De Karlo, who wrote the music and his own English lyrics for "Mister Franklin D.," proclaimed, "With you America will win a great victory," and assured Roosevelt that "In gay Latin America / Your good neighbors strongly stand / To hold instead of a guitar, a gun, / And fight for Uncle Sam." The English text for Xavier Cugat's "Viva Roosevelt!" was by New Yorker Al Stillman, writing from a Latin American point of view. He calls the president "a real amigo" and uses a conga line metaphor for the twenty-one Pan-American countries getting behind Roosevelt in the war effort, shamelessly punning on the name of the dance: "Latin nations, / Take your stations, right behind the leader / . . . We're gonna follow you Franklin D. / Begin the Panamericonga / Fall in the line of Liberty." One expression of support for FDR from the African American songwriting community was lyricist Andy Razaf's "Three Cheers For Our President" (Joe Davis Music, 1942), with music by white publisher/composer Davis. The lines "Let's remind him, we're behind him, / Pledging all our loyalty" refers to all Americans, but that "we're" could also be one of Razaf's many subtle references to American blacks in his wartime lyrics. And the line in which Razaf calls FDR "Friend of all humanity" suggests that he meant all ethnicities and races, including his own, though Eleanor in fact did more than Franklin to improve race relations in America.

Two of the other songs about FDR in 1942 were Tin Pan Alley pro-am efforts. Early in the year, the Alley's frequent collaborators Vic Mizzy and Irving Taylor teamed with professional songstress but amateur lyricist Mary Small to write "Thank You, Mister President" (Santly-Joy-Select, 1942). The sheet music says the number was "Introduced by Mary Small and respectfully dedicated to the Committee for the President's Birthday," Roosevelt having turned sixty on January 30 of that year. Small's song with Mizzy and Taylor obliquely references FDR's leadership during the still-young war by thanking him "for all the hope and strength you give." For the same occasion, incidentally, bandleader Glenn Miller asked Irving Berlin to write a number, the result of which was "The President's Birthday Ball" (Irving Berlin Inc., 1942), premiered by Miller and his orchestra on January 8. The number, however, is not war-connected but rather a very explicit fundraising pitch for the March of Dimes of the Infantile Paralysis Foundation (see Kimball and Emmet 374). The second pro-am effort involved the collaboration of an apparently amateur songsmith, Sig. G. Hecht, with the long-time professional husband-and-wife team of Alma Sanders and Monte Carlo (no kidding!), best known for some songs in the "Irish genre" like "That Tumble Down Shack In Athlone," back in the 1910s and '20s. This threesome came up with the prayerful "God Bless Our President" (Mills Music, 1942), which, while not memorable, has a tone of quietly sincere reverence for Roosevelt: "many heads in silence bend; / A million lips a prayer will send." Also in 1942 Nationwide Songs, a BMI affiliate, published Clarence Kelley, Frank B. Stanton, and Bob Matthews's "There's An F-D-R In Freedom." According to *Variety* it got plugged on the networks five times in the week prior to January 27, 1943, and fifteen times the week after that. As its title implies, the song virtually equates Roosevelt with the American ideal of freedom— "There's an F. D. R. in freedom, we have both in the U. S. A."—and proclaims "he'll bring freedom to the whole wide world." Except for this song, every tribute to FDR in 1942 had at least one established professional on the writing team, yet none had widespread popularity.

In 1943, two more songs about Roosevelt appeared, both by professionals and both very different from those that came before. Each dealt with FDR's participation in a specific event that helped chart the course of the war or present ideals for the world after the war. For the musical revue *The New Meet the People,* composer Jay Gorney and his two usual lyricists in the '40s, Henry Myers and Edward Eliscu, wrote "The Four Freedoms" (Mills, 1943), a piece about the historic meeting between FDR and Winston Churchill that took place on ships in Placentia Bay off the coast of Newfoundland on August 12, 1941. During that meeting the two heads of state framed the document outlining postwar principles for peace and freedom known as the Atlantic Charter, which was later the basis for the United Nations Charter. As we will see, in some ways the song is lousy history, but thanks to lyricists Myers and Eliscu's penchant for playfulness, the number depicts Churchill and Roosevelt's first meeting in a casual way that is eminently entertaining as well as respectful of the men and serious about "The Four Freedoms." "Said Mister Roosevelt to Mister Churchill: 'Let me have your fountain pen. / What we ought to write is something like your Magna Carta / Something for humanity, so for a starter what ya say we call it the Atlantic Charter?'" History starts getting skewed when the song credits the Atlantic Charter as the source of the famous Four Freedoms—freedom of speech and expression, freedom of religion or "of every person to worship God in his own way," freedom from fear, and freedom from want. Actually, these were first enumerated in FDR's address to Congress on January 6, 1941, more than eight months before Roosevelt and Churchill met. The song says Churchill and Roosevelt jointly coined all four while they "were sitting on a boat." The Atlantic Charter itself contains only two of the four freedoms when it speaks of a postwar peace that will allow people globally to "live out their lives in freedom from fear and want." Also, Myers and Eliscu have FDR tell Churchill, "We will meet in Casablanca in the early Spring," something they in fact didn't do until the winter of 1943, which the lyricists must have known.

The team responsible for the enormously popular peace-and-ease hit "When The Lights Go On Again (All Over The World)," Bennie Benjamin, Eddie Seiler, and Sol Marcus, also looked to better times after the war in a celebrity song and love song oddly rolled into one. Its title, "When They Met In Casablanca" (Words and Music, 1943), sounds as if it will be about Bogart and Bergman in the film, when in fact it's about Franklin and Winston's less romantic meeting in that exotic locale. This is seen immediately on the sheet music cover from the silhouettes of the two statesmen flanking a man and woman looking at a map of Morocco. If the Churchill/FDR meeting off Newfoundland had been about ideals and principles, the Casablanca Conference was about priorities and strategies for the war itself. They determined to concentrate on Europe initially, first through Sicily and Italy in 1943 rather than an immediate invasion on the French coast, largely leaving Pacific operations against the Japanese to American forces for the time being. But they also agreed to do this without sacrificing U.S. participation in the European theatre (see *Life's*, 147). What the public most remembered from the conference was Roosevelt's apparently offhand remark about settling only for "unconditional surrender" from the Axis, the phrase soon becoming a great morale booster and rallying cry for the Allies. Benjamin, Seiler, and Marcus's song is short on historical detail and long on emotion. A GI overseas sings to his girl back home, "When they met in Casablanca / They brought new hope / . . . I felt right then / That, soon after Casablanca, / I'd be with you again," evoking the confidence Americans and the other Allies had in Churchill and Roosevelt. "When They Met In Casablanca" was the last musical celebration of the war years' public figures in conjunction with specific events, but from Pearl Harbor to the Japanese surrender a few songs also commemorated some historic events themselves.

### "Cheer Up, Blue Hawaii": Commemorating Events of the War

For decades before Pearl Harbor, the Hawaiian Islands had inspired legions of popular songs, from silly novelty numbers like Irving Berlin's 1916 "I'm Down In Honolulu Looking Them Over" to languid love songs like Harry Owens's 1937 "Sweet Leilani," which Bing Crosby crooned in the movie musical *Waikiki Wedding* and on a million-selling Decca disk. Indeed, with the kind of irony only hindsight offers, just a few months before the Japanese attack inspired Sammy Kaye and Don Reid's "Remember Pearl Harbor," Sammy and Billy Kaye (relationship to Sammy unclear) had written the lyrically romantic "Hawaiian Sunset" (Republic, 1941). Kaye and Reid's "Remember Pearl Harbor" wasn't a song about the event; it was a battle cry of retaliation that employed its title phrase the way past wars had used "Remember the Alamo" and "Remember the *Maine*."

Some songs about Pearl Harbor were styled as romantic ballads commemorating the event not just immediately after it happened but also later in the war. Although Tin Pan Alley songwriters were responsible for five of these six Pearl Harbor songs, most at best are of historical interest for one reason or another. All except one are mediocre lamentations over December 7 using similar language; all also offer some hope to the once tranquil islands. And these songs were as unsuccessful as they were mediocre. Mills Music, publisher of Alfred Bryan, Willie Raskin, and Gerald Marks's "We'll Always Remember Pearl Harbor" (Mills, 1941), tacitly admitted the song's failure in an ad for some of its publications (including two other war-related numbers) on page 38 of *Variety* on February 4, 1942. In addition to hyping its sheet music, Mills's ad listed available recordings of three songs, but none for "We'll Always Remember Pearl Harbor," obviously because no one had recorded it! The ad calls the song "*A Warm, Beautiful Ballad*," but it's also a peculiar one, especially since it was presumably written for the broad spectrum of people on America's Protestant, Jewish, and Catholic home front. Its first chorus ends with the very parochial lines "Our lips will be saying 'Pearl Harbor' / On each bead of our Rosary." Al Bryan must have been Catholic; Raskin and Marks sure weren't! But, more to the point, perhaps the song's parochialism kept some performers and recording companies away from it.

Other early lyrical commiserations with Hawaii include Meredith

Willson's "Remember Hawaii" (Mayfair Music, 1942), which says little more to the islands than "For you each heart is praying, / For you the world is saying, / We will REMEMBER HAWAII," and Bobby Worth's "Cheer Up, Blue Hawaii" (Greene-Revel, 1942). Worth's title clearly traded on the ongoing popularity of Leo Robin and Ralph Rainger's Academy Award–winning "Blue Hawaii" from 1937, which, like "Sweet Leilani," Bing Crosby popularized in *Waikiki Wedding* and on a Decca record. Of course Worth's "blue" meant something very different from its sense in the original song, his single message being "Tho' your golden sands are grey / . . . It won't be long till we are there. / So, cheer up, blue Hawaii / Though steel guitars are silent today." Arthur Freed and Nacio Herb Brown were songwriters mostly for Hollywood (Freed was a producer as well); their best-known song together is probably "Singin' In The Rain." In "We'll Meet Again In Honolulu" (Variety Music, 1943), they depicted a vision of a redeemed world after the war. The idea of the number is that "Though the song has gone from Honolulu," after the war "It will sing again a happy melody" and "We will meet again in Honolulu / When ev'ry heart is free."

The one standout among Pearl Harbor commemorations, not for its popular success so much as for its forthright content, came from hillbilly music. During the war years country singer/songwriter Fred Rose and the acclaimed Roy Acuff formed Acuff-Rose music publishers, which became the foundation for Nashville's later preeminence as one of the epicenters of the American music industry. The two collaborated on numerous songs for Acuff and others to perform and record, and Rose also wrote many on his own, including "Cowards Over Pearl Harbor" (Acuff-Rose, 1943). Not Axis-bashing or a militant war song, Rose's piece looks back at Pearl Harbor from a distance of nearly two years, assessing the sneak attack as "A coward's desire" that materialized into "hawks of destruction, / Piloted by disciples of hate." In an unusual stroke of songwriting, the number ends by looking at the event not from the American standpoint but from inside the consciences of the Japanese who carried out the attack: "Oh what will they say to all of their children, / And how can they look themselves in the face; / . . . They must go down in mortal disgrace." Like so many hillbilly pieces, Rose's song pulled no punches as it sang of Pearl Harbor not from a military standpoint but from a moral and ethical one.

About a month and a half before Pearl Harbor, on October 31, 1941, a German U-boat in the North Atlantic torpedoed and sank an American destroyer on escort duty with a convoy taking supplies to Britain. The *Reuben James* thus became the first U.S. Navy ship sunk by hostile action in World War II, even before America had entered the war. In the terse, unsentimental style of so many narrative folk songs, Woody Guthrie memorialized the calamity in the now classic "Sinking of the *Reuben James,*" repeatedly bringing the event down to the personal level in its refrain of "What was their names, tell me what was their names / Did you have a friend on the good *Reuben James?*" It's unclear just when Guthrie wrote the piece, but it had to have been long before his first recording of it on April 25, 1944, which itself wasn't released until it appeared on the Folkways LP *Bound for Glory* in 1956 (Logsdon 13). Presumably, Guthrie would have sung it in live or radio performances during the war years.

Besides Guthrie's song, a few others were written and published about the European theatre of war, but songs about places and events in the Pacific were more prevalent. The card catalogues of the U.S. Copyright Office contain registration slips for literally dozens of songs called "D-Day," as might be expected since the Allied landings at Normandy on June 6, 1944, constituted one of the most impressive and strategically vital events of the war. Yet, as far as I can tell, only one song of that title was ever recorded and then only on an electrical transcription for radio broadcast, not for a commercially available record. This "D Day" (no hyphen) has words and music by Nat Cole and was recorded at the C. P. MacGregor Studios in Los Angeles during July 1944 by the King Cole Trio with Nat "King" Cole on vocal and piano (Teubig 89). (It was released commercially only much later on the Intersound CD *Swing Out to Victory!*—along with the misinformation that Cole recorded it in October 1943.) It's a jump tune, and his trio's jazz styling supports Cole's words, which combine celebratory, cautionary, and hortatory messages in one short lyric. It first declares there "never was a finer sight" than our boys hitting the beaches at Normandy, but then it cautions Americans that to defeat the Axis "It'll take more than a weekend, so let's be patient and calm," and it concludes by reminding the home front that "We're in it too," urging listeners to "buy those bonds, and I do mean you!" This is a good example of the numerous wartime songs of every kind that worked in a War Bond pitch, usually at the end. On July 5, 1944, Dorsey Brothers Music, the bandleader brothers' publishing firm, placed a half-page ad in *Variety* to plug a "*STIRRING!—TIMELY!* . . . TRULY GREAT BALLAD," Don "Remember Pearl Harbor" Reid and Irving Miller's "The Bells of Normandy (Are Ringing Again)," a song celebrating the Allies retaking of Normandy from the Germans (31). Despite the effort and expense of the Dorseys' ad, the number rang few bells with the American public and was rarely heard thereafter.

The last and most entertaining number dealing with the war in Europe is one of those songs that led writers on World War II to decide what it was about just from the title, not the lyrics. In *Don't You Know There's a War On?* Richard Lingeman states that Hal Block and Bob Musel's "The U. S. A. By Day And The R. A. F. By Night" (Paramount Music,

1944) was "the first song ever written about a bombing pattern" (215), words echoed verbatim by Kathleen E. R. Smith (29). In fact, the number applauds the heavy air strikes on Germany by Britain's Royal Air Force and the Army Air Force of the United States, specifically the strikes on the Ruhr that began on March 5, 1943, and the saturation bombing of Hamburg that started on July 24. But what's so entertaining about the number is that it celebrates these air attacks with the sardonic humor of an Axis-basher. Several members of the German High Command, from Hitler and Himmler to Rommel and Von Runstedt, are getting frantic over the results of the bombings day and night. The song gets specific, observing that Germany's strategically important industrial area "Der Ruhr is such a shambles" and having one officer ask the great arms manufacturer, "Krupp, why are you worried, / What is your fact'ry's plight?" Krupp replies, "It was standing here one day, then it disappeared one night." Indirectly praising the British and American airmen through the comically horror-stricken remarks of the German officers is a device unique in all World War II songwriting. Of course, with the number's roots in Axis-bashing, Block and Musel couldn't let go without getting in the inevitable Il Duce joke, when Goering tries to explain the air supremacy of the British and Americans over his Luftwaffe, "They paid us back ten bombs for one then threw in Mussolini."

Back in the Pacific, songs were much more serious—triumphant, but serious, in accordance with the events. On February 19, 1945, the 3rd, 4th, and 5th Marine Divisions hit the beach on Iwo Jima, an island that had to be taken if B-29 bombing missions to Japan were to succeed. After twenty-six days of hard fighting and an enormous death and casualty toll among the American troops, on March 16 the U.S. forces captured the island and the few remaining Japanese, about 1 percent of Iwo Jima's 22,800 defenders (*Life's* 338). Most Americans born after the war assume that the raising of Old Glory on Mt. Suribachi signaled the American victory on Iwo Jima, when in fact that handful of courageous Marines and one Navy man climbed up the mountain and raised the flag on February 23, just four days after the battle had begun. That notable flag raising was commemorated immediately in Joe Rosenthal's famous photograph and not long after in C. C. Beall's equally famous painting based on it; ultimately the moment was given permanence in Felix W. De Weldon's sculpture near the Arlington National Cemetery. But shortly after the event there were also some musical tributes to Iwo Jima, notably one song each by prominent hillbilly and Tin Pan Alley songwriters, the hillbilly number again getting the most public attention. Alleymen Harold Adamson and Jimmy McHugh's "There's A New Flag On Iwo Jima" (Leeds, 1945) both celebrates the victory and memorializes its costly toll on American lives, as does country songwriters Bob Wills and Cliff Johnson's "Stars

And Stripes On Iwo Jima" (Hill and Range Songs, 1945), but with much less overt emotion than the hillbilly number. For example, whereas Adamson's lyric says "They're immortal the boys who died there / Let's give thanks to them in ev'ry pray'r," Wills and Johnson's song contains heart-tuggers like "When the Yanks raised the STARS AND STRIPES ON IWO JIMA ISLE, / There were tears in their hearts tho' they smiled." Wills himself and the Sons of the Pioneers recorded "Stars and Stripes on Iwo Jima," Wills's record a *Hot Charts* Extra for June through October 1945, with the Sons of the Pioneers joining him in September and October.

Though Harold Adamson and Jimmy McHugh's Iwo Jima song didn't make waves, they had a huge hit in a number they wrote just after the war that was in part about a wartime event. Perry Como first sang their jive-talking swing tune with the hip but innocuous title "Dig You Later (A-Hubba-Hubba-Hubba)" (Twentieth Century Music, 1945) in the 20th Century-Fox picture *Doll Face.* On October 13, 1945, Como recorded it for Victor with Russ Case's orchestra, the Satisfiers, and an uncredited girl soloist who may have been part of that singing group. By the last two weeks of 1945 the record had soared to become 6th and then 5th top-seller on *Billboard*'s weekly charts and 9th in jukebox plays, and the number's popularity carried well into 1946. I won't try to claim Adamson's lyric accounted for the song's appeal, but at least the first chorus didn't turn people off to the song. The early part of "Dig You Later" gloats smugly and, in terms of 1945 sensibilities, comically over dropping the atomic bombs on Hiroshima and Nagasaki. The lyric is a dialogue; in reply to the Satisfiers asking in chorus, "Say, whatever happened to the Japanese?" Como replies in part, "It was mighty smoky over Tokio," and goes on to say, "A friend of mine in a 'B-twenty nine' dropped another load for luck, / As he flew away, he was heard to say, A-hubba-hubba-hubba, yuk! yuk!" "Dig You Later" was the only song celebrating a wartime event or celebrity to become a genuine hit.

### "Praise The Lord And Pass The Ammunition": Singing of Unsung Heroes

While examining the World War II sheet music in the John Hay Library and the Library of Congress, I came across quite a few amateur songs about actual men in the service written by a relative (usually a mother or father), almost always with a photo of the serviceman on the cover. Most of the numbers admired or thanked the man for fighting for his country, and a few praised him for a heroic action, while far too many others memorialized his death in combat. These songs were often painful to read, as the writers so publicly gave voice to their grief in elegies to a loved one killed in action. Nearly all amateur songs were published by small local publishers or privately by their authors or composers, so no such numbers reached far enough beyond the writer's circle of family and friends to make a public hero of a private one, but each piece served its writer well as a cathartic outlet for feelings about a loved one, whether of pride and admiration or of loss and sorrow. Tin Pan Alley turned out a number of songs paying tribute to fictional or "generic" GIs (see the last section of chapter 8), but songs by professionals about actual men in combat were extremely rare. Yet two Frank Loesser songs about hitherto unsung servicemen are among the most affecting, popular, and best-remembered songs of the war.

Legends beget legends. And with some songs connected to World War II, the more popular the song, the more the legends strayed from actual facts, as seen in the tangled tale of "Lili Marlene" in chapter 4. This was almost as true of Loesser's "Praise The Lord And Pass The Ammunition" (Famous Music, 1942), though its story can be told more briefly than Lili's. During the war, the fate of Loesser's song was a little controversy and a lot of popularity, the number finally selling two and a half million records and 750,000 copies of the sheet music (Kimball and Nelson 92). Only after the war did writers begin to embellish or distort both the origin of the song's content and its public reception.

The line "Praise the Lord and pass the ammunition" is attributed to Captain William A. Maguire, who was at Pearl Harbor as fleet chaplain for the Pacific Fleet; he later became senior chaplain at the San Diego Naval Training Station (*Life* 2 Nov. 1942: 43). When the Japanese attacked, Captain Maguire was on a dock and "managed to reach his own ship where he took up a battle station in the stern of the vessel . . . and helped men who carried ammunition up a narrow ladder which led to the blazing guns," although the reverend never actually fired any artillery himself. As to whether Maguire ever actually spoke the now-famous phrase, he told *Life,* "If I said it, nobody could have heard me in the din of battle. But I certainly felt what that statement expresses" (43). Whether he said the words or not, someone there with access to the press must have thought he did, since Loesser's inspiration for the song came from a newspaper clipping crediting Captain Maguire with them (Kimball and Nelson 92). As corroborated by Maguire himself, those are the barebones facts about the chaplain's role at Pearl Harbor that inspired Loesser's song. But later writers, and not just writers about popular song, couldn't leave it alone. The authors of *WWII: Time-Life Books History of the Second World War* came up with this inanity: "a Navy chaplain, who had been setting up his altar for an outdoor mass, rushed for a machine gun. He set it up on the altar and began firing" (164). Even if a machine gun could be stable on a portable outdoor altar, the "pass the ammunition" makes it clear the phrase (and the song) is about the huge shells used in heavy artillery. Maguire's telling *Life* that he "certainly felt what that statement expresses" plus his cover picture on that week's issue effectively negate music historian David Ewen's claim that "Father Maguire expressed displeasure at being associated with the now famous slogan" (429).

If not the stuff of legend per se, the popular reception accorded "Praise The Lord" was legendary in a more casual sense. Throughout the fall of 1942, *Variety's* usually cool, unflappable prose was filled with increasing astonishment in articles tracing the trajectory of Loesser's song to national popularity. As early as September 30, a piece described how radio's *March of Time* spotlighted "Praise The Lord" the previous week "because it highlights, among other things, that we are fighting on God's side." *Variety* called the radio show "a songplugger's dream come true" that had already resulted in 21,000 copies of the sheet music and 100,000 copies of Kay Kyser's recording sold, "with orders for 150,000 platters more" (45). The saga continued on November 4 under the two-part headline "'Praise the Lord's' Great Press—Unusual National Attention—170,000 Copies Sold and Can't Fill Record Orders" (41). The 170,000 refers to sheet music sales; record sales were almost uncountable, to the point that "Columbia can't press the Kay Kyser platter fast enough." The piece also confirms the notice on the sheet music that Loesser would be donating all his royalties from "Praise The Lord" to the Navy Relief Society, a clear tribute to Navy Captain Maguire as the song's inspiration, since by then Loesser himself was an Army Air Force private. By November 18, *Variety's* headline was shouting, "'Praise the Lord' Wow—450,000 Copies Despite Frowns From the Clergy" (3). The article said the song "has sold over 450,000 copies and may come near the 1,000,000 mark before winter is over," despite some conservative, mostly Protestant, clergy who were complaining about the song's linking God and ammunition in one breath. On the other hand, the Liberal Church of Denver and a "large Brooklyn Jewish temple" incorporated "Praise The Lord" into their worship services. The controversy among the clergy may in fact have helped the song's sales, just as later clerical skirmishes helped boost ticket sales for the musical *Jesus Christ Superstar* and Mel Gibson's film *The Passion of Christ.*

The *Variety* and *Billboard* charts corroborated what *Variety* was saying in prose about the ascent of Loesser's song. To summarize chart data from mid-October 1942 through mid-January 1943, "Praise The Lord" was always just behind (and sometimes just above) "White Christmas," in the top two or three slots of record and sheet music sales and jukebox plays, and it was on *Your Hit Parade* for twelve weeks, five times in 2nd place. That "Praise The Lord" challenged "White Christmas" as successfully as it did and at precisely the same time says much about the song's appeal to the American public.

   Legends abound about "Praise The Lord" vis-à-vis the radio networks.
The story most often bandied about is that because the Office of War Information liked the song and wanted to prolong its popularity, the OWI
wound up "forbidding that it be played too frequently on radio lest it be
plugged to death, an attempt to breathe life into it beyond the usual span
of a hit song" (Lingeman 212). David Ewen's slightly more temperate version is that the OWI "*requested* radio stations to limit its use to no more
than once every four hours" (429, italics supplied). The most extreme
version comes from Robert Kimball and Steve Nelson, in their edition of
Loesser's complete lyrics: "The song was so popular that the Army asked
radio stations not to play it more than once every four hours" (92). While
the civilian OWI did intervene or express an interest in restricting airplays, there is no evidence of intervention by the U.S. Army. Nor is there
evidence for Jody Rosen's take on the whole matter, since he gets it absolutely backward when he writes, "under orders from government officials, radio stations bludgeoned ["Praise The Lord"] into popular favor,
playing it tens of times a day" (143–44). What in fact happened was that
Loesser's publisher, Famous Music, was "making every effort to restrict
the number on the networks. . . . Famous requested every four hours as a
means to preserve the longevity of a war song which may become one of
the truly significant battle cries of World War II" (*Variety* 4 Nov. 1942:
41, 47). To which one might add that the longer the tune remained popular, the longer Famous would turn a profit from it. Although the OWI
concurred with the publisher about prolonging public interest in the song,
the actual request for reducing the frequency of airplays came to radio stations from the music biz itself, not from Washington. Considering Loesser's
music and lyrics, it's no wonder "Praise The Lord" was such a success for
so many months. The tune is robust, muscular, and just repetitive enough
that it's easy to remember and hard to forget, and the lyrics are just as
tough and energetic, yet filled with a playfulness that keeps the song
entertaining, not just belligerent: "Yes the sky pilot [chaplain] said it /
You've got to give him credit for a son of a gun of a gunner was he."
   Frank Loesser was a songwriter who almost instinctively made his
words and music appropriate to a setting or situation, whether the number was in a film or Broadway show or was simply a stand-alone popular
song. This ability shines through in the contrast between his two greatest
war songs, "Praise The Lord And Pass The Ammunition" and "Rodger
Young" (Bob Miller, 1945). While "Praise The Lord" is a gung-ho, militant battle cry, "Rodger Young" is a quiet, understated elegy for a soldier who sacrificed his life so "a company of men might live to fight."
The song's account of Rodger Young's heroism is based on his true story,
as recounted in *Life* and elsewhere, including the back page of the sheet
music. Much of the sheet music's account is quoted from the citation

signed by President Roosevelt that accompanied Young's posthumous Congressional Medal of Honor. Rodger Young was born in Tiffin, Ohio; at eighteen he enlisted in the National Guard and even before Pearl Harbor went on active duty with the 37th Infantry Division. On July 31, 1943, Young's platoon on New Georgia in the Solomon Islands "was pinned down by an enemy machine gun firing on it from a pillbox seventy-five yards away." Young, already wounded, began crawling toward the machine gun, firing his rifle at it; wounded again, he still kept crawling and firing, drawing all the attention of the Japanese so the rest of the men could pull back to safety. Finally within hand grenade range, Young threw his grenade and destroyed the Japanese installation just as "a final burst of fire killed him." Rodger Young posthumously received "the highest decoration this country can bestow on one of its citizens" for "distinguishing himself conspicuously by gallantry and intrepidity above and beyond the call of duty in action with the enemy" ("Rodger Young" 6).

Just how Loesser came to write this singularly moving song is shrouded in more legends. There is some agreement that the U.S. Infantry asked Loesser to write an infantry song, or, according to Loesser's daughter Susan, a "'proper' infantry song" (qtd. in Kimball and Nelson 123), which suggests that the brass didn't think "What Do You Do In The Infantry?" was especially "proper," even though the 264th Infantry Regiment had adopted it as its official marching song (Radio Hit Songs, vol. 3, no. 6, June 1944). But one source suggests the request was more personal, coming from a friend of Loesser's, "writer E. J. Kahn, Jr., then a public relations officer for the Infantry" (Lindsay 47). Loesser decided he wanted to write the number about a Medal of Honor winner, so he either contacted Washington for a list of infantrymen who had been awarded the medal posthumously (Ewen 429), or, again according to his daughter, somehow "got hold of a list . . . to search for a name that would scan." My guess is he also sought for a soldier whose story could be dramatized compellingly in song. However it was that he finally lighted on Young, Loesser's sense of the appropriate guided him to write a fitting tribute to a hero most Americans never knew about before the song appeared.

Loesser's melody emulates folksong, so it's only fitting that Earl Wrightson, accompanying himself on guitar, introduced the song on Meredith Willson's NBC radio program, and that the first and greatest recording was by Burl Ives, one of the finest folk artists at the time. In the spirit and method of the best folksong writing, Loesser crafted Young's story into a lyric that is spare, terse, economical, and, above all, written from the detached, unsentimental narrative stance of a folk ballad, with music to match: "Caught in ambush lay a company of riflemen, / Just grenades against machine guns in the gloom, / Caught in ambush till this one of twenty riflemen / Volunteered, volunteered to meet his doom." In great part, Loesser's eschewing of emotion is what makes "Rodger Young" so moving.

This simple but affecting song touched countless Americans in 1945 and has continued to do so. Indeed, the number made such an impact shortly after it was published (either that, or the infantry's public relations officers were working overtime) that *Life* devoted pages 111 through 117 of its issue for March 5, 1945, to a photo spread on Rodger Young the man, "Rodger Young" the song, and Frank Loesser the songsmith. *Life* prefaced a list of many of his varied war-related songs with "Pfc. Frank Loesser [is] the nearest thing to a George M. Cohan that World War II can boast" (117). (Irving Berlin must have loved reading that!) Shortly after Loesser wrote the piece, the army created the Combat Infantry Band specifically to play "Rodger Young." The band first performed the song, appropriately, in Rodger Young's birthplace, Tiffin, Ohio, "then on every radio station in the country" (Lindsay 47). Yet as popular as it became, the song never made any charts tracking the commercial success of songs. One reason might be that no one expected it to. Burl Ives singing "The Foggy, Foggy Dew" was the featured side of the record and became one of Ives's standards; "Rodger Young" was on the flipside of that record, riding the coattails of the other song's success (Kinkle 1: 413). Other than those who heard it on the radio, most people who discovered "Rodger Young" probably did so quite by accident, on the other side of the song they had actually bought, so charts of record sales may not have accurately tracked its popularity. Sometimes in the absence of concrete evidence of the popularity or the impact a song had on contemporary listeners, one must fall back on oral history, and in this case it has to be my own. I first heard "Rodger Young" when I was four years old, in 1945. A few years ago I was planning to quote part of the song in a book I was writing and wanted to be sure my quotation was accurate. With the lyrics and melody of "Rodger Young" racing through my head, I drove to the John Hay Library to look at the text. When the sheet music was brought to me, I discovered with goose bumps that I had remembered with absolute accuracy every word of the song, all verses and refrains in order, even though the last time I heard "Rodger Young" I was no more than five. For me to retain it so well, I either had to have heard it on the radio a lot, or my parents had bought the record. Much later, when I merely mentioned the title "Rodger Young" to a friend, she began singing the ballad from the top. Judith was eight when the song came out in 1945 and to the best of her knowledge has also never heard it since. However popular "Rodger Young" became, it clearly had a lasting impact on some children of the home front.

# "In The Army, In The Navy, In The Marines"

## Saluting the Services

On the eve of World War II most Americans could hum at least a few bars of the venerable musical tributes to three of the armed forces—"Anchors Aweigh," "The Marines' Hymn," and "The Caissons Go Rolling Along." Fewer knew the coast guard's "Semper Paratus," though it had been around since 1927, and while "The Army Air Corps" was written in 1939, only during the war did it become one of the most popular service tributes in the history of American military music. But these service songs were just the tip of the iceberg. The war occasioned an explosion of salutes to the armed forces and to some civilian groups, but since most were written for the intramural use of military or home front organizations as morale boosters, or to give the groups a strong sense of identity, the public rarely heard these songs. Nevertheless, by the end of the war ASCAP, BMI, and SESAC publishers released over 240 service salutes by professional and military songwriters.

### "Anchors Aweigh": Three Oldies, a Contest Winner, and a Bunch of New Service Songs

"They don't write 'em like they used to anymore" pretty much sums up the public's rationale for dismissing most of the seventy-five tributes to the branches of the armed forces written during the war, while continuing to embrace the old familiar ones. "The Marines' Hymn" is the oldest, but the lyricist and its precise date of composition are vague. What *is* known is that the music wasn't by an American, but by Jacques Offenbach, the prolific German-Jewish composer of Parisian opéra-bouffe. Two gendarmes in Offenbach's *Genevieve de Brabant* first sang the melody in 1859. When the piece was revived in 1875, Major Richard Wallach of the U.S. Marines heard the tune and brought it back to the states with him. There's no clear record of precisely when the Marine Corps adopted as its official song this "hymn" that's really a march, other than its copyright registration of August 19, 1891 ("Marine Corps").

The other service songs were written in the twentieth century but came about in very different ways. In 1906, Midshipman First Class Alfred Hart Miles asked Lieut. Charles A. Zimmerman, bandmaster at the U.S. Naval Academy, to write a new march that could double as a football song, with Miles writing the lyrics. Miles's lyrics were definitely those of a football fight song: "Sail Navy down the field and sink the Army, sink the Army Grey." During the 1920s, George D. Lottman revised the lyrics to include the more familiar "Anchors Aweigh, my boys, Anchors Aweigh" and turn the number from a football song into a drinking song: "Through our last night on shore, drink to the foam / . . . Everybody drink up while you may" ("Anchors Aweigh"). The navy adopted the number as its official song sometime in the 1920s, but when and with which set of words remains unclear.

Written specifically as a tribute to the army's field artillery, the story of "The Caissons Go Rolling Along" is simpler. Hearing the rattle of horse-drawn gun-carriages and caissons (ammunition containers) along dirt roads while on duty in the Philippines in 1908, Brigadier General Edmund Louis "Snitz" Gruber (with an anonymous assist from some army buddies) wrote both the music and words of the still familiar and popular "Over hill, over dale / As we hit the dusty trail." While strictly speaking a song for the field artillery, during the war years "Caissons" became an all-purpose army song. The army had no official song until 1956. After unsuccessful song contests in 1948 and 1952, the army finally agreed to a rewrite of General Gruber's "Caissons" as its official song. Still, "most folks sing the old words," probably not just because they're familiar but because they're a whole lot better ("Army Goes").

The story of the official coast guard song is the simplest; it was commissioned for its newly formed Coast Guard Band in 1926. Taking its title from the coast guard's motto, meaning "Always Ready," Captain Francis Saltus Van Boskerck's "Semper Paratus" was the winner, and the march became the coast guard's official song in 1927. It's rather a shame the song hasn't become as familiar to the American public as all the rest, since its music is just as stirring.

The "youngest" service song was the most successful war-related song ever to come out of a prewar or wartime song contest. Before and during World War II, the Army Air Corps (otherwise known as the Army Air

Force or Army Air Forces) was not a stand-alone branch of the military but a part of the U.S. Army. In 1937 the Air Corps decided it wanted its own song. With *Liberty* magazine putting up a $1,000 prize, the corps sponsored a song contest that attracted "no fewer than 650" entrants, including "young Meredith Willson." The judges, chaired by Mildred Yount, wife of Brigadier General Barton K. Yount, were given until July 1939 to pick a winner. At the proverbial eleventh hour, a man who was both a Julliard-trained professional singer and a civilian pilot sang for Mrs. Yount a song he had made up but had yet to write down. She was riveted by what she heard and made him write out the words and music in accordance with the contest rules. Titling the piece "The Army Air Corps" herself, Mrs. Yount put the manuscript in a pile of other semifinalists, and the judges unanimously selected Robert M. Crawford's song the winner. Frequently played at Army Air Corps functions, it was sometimes sung by Crawford himself, whom *Time* dubbed "The Flying Baritone." Though adopted as the corps's official song almost immediately, widespread public awareness of it began only after the United States entered the war. Songwriter-pilot Crawford enlisted and "flew thousands of miles for" the Air Transport Command, and the revised 1942 edition of the Carl Fischer sheet music henceforth credited "The Army Air Corps" to Captain Robert Crawford (Green; *New York Times* 13 Mar. 1961: 29).

The heightened popularity of these pre-existing service songs in wartime America attests to their excellence. It is purely a coincidence, but all begin with vivid images of strong, forward-moving actions that inspire confidence in each of the fighting forces: "From the halls of Montezuma to the shores of Tripoli"; "Anchors Aweigh, my boys"—"aweigh" signaling that the anchor has been lifted and the ship is ready to sail; "Over hill, over dale / As we hit the dusty trail"; "Off we go into the wild blue yonder, / Climbing high into the sun"; and even the less familiar opening of "Semper Paratus," "We're always ready for the call, / . . . Through howling gale and shot and shell."

The trade paper charts and *Hot Charts* suggest what sparked and sustained the resurgence of home front civilians' enthusiasm for these service songs. First came new records by some of the top big bands and other recording artists. One disk of a service song even took off for a time two months before Pearl Harbor, when Ozzie Nelson, a bandleader and singer before he was a TV sitcom dad, recorded an "Anchors Aweigh" that is a *Hot Charts* Extra for October 1941. During the war, Tommy Dorsey, Glenn Miller, Bob Crosby, and Rudy Vallee's U.S. Coast Guard Band followed with more popular recordings of the navy's song. But Gene Krupa's swing versions with Johnny Desmond's vocals of "The Caissons Go Rolling Along" and "The Marines' Hymn" were the earliest big band recordings of service songs once we were in the war, both recorded on January

23, 1942, and released back to back on the Okeh label. Krupa's "Marines' Hymn" is a *Hot Charts* Extra for March through June 1942, joined by the very different Kate Smith and Tony Pastor recordings. Other "Caissons" by Shep Fields and Horace Heidt rolled along, making the Extras list for July. But perhaps because of its newness and "modernity," "The Army Air Corps" soared above the other service songs. Glenn Miller and Bob Crosby recorded it, Crosby's version a *Hot Charts* Extra from January through May 1943, but the biggest seller was Alvino Rey's with vocal by Bill Schallen and the King Sisters. The selling streak of Rey's "Army Air Corps" was fairly strong for a very long time. It's a *Hot Charts* Extra every month from March 1942 through December 1943, except for May 1943, when it ranks 33rd. After that string of twenty-two months, Rey's record returns as an Extra from May through July 1944. In terms of record sales, no other service song came close to the success of "The Army Air Corps," and the sheet music had a long run on both the *Billboard* and *Variety* charts. With their almost inexplicable discrepancies, *Billboard* twice ranked it as high as 8th, and *Variety* once as high as 3rd, on October 7, 1942. While played often on the radio as patriotic, morale boosting, or motivational numbers, service songs on the air were in no sense plugs; *Variety* realized this fairly quickly, and dropped them from its plug charts.

Analogous to the rationale for playing service songs on the radio was their part in wartime films, not to sell records or sheet music but to instill empathetic support for the troops among moviegoers, whether or not the numbers were relevant to the film's story. Perhaps the most extravagant of Hollywood's treatments of service songs was the finale of the Republic musical variously titled *Ice-Capades* or *Ice-Capades Revue,* released in December 1942. For no reason other than a lavish display of wartime patriotism (and skating), *all four* major service songs were sung, while skaters in military uniforms and other patriotic garb executed "an elaborate routine ending with a V-formation" (Shull and Wilt 309).

While *Variety* stopped charting airplays of service songs after nine months since they were of no commercial use to publishers, one segment of the plug charts is of more than casual interest historically in revealing the intersection of an event of the war with radio musical broadcasts. Like the other service songs, "Anchors Aweigh" generally received between six and eight plays a week between March and May 1942, when it was aired twelve times a week twice and thirteen once in the three weeks immediately following the decisive American defeat of the Japanese fleet at the Battle of Midway. These more frequent broadcasts of the number obviously weren't a stepped-up effort to sell the song but broadcasters' way of honoring the U.S. Navy's success in the first major American victory of the war.

Since the wartime American public was clearly attached to the service songs already adopted officially or informally by the several branches of the armed forces, why were so many new tributes to the individual services written in the war years? Even excluding eleven songs jointly saluting all of the armed services and another seventy-five or so written for specialized units within each service (see the next section), there were at least twenty-two written specifically for the army (primarily the infantry), nineteen for the Army Air Corps, seven for the navy, eleven for the marines, two for the coast guard, and five for the U.S. Merchant Marine, one of which became its official song in 1943: "Heave Ho! My Lads, Heave Ho! (Song Of The Merchant Marine)" by Jack Lawrence, Lt. (jg) USMS (Kaycee Music, 1943). Yet established Tin Pan Alley or Broadway writers wrote only sixteen of these sixty-six new service tributes; six were for Hollywood films and four were by Irving Berlin for various editions of *This Is The Army*. Top professionals most likely wrote so few service songs because they recognized their limited commercial appeal. The remaining fifty songs by lesser-known professional or occasional writers were often released by relatively minor ASCAP, BMI, or SESAC publishers. That lesser and essentially amateur writers wrote three-fourths of the service songs suggests that their primary motive (like that of the writers of traditional patriotic songs) was to express their patriotism.

A few writers wrote potentially morale-building service songs. Before Pearl Harbor, Bill Coleman of the Radio Branch of the War Department's Bureau of Public Relations wrote "Keep 'Em Flying!" (Broadcast Music, 1941), "Dedicated to the United States Army Air Corps." Recorded by Gene Krupa with Johnny Desmond's vocal on November 25, 1941, the fortunes of war made the number take off quickly, ranking 46th in December, according to *Hot Charts*. While it doesn't rank again, Krupa's swinging salute to America's fliers remains an Extra during January and February 1942, joined in the latter month by Glenn Miller's disk. The other big wartime tribute to pilots, Johnny Mercer and Harold Arlen's "Captains of the Clouds" (Remick, 1942), had its main impact in the movie from which it took its name. The Warner Brothers film, starring James Cagney, was actually about the Royal Canadian Air Force, but combined with Arlen's dynamic and infectious music Mercer's vivid lyric could apply to any pilots of the Allies. As a morale booster, one new service salute attracted jukebox players from bobbysoxers to guys at the corner tavern: the Andrews Sisters' hit "Here Comes The Navy" (Shapiro, Bernstein, 1939, 1942, 1943). With music by Jaromir Vejvoda, the song began life in English with lyrics by Lew Brown as "Beer Barrel Polka" in 1939, also a big Andrews Sisters hit. Come the war years, the tune was given entirely new words by Lt. Commander P. Oakes, U.S.N.R. The Andrews Sisters both recorded the new naval version and sang it as the finale of their Universal musical *How's About It,* released in February 1943. *Variety's* charts indicate that their record received a lot of plays on the country's jukeboxes between November 11, 1942, and February 3, 1943, even before the film's release.

Non-professional songwriters in the military also wrote service tributes, the quality of which varies greatly. And yet at their best the lyrics contain vivid, gritty language that is rare among civilian writers, as in Major General Edwin F. Harding's "That's The Infantry," with music by Dorothy Godfrey (Shapiro, Bernstein, 1943): "The roads are clogged with trucks and jeeps / With cannon and with men / We're marching God knows whither / And we'll get there God knows when." Despite music by Richard Rodgers, even master lyricist (but civilian) Oscar Hammerstein's attempt at an infantry song, "We're On Our Way" (Williamson Music, 1943), sadly pales by comparison: "The infantry's movin' in, / . . . Yea, brother! / Verily, yea!" Among the professionals, Pfc. Frank Loesser struck the right note in his classic combination of humor and pride, "What Do You Do In The Infantry?" discussed in chapter 5. And while the Music War Committee was turning out forgotten infantry salutes by Alleymen such as George Vail, Robert Sour, and Carl Kent's "Till The Infantry Moves In" (Broadcast Music, 1944) and Charlie Tobias and Abel Baer's "You've Gotta Have Oomph In The Infantry" (Tobias and Lewis, 1944), late in 1943 Loesser's playfully proud infantry tribute was having strong record and sheet music sales and ten weeks of radio plays on its way to immortality.

### "Hit The Leather": Special Songs for Specialized Servicemen

If general service songs had a limited public during the war, even fewer songs saluting the specialized commands, corps, divisions, services, and other units within the branches of the military found any civilian audience at all. Never intended to be commercial, these specialized service songs were more designed for the sole purpose of morale boosting than any other group of songs during the war. At least seventy-six of these specialist salutes were published in the war years, making them the largest group among the roughly 240 service songs of all kinds, plus thirty-one more saluting another special group of service personnel, the women of the armed forces (see the next section). The writing of so many songs of this kind reflects contemporary thinking that any specialized group fighting the war deserved a song.

Best known as the bandleader and choral conductor of Fred Waring and His Pennsylvanians, Waring had something of a service-song cottage industry going during the war. Usually teamed with lyricist Jack Dolph,

Waring composed over fourteen of them, and his Words & Music firm published them. Among these were songs for the army's Quartermaster Corps, paratroopers, Military Police, and Armored Command, the navy's Naval Aviation, airships (blimps), and Seabees (Construction Battalions), and the Air Corps's Air Transport Command. Waring understood the audience and need for such songs. His large ad in *Variety* on May 26, 1943, doesn't even hint at commercial possibilities for them. Instead, under the headline "Salute them by their *first name!*" is a drawing of servicemen around a radio, captioned "PROGRAM SERVICE SONGS — HELP BUILD TRADITION FOR EACH INDIVIDUAL BRANCH," followed by a list of Waring's service songs. Here Waring implicitly acknowledges that these songs were to serve the services, not the music-buying public, even though Words & Music published commercial sheet music of all of Waring's specialized service songs.

An article called "American Songs Go To War" in the October 1944 issue of *Song Hits* focused on Hammerstein's Music War Committee. It reported that in "recent months the Committee has been giving more and more attention to special requests from the armed services, and at its last meeting the Music War Committee voted to direct its attention almost exclusively to such requests" (20). That vote indicates that many more professional songwriters than just Waring and Hammerstein recognized the need for specialized morale-building numbers in the armed forces. More importantly, it said that Alleymen and women were ready to devote some of their time and talent to them, even with little likelihood of realizing much remuneration for their efforts.

Long before the MWC voted to focus its attention on specialist service songs, professional songwriters recognized both the clientele and the need for them. Even without Fred Waring's fourteen-plus songs, well-established and even prominent Tin Pan Alley and Broadway writers turned out at least twenty-eight published salutes to specialized service units between 1938 and 1944, mostly in 1943. With the exception of a few perfunctory pieces that never got off the ground, like Richard Rodgers and Lorenz Hart's song for the Army Air Corps bomber crews, "The Bombardier Song" (Chappell, 1942), and Cole Porter's leaden salute to glider pilots, "Glide, Glider, Glide" (Chappell, 1943), Tin Pan Alley and Broadway's top-notch pros put some real creativity into songs that would be heard only by a comparative handful of people. Rodgers and Hammerstein did far better than their generic and old-fashioned infantry salute in "The P. T. Boat Song (Steady As You Go)" (Crawford Music, 1943). Hammerstein crammed the song with apropos language describing those fragile but feisty little boats and their crews: "we are burning up the seas in a flock of flying splinters / The P. T.'s are the peewees, the midgets of the fleet, / But the biggest one the enemy's got is the one we run to meet."

Herman "As Time Goes By" Hupfeld wrote the official song for the Transportation Corps of the U.S. Army, titled appropriately, if predictably, "Song Of The Army Transportation Corps" (Chappell, 1943). And Johnny Burke and Jimmy Van Heusen once found themselves writing for a very small contingent of servicemen, but they did so with vigor and wit in "Duke The Spook" (Mayfair Music, 1943), named for the mascot of the 400th Bombardment Group of the U.S. Army Air Force, to which the number was dedicated.

A couple of specialized service salutes had some public exposure, if not commercial success. With standards like "Georgia On My Mind," "I Get Along Without You Very Well," "Lazybones," "Stardust," and "The Nearness Of You" to his credit, Hoagy Carmichael is best remembered for his songs on the mellow side, but his musical moods could swing to the manic too, as can be seen in the title of the wackiest specialized service salute of the war, "The Cranky Old Yank (In A Clanky Old Tank)" (Beverly Hills: Carmichael Music, 1942). Dedicated to the U.S. Armored Forces, this entirely comic service salute was premiered by Carmichael himself at Desert Center, California, after which Bing Crosby first sang it to the American public on NBC's *Kraft Music Hall* on October 22, 1942, and again on February 25 and October 14, 1943 (Morgereth). Crosby's repeat performances of "Cranky Old Yank" suggest that the public's response to its first broadcast was at least cordial, perhaps even enthusiastic. No one recorded the song commercially, but the transcription of Crosby's October 14 performance was included on a V-Disc for the armed forces (Sears 164). The improbable situation in the song has an American GI roaring through Japan in his tank, doing so to some of the silliest rhymes at Carmichael's disposal: "And when I set my khaki down in old Nagasaki, I'll be singing like a wacky Jackeroo, / And you can bet, by cracky, ev'ry Sukiyaki lacky will be lookin' mighty tacky when I do." That Carmichael intended his off-the-wall Armored Forces tribute also to be a bit of a Japan-basher is apparent in the comic cover art of the sheet music, which featurs a cartoon of a Japanese officer in a Nazi uniform saying "Scuse pleez! Bad Song. Don't Buy!" A more conventional but lasting specialist tribute had at least as much home front exposure when Alley veterans Sam M. Lewis and Peter De Rose's "The Song Of The Seabees" (Robbins, 1942), already the Navy Construction Battalions' official song, was featured in the 1944 Republic war film *The Fighting Seabees,* starring John Wayne and Susan Hayward.

Of the Alleymen in the service during the war, a few wrote specialized salutes along with their war-related and other popular songs. Usually these songsmiths' special tributes were for the groups within the branches of the service that they themselves were in, though not necessarily their own special units. Capt. Meredith Willson wrote songs for two groups in the army, "Hit The Leather" (Carl Fischer, 1943) for the U.S. Army Cavalry and "Fire Up (Marching Song of the Chemical Warfare Service)" (Words & Music, 1943), but he didn't write one for the Armed Forces Radio Service, to which he was assigned. While in the navy, frequent collaborators Seamen First Class Irving Taylor and Vic Mizzy wrote "Take 'Er Down" (Santly-Joy, 1943) for the Submarine Force. The army's Pvt. Hy Zaret and the coast guard's Ben Machan collaborated rather ecumenically to write "Soldiers of God (Official Chaplains' March)" (Remick, 1944) for the men whose ministries spanned all faiths and all branches of the armed forces. Pvt. Harold Rome and Pfc. Frank Loesser, the two most prominent Alleymen turned servicemen, each wrote a song for the largely unsung vast and vital segment of the army to which they belonged, the Army Service Forces. The AFS organized and ran essentially every noncombat function of the army, from procurement, supply, and transportation through medical care, cryptography, and the Military Police to the chaplaincy, service clubs, recreation, and entertainment. Both Rome and Loesser were in Special Services, that corner of the ASF that "handled recreational and morale activities" (438), which for men like Rome and Loesser meant writing songs, camp shows, and other entertainments. Seeing firsthand the critical functions of the ASF, Pvt. Rome wrote "The Army Service Forces" (Leeds Music, 1944), and Pfc. Loesser "Salute To The Army Service Forces" (Hollywood: Saunders, 1944), acknowledging the indispensable work of this relatively silent partner to the ground and air forces.

Not only Tin Pan Alley songsmiths responded to a need for songs for specialized units of the armed forces. That the military itself saw the morale-building value of such songs is dramatized by the fact that, even excluding numbers by songwriting professionals in the service and songs saluting the women's branches of the service, major publishers issued at least twenty-one specialized service songs by songwriting members of the military. Most were ranking officers, some career soldiers: from the army, one brigadier general, one lieutenant colonel, four majors, three captains, and four lieutenants; from the navy, one lieutenant commander and a lieutenant. They wrote songs for groups within the armed forces both great and small. "Bomber Command" (Carl Fischer, 1942), with words by Lt. Col. Ellis O. Keller and Gene Marvey and music by Paul Taubman, paid tribute "To all U. S. Army Air Force Bombardment Units," a huge group of flying servicemen, just as Lt. Don Thornburn, U.S.N.R., and Charles Wolcott's "Sailors Of The Air" (Southern Music, 1942) and Lt. Commander Guy E. Wyatt, U.S.N.R., and Joseph Hewitt's "Wings of Gold" (Cleveland: Sam Fox, 1942) both saluted Naval Aviation, the navy's large airborne fighting force. Some songs honored groups that were much smaller but equally important to fighting the war. Major William J. Clinch gave the Cadet Battalion of the West Point of the Air its official song in "Spirit Of The Air Corps" (Broadcast Music, 1941). Lt. Harold P. Wood, and Arthur A. Allen's "The Spirit of Aberdeen" (Boston: Evans Music, 1942), whose title alone led Kathleen E. R. Smith to list it with songs saluting our British Allies (63), in fact saluted the small but vital group of men and women who tested cannon and other ordnance at the Aberdeen Proving Ground in Maryland. The best-known non-professional serviceman/songwriter of specialized unit salutes is Captain Robert Crawford, who as a civilian had written "The Army Air Corps," which the corp adopted well before we entered the war. Once in the Air Transport Command, in addition to his infamous "Kill The Bastards," Crawford wrote for airplane ground crews "Mechs Of The Air Corps" (Robbins, 1942); "Born To The Sky" (Carl Fisher, 1945), the Air Transport Command's official song; and "Cadets Of The Air Corps." Like their best general service salutes, the specialized ones by career servicemen pack in the kind of detail, honesty, and grit that few civilian lyricists could capture. A few lines of Captain Crawford's literally gritty appreciation of what airplane "mechs" do are typical of the best of such writing: "We rev up the motors, we change the plugs and all of the jets we drain, we know very well when she's running swell, you'll crack her up again! / . . . We're the guys who make 'em fly, the grease balls of the Air Corps." With so many specialized units in the armed forces and the military brass saying each one should have its own song, songwriters in and out of the service undoubtedly supplied many more numbers of this type than just those published commercially, the rest existing only in copies for the use of the specialized personnel for whom they were written.

The verso of the sheet music cover for Pvt. Hy Zaret and Lou Singer's "Song Of The Army Nurse Corps" (Leeds, 1944) reproduces a brief undated letter on War Department stationery from Colonel Florence A. Blanchfield, A.N.C. Superintendent. While some specifics in Colonel Blanchfield's remarks pertain only to armed forces nurses, in spirit her words are perhaps the most eloquent by any military officer expressing the vital role of song among all servicemen and women in time of war: "There is no burden so heavy, no night so long that it cannot be eased by music. The members of the Army Nurse Corps should be encouraged to sing, for in song there is a contentment that means happier times, good fellowship, better care for their patients and a more optimistic outlook for the entire Corps." Zaret and Singer wrote the Army Nurse Corps's "Official Anthem" late in the war, but other professional songwriters and songwriting servicemen and women had been writing songs for the women's branches of all the armed forces since their inceptions.

### *"They're All Miss Americas Now": Singing the Praises of Women at War*

If by today's standards the title of Jack Frost and Frank Worth's song (Mills, 1943) has a slightly sexist ring to it, rest assured that the first four lines unequivocally turn the criteria for becoming a Miss America from traditional aspects of feminine charm to serving in the military: "There goes Kitty from Kansas City, her bathing suit was a wow, / But she's wearing khaki and joined the Waacs, She's a real Miss America now!" In fact, in over thirty songs written in praise of the women's armed forces, sexism is virtually absent, as is any trace of condescension. Instead, most of the songs intended for a wide home front audience were characterized by pride and some amazement. While not engaged in combat, these women still sacrificed the comforts of home and family (and even well-paying defense work) to serve in the military. The songwriters' pride naturally extended to songs about women in the specific services, and some of these, predictably all by men, occasionally mixed pride with sentimentality.

Even before the formation of the women's service corps, songwriters began praising the work of Red Cross nurses. Irving Berlin was the most successful in "Angels Of Mercy" (American Red Cross, 1941). The song eschewed sentimentality, raised a lot of money for the Red Cross, and is a *Hot Charts* Extra for February 1942 on disks by singer Barry Wood and the big bands of Glen Gray, Glenn Miller, and Charlie Spivak. Not long after came "The Girl Behind The Boy Behind The Gun" (Song Hit Guild, 1942). Albert F. Miller's lyric to Vic Mizzy's music takes a wholly sentimental approach to describing the Red Cross nurse: "An angel picked a flower from our own native bower / And placed it somewhere 'Over There.' / Now, no matter where she grows, she's the doughboys' fav'rite rose; / The world has never seen a flow'r so fair." Ricky Serras's picture of the Red Cross nurse was a more balanced blend of praise and sentiment in "An Angel In White" (Excelsior Music, 1943); after eight lines describing the unflagging and cheerful nurse's daily duties for men wounded in combat, the number concludes with "For the boys missing, an angel in white / Often sheds tears in a chapel at night."

The music of one servicewomen's song is more sentimental than its words. The lead writer of "The Girl of the Year is a SPAR" (Cleveland: Sam Fox, 1944) was Lieut. Rudy Vallee, U.S.C.G.R., who then was the conductor of the Coast Guard Band and who for decades in civilian life had been a popular sentimental crooner on radio and records. All coast guardsmen, the other writers of the tune were Red Harper, Bill Marcus, and Eddie Hunt. The lyrics are a bit romantic ("She's the girl you adore and lives next door / A Betsy Ross in Coast Guard blue"), and, as sung by Vallee, the music is syrupy enough to throw one into insulin shock. Fortunately, the SPARS had other, sprightlier tunes.

As did all the women's corps. At least ten songs were written for the WACS (including one specifically for the AIR WACS assigned to the Army Air Force), six for the WAVES, and three for the SPARS; the Women Marines even got one, though still no acronym. The numbers of songs seem more or less proportionate to the number of women in each corps. By the end of the war "more than 143,000 women served in the WAC," with proportionally fewer in the other services. The estimated number of women in all of the branches during World War II reached upward of 200,000 (Bailey 68, 50). Whether they were by professionals or military personnel, at the core of nearly all songs for the women of the individual services is a celebration of one or both of their primary roles as WACS, WAVES, SPARS, or Women Marines. The first, often expressed by variants of the "girl (or woman) behind the man behind the gun" imagery dating back to many wars before World War II, commends the women for providing behind-the-lines and stateside auxiliary services necessary to support men in combat. Sometimes such commendation is general, as in Johnny Mercer and Harold Arlen's "Here Come The Waves" (Famous Music, 1944), from the Paramount picture of the same name: "Any time there's a job to be done, / You'll find the gal behind the guy behind the gun." But the most vivid servicewomen salutes contain wonderfully detailed descriptions of what they did. It's unclear whether Margaret Bristol was a SPAR herself, but her lyric for "True Blue And Always Ready (SPAR Song)" (M. Baron, 1944), with music by Marion Ohlson, is filled with such specifics: "We're cam'ra men and craftsmen, we drive a truck or jeep; / We're pastry cooks and draftsmen; on tower watch we never fall asleep / . . . We're aides to nurse and doctor, we map out the sea and skies, / Bake hot-cross buns, clean and test the guns," and more. Tin Pan Alley's Pvt. Hy Zaret had a close-up view of WACS and their duties that he put into "Song of the WAC" (Remick, 1944), with Arthur Altman's music: "planes go zooming by; / Inside the tower there's a WAC! / When supplies are due, trucks go roaring thru; / Behind the wheel you'll find a WAC!"

According to several songs, the other main role of each woman who enlisted was to free a serviceman for combat duty by taking over his previous, non-combat duties. Two lines in Fred Waring and Jack Dolph's "WAVES In Navy Blue" (Words & Music, 1943)—"For every WAVE in Navy blue, / There's a sailor on the sea"—led Kathleen E. R. Smith to claim that the song's "message was controversial," in that it could retard the recruitment of women by implying that by enlisting a woman might take a man "from a safe stateside job" and send him to his death in combat (115, 116). This claim is totally unsupported by the facts. In addition to Dolph and Waring's number, seven other prominent servicewomen salutes made their central theme the freeing of men for active duty. Of those seven, women wrote five, all but one of them in the women's armed forces themselves, and the writers of "True Blue And Always Ready" may have been also. Since servicewomen wrote songs with this message, since that message is always vigorously expressed, and since there were no orders from Washington to cease and desist, it's doubtful the Pentagon or OWI worried about such songs putting the kibosh on the recruitment of women.

Servicewomen songwriters found varied ways to express their common theme. In "The Navy's Women In Blue (The WAVES' Song)" (Bell Music, 1943), Mary Monett of the U.S. Naval Reserve directly addressed sailors: "Yes, the WAVES will do your work on the shore, / We'll take over while you fight the war." Lyricist Ensign Jane Leeds and composer Ensign Ruth Simon in their "Song of the WAVES" (Mercury Music, 1943) played with professional aplomb on two meanings of a single word in a single line to make their point: "We will free our Navy's men who will free the world." Two other Navy women, Ensigns Betty D. St. Clair and Elizabeth K. Ender, wrote "Waves Of The Navy" (Sam Fox, 1943) from the active duty sailors' point of view: "every hero brave / . . . will find ashore his man-sized chore / Was done by a Navy Wave." The army's prolific writer of songs for and about WACS, Lieutenant Ruby Jane Douglass, took the direct approach in "The WAAC Is A Soldier Too": "We didn't join the WAAC for fun or beauty, / But to release a man for combat duty." And, SPARS or not, Margaret Bristol and Marion Ohlson's novel angle in "True Blue And Always Ready" was to tell home front Americans, "When you see the Spars, thank your lucky stars, / There's another gob at sea!"

In 1944, Pfc. Frank Loesser wrote his solemn "The WAC Hymn" (Famous Music, 1944) for the WAC show *P. F. C. Mary Brown*. That same year, in a more playfully patriotic mood, Loesser wrote "One Little WAC" (Hollywood: Saunders, 1944) about how just one WAC could win the war by freeing a man for combat: "ONE LITTLE WAC, a khaki covered cutie, ONE LITTLE WAC, released a man for duty, / One little man, he flew thru the flak to Berlin and back with bombs in his rack, / . . . That was the bomb that broke Hitler's back / A score for the Yanks, thanks to ONE LITTLE WAC."

### "Thank You Joe": Saluting Our Servicemen, One at a Time

Of the 185 general and specialized service tributes, only about eleven general ones, like Harry Tobias and Pinky Tomlin's "In The Army, In The Navy, In The Marines" (Variety Music, 1943), and a dozen others in Hollywood films were written with the hope of appealing to the general public. Most of them didn't, but a different kind of service salute occasionally did. Since nearly every American who wasn't fighting in the war was related to or knew someone who was, the more personal songs saluting an individual "generic" serviceman had the most popular appeal. A few even became hits.

War being what it is, salutes to individual fictional servicemen either commended GIs or memorialized them. Twenty-nine professional salutes to living servicemen and eleven elegies to men who died in combat were published during the war; some of each kind found an audience on the home front.

Quite a few numbers extolling a typical hometown boy fighting in the war contain a nostalgic glance back at his childhood and youth. Seeing every "GI Joe" as just an "average Joe" before he entered the service was a hook that let listeners associate the song's GI with someone they knew. One of the lighter of these songs, Harry Pease, Ed G. Nelson, and Jimmy Dupre's "He's a Real All-American Now" (Leeds, 1942), has a do-it-yourself gimmick built in. The song's conceit is obviously college football—"He used to hold that line for old Notre Dame / Now he's hitting that line for Uncle Sam." But while the song names numerous football teams, it provides places where a person can plug in the college a soldier friend or relative once played for. Typical of the more sentimental Tin Pan Alley serviceman tributes is "He Looks Like An Angel (But Fights Like The Devil)" (Miller Music, 1943), by Al Hoffman, Allan Roberts, and Jerry Livingston, who actually invite listeners to make personal associations: "It's dollars to doughnuts you'd know him if I ever mentioned his name." They then describe the "kid in the Infantry" as a "Bible readin' kid," always as "shy as a kitten," yet now he "Fights a battle ev'ry day, [but still] writes his mother just to say / 'Please take care of yourself.'"

Most salutes to an individual GI that look back to his civilian life came not from mainstream Tin Pan Alley but from hillbilly songwriters, who were just as conspicuously absent from musical tributes to servicemen in the aggregate. Those who wrote hillbilly songs seemed again to be most comfortable focusing on individuals rather than groups, as they did in their highly personal approach to patriotism in "There's A Star Spangled Banner Waving Somewhere" and similar numbers. Fully eight of the twenty-nine songs celebrating living servicemen and five of the eleven elegies are hillbilly or faux hillbilly songs. These pieces also exemplify a trend occurring within all hillbilly music in the 1940s, a shift from hill country songs to western numbers. While other war-related hillbilly songs dealt with such matters as mountain boys enlisting or getting drafted (see chapter 5), each of the eight personal tributes to a serviceman concerns a cowboy turned soldier, marine, or, in most cases, airman, as is seen in such titles as "Pony Boy Is In The Army Now," "Salt Water Cowboy," and "Cowboy In The Clouds." Songwriters found the airman image especially congenial because of the analogies they could draw between riding a horse across the range and piloting a plane across the sky, a comparison that occurs in most of the numbers, often with a wistful look back at the cowboy's prewar life. While praising the exploits of a friend who changed his "bronco for a fighter plane," the singer in Buck Ram's "A Cowboy Ridin' High Over There" (Noble Music, 1942) also admits, "Tonight I sort of miss you pal / Your cheerful voice is missing from the old corral," and country singer/songwriter Polly Jenkins's "The Kid With The Guitar" (Kelly Music, 1943) lets its audience know not only that the boy's sweetheart and mother are proud of him and eagerly await his return but also that "His pinto hopes that he is safe across the sea."

The commercial fate of hillbilly songs is almost impossible to know since the trade papers didn't track their popularity. But it's a matter of record that at least two serviceman salutes had some public exposure on radio. The earlier of the two is about the most faux a hillbilly song could be, having a thoroughly British pedigree. The words for "There's a Cowboy Ridin' Thru The Sky" (London: Peter Maurice; New York: Shapiro, Bernstein, 1942) were by English lyricist and playwright Jack Popplewell and the music by Michael Carr, "the only British songwriter to successfully imitate American cowboy ballads," perhaps because he worked for a time as a "Montana cowhand" while living in the United States from 1924 to 1930 (Harrison 83). Carr's western music is almost matched in authenticity by Popplewell's words, in lines like "Tho' he misses his cattle, he thrills to the rattle of his gun." But the lyric gives away the song's English origins when it claims, "There's a Spitfire where his bronco used to be," improbably having the American cowboy piloting a fighter plane used by the R.A.F., not the U.S.A.F. Although Kate Smith never recorded the number, her photo on the American sheet music suggests that the home front heard her sing it at least once on her radio show. Similarly, Bing Crosby's music supervisor Perry Botkin, Bernie Schwartz, and Jon Bushallow Jr. heard their faux western "Ridin' Herd On a Cloud" (Hollywood: Saunders, 1943) broadcast to a national audience that most actual hillbilly numbers never reached when Crosby introduced it on *The Kraft Music Hall* on August 12, 1943, and encored it on September 2 (Morgereth). Characteristically combining wistfulness and pride, the song describes how the cowhand "Left his spurs and his saddle on the range with his cattle," and ends with wartime homefolks' typically mixed feelings of pride and apprehension about their men overseas: "Someone back home feelin' mighty proud / Prays for him RIDIN' HERD ON A CLOUD tonight."

Not at all a hillbilly number, the one hit salute to a fictional serviceman linking his childhood to his war record was "Johnny Zero" (Santly-Joy, 1943), with lyrics by Mack David and music by Vee Lawnhurst, one of Tin Pan Alley's more admired woman composers of the 1930s and '40s. Johnny was the dumb kid in school, and the other children taunted him with "Johnny got a zero" every time he got failing marks on his school-work. But now that he's a fighter pilot shooting down Japanese fighter planes, people cheer, "Johnny got a Zero; he got another Zero, hooray! / JOHNNY ZERO is a hero today." David's simple narrative lyric, Lawnhurst's catchy melody, and the always popular fairytale motif of the least likely kid succeeding beyond anyone's wildest dreams helped "Johnny Zero" take off faster than an F6F Hellcat from an aircraft carrier. Heavily plugged beginning April 7, 1943, the sheet music of "Johnny Zero" already appeared on the *Variety* chart of April 21 as the 14th best seller; it shot up to 4th the following week, where it stayed for eighteen weeks more, only gradually declining in popularity through August; on September 8 it was back at 14th, before it fell off the chart. The hit a capella Decca disk of "Johnny Zero" by the Song Spinners (the musicians' union recording ban was still on) took off later than the sheet music, but by June 23 *Variety* was reporting numerous jukebox plays, and *Billboard*'s chart of top-selling records first noted it on July 10, ranking it 7th. *Hot Charts* ranks the Song Spinners' "Johnny Zero" 16th in June, 7th in July, and 20th in August 1943.

Not that the Song Spinners' recording couldn't have succeeded on its own, but their disk about Johnny and his feisty little fighter plane got a piggy-back lift in the popularity rankings from Harold Adamson and Jimmy McHugh's bomber with "one motor gone" that managed to "limp thru the air" back to base "With our full crew aboard," "Comin' In On A Wing And A Prayer" (Robbins, 1943). I can just picture the Decca execs tearing out their proverbial hair when they discovered they had issued two substantial hits as the A and B sides of a single record! Sheet music sales of the two songs were totally independent of one other. Both hit the charts around the same time, and the charts make it clear from the start that more record buyers were requesting "Wing And A Prayer" than "Johnny Zero." It rose from 10th in *Billboard* on June 19, 1943, to 2nd the following week and 1st on July 3, where it stayed for a while. Willie Kelly's recording first attracted attention and is 31st in May in *Hot Charts,* but once the Song Spinners' record was released—listed as 2nd in both June and July and 10th in August—Kelly's never got back above 23rd; recordings by the Golden Gate Quartet and the Four Vagabonds never rose out of the thirties and forties. "Wing And A Prayer" is one of the very few salutes to individual fictional servicemen that don't look back at the GI's prewar life. The pilot's heroism not in battle but in saving his plane and crewmen, plus his "trust in the Lord," were all it took for "Comin' In On A Wing And A Prayer" to be on *Your Hit Parade* for eighteen weeks, in first place for three, and to sell over a million records, making it one of the biggest-selling war-related songs of World War II.

A small number of songs honoring heroes who gave their lives for their country achieved the status of minor hits. Of eleven songs memorializing dead GIs, only two were by prominent Tin Pan Alleymen, both exercising considerable restraint in the sentiment department, while five were by hillbilly songwriters exercising far less. Under his occasional pseudonym Dick Howard, lyricist Howard Dietz of the noted Broadway team of Schwartz and Dietz wrote "I Had A Pal On Guadalcanal" (Shapiro, Bernstein, 1943) with music by "White Cliffs Of Dover" composer Walter Kent. This unusual song is written from the point of view of a soldier who lost a friend, and the singer expresses his feelings with understated stoicism: "He may be gone but I'll carry on / Till the last foe of freedom shall fall." Al Dubin, best remembered for his lyrics to the many songs he wrote with Harry Warren, like "Lullaby of Broadway," wrote with composer Pierre Norman a very different kind of lullaby during the war in "Thank You Joe" (Mills, 1945). More openly emotional than "I Had A Pal," Dubin's lyric expresses both personal loss and pride in the fallen soldier, and the singer speaks directly to him: "There is a girl you used to know, / She'd like for me to say 'Hello,' And THANK YOU JOE." According to the sheet music, the song was "Featured by GUY LOMBARDO and his Royal Canadians," which seems appropriate, since Lombardo ran more to the "sweet" sentimental sounds of the '40s than to swing.

Of all the country numbers on this theme, one is very sentimental yet extremely effective because of the drama it plays out—Bill Showmet's "Did You See My Daddy Over There?" (Peer International, 1944). The first verse describes a little boy coming up to a soldier and, in the chorus, asking him, "Did you see my Daddy, Mister Soldier, / When you were fighting over there." In the second verse, the boy's face makes the soldier recall "A buddy lost in action, the best he ever had, / [who] Till death had carried o'er his heart a picture of this lad." The chorus repeats, but quite brilliantly there's no third verse, the song ending before the grief-stricken soldier has to tell the child his father was killed in action. By contrast, one hillbilly elegy, Bob Wills, Cliff Sundin, and "Cactus Jack" Cliff Johnson's "White Cross on Okinawa" (Hill and Range, 1945), overall is fairly flat and emotionless, but its one mention of the "gold star" would have moved many listeners: "Some Mother's heart feels deep sorrow, silent her prayers cross the foam. / There's a WHITE CROSS TONIGHT ON OKINAWA, / And a gold star in some Mother's home." Gold Star Mothers were those whose sons had died in combat, and they are featured in a number of other songs, such as Tex Ritter and Frank Harford's emotionally restrained "There's A Gold Star In Her Window" (Southern Music, 1944) and Floyd Wilkins, Ray Marcell, and Russ Hull's more sentimentally charged "There's A Gold Star Hanging In The Window (Where A Blue Star Used To Be)" (Chicago: Country Music, 1943), with its lines like "May the good Lord bless this little mother / She has given all that others might be free." But most sentimental and biggest selling among these songs was "Soldier's Last Letter" (Hollywood: Cross Music, 1944), with words and music by country singer Ernest Tubb and Sgt. Henry Stewart. An unabashed tear-jerker, the song describes a mother reading a letter from her GI son. As the mother continued to read, her "old hands began to tremble / And she fought against tears in her eyes / But they came unashamed for there was no name / And she knew that her darling had died." Tubb's own record is a *Hot Charts* Extra from May through July, ranked 35th in August, and then was an Extra again from September 1944 through January 1945.

### *"Fighting On The Home Front, WINS": Salutes to Civilians Who Served*

For home front volunteer organizations Tin Pan Alley professionals wrote at least nineteen marching tunes, morale-building anthems, and other songs praising the work of their members. Two of these reached a broad public through a Hollywood film and phonograph records. But, like the specialized service songs, most were written primarily to build morale among the organizations' members and stir their sense of identity, purpose, and pride as volunteers.

With few exceptions, the songs for home front volunteer organizations and similar groups are far less interesting for their content than as documents of home front history. Just a small selection shows how varied the organizations were, as well as the songwriters. Even before the United States entered the war, American songsmiths wrote numbers for two groups that were more or less international in scope. For the "V" Clubs of the British-American Ambulance Corps, Inc., Alleymen Al Lewis, Larry Stock, and Vincent Rose wrote their official song, "Let's Keep A 'V' In Ev'ry Heart" (Chappell, 1941). Bundles for Britain got its own official song, "The 'V' Song" (Dash, Connelly, 1941), by Bill Livingston and Saxie Dowell, the latter given nonsense-song immortality for his "Three Little Fishies." Kent Cooper, an ASCAP member known more as the founder of the Associated Press than as a songwriter, wrote "America Needs You" (Broadcast Music, 1941) for the Girl Scouts of America. A less-remembered young people's wartime organization, United Youth for Defense, had "There'll Always Be A U. S. A." (Embassy Music, 1942) written for it by the lesser-remembered Leonard J. Silver and Dr. Irving Epstein. Another minor professional, Daniel Wolf, wrote music to the words of Louise Richardson Dodd's "Stand By The Navy," the official song of the National Women's Council of the Navy League, a civilian support group for naval officers and enlisted men. Other published songs were written for groups as diverse as the Citizens Committee for the Army and Navy and the Civil Air Patrol.

Six home front tributes—about a third of the total—saluted the cheerfully untiring work of volunteer hostesses at USO centers and the Junior Hostesses of the American Theatre Wing Canteens. The most famous of these were midtown Manhattan's Stage Door Canteen and the Hollywood Canteen. To be perfectly frank, the worst song of this bunch is "(The) Spirit Of The U.S.O.," written as the official march of the USO (United Service Organization) by Wolcott D. Street, Prescott S. Bush, and Albert Godlis (Bob Miller, 1942). The number, which embraces all of the functions of the USO, is a bland, generic, humorless piece, simply telling the world, "We'll do what we must do / We'll go where they must go / . . . That's the spirit of the U. S. O." The remaining five songs focus on the canteen hostesses themselves, not equally well to be sure, but all with some degree of charm, wit, or humor, and a lot of pride in the often thankless work these women did for servicemen's morale. That pride is perhaps best summed up in one striking line of a number that's for the most part pretty conventional, Alleymen Abel Baer and Cliff Hess's "The Hostess In The U. S. O." (unpublished, copyright July 8, 1943): "We'll win this war, you said it, but who will get the credit? / The Hostess in the U. S. O." Who doesn't believe morale helps win wars?

Two hostess tributes reached large audiences in the 1944 Warner Brothers musical *Hollywood Canteen,* both sung by the Andrews Sisters in praise of the canteens and their unflappable hostesses. The film's title song, by Ted Koehler, Ray Heindorf, and M. K. Jerome (Remick 1944), just describes the canteen as a comfort zone for servicemen; unseen, the Andrews Sisters sang it during the opening credits. But Leah Worth, Jean Barry, and Dick Charles's richly comic "Corns For My Country" (Remick, 1944) was a fully staged performance by the sisters. In the song a beleaguered canteen hostess, "a patriotic jitterbug," bemoans being trod upon and squeezed by clumsy servicemen trying to dance: "I'm getting CORNS FOR MY COUNTRY, you should see the pounds fly, / I'm getting down the waistline and I don't even try, / . . . 'cause my weight's been taken over by the army air force." But for all her griping, "When I think I can't go on I find I can't get enough," and the intrepid hostess is ready for another tour of duty. The Andrews Sisters' recording of "Hollywood Canteen" was issued only on a V-Disc for the armed forces, but they recorded "Corns For My Country" for Decca on August 24, 1944, and it was a brief hit, a *Hot Charts* Extra for December 1944 and ranked 43rd for January 1945.

An article in the March 1943 *Ladies' Home Journal* began, "You are in charge at home for the duration: twenty million of you, with no uniforms or titles; on twenty-four hour duty, with no days off, no furlough till it's over" (25). Thus the magazine launched Women In National Service (WINS), the largest, most informally structured home front organization of the war years; all "homemakers" were automatically members without applying, paying dues, or attending meetings. Made up of "Twenty million American housewives and their teen-age daughters," WINS had as honorary national chairman Mrs. William O. Douglas, wife of the associate justice of the Supreme Court. Through articles in the *Journal,* government pamphlets, and other publications, housewives could learn how to help win the war through efficiency and conservation on the home front of their own homes. And while WINS may have had no regalia, they did have a song by Kay Swift, prominent woman composer of "Fine And Dandy" and other Broadway and Tin Pan Alley numbers. Swift's lyrics in "Fighting On The Home Front, WINS: The National War Song Of The American Housewife" (Chappell, 1943) are as specific as the best of those for women in the service. The number unsentimentally details the real work of millions of women behind the men behind the guns: "We're the dustpan crew standing back of you / . . . In ev'ry kitchen, we've got to pitch in, / If we're to save the food we're rich in / . . . Budgeting and spending, / Home repairs, Patching up and mending / . . . This is our war too, and we're there with you."

# 9:

## "Don't Forget There's A War Going On"

### Pitching In and Coping on the Home Front

Coming out of the Great Depression, war preparedness and then the war itself became America's great employment agency. The stepped-up defense economy that helped end the depression brought the country to almost full employment and stimulated its economy and industries. But ironically all that happened thanks to the most destructive war the United States ever fought. For most people the war years were prosperous, despite the rationing or shortages of many items. Nylon stockings, vacuum cleaners, flashlight batteries, and automobiles were unobtainable, but people still got dressed up, went out, and spent their new disposable income on something there was an abundance of—entertainment. FDR himself espoused "a variety of public amusements," since "off-duty recreation was a salubrious thing, so long as it did not cut into efficiency" (Lingeman 271–72). Official Washington encouraged "the movies, radio, popular music, baseball, football, and so on" as long as these entertainments paid their taxes, didn't deal with the black market, participated in bond drives and other events, and made their personnel available if needed for conscription into the armed forces (272).

The ready availability of diversions from baseball games to nightclubs, plus the discretionary income to spend on them, created an unprecedented entertainment boom in the war years. Popular music played a part in nearly all leisure activities with the possible exception of golf—the single biggest participatory sport for both men and women. Even though over 4,000 of baseball's 5,700 professional players were away in the armed forces, ballpark attendance reached its highest figures ever (Lingeman 311), with ballpark organs wheezing out snatches of tunes. Despite rising prices, nightclubs and cafés packed in patrons. In 1942 alone, New York's fifty-plus nightclubs grossed $85 million, and, throughout the war years, nightspots nationally did an annual business of around $250 million (Blum 96; Lingeman 281). These places usually featured floor shows filled with popular songs.

More than ninety million Americans went to the movies every week (Doherty 9). Besides songs in Hollywood musicals, Tin Pan Alley provided title songs and incidental music for other feature films, short subjects, and animated cartoons. Live theatre, including musicals, did very well on Broadway and on national tours. Teenagers and young adults thronged to personal appearances by popular singers and dance bands on stage or in dancehalls nationwide. And when people didn't go out for music, they brought it home with them. The demand for hit phonograph records often outstripped the capacities of recording companies to supply them, not just because of the volatile shellac shortage (see chapter 1) but because of sheer public demand. Sheet music sales of popular music alone (not classical, choral, or sacred) reached a ten-year high in 1943 (Blum 96). Publishers worried about a paper shortage (which never materialized) took steps to conserve. In one charming effort, for one edition of Frank Loesser and Ted Grouya's big 1943 hit "In My Arms" (see Chapter 11), Saunders Music replaced the cover photograph with the first page of the song's words and music, along with a little rhymed note: "Paper shortage getting worse, / Here is where we start the verse." And radio gave people all the music they could want absolutely free.

For virtually everyone on the home front, the war was a constant reality. It was on the radio, in magazine advertisements, in newsreels, or just in a trip to the grocery store, where the shortages of particular foods and other goods became apparent. An ongoing barrage of war-related messages ensured the cooperation and support of American citizens. Doing its bit for Uncle Sam, Tin Pan Alley wrote literally hundreds of songs advocating everything from national unity to scrap metal drives. Such songs appeared alongside the hits of the day in bands' live performances, in movies, and on the radio shows of popular personalities. Many were published as sheet music, but because of their limited subject matter few became commercial hits. Still, Tin Pan Alley's songs for and about the home front were the nucleus of its morale-building blitz. What's remarkable is how terrific so many of them are.

### "This Is Our War!": Singing of National Unity

"You could almost hear it click into place," wrote *New York Times* correspondent and columnist Arthur Krock of the "national unity [that] was an instant consequence" of Japan's attack on Pearl Harbor (*New York Times* 8 Dec. 1941: 6). Writing those words the very day it happened, Krock based his remarks on the immediate reactions of Congressmen, government officials, and others in Washington on that fateful Sunday. Conceding that the lives and property lost in Honolulu were a "heavy price to pay for anything," Krock nevertheless concluded, "they were not spent in vain, for national unity—which has been a distant and unattained goal since and before Hitler invaded Poland in 1939—seemed visibly to arise from the wreckage at Honolulu." The unsigned lead editorial in the *Times* on Tuesday, December 9, concurred: "Congress has spoken—no, thundered—its answer to the madmen of Japan. Gone is every sign of partisanship in the Capitol of the United States. Gone is every trace of hesitancy and indecision. There are no party lines today in Congress. There are no blocs, no cliques, no factions. The house-divided-within-itself has ceased to exist in Washington. . . . This swift and heartening demonstration of American unity meets with a reverberating echo outside the halls of Congress. From every section of the country, from every walk of life, come pledges of support for the Administration. Even before Congress had spoken, Mr. Hoover and Mr. Landon, leaders of an opposition which now takes its place at the President's side, had urged Congress to make the decision which has now been made in the name of the American people" (30). The editorial gives as examples the far-right America First Committee and a far-left labor union publicly coming together for national unity.

Of the roughly forty-five national unity songs by Tin Pan Alley or hillbilly songwriters, at least twelve were written and published before the war, from 1939 to late 1941. Like most patriotic numbers from those years, most of the prewar national unity songs aren't very good. A key difference between the pre- and post-Pearl songs is that many early ones *urged* national unity among the American people, whereas after December 7, 1941, they were able to proclaim it as a given.

Two pre-Pearl national unity songs by very skilled Alleymen were substantially better than the rest, and both got wide exposure in films, if not in record and sheet music sales. For the Republic picture *Sis Hopkins*, released in April 1941, Frank Loesser and Jule Styne wrote "That Ain't Hay (It's The U.S.A.)" (Mills, 1941), encouraging an egalitarian look at the United States as "a great big army of little people." Even earlier, Leo Robin and Ralph Rainger's "We're All Together Now" (Famous Music, 1939) first appeared in the Paramount animated film *Gulliver's Travels*. While undoubtedly written to fit the plot, the number was such a succinct and jaunty affirmation of national unity that Famous reissued the sheet music during the war. Its new cover was a photo montage of throngs of people outside the U.S. Capitol, combat troops, warships and planes, servicemen marching in dress uniform, the Statue of Liberty, and more, all within the outline of a large star. Robin and Rainger's crisp, colloquial lyric is effective: "We're all together now / . . . Ready to do, ready to dare / Whada we, whada we, whada we care / . . . There's a war that must be won."

Not surprisingly, once the United States was in the war, nearly all of the national unity numbers were published in 1942, many in the months just after Pearl Harbor. In the vanguard and doing a very patriotic turnaround was prewar leftist and isolationist songwriter Harold Rome with "This Is Our War!" (Musette, 1942), a song partly urging, but mostly proclaiming, unity, and doing both with the immediate impact of a thunderclap: "THIS IS OUR WAR, MISTER! Yours and mine and the man's next door. / THIS IS OUR WAR, MISTER! His and hers and the millions more." Even before Rome's song was published, on a radio program on December 23, 1941, dedicated to the American reaction to Pearl Harbor, Carl Hoff's orchestra with Al Noble on vocal premiered the first of what would be three versions of E. Y. Harburg and Burton Lane's "The Son Of A Gun Who Picks On Uncle Sam." With his usual offbeat wit and ingenuity, lyricist Harburg wrote of Americans putting aside their home front rivalries to unite behind the war: "The Giants how they love to cripple the Dodgers, The Dodgers how they love to scuttle the Cubs. / But the Dodgers and the Giants and the Cubs'll take a wham / At the son of a gun who picks on Uncle Sam." Subsequent stanzas cite the skirmishes among college football teams, city dwellers and country folks, and ethnicities and nationalities as personified in the Cabots, the Kellys, and the Cohns (broadcast information and unpublished lyrics courtesy of Yip Harburg Foundation archivist Nick Markovich). Harburg revised the number into a straightforward militant war song for the MGM musical *Panama Hattie,* released in September 1942. Yip's third lyric, in the 1942 Chappell sheet music, replaces the groups in the radio version with a different cast of characters: "Oh Capital may take a wallop at Labor, The C.I.O. may slug the A. F. of L. / . . . Though our melting pot may boil red hot with a thousand different types / Though we Lefts and Rights may have our fights, / We all stand pat on the no good rat who belittles the Stars and Stripes." This kind of writing brings the concept of national unity down to a concrete level everyone could appreciate.

Several other Tin Pan Alley songsmiths got on the national unity bandwagon, the best of them adding special nuances to the idea. In "Let's Bring New Glory To Old Glory" (Twentieth Century Music, 1942) from the 20th Century-Fox film *Iceland,* Mack Gordon and Harry Warren explicitly linked home front unity to America's fighting forces: "High in the sky, on the land, or the sea, / On a farm, in a mine, or munitions factory, / . . . Let us make this song our song of unity." Like Lew Pollack and Tony

Stern's militant "The Yanks Are Coming" (see chapter 6), Don Reid and Henry Tobias's "We've Just Begun To Fight" is unusual for openly recognizing the setbacks for American forces early in 1942: "Just when ev'rything is really tough / That's the time we always start to show our stuff." As the lyric unfolds, it's not just the combat troops but everyone from "the soldier to the sailor, the grocer to the tailor" who must "fight" as well. As a song, "We're All In It" (Broadway Music, 1942) isn't bad, though it's littered a bit with what were becoming national unity clichés, like "The banker, the broker, the playboy, the stoker." What's interesting about the song is that its writers were civilian Alleymen Leonard Whitcup and Paul Cunningham teamed with Major Harold G. Hoffman of the U.S. Army.

Somewhat later in the war Buck Ram, in "That Democratic Feeling" (Noble Music, 1943), and Irving Caesar, in "There Ain't No Color Line Around The Rainbow" (Chappell, 1943) from Caesar's short-lived Broadway musical *My Dear Public,* used the national unity theme to promote racial harmony and tolerance to help fight and win the war. Ram's song, the stronger of the two (and the one sponsored by the Music War Committee), makes racial unity the essence of democracy: "I get that democratic feelin' when I see people working side by side, / Every one, black and white, backing up the men who fight. Yes siree that's the way it ought to be." In Caesar's song, just as natural wonders from rainbows to roses exist for everyone regardless of color, so too should opportunities for all Americans.

The nation's unanimity of purpose excited very tangible responses from the home front. In fact, the national unity subscribed to by nearly every American made everything else on the home front possible. Without this nationwide dedication a common cause, all the plans and programs for coping with the exigencies of wartime daily living and contributing to the war effort would have been virtually impossible to implement. Though it is perhaps less remembered than tangibles like scrap drives and rationing, moral support for the troops was another responsibility of home front Americans.

### *"Say A Pray'r For The Boys Over There": Home Front Support for GIs*

During the war over a million women volunteered as hostesses to provide "food, entertainment, company and good cheer for lonely servicemen at USO centers across the nation" (Bailey 92). The good they did for stateside serviceman morale is inestimable. But the number of them in need of cheering up was small compared to the number of American troops abroad, at most times during the war estimated at over ten million. That task fell to all Americans. A handful of songs, most pretty ordinary but one that became a minor wartime classic, suggested ways for the home front to touch the front lines.

Even with only eighteen numbers in it, the group of songs encouraging Americans to offer spiritual support and otherwise keep up the morale of servicemen visibly displays a progression in the songs' subjects and tone as the war went on. In 1941 in the City of Brotherly Love, the prestigious *Philadelphia Inquirer* sponsored a "Smokes for Yanks Fund." To encourage cash contributions for sending cigarettes to GIs, Harry Filler and Frank Capano wrote the fund's official theme song, "Smokes for Yanks" (Philadelphia: Tin Pan Alley, 1941). The lyrics put servicemen having their cigarettes on a par with defense industries: "Keep your eye on plane production, / And we need those ships and tanks, / But remember, keep 'em smokin', / Don't forget those smokes for Yanks." In the 1940s almost all adult Americans smoked, and, except in combat scenes, one rarely sees a photo of a GI without a cigarette.

In 1942 four peppy morale-boosters of the "When you're smiling, the whole world smiles with you" variety burst onto the scene, encouraging people to laugh and sing so that our troops would somehow infectiously do the same. Three of them were by major songwriters. Harry Pease, Ed G. Nelson, and Reidy Reid's "Yankee Doodle Rainbow" (Joe Davis Music, 1942) exhorted people to "Smile, buddy, smile, keep your chin up high." Billy Rose and Milton Ager's "Keep 'em Smiling" (Ager, Yellen & Bornstein, 1942) encouraged doing what the title says, the "'Em" referring to our fighting GIs, "for if you do / They'll come smiling through." The best of these cheerful ditties was by Danny Kaye's wife, Sylvia Fine, a multitalented producer, writer, actress, composer, and lyricist. Written as an "Official U. S. O. Song," "Keep 'Em Laughing" (Harms, 1942) urged USO hostesses—and, by extension, all Americans—to help keep up our GIs' sense of humor, which was vital to winning the war. Fine's playful rhymes include "they'll win it in a gallop if we keep that old morale up."

Also in 1942 came the first wave of songs encouraging letter writing to GIs; the second came in 1944, with no perceptible differences in content or tone, except perhaps for a greater sense of urgency. The sameness of the six songs is reflected in their titles, which in most cases provide all the clues one needs as to the content of the lyric: from 1942 there's "Dip Your Pen In Sunshine (And Drop The Boys A Line)," "Don't Forget Your Buddy," and "Remember to Write To The Boys," and from 1944 "Have You Written Him Today?" and two different songs called "If You Don't Write You're Wrong," apparently a wartime slogan encouraging home front letter writing to GIs. A few of the numbers are maudlin, appealing to Americans' guilt about *not* writing to servicemen. Much better as songwriting and propaganda are those that take an upbeat approach, none better than one of the earliest, "Dip Your Pen In Sunshine" (Mutual

Music Society, 1942), by the songwriting twins Kay and Sue Werner and Sammy Mysels, and featured by Hal McIntyre's orchestra. The number focuses on what to write: "Fill the page with laughter, and a kiss or two to keep 'em smiling while they keep 'em flying for you." The song even urges corresponding with casual acquaintances in the service, because every GI could use the lift of a letter: "You don't have to be his father or mother, he needn't be your sweetheart or your brother."

Early in 1942 Cliff Friend and Charlie Tobias's "Wherever You Are" (Miller Music, 1942) urged spiritual support of our boys overseas through prayer. Their song was sufficiently strong for records by Dick Jurgens, Joe Reichman, and Freddy Martin to appear as *Hot Charts* Extras for March 1942. The chorus lets GIs know in the simplest terms that "All thru the darkness our faith is your guiding star, / May God bless you all / Wherever you are." We'll never know what triggered five more prayerful popular songs in 1943, though one factor may have been that by then American forces were heavily engaged in both the Pacific and in Europe, once the Allied invasion of Sicily began in July. Whatever sparked this turn toward spirituality, the results were mixed. Fred Waring, Jack Dolph, and Roy Ringwald's "Army Hymn (A Prayer For Soldiers)" (Words & Music, 1943) is a prayer for the troops, not a song encouraging Americans at home to pray for them; it's filled with heavy doses of "Thou," "Thy," and a pompous religiosity. At the other end of the spectrum is a parent's personal prayer for the wellbeing of a soldier son, Billy Post and Pierre Norman's "Son O' Mine" (Mutual Music Society, 1943), "As sung," so says the sheet music, "by Frank Sinatra." Three other songs asked Americans to pray for our troops in very similar language. The chorus of Morty Berk, Billy Hays, and Joe Frasetto's "Just A Prayer" (Mills, 1943) begins "Say a prayer, JUST A PRAYER / For someone over there," and the chorus of Steve Nelson's "Let's All Say A Prayer Tonight" (Rainbow Music, 1943) follows the title phrase with "For those ev'rywhere tonight." Both numbers are warm and sincere, but the song whose first line was its title, Herb Magidson and Jimmy McHugh's "Say A Pray'r For The Boys Over There" (Southern Music, 1943), transcended the rest in every way.

Magidson's lyric is strong, if a bit sentimental, but it's Jimmy McHugh's radiant music that set "Say A Pray'r" apart from the others and helped make it a minor hit for a time. Magidson's verse is the only direct statement I've seen in any song saying that while Americans' "working hand in hand" is important for the war effort, still "there is something more we all can do that will help to bring our loved ones safely through." To quote just Magidson's lyric of the chorus, good as it is, hardly does it justice without McHugh's soaring, legato melody, seemingly tailor-made for the soprano voice of Deanna Durbin, who sang "Say A Pray'r" in the Universal film *Hers To Hold* and recorded it. Still, the opening lines give an idea of the flavor and intent of the whole: "SAY A PRAY'R FOR THE BOYS OVER THERE / When they play the Star Spangled Banner." With its wonderful fusion of words and music, "Say A Pray'r" demonstrates that this sort of song could be majestic and moving without being artificial or overblown. The various issues of the sheet music display photos of the people who sang or played it live, on radio, or on recordings: Vaughn Monroe, Bobby Sherwood, Sonny Dunham, Ray Heatherton, Jimmy Dorsey (with vocalists Bob Eberly and Kitty Kallen), and, of course, Deanna Durbin herself. While Durbin's Decca recording is a *Hot Charts* Extra for only the month of January 1944, *Variety*'s charts show "Say A Pray'r" had consistently frequent airplays from early September 1943 through mid-January 1944. More importantly, because people wanted to participate actively in its message and sentiment rather than passively listen to it, they bought the sheet music abundantly. Both the *Billboard* and *Variety* charts show that for the same twenty weeks as the airplays, "Say A Pray'r" was never lower than 14th and frequently as high as 6th on a weekly basis in national sheet music sales.

### *"Ac-Cent-Tchu-Ate The Positive": Keeping Up Home Front Morale*

Home front Americans were eager to help boost the morale of servicemen and women here and abroad, but sometimes the home front also needed a spiritual lift. In the first half of 1942 people were disheartened by constant news of American defeats and setbacks in the Pacific and were learning to cope with shortages and rationing. In that year, songwriters produced eleven of the eighteen songs intended for general home front inspiration, but the one mammoth hit came as late as 1945.

Most home front morale songs written in 1942 are flat and colorless for the same reason that the majority of national unity songs at the same time were equally bland—they tried to address a general concern in general terms rather than with the specificity and vivid imagery that make for effective lyrics. Writers who got down to individual cases wrote the more compelling songs. Taking a break from his usual wartime occupation of Axis-bashing, country songwriter/singer Carson J. Robison recorded his "Plain Talk" (Bob Miller, 1942) for Bluebird Records on April 16 to shake up complacent Americans and get them involved in the national effort. The opening sets the tone: "The hands that fit a golf club will also fit a hoe." As an example to civilian men who gripe or just don't get involved, Robison's second verse offers the American woman who watches her boys go off to war, works in a defense plant, and still manages a household, ending with these powerful lines: "What did we [men] ever have to give up to compare to her sacrifice? / Did you ever hear her squawkin' 'bout a spare tire for the car? / If it's inspiration we're needin' we don't have to look very far." In mainstream Tin Pan Alley, Kay Twomey and Al Goodhart took a similar, though lighter, approach in "My All American Family" (Irving Berlin Inc., 1942). Twomey is at her cleverest in the song's overall concept and the lyric itself. Each chorus is essentially a list: the first is of a child's immediate family's war involvement: "My daddy is a captain in the Army / My Mummy helps the Red Cross every day," The kid ends by making a pitch: "I tell the kids that play with me / To tell their folks to be / Like My All American Family." The second list shifts from the nuclear to the "All American Family" of all Americans, Twomey deliberately placing ethnic American GIs in unlikely places: "Giuseppe has a boy that's in Hawaii, / . . . And Abe the tailor's son is now in Ireland." And to show the involvement of *all* real Americans, the third list proclaims, "Oh, Dumbo's busy flyin' bombs to Burma" and continues with five more cartoon characters, including Donald, Mickey, and Minnie, all of whom "deserted Dis-aney / To fight for Liberty"—so, in a word, you can too.

A few songs weren't just concrete but were narrowly focused too. They suggested specific programs of activity or behavior to help keep up morale. For two teams of songwriters the key to maintaining a cheerful outlook and productivity was physical fitness. From Gene Carroll and Glenn Rowell's *Gene and Glenn's "Morale Songs,"* "Keep Fit, Fella" advocated a healthy diet and regular exercise. Abel Baer and Lou Handman's "Patriotic Rhythm" (Bregman, Vocco and Conn, 1942) listed forms of exercise from baseball and bowling to golf and working out as ways to maintain a healthy attitude and a healthy body, since "Good health means good defense." One of the stranger songs offering a specific plan for keeping up morale was "Dress Up, Baby (And Smile)" (Irving Berlin Inc., 1942), with words by Buddy "A-You're Adorable" Kaye and music by David Saxon. Kaye's lyric tells the women of America that when they aren't on the job in the plant or in the home, they should "Turn in those baggy slacks," then "Wear all the things you love, and smile." Dressing up and looking good will help raise the women's spirits and also "Keep up Johnny Jones' morale—so DRESS UP, BABY and smile." Equally unusual is a little morale number from 1943 that brought children into the equation. Written by Bobby Worth and Stanley Cowan and, according to the sheet music, "Featured by EDDIE CANTOR," presumably on his radio show, "Be Good! Children, Be Good!" (West'rn Music, 1943) lays a heavy burden on kids: "Love your Mommy and guide her / You're the angel heaven sent to stand beside her. / . . . Don't be bad, children be good! / Don't forget 'over there' / Daddy waits to hear your pray'r"—words guaranteed to make children feel really bad about not being good.

Late in 1944 in the Paramount musical *Here Come the WAVES* and on some smash recordings came along Johnny Mercer and Harold Arlen's "Ac-Cent-Tchu-Ate The Positive," the war's one great feel-good morale number. Although it never mentions the war, home front morale had to have been at the back of the writers' minds when they admonished people to "E-limynate the negative, / Latch on to the affirmative / Don't mess with Mister Inbetween." And since the song was written for a war-related film set on the home front in which Bing Crosby and Sonny Tufts played sailors who sing the number (in blackface!) in a show for both civilians and service personnel, its relevance to both home front and overseas morale could hardly have escaped the song's large audience. By December 1944 some home front war-weariness was only natural for a country entering its fourth year in the war, even though most news from Europe and the Pacific had been generally good for months. Then, on December 16, right around the time "Ac-Cent-Tchu-Ate The Positive" debuted both on screen and on records, American troops in northern France, Luxembourg, and Belgium found themselves mired in the prolonged and bloody monthlong Battle of the Bulge. There's no way to prove that the sudden German offensive was an impetus for the song's initial popularity, any more than that the Americans' ultimate victory—at a cost of 77,000 Allied lives—on January 16 was responsible for its continuing success into the spring months of 1945. But "Ac-Cent-Tchu-Ate The Positive" stayed twelve weeks on *Your Hit Parade*, in 1st place for four. The most popular record was Johnny Mercer's own with the Pied Pipers and Paul Weston's orchestra, which *Hot Charts* ranks 2nd, 3rd, and 4th for January, February, and March, followed by Bing Crosby and the Andrews Sisters at 11th, 4th, and 8th for those months. Impressive sheet music sales show that people wanted to sing a really good morale-booster as much as listen to it.

Fred Waring's "The Time Is Now" (Words & Music 1943) is as vapid as a morale builder can get, saying nothing more than "hear that call, / That call to give your all." But the riveting sheet music cover art could have been the poster child for home front support of the war. A drawing of Uncle Sam's clenched fist is slamming down on the front page of a newspaper whose partially covered headline reads "WAR EFFORT," and below it are articles headed "Buy Bonds," "Write the Boys," "Support Charities," "Economize," "Keep Healthy," "Give Your Blood," "Do A Spare-Time War Job," "Kill Black Markets," "Buy Stamps," "Kill Rumors," "Save Vital Materials," and "Share with Your Neighbor." Though Waring, his own lyricist this time, included none of these specifics from the cover art in this song, many other songwriters did, making them and similar topics the timely and often entertaining subjects of motivational songs for home front Americans.

### "Citizen C. I. O.": The Workers behind the Men behind the Guns

As early as 1939 the needs of defense production increased employment markedly and brought back into the labor pool many whom the Great Depression had left stranded on the public dole. Yet by March of 1940 more than eight million Americans were still unemployed (Stillman 390), and even at the end of 1941 "Somewhere between 5,000,000 and 7,000,000 remained out of work" (Perrett 176). But four years later over sixty-four million Americans were in the labor force, including the ten million or so in the military. That brought unemployment in 1944 to an all-time low of 800,000, meaning that close to "7,000,000 of the 8,000,000 unemployed in 1940 had been siphoned into the employed" (Lingeman 136), and almost all because of the war. There are no good records of the total number employed specifically in defense industries, but overall during the war years seventeen million new jobs were created (Blum 91). A good feel for the number of war workers and their unprecedented productivity can be derived from the fact that between the fall of France in 1940 and the Japanese surrender in 1945 American industries turned out 86,000 tanks, 296,000 airplanes, fifteen million rifles, pistols, and machine guns, over forty million bullets, four million tons of artillery shells, 64,000 landing craft, 5,400 merchant ships, and 6,500 naval ships (Perrett 399). And of course war matériel productivity must also factor in uniforms, helmets, belts, boots, field rations, radar and radio equipment, and medical supplies—not to mention jeeps—along with everything else that keeps armies and navies on the move. No wonder a lot of songwriters thought war workers were worth singing about.

Americans in war work attracted the attention of some of Tin Pan Alley's finest, including Frank Loesser, Harold Rome, Ray Henderson, Irving Caesar, Johnny Mercer, Harold Arlen, Kay Twomey, Al Goodhart, Don Raye, and Gene De Paul. Alley, hillbilly, and folk songwriters wrote roughly thirty songs on defense work, making it the second biggest group of home front motivational songs next to the fifty-six promoting War Bonds and Stamps. These home front numbers are also second for most songs by Tin Pan Alley writers within any one group—twenty-four. Most of their songs are neither dull individually nor monochromatic collectively. Professional songsmiths displayed considerable creativity along with commitment to the war effort in their approaches to defense industry songs and the subtopics or angles they wrote about. The earliest pieces were fairly general, most often praising war workers or cheering for the terrific output of our defense plants, factories, and shipyards. Typical is Alley veterans Bud Green and Ray Henderson's "On The Old Assembly Line" (Green Bros. & Knight, 1942), though it goes farther than others in candidly remarking that it's American workers and American money that together will win the war: "When the overalls combine / With the mighty dollar sign, / There'll be miles and miles of American smiles / From the fac'try to the mine." That same year, for Paramount's *Priorities on Parade,* released in July, Frank Loesser and Jule Styne wrote an elaborate piece called "Payday" (unpublished; see Kimball and Nelson 88) that hints at the kinds of complex numbers both men would go on to write for Broadway. While it touches on pride in our war industries, the number is mostly about workers' loyalty to the war effort: a factory worker who likes his beer or two after work sings "as long as the soldiers over there / Need the soldiers over here, / Then I'd go right on / Rushing those props—Moving those motors— / . . . I'd go right on fighting this fight / If never was no more beer." Also in 1942, Kay Twomey, Al Goodhart, and Irwin S. Joseph fused defense work with ethnic unity in "The Smiths and Jones (The Kellys and Cohens)" (Crawford, 1942): "Who's building the tanks, who's building the planes, who's building the ships by the tons? / It's the Smiths and the Jones and the Kellys and the Coh'ns / They're all America's sons." Hillbilly music lent vocal support to defense work in the second verse of Smiley Burnette's "Gotta Figure There's A War" (Broadcast Music, 1944)—the first verse is an Axis-basher—and from folk music, Tom Glazer's "Citizen C. I. O." rose right from the union rank and file, the song's own intended audience. It's not known when Glazer wrote it, but he recorded it with the Almanac Singers on June 19, 1944, for release by Asch Records in the album *Songs for Citizen C. I. O.* (Logsdon 3, 13). The lively song's message is that the members of the C.I.O. are proud to represent virtually every ethnicity and race in working for the war effort.

One Tin Pan Alley songwriter with strong union ties in the '30s was also proud to work for the war effort. With proletarian and pro-union roots going back at least to writing the songs for the International Ladies' Garment Workers Union show *Pins and Needles* in 1937, Harold Rome was appropriately the most prolific Alleyman or woman writing songs about and for workers in the war industries. Most of these were for the American Theatre Wing's traveling *Lunch Time Follies,* presented on the job to war workers (see chapter 1). Rome published six songs, five from *Follies,* that featured defense workers. "On That Old Production Line" and "Victory Symphony Eight To The Bar" (both Kaycee Music/Leeds, 1943) lavish praise on the nation's defense workers, the latter to a boogie beat. Rome's songs about more specific aspects of war work are cleverer and sound as if he had more fun writing them. Like Johnny Mercer and Harold Arlen in "On The Swing Shift" (Famous, 1942) from Paramount's *Star Spangled Rhythm,* Rome combined war work with romance in "On Time" (Kaycee/Leeds, 1943). Mercer's lyrics, like "On the line with my baby on the swing shift, / It's the nuts there among the nuts and bolts / Plus a hundred thousand volts shining from her eyes," keep "On The Swing Shift" an innocent depiction of a boy and girl in love and at work in the same airplane plant. By contrast, Rome's comic number, sung by a woman, is packed with slightly more than borderline risqué double meanings in the singer's demand for a man who follows industrial workplace rules: "I am wise to the stay away, want to play, skip a day guys. / The man who is careless, doesn't work hard, / Will never get employment in my shipping yard. / No sir, I want a man who comes to work on time." In a more serious mood, Rome sets up a conscientious and safety-conscious worker as an exemplar to others in "That's My Pop" (Kaycee/Leeds, 1943).

With sardonic humor Rome's "The Ballad of Sloppy Joe" (Kaycee/Leeds, 1943) tells the mock mournful tale of a worker who disregarded safety regulations and died as a result: "We put what we could find of Joe into a very lovely coffin." Funny as the song is, plant safety was no laughing matter. According to historian Geoffrey Perrett, the "physical cost of war production exceeded the battle casualties." By the end of the war close to 300,000 workers had died in industrial accidents, over a million were permanently disabled, and three million more "nursed lesser wounds" (Perrett 399). Other songwriters took up the cause of plant safety. The subject naturally attracted Irving Caesar, writer of so many safety songs for children. Caesar and Gerald Marks's "Father In That Factory" (Irving Caesar, 1943) featured a child asking his parents, both war workers, to be careful. He even gives his mom some safety advice: "Wear those overalls of blue / They are safer than a skirt."

Some writers focused on quite narrow aspects of defense work. Probably the most parochial was Fred Waring and Jack Dolph's "We'll Do It!" (Words & Music, 1943), which cheered the efficiency of workers at the great shipbuilding firm of Kaiser Industries; the sheet music dedicates the song to them. An army chaplain named Captain Joseph P. Connor got together with Jack Arnold Press and Harry "By The Beautiful Sea" Carroll to write a song about the perils of absenteeism. The lyric of "You Can't Spell Victory With An Absent 'T'" (Mutual Music Society, 1943) isn't as clever as the title.

Three songs late in the war targeting specific aspects of defense work went beyond clever; they were outright funny. And in one case, funny spelled hit. Of all the songs about defense work, Don Raye and Gene De Paul's "Milkman Keep Those Bottles Quiet" (Leo Feist, 1944) is the most personal, dealing with something everyone could relate to. It's written and sung from the standpoint of an individual war worker, male or female, who works the swing shift and needs a good sleep to do a good job. This is why the poor sleep-deprived riveter keeps yelling at the milkman in jive-talk lyrics and swingtime music. In those days dairies still delivered milk and the milk still came in bottles, *very* early in the morning. The song's hip swing-shift worker unleashes a hilarious harangue at the milkman for making sleep impossible: "Milkman, stop that Grade A riot! / . . . Now the noise of the riveter I don't mind it, 'cause the man with the whiskers has a lot behind it, / But I can't keep pitchin' with that vict'ry crew when you're makin' me punchy with that bottled moo." That bottled moo was, as they say, a cash cow, especially for Ella Mae Morse's hit record during the spring and summer of 1944. Morse's association with Raye and De Paul was taking on bovine overtones—her previous big hit was their "Cow-Cow Boogie." Morse's record ranks in *Hot Charts* for five consecutive months, as high as 14th in June. The Four King Sisters and Woody Herman also had strong selling disks of "Milkman." This was the only song about defense work that had wide audience appeal.

Two other songs didn't reach as widely but dug deeply and humorously into the widespread repercussions of the mammoth growth of war industries. During the vast migrations of Americans during the war, about nine million people (four million workers and their families) "left their homes for employment in war plants" (Blum 102). Large numbers came from the south and the border states (West Virginia, Kentucky, and so on) and equally large numbers from America's heartland, what had been the Depression era's Dust Bowl. It was for this region that Eddie Cherkose and Jacques Press wrote their "western" lament "There's Nobody Home On The Range" (Hollywood: Boris Morros, 1944), about how the cowpokes and country folks had left the prairie a virtual ghost town. The choruses keep getting funnier, with lines like "Grammaw doesn't ride her geldin', / She's out at Lockheed weldin'," and "All the pistol packin' mamas are at Douglas buildin' bombers." But for all the fun, the song ends on a note of patriotic war industry cooperation: "Ev'ryone is in the battle, / Punchin' time clocks, 'stead of cattle."

The population shifts during the war worsened the housing shortage that had begun during the Depression. In defense plant boomtowns, some landlords rented a single room or apartment for twelve- or eight-hour periods to two or three workers on different shifts (see Bailey 143). With an eye for the ridiculous about such living arrangements, long-time lyricist L. Wolfe "Waiting For The Robert E. Lee" Gilbert and composer Ben "I'll Take Romance" Oakland concocted an amusing piece about a man and woman defense worker sharing a single flat at different times of day, called, appropriately, "He Went To Work In The Morning (She Went To Work In The Night)" (LaSalle Music, 1944). The sheet music is labeled "Radio Version," suggesting Gilbert and Oakland first wrote a naughtier one the airwaves wouldn't allow. The two shift-workers coexist by leaving notes for each other and sharing chores based on the time of day ("She would take in the milk in the morning, / And he took out the dog at night").

## *"Rosie The Riveter": Women Who Worked and the Songs That Loved Them*

By the fall of 1943, besides the roughly 200,000 women in the military, seventeen million others were working, "a third of the total workforce, and of those about 5,000,000 were in war industries" (Perrett 343). Even more women were "unpaid volunteers who gave of their own time to perform vital services on the home front" (Bailey 92), over three million with the Red Cross alone and millions more through the Office of Civil Defense, American Women's Voluntary Services, the United States Crop Corps, and similar agencies. No gender breakdown of volunteers is available, but it's estimated that by mid-1943, twelve million Americans were actively volunteering in civil defense–related activities alone (Lingeman 59), the majority of them women. Tin Pan Alley paid scant attention to the women doing volunteer work, but the Office of Civil Defense did wind up with two songs calling for women recruits. "Song Of The O.C.D." (Robbins, 1943), by composer Peter De Rose and his Hawaiian-born lyricist wife, May Singhi Breen, is just a call for women to become "A home front soldier," but Johnny Graham's "Volunteer For Victory" (Barton Music, 1942) enumerates in detail some of the things women could do to help: "If you can cook or you can sew a stitch," "If you can tell the children fairy-tales" (alluding to day care centers), or "If there is nothing special you can do, / Why not join the air raid warden crew?"

From the millions who volunteered to the millions working in civilian jobs that freed men for military service, women in defense industries got the most national attention. Among the inscriptions on the World War II Memorial in Washington are President Roosevelt's words about women contributing to the war: "They have given their sons to the military services. They have stoked the furnaces and hurried the factory wheels. They have made the planes and welded the tanks, riveted the ships and rolled the shells." In its dozen or so serenades to Rosie the Riveter and her sisters, Tin Pan Alley wasn't quite as eloquent as FDR, but the songs all share Roosevelt's pride in this over-and-above contribution to the cause, often by women who previously hadn't known a rivet from a trivet. The songs praising women in the work force are more vocal than those praising women in the military, perhaps because there were so many of them that they were more visible on the home front, or because it was novel and astonishing to see what women could do in jobs traditionally held by men.

Admiration for workingwomen varies only slightly in the form it takes from song to song. Musical pride in women's work first surfaced here during the war in an English import, Gordon Thompson and David Heneker's wacky "The Thing-Ummy Bob" (London: Francis, Day & Hunter, 1941, 1942; sole U.S. agent, Robbins Music). Popular English singer and comedienne Gracie Fields popularized the number here, as she had in Britain.

The lyric is mostly gibberish, as an assembly-line girl tries describing what she does to help make something she doesn't understand: "It's a ticklish sort of a job / Making a thing for a thing-ummy bob / Especially when you don't know what it's for." But ultimately she ends on a note of triumph: "And it's the girl that makes the thing that holds the oil that oils the ring / That works The Thing-ummy Bob that's goin' to win the war." A later American song also from the point of view of a self-congratulating woman is Inez James and Sidney Miller's "We're The Janes That Make The Planes" (Universal Music, 1944), from the Universal musical about defense work and bond rallies *Sing a Jingle,* released in January 1944: "We're the Janes who make the planes and we're givin' ev'ry fightin' man a chance. / We're the girls who clipped our curls and from now on we're the ones who wear the pants!" Other than Ms. James, whose best-known song is the Les Paul and Mary Ford hit "Vaya Con Dios," the only Tin Pan Alleywoman to write about women in defense work was Ann Ronell, in "The Woman Of The Year" (Chappell, 1942) from her short-lived Broadway musical *Count Me In,* with book by Leo Brady and the later great drama critic Walter Kerr. Each of the song's complex stanzas allusively describes the woman of the day, of the week, and of the month in phrases like "The woman of the day is the woman behind the beat behind the drum," but each chorus ends by repeating, "And the woman of the year is the woman behind the man behind the gun!"—literally, here, the woman defense worker making munitions and weapons for our armed forces overseas.

The songs by men about women in defense work reflect various male points of view. Though none outright criticizes workingwomen, some songs' praise does seem rather halfhearted. Alfred Eiseman, Buddy Kaye, and Howard Steiner are ambivalent in "Sweethearts In Overalls" (Edwin H. Morris, 1943), first praising the woman "with a smudge on her chin, and a victory grin, / Proudly helping them to win, Over There!" but then hoping that "some day she'll settle down, And put on her gingham gown, / When it's all over." Humor is the saving grace of the one hillbilly entry into the field of women at work. While admiring women's new independent role in society, Billy Hayes, Zeb Carver, and Jack Rollin still ask the musical question "How Will We Get Her Back In The Kitchen? (After We've Won The War)" (Peer International, 1945), not to mention "How will we stop her fingers from itchin' / To earn that fifty bucks a week or more." And Miss Assembly Line isn't just missed in the kitchen, but in more intimate spaces as well: "She used to sit in satin gowns / Behind a bedroom screen, / But now she stands in overalls / Over a milling machine." Yet for all its comic ambivalence, the number ends with the highest possible admiration for women in defense work: "The hand that rocked the cradle / Is the hand that rules today."

That's the point of view of the remaining songs by men. Harold Rome's

"The Lady's On The Job" admires and appreciates the role she plays in the big picture of the war: "The lady fair's setting the pace, / Doing her share, filling the place of somebody over there." Similarly, while the bulk of Eddie Seiler, Sol Marcus, and Fred Jay's "A Guy 24 And A B-29" (Shapiro, Bernstein, 1943) is about a bomber pilot's exploits, the second verse shifts to his sister and reveals admiration for women in defense work: "He's got a sister doing fine who works on the assembly line / She works all night and knows no play so that he can fly till Vict'ry day." Two other numbers were more effusive. In "Minnie's In The Money" (Twentieth Century Music, 1943), Leo Robin and Harry Warren express total astonishment that "Minnie's in the dough re mi": "Take my word that Minnie's in the money, / She hasn't got a guy who's got a diamond mine; / But she's a welder on the old assembly line." Several songs remark on the astounding ninety cents an hour women were paid in defense plants, but equality of pay with men doing the same job was still a long way off. The most famous defense-plant woman had the earliest song written and the most praise lavished on her—Redd Evans and John Jacob Loeb's "Rosie The Riveter" (Paramount Music, 1942). "Rosie" was also the only such song that even briefly caught on with the public, with records by the Four Vagabonds and Allen Miller making the *Hot Charts* Extras list for March and April 1943. The verse alone is testament enough to the whole song's outpouring of genuine male pride in the "new" wartime woman. "While other girls attend their fav'rite cocktail bar / Sipping dry Martinis, munching caviar / There's a girl who's really putting them to shame / Rosie is her name." And not only that, "That little frail can do / More than any male can do"—an instance of the hyperbole to which praise could stretch. The ending of the song also praises Rosie because she "buys a lot of War Bonds," at which point the song turns to a War Bonds pitch, like numerous others during the war. Over fifty other numbers did nothing but pitch bonds, many by some of the nation's finest songwriters, who produced some truly outstanding songs, as unlikely as the subject was.

### *"Dig Down Deep": Bond Drives and Other Money Matters*

Most Americans participated in the war effort not by working in defense plants or volunteering but by buying Defense Bonds and Stamps before Pearl Harbor, War Bonds and Stamps during the war, and Victory Bonds and Stamps after the Japanese surrender. Essentially, the bonds were loans to the government to help defray the cost of the war. That cost was high: over $330 billion in military and related expenses for the roughly four years the United States was in the war (Bailey 108). During that time Americans bought about $135 billion in bonds, much of the total purchased by "banks, insurance companies, and other big corporations," but Mr. and Mrs. Average Citizen and their kids bought $36 billion worth of the smaller denomination Series "E" Bonds (108). And the kids' investment in America wasn't small potatoes: "During the War, U.S. schoolchildren accounted for more than a billion dollars' worth of stamps and bonds"; to visualize this concretely, in just 1944 bonds and stamps sold in the country's schools purchased "11,700 parachutes, 2,900 planes, and more than 44,000 Jeeps" (122, 120).

Corporate bond purchases aside, for the federal government to raise such enormous sums of money by selling War Bonds and Stamps to private citizens entailed a gigantic public relations campaign. Most of the job fell to Treasury Secretary Henry Morgenthau Jr., who, even before Pearl Harbor "decided, . . . with an insight advertising men commended, 'to use *bonds* to sell the *war,* rather than *vice versa*'" (Blum, and Morgenthau qtd. in Blum, 17). Morgenthau seemed to relish the challenge of working with media and entertainment types to sell Americans on buying a piece of America. The treasury secretary gave his blessing to bond rallies with live entertainment in Madison Square Garden and similar venues elsewhere. He supported special bond drive shows on the radio, such as Kate Smith's on September 21, 1943, from which she emerged the undisputed bond-raising champion, selling close to forty million dollars worth in sixteen hours on the air (Perrett 299). In addition to giving its support to such occasional radio programs, the U.S. Treasury had its own weekly show. "Presented with the cooperation and direction of Secretary of the Treasury Henry S. Morgenthau, Jr.," *Treasury Hour* was broadcast on Tuesdays at 8 P.M. EST on the NBC-Blue Network, reaching about a hundred affiliate stations around the country. Morgenthau and Co. backed the program in every way but financially, the airtime paid for by "Bendix Aviation Corporation as a contribution to national defense" (*Radio Hit Songs* Feb. 1942: 5). The show, with its own twenty-five-piece orchestra and fourteen-voice chorus conducted by Leonard Joy, mostly alternated popular musical numbers sung by many guest artists with pitches for War Bonds. Morgenthau also worked with Hollywood studios to make short subjects about War Bonds for the nation's millions of moviegoers to watch along with the double feature, cartoon, and newsreel. Overall he engaged not just the cooperation but the creativity of people in every branch of the media and entertainment industries, not the least of these being songwriters. Morgenthau occasionally commissioned a song from a specific writer but more often reviewed songs sent to the Treasury Department, and, if they were suitable to a bond drive, gave his imprimatur in variations of the phrase "Approved by The United States Treasury" on the sheet music. When a song's profits were to go entirely and directly to the government, he'd copyright the number in his own name, the sheet music reading "Copyright by Henry Morgenthau, Jr., Secretary of the Treasury, D. C.," with no publisher given.

Irving Berlin wrote the granddaddy and biggest hit of all bond songs well before Pearl Harbor. In addition to Secretary Morgenthau's copyright notice, the sheet music cover of "Any Bonds Today" proudly proclaims, "Theme Song of the National Defense Savings Program." Berlin wrote it "at the request of" Morgenthau to promote the Treasury Department's Defense Bond and savings stamp drive very early on; the copyright date is June 16, 1941. Morgenthau later wrote to Berlin to thank him: "This is just to tell you that 'Any Bonds Today' is proving to be a wonderful help to us in our Defense Bond program. You have given a real lift to American morale by writing and contributing this song. . . . I am just about the proudest copyright owner you ever saw" (qtd. in Kimball and Emmet 371). Savvy songsmith that he was, Berlin wrote a snappy lyric and razzmatazz ragtime tune almost guaranteed to lift morale. The melody has so much to do with this, as is true of the other truly great bond appeal songs, that a snatch of lyric hardly does justice to the whole. But a few lines give an idea of Berlin's blending of the patriotic with the colloquial for some very effective songwriting: "Any Bonds today? / All you give will be spent to live in the Yankee way / Scrape up the most you can, Here comes the freedom man." "Any Bonds Today" never made *Your Hit Parade* or the trade paper charts, but in the big picture it did extremely well. Barry Wood premiered it on radio "in late June 1941" (371), and his record is a *Hot Charts* Extra from June 1941 through March 1942, moving up to 50th for January 1942. Dick Robertson and Kay Kyser's records also did well. But the most interesting was Decca 4044, a disk for people who liked the song so much they could hear the Andrews Sisters' rendition on one side and Tommy Dorsey's orchestra with vocals by Bob Eberly and Helen O'Connell on the other.

Professionals wrote fifty-one songs whose sole or primary purpose was a bond appeal. Of these, prominent Tin Pan Alleymen wrote thirty-four (and I mean "Alleymen" literally; inexplicably, none of the Alley's major women wrote songs about bond drives). Even Hammerstein's Music War Committee got in the act, straying again from chasing the chimera of an all-purpose war song to publish bond appeals by established Alleymen Ervin Drake, Bob Russell, and Buck Ram. Yet there's not much to say about most of the songs since the content and purpose of all are nearly identical: War Bonds and Stamps, and selling them. But a half dozen or so numbers rise above their peers as outstanding popular songwriting. Briefly and chronologically, on June 17, 1942, Tommy Dorsey with Frank Sinatra and the Pied Pipers on vocal recorded Alley veterans Walter Hirsch, Sano Marco, and Gerald Marks's "Dig Down Deep" (Yankee Music, 1942), asking Americans to do just that for bonds in the idiom of a big-band swing number: "So, DIG DOWN DEEP! / The boys are giving all for you, / And so, the least that you can do / Is DIG DOWN DEEP." The sheet music notes that "This song has been prepared by its owners on behalf of the United States Treasury War Bonds and Stamps Campaign," but it's not clear whether the profits went solely to the Treasury Department or if the song was a commercial venture. Either way, *Variety*'s jukebox charts show the very danceable tune had a lot of plays between September and November, and Dorsey's record is a *Hot Charts* Extra for October and November 1942.

Equaling Berlin's prototype in its superior music and lyrics was Tom Adair and Dick Uhl's "Ev'rybody Ev'ry Payday" (copyright 1942 by Henry Morgenthau Jr., 1942), all proceeds going to the Treasury Department. Uhl's bouncy tune aside, Adair's felicitous way with words shines out, even when he's hawking bonds: "EV'RYBODY, EV'RY PAYDAY, / Ev'ry farmer, ev'ry hay day / Top the crop with dimes for Uncle Sam. / Ten per cent! That's the rent! / Ev'ryone can pay / For a home in the U.S.A." In November 1942 Barry Wood made an electrical transcription for radio broadcasts, then later a commercial record, as did Tommy Tucker and Guy Lombardo, with special dispensation from Petrillo's recording ban because of the song's subject and purpose (Weiner).

The lyrics of Frank Loesser's "The Road To Victory" (Saunders, 1943) look repetitive, but when the words are attached to his very insistent melody, this bond appeal becomes a tune you can't get out of your head until you exorcise the demon by running out to buy a bond or two (which may have been Pvt. Loesser's intention): "Get on, get on, get on THE ROAD TO VICTORY, / Get off, get off, get off the rusty dusty / And get on, get on, get on THE ROAD TO VICTORY / And buy another Bond today." The sheet music provides the history: "Published by request of the UNITED STATES TREASURY DEPT. In connection with the THIRD WAR LOAN" and "Entire proceeds of This Song to Be Turned Over to the NATIONAL WAR FUND." Loesser's was the first of two bond songs millions heard sung by America's most popular male vocalist, Bing Crosby. Crosby sang "The Road To Victory" twice on his *Kraft Music Hall* radio show, on September 16 and October 7, 1943, and also performed it in a Warner Brothers short subject of the same name released in May 1944. In another short film—*All Star Bond Rally*, released by 20th Century-Fox in June 1945—Crosby sang Harold Adamson and Jimmy McHugh's "Buy a Bond" (Chappell, 1945), just about as infectious and upbeat a song as anyone might imagine, whether about bonds or anything else. McHugh wrote a highly imaginative march in ⅝ time, and Adamson wrote lyrics to match: "Buy, Buy, Buy, Buy a bond / And you'll be standing by the vict'ry arch when Johnny comes marching home again. / . . . 'Til the lads come back again, back the old attack again / And Buy, Buy Bonds." The drives continued even after the Japanese surrender, now for Victory Bonds to help pay for the war just ended. And the songs continued as well, including Sammy Cahn and Jule Styne's "Buy A Piece Of the Peace," performed by Frank Sinatra with Axel Stordahl's orchestra on the Treasury Department's *Music For Millions #5* radio fundraiser on September 9, 1945 (Weiner). All that quality talent expended on selling War Bonds, and for virtually no monetary compensation.

The six "big" bond numbers just discussed were written and performed by some of the biggest names in the business: writers Irving Berlin, Tom Adair, Frank Loesser, Harold Adamson, Jimmy McHugh, Sammy Cahn, and Jule Styne, and performers Barry Wood, the Andrews Sisters, Kay Kyser, Tommy Dorsey, Bob Eberly, Helen O'Connell, Guy Lombardo, Bing Crosby, and Frank Sinatra—a pretty impressive list of some of the war years' top music talent. Other prominent Alleymen who wrote songs for War Bond drives were Oliver "Der Fuehrer's Face" Wallace, Herman Hupfeld, Andy Razaf, Harold Rome, Lew Brown and Ray Henderson, and Johnny Burke and Jimmy Van Heusen, all, like the others above, on their own time with no monetary reward. Some of America's most successful and finest songwriters channeled a lot of energy into writing not perfunctory songs for something as non-commercial (for them) as bond drives but instead imaginatively and creatively excellent popular songs. That they did this with no expectation of financial gain says a lot about Americans' readiness to voluntarily participate in the war effort. Anyone familiar with 1940s popular music idioms listening to any of the six big bond songs would recognize *this* as outstanding songwriting, regardless of the subject.

The few songs dealing with fiscal matters other than bond drives are a footnote on history and scarcely worth mentioning except to show Alleymen at work writing about various facets of financing the war. Irving Berlin again led off, with "I Paid My Income Tax Today" (Henry J. Morgenthau Jr., Secretary of the Treasury, Washington, D.C., 1942). As with "Any Bonds Today," all royalties went to the Treasury Department, and once again Secretary Morgenthau was very grateful to Berlin: "It wasn't an easy assignment to make people sing about taxes, but you have done this beautifully, and you have also hit the nail on the head as far as the Treasury policy is concerned" (qtd. in Kimball and Emmet, 373). The policy alluded to by Morgenthau was that the income tax (and its wartime 5 percent surcharge) was designed not just for revenue to fight the war but to make *all* Americans aware that they shared in a common cause: "You see those bombers in the sky? / Rockefeller helped to build them; so did I— / I paid my income tax today." Inflation was both a great fear and a great reality during the war, and part of the government's rationale for War Bonds and the income tax was to fight inflation; people would invest in or pay a tax directly to the government rather than spend their surplus money. Another inflation fighter was personal savings, and the case for it was put directly in "Save The American Way" (Mills, 1942), with words by Richard Litton and music by eminent bandmaster and march composer Edwin Franko Goldman. And very late in the war, Robert Sour even managed to explain inflation in terms just about anyone could understand in "Your Pot Of Dough (And My Pot O' Dough)" (Broadcast music, 1945): "If you spend your pot o' dough, / And I spend my pot o' dough, / We'll just send the prices sky high. / If we're not thrifty, five gets you fifty / Old debbil inflation will get us."

### *"Dirty Overalls": Salvage and Tillage for Victory*

To curb inflation and preserve precious resources, home front Americans gave not just their money but their time and physical labor to collect and conserve vital materials and to plant, cultivate, and make their Victory Gardens grow. The bombing of Pearl Harbor signaled almost immediate calls for civilian participation in the war effort that was more active than investing in War Bonds. Not far behind those calls to action, Tin Pan Alley richly acknowledged such home front activities. Appeals for scrap metal began even before Pearl Harbor, the campaigns for steel very successful, those for aluminum a disaster. For the latter, mountains of old pots, pans, and other stuff piled up at collection points outside "courthouses, fire stations, and city halls," with no one willing to cart it off once it was learned that only "virgin aluminum" could be used in aircraft manufacture. So all the scrap aluminum was useless—except to be melted down and recycled into yet more pots and pans (Perrett 194). But as the war went on, military uses were found for scrap aluminum, as well as steel, iron, and other metals, and people kept collecting it for salvage. It's not clear when the call first went out for scrap paper, but it had to have been very shortly after Pearl Harbor, since Fats Waller recorded his "(Get Some) Cash For Your Trash" (Leo Feist, 1942) on December 26, just nineteen days after the attack, and Ed Kirkeby's wonderfully funny lyric mentions both paper and metal. The number also illustrates that in the early days of salvaging metal, people could sell it to "junk dealers": "Save up all your iron and tin, / But when you go to turn it in, / Don't give it away, No, no! / Get Some Cash For Your Trash." Another form of trash people could get cash for throughout the war was kitchen fats of all kinds, "from deep-fat frying, meat drippings, and the rendered trimmings from steaks and chops." Fat was a key ingredient of the glycerin used in the manufacture of explosives and munitions; "a pound of fat from every home each month would make more than 500 million pounds of smokeless powder a year" (Hayes, *Cooked* 152). People took their fat to a butcher, "who would pay the prevailing price for it in cash or ration stamps depending on the program that was in effect at that time" (152). Vital as kitchen fats were, they never got their own song, as far as I can tell. But in "On That Old Production Line," Harold Rome at least gave a casual nod to them as part of housewives' contributions to the war effort: "Pop is in the shop helping their output increase, / Mom is in the kitchen saving kitchen fats and grease! / Sister's gone to work in her overalls and cap, / And kid brother is out collecting scrap."

And was he ever! America's children were the champion scrap collectors, and, unlike many adults, "enlisted for the duration . . . [and] never let up until the War was over" (Bailey 120). Butchers paid for kitchen fats, but many kids collected them for fun and contributed them for free; good thing, because a thirteen-year-old boy in Maywood, Illinois, didn't just scrounge up over a hundred tons of paper between Pearl Harbor and D-Day but "somehow also found the time to round up a ton and a half of waste fats" (Perrett 394). If he had sold it, he could have retired in tenth grade. Both in organized groups and casually, children were prime movers in scrap collection, and their efforts did not go unnoticed by songwriters. "Children of America," by Nelle W. Godfrey, Ann Godfrey, and Helen Meyers (Irving Berlin Inc., 1942), celebrated the kids' efforts from their own point of view: "We're the CHILDREN OF AMERICA, / We're in the scrap today. / . . . We can gather up the copper, the rubber and the rags, / And ev'ry piece of iron and steel, and the rope and burlap bags." Probably alluding to the Junior Commandos, the boys' and girls' groups structured on paramilitary lines to collect scrap and participate in war games and patriotic exercises, Gene Carroll and Glenn Rowell's "Join The Junior Legion," from their 1942 *Morale Songs,* was a motivational number to get kids involved and doing their best: "Private Slim and Sergeant Stout, / Get your little wagon out / . . . Gather papers and old junk / Show the world we kids have spunk," concluding with a pitch for children to buy War Savings Stamps every week. Later in the war, when the War Production Board organized the Paper Troopers for kids in scrap-paper drives, Alleymen Sunny Skylar and Henry Sylvern wrote them an official song with the group's name as its title (Robbins, 1944). The kids really did their job: in five months in Chicago, "thousands of children took to the streets" and collected 18,000 tons of newspaper (Bailey 120). When FDR issued the call for scrap rubber in 1942, Boy Scouts alone "collected more than 54,000 tons" (126). "My Rubber Dolly" (Reising Music, 1943), by Seldon Reising and Rose Marlowe, charmingly captures the naïve sincerity of a little girl wanting to help a scrap rubber drive: "I'm glad I gave my rubber dolly to Uncle Sammy / 'Cause he needs it more than I do / It was all I had but I was glad / To do it for the Red White and Blue."

While songs about scrap weren't many, something as prosaic as junk sparked some pretty inspired songwriting by a few less-well-known Alleymen, one song becoming the "official" junk song of the war. The sheet music of Austen Croom-Johnson and Alan Kent's "Junk Ain't Junk No More ('Cause Junk Will Win The War)" (Bregman, Vocco, and Conn, 1942) identifies the number as the "Theme Song of the NATIONAL SALVAGE CAMPAIGN under the auspices of the CONSERVATION DIVISION OF THE WAR PRODUCTION BOARD." The cover photo is captioned "Featured by Bing Crosby," which indeed this little song was, but in a rather unusual way. According to *Song Hits Magazine* for October 1942, "Junk" is so short because it "was not written primarily as a popular tune but as a quick musical expression of an idea . . . [that] would not interfere with station broadcasting schedules" (12). Crosby made an electrical transcription of "Junk" to be distributed to radio stations nationwide as a spot announcement promoting scrap collection, the songwriters and publisher turning over all sheet-music royalties and profits to the USO (12). As the title suggests, the song took a lighthearted approach to the serious business of scrap salvage, concluding with the playful rhyme: "Take a tip from Uncle, / Junk'll Win The War."

Given the myriad items encompassed by junk, scrap metal gave the impetus to a few list songs, some mostly for fun, others with more point and purpose. Of the former variety is Justin Herman and Dudley Wilkinson's "Savin' All The Tin I Kin" (Famous Music, 1943), which rattles off "Ash cans, trash cans, corned beef hash cans, soup cans and tomaters; / Thick foil, thin foil, any old tin foil helps foil the dictators!" By contrast, Hammerstein's MWC published Milton Drake, Al Kaufman, and Leonore Glasner's "We're Melting All Our Memories" in 1943. It's a lyrical piece in which an older married woman's scouring the home for scrap elicits both wistful humor and poignancy: "The shiny cocktail shaker that held enough for two. / The trains I bought for Junior that I should have bought for you! / . . . I'm clinging to your picture, but the frame is on the heap." One sequence in this touching song puts all of the home front's sacrifices in perspective: "Some things that we forgot we had, a lot of things we'll miss. / But after all, it's not so bad, / Those youngsters on Bataan gave up a great deal more than this."

One of Washington's stated aims for scrap drives was to keep people in close, active touch with the war. The same held true for Victory Gardens. My father's only hobby was gardening—tulips, roses, zinnias, dahlias, and chrysanthemums that he planted and tended every spring and summer in our suburban Chicago backyard. But like millions of other gardeners (and non-gardeners), Dad mostly turned from flowers to vegetables for the duration and joined the neighbors in clearing, tilling, and parceling out Victory Garden plots for each family on two vacant lots across the street from our house. As a child during the war, I'd trot over there, salt shaker in hand, to pluck and eat a sun-warmed tomato right off the vine. No one bothered much with pesticides, and the pests didn't seem to bother the veggies much either—maybe even the bugs knew there was a war on. Not long after Pearl Harbor Secretary of Agriculture Claude R. Wickard proposed the idea of Victory Gardens, "even though American farms already were producing enough to feed half the world" (Bailey 108). Victory Gardens still had their uses, beyond the obvious morale-building use of promoting national unity by getting neighbors to talk to each other. A great deal of American produce, meat, and dairy products fed our own troops and those of the Allies, so by maintaining a high crop yield of homegrown vegetables, Victory Gardens helped control the prices of those that were commercially grown, thus helping to curb inflation. The home front took to Victory Gardens with an enthusiasm unequaled by any other form of participation in the war effort. From pots of tomatoes on urban rooftops to acres of rural corn, in 1943, the peak year of participation, Americans planted over twenty million Victory Gardens, yielding over a million tons of vegetables valued at $85 million and accounting for 40 percent of all produce consumed in the United States in '43 (Bailey 108; Lingeman 251). Children, mostly in organized groups, played a major role in the success of Victory Gardens and other home front agriculture. In just the first year of the war "a million and a half 4-H boys and girls harvested 3,000,000 bushels of vegetables from victory gardens and preserved 14,000,000 jars of food. On larger farms and ranges, 4-H children in 1942 raised 6,500,000 chickens [chicken wasn't rationed, incidentally], 300,000 hogs, and 65,000 dairy cattle" (Hoehling 71).

The gardening bug bit the home front immediately, but songwriters at first seemed almost immune, producing only two of the war's total of fifteen songs about Victory Gardens and other agriculture in 1942, and neither of them particularly noteworthy. But in 1943 and 1944 Tin Pan Alley yielded a larger crop of horticultural songs. Most were of the average garden variety and none ever made the trade paper charts or even the retrospective *Hot Charts,* but some of the best gained wide exposure in the movies. Also, the Music War Committee published two such numbers, showing the MWC's support of the war with all sorts of songs, not just militant marching tunes. In the first of these, folksong and popular music came together when Woody Guthrie and Earl Robinson wrote "Dirty Overalls" (Music War Committee, 1943), not about the country's "dilettante" Victory Gardeners but about a dirt farmer whose family farm helps support the war: "This piece of land I stand on is my battlefield and home, / And my plow and my hoe are my gun / . . . And my uniform is my Dirty Overalls." For the 20th Century-Fox Betty Grable musical *Pin Up*

*Girl,* released in April 1944, Mack Gordon and James V. Monaco picked up on this idea in "Yankee Doodle Hayride" (Triangle Music, 1944), a number about volunteer harvesters such as those in the Crop Corps: "Soldiers in khaki, sailors in blue, cannot be any prouder than you, / A pair of overalls is a uniform too." The other MWC agricultural offering is one of several Victory Garden songs that found seemingly infinite numbers of rhymes for vegetables. The lyrics of Leonore Glasner and Ernest Gold's "We've Gotta Dig For Victory" (Music War Committee, 1944) try to do the nearly impossible by having three two-syllable rhymes in each half of every stanza—and it almost succeeds but strains a bit. (Lorenz Hart achieved this effortlessly in "Manhattan," but few others have done it as well.) Urging people to plant Victory Gardens after their decline following the 1943 bumper crop, one of Glasner and Gold's better triple rhymes is "Don't hang around that hotel lobby / Go and plant some fresh kohlrabi / Make your garden work your hobby / We've gotta dig for Victory!"

Hollywood's three remaining Victory Garden songs took very different approaches, each of which could have been very effective at the time. For the 1944 Paramount musical *And the Angels Sing,* Johnny Burke and Jimmy Van Heusen focused on the social value of Victory Gardens in "How Does Your Garden Grow?" (Famous, 1944). Sung by Dorothy Lamour, Betty Hutton, Diana Lynn, and Mimi Chandler, the number remarks how "Old fashioned friendship is in style again / The folks on the corner find time to meet with the folks next door or across the street," with talk turning to their gardens: "They say there may be rain. / Just think what that will do for our romaine"—in a word, Victory Gardens bonded people in national unity on the neighborhood scale. The previous year, Johnny Mercer and Harold Arlen also showed the socializing value of Victory Gardens, but on a personal level, when "a small four 'F'" becomes a home front hero as "Harvey The Victory Garden Man" (Edwin H. Morris, 1943) in the 1943 RKO film *The Sky's The Limit.* Harvey isn't just the envy of other Victory Gardeners and suddenly a desirable catch for the girls, he's also held up as a model for hip would-be gardeners in one of Mercer's most outrageous rhymes: "Come on you cats, aristocrats, and dig, dig, dig, . . . Forget all your troubles among the 'vegetubbles.'" But the most ingenious of all Victory Garden songs for Hollywood or otherwise was by composer Jay Gorney and his two irrepressibly wacky lyricists, Henry Myers and Edward Eliscu. It was originally sung in the 1943 Columbia release *The Heat's On* by Victor Moore, who had made a career of playing droopy, sad-eyed nonentities all the way back to Vice-President Alexander Throttlebottom in the 1931 musical *Of Thee I Sing.* Singing the hilariously mock-doleful "They Looked So Pretty On The Envelope" (Mills, 1944), Moore was the Everyman of would-be backyard gardeners who had no knack for growing things. Through three long verses of Myers and Eliscu's screwball gags, he tells of how "my only stalk of celery was rejected by the cow," "my vegetables look like rope, / They feel like jello, and they taste like soap," and—in the song's most inspired bit of nonsense—"The way my peas grow littler, / You'd think I work for Hitler." In the happy ending, the poor schlemiel discovers that his onions manage to grow, so he goes on planting nothing but. Such a song might appear counterproductive to getting people to make their gardens grow, but in fact it falls right in with a large and frequently wonderful body of numbers that didn't encourage proactive participation in war-related activities but instead offered ways of coping with or feeling better about the restrictions, regulations, and limitations imposed on home front living. The best of these songs, like Gorney, Myers, and Eliscu's Victory Garden one, did so through humor.

### "You Can't Get That No More": Coping with Home Front Conditions

In their 1938 musical *Knickerbocker Holiday*, Maxwell Anderson and Kurt Weill defined the American character by its fierce independence, especially in the face of government rules and regulations. One song asks "How Can You Tell An American?" and answers, "It's just that he hates and eternally despises / The policeman on his beat, and the judge at his assizes, / The sheriff with his warrants and the bureaucratic crew / For the sole and simple reason that they tell him what to do; / . . . He insists on reading, he insists on thinking—free of governmental snooping or a governmental plan— / And that's an American!" (Anderson 27). There was a lot of truth to this vis-à-vis government controls and directives during World War II, and many Americans had trouble adjusting.

The attack on Pearl Harbor said to Americans that it *can* happen here, making air raid and blackout drills a serious business in most communities, even if it meant swallowing our feisty American individuality and following pretty stringent directives. While most of the country cooperated exceedingly well with activities planned or suggested by the Office of Civil Defense, scattered individuals and some entire parts of the country, such as Buffalo, New York, and most of the state of Kansas, remained recalcitrant, apathetic, or just plain lazy about such things (Lingeman 61). Such attitudes may explain why the majority of songs about air raid wardens and blackouts either urge cooperation or patiently detail the procedures to follow during a blackout or air raid drill. The tone of Tin Pan Alley's half dozen or so air raid and blackout songs—all, incidentally, written and published in 1942—is uniformly serious, quite different from songs on these subjects that entertained our English allies even during the height of the Blitz. The English, especially in and around London, experienced bombings firsthand and so learned how to carry on through repetitions of them. In those circumstances, humorous and romantic songs about the situation provided momentary relief from blackouts and air raids that weren't drills but the real thing. With their serious messages designed to keep people informed and in a state of preparedness, American civil defense songs were never as lighthearted as English ones, like the outrageously funny if politically incorrect "Mr. Wu's An Air Raid Warden Now," the slyly risqué "The Deepest Shelter In Town," or the swing-time ballad "They Can't Black Out The Moon."

"The Air Raid Warden Song," "Co-Operate With Your Air Raid Warden," "Shake Hands With Your Air-Raid Warden," "If There's A Blackout Tonight," "When You Hear The Sirens Blow," "Don't Let A Blackout Give You a Knockout"—these titles suggest the similarity of the songs. The numbers are distinguishable only by their varying quality, even though major Tin Pan Alley writers wrote them all. In terms of cleverness and entertainment value, which were scarce commodities in civil defense songs, Herb Magidson's lyric for "Co-Operate With Your Air Raid Warden" (Famous, 1942), with music by Jule Styne, is the winner. Sung by Ann Miller in the Paramount musical *Priorities on Parade* (Shull 320), Magidson's skilled lyrics give a little lift to the usual instructions about turning out lights and pulling down shades: "If you don't wanna cross that river Jordan / Co-operate with your air-raid warden." Of the rest, the best were by Irving Caesar and Gerald Marks, writers of numerous children's songs about safety. In fact, they wrote "Shake Hands With Your Air-Raid Warden" and the first verse of "When You Hear The Siren Blow" (both Irving Caesar, 1942) for an audience of children, the second verse of the latter for their mothers. The sheet music features identical cover art: a photograph, from the rear, of two adorable young children (perhaps age three to five) bundled up in snowsuits and looking at a drawing of an iron fence with a large poster of instructions headed "AIR RAID PRECAUTION BULLETIN." Like Caesar's familiar "Remember Your Name And Address," his lyrics for the two air raid drill songs for children are written in simple, easy to understand, and—most importantly—entirely non-threatening language. Caesar even defines terminology for the kids: "'Air-Raid warden' is a phrase that's new, / And it may need explaining, / Warden means protector, / And ev'ry one gets special training." When he speaks to the kids' mothers, Caesar gets down to more specific actions to take: "If a raid should come by day, from the school please stay away, / Teachers know what to do; And if a raid should come by night, shut off the gas, turn out the light, / Then you won't give a plane in flight, one little sight of you." Irving Caesar wrote only a few great songs (like "Tea For Two"), but his almost obsessive devotion to instructing children about safety in song and his talent for doing so in gentle, reassuring ways earn him a place of importance in helping home front children cope with the often puzzling life during the war.

The Office of Civil Defense took the matter of citizens' participation in rumor control as seriously as it did air raid preparedness. Tin Pan Alley took it seriously too, but songwriters had a whole lot more fun in the ways they wrote about it. Only two of the seven numbers dealing with rumor control were wholly serious, Gene Carroll and Glenn Rowell's "Silence Is Golden," from their 1942 *Morale Songs* collection, and Lew Pollack and Herman Ruby's cautionary "Zip Your Lip!" (Southern Music, 1942): "If you have a boy in uniform, / You should be very proud; / If you happen to know where he is to go, / Don't dare to say it out loud." Fear of enemy agents, spies, and sabotage was very real throughout the war, though actual incidents of Axis infiltration into the United States were few and inconsequential. Nevertheless, like the government, Tin Pan Alley treated such possibilities as a clear and present danger, especially early in the war—all but one rumor-squelching song appearing in 1942. Two became brief hits, and even those that didn't were pretty good songs. At one point, Harold Rome's "Mr. Chucklehead" (Musette, 1942) zooms in on rumors and idle talk. Mr. Chucklehead is a guy who "warns you that our allies are gonna pull a fast one / Who says that he hates rumors, then gives out with the last one!" In a very different style was "Shut My Mouth (I Ain't Talkin')" (Edward B. Marks, 1942), by singer Frances Faye, Ruthe Bryer, and Roslyn Hershenson. In 1939, Ms. Faye had collaborated with Don Raye and Dan Howell on "Well, All Right! (Dig! Dig! Dig!)," a singularly groovy jump tune and a major hit for the Andrews Sisters. In 1942, Faye and her female collaborators playfully enlisted hip, jive-talking lyrics and swing music in the serious cause of rumor control: "SHUT MY MOUTH I ain't talkin' / I SHUT MY MOUTH I ain't squawkin', / When I hear an idle story I'm no mocking bird, / I SHUT MY MOUTH for dear old Glory, / Sh! Sh! Mum's the word." It's a good song, but two others around the same time were just better enough to gain some national popularity. It didn't hurt that Alan Courtney, Earl Allvine, and Walter Bishop's "Shh, It's A Military Secret" (Alan Courtney Music, 1942) was recorded by Glenn Miller, with vocals by Marion Hutton and Tex Beneke. And, of course, the last-minute shift from rumor-squelching song to love song probably had a bit to do with its popular appeal: "Let's just talk about love. / 'cause that's what I'm thinking of / And it's no MILITARY SECRET that I love you." Miller's record, along with one by Terry Shand, is a *Hot Charts* Extra for May 1942. Even without a romantic angle, Duke Ellington's record of Luther Henderson Jr. and Mercer Ellington's jive-talking "A Slip Of The Lip (Can Sink A Ship)" (Tempo Music, 1942) was the biggest-selling rumor-control song, a *Hot Charts* Extra from August through December 1942, except for October, when it ranks 32nd. The smooth swingtime music and stylishly hip lyric most likely accounted for the song's success: "Shh! Don't see too much. / Shh! Don't jive too much. / Jack! Don't be too 'hip,' 'cause a SLIP OF THE LIP might sink a ship." After 1942, the only rumor-control song was Milton Drake's "Your Tail Is Showing" (Music War Committee, 1943), which simply says that if you believe or spread rumors, then your tail is showing and "Hitler made a monkey out of you."

Having to obey air raid and blackout regulations and be wary of unsubstantiated rumors were only periodic annoyances for Americans, but the rationing or unavailability of creature comforts most people took for granted was a daily aggravation and inconvenience, if not an actual hardship. Right after Pearl Harbor, rumors of imminent "shortages, rationing, and controls" of consumer goods began, and the immediate response for millions was hoarding. A fourteen-city study found people squirreling away everything from sugar, coffee, canned goods, and spices to rubber products like tires, garden hoses, and golf balls (Blum 94). In pursuit of the hoarders came some "no-no" songs like Gene Carroll and Glenn Rowell's "You're Out Of Order, Mrs. Hoarder," from their 1942 *Morale Songs,* Mickey Gillette and Dick McCaffrey's "The Bad Little Piggie" (Hollywood: Variety Music, 1943), and Harold Rome's "Johnny Is A Hoarder," from his ill-fated musical revue *Let Freedom Sing,* which closed after eight performances. Not many people heard these songs, nor, apparently, did hoarders hear more official appeals to cease hoarding until conditions made it practically impossible.

Those conditions came soon enough as the reality of shortages and rationing replaced the rumors. Every week for the first three months of 1942, *Business Week* ran lists of the government-ordered cessation or, occasionally, reduction of the manufacture of consumer goods and materials. Among the long list's items were bicycles, over fifty types of appliances, including toasters, waffle irons, and percolators, materials for making flashlights and batteries, and metals used in household furniture, toys, and other "nonessential" goods. Anyone who used toothpaste or shaving cream in tubes had to bring in a used tube in order to buy a new one (Lingeman 115–16). What really hurt this nation of drivers was Washington's order to "auto makers to stop building family cars in 1942" (Bailey 156). This, along with the rubber shortage and gas rationing, greatly altered the lifestyle of most Americans. But Tin Pan Alley's songwriters kept pace with current events and did their humorous best to keep up morale. The earliest such songs of any significance had to do with gas, rubber, and cars, and offered whimsical or romantic solutions to Americans' displeasure over their restricted driving habits. The silliest solution came in the early 1943 Disney cartoon *Victory Vehicles,* in which Goofy demonstrated some goofy conveyances, opting for the one in Ned

Washington and Oliver Wallace's accompanying "Hop On Your Pogo Stick" (Southern Music 1942): "Who needs a limousine that's always out of gasoline, / Hop on your pogo stick and laugh your cares away!" In the 1942 Universal musical *Get Hep To Love,* Al Hoffman, Mann Curtis, and Jerry Livingston had Gloria Jean console Donald O'Connor about his jalopy's flat tire in "Let's Hitch A Horsie To The Automobile" (Leeds, 1942), a gas-saving measure with the added incentive of backseat necking: "Our nation needs its gasoline, the situation's pretty keen / . . . So let's hitch a horsie to the automobile / And we'll kiss as he clippety clops along."

Nearly everything was interconnected in wartime rationing and shortages, a principle worth remembering when trying to understand gasoline rationing because gas seemed plentiful enough. Canned beer was scarce or totally unavailable not for the lack of beer but the lack of cans—tin was a critical material diverted to war industries for the duration (Lingeman 253). Similarly, gasoline wasn't rationed because there wasn't enough of it; the reason "was the dire American shortage of rubber . . . [which] made it necessary to conserve rubber in automobile tires and to divert petroleum stocks" for making artificial rubber (Blum 23). And *that* explains why the singer of Jesse Greer and Alex Gerber's very amusing "I've Got Four New Tires" (Broadway Music, 1942) uses them "And a brand new spare" he inherited from his uncle as a very attractive incentive when courting (or seducing?) a girl: "We don't need a penthouse on Park Avenue / I've got four new tires and they're all for you." The boy establishes the wartime worth of those tires when he tells his girl, "When I join the army fighting every Jap / Keep the four new tires, sell the car for scrap." Country singer Carson Robison's homespun satiric wit triumphed among the gas and rubber songs in "The Old Gray Mare Is Back Where She Used To Be" (Bob Miller, 1942), a *Hot Charts* Extra from January through June 1943, and ranked 36th in March. Starting with "The old spare tire it ain't what it used to be, / . . . You can't tell now where the retread used to be," the song's three verses and choruses extol the superiority of the horse over the car: "She may be old and lean, but she don't need gasoline, / Oh she flips her tail at a Ford and a Cadillac, / Kicks at a Pontiac," and now during the war is "Gettin' more attention than a widow with a pension." Of all Robison's war-related pieces, this is his folksiest and one of his funniest.

Of all forms of rationing, none directly touched Americans more than those having to do with food products, and this touched them not just materially, by making them alter their eating habits, but psychologically and mentally as well. Women in wartime America did most of the grocery shopping, whether as housewives or as single women. Mastering the complexities of rationing and learning how to use ration coupons wisely was often challenging and frustrating. The details go far beyond present purposes, but, briefly, there were four kinds of rationing: Certificate Rationing, "for equipment and metal goods"; Differential Coupon Rationing, for gas, oil, and other products "some people needed more than others"; Uniform Coupon Rationing, for such things as sugar and coffee that didn't vary much within their category; and Point Rationing, the most complicated, for meats, cheese, fats like butter and margarine, and canned goods (Hayes, *Cooked,* 4). Coping with these bits of colored paper for a trip to the market was not unlike drawing up plans for the D-Day invasion, and believe me, I know—I watched my mother do it often enough. Sugar rationing came first and early (various sources put the start between late March and May 5, 1942), and it stayed late, all the way through 1946, at first allowing eight ounces, then later twelve ounces per person per week (yes, that sounds like an awful lot of sugar today, but there was much more home baking in the 1940s than now). Coffee rationing began in November 1942, not because it was scarce but because the ships that brought coffee beans from South America had been diverted for military purposes (Lingeman 246; Bailey 110). The meat rationing that started on March 29, 1943, hurt the carnivorous home front the most. Initially each person was allowed two and a half pounds per week (soldiers got four and a half a week and sailors seven) (Lingeman 256, 254). The few items that were never rationed included poultry, fish, and milk, except for canned milk, because of the cans.

The earliest song touching on controls on food items did so when the government was preparing the public for imminent sugar rationing. Carmen Lombardo and John Jacob Loeb's "There Won't Be A Shortage Of Love" (Leo Feist, 1942) was one of several songs suggesting that romantic relationships lessen the sting of rationing and shortages: "Oh, there may be a shortage of sugar, of Aluminum pots and such, / But There Won't Be A Shortage Of Love / When we love each other so much." The song had some success and was recorded in February 1942 by Dolly Dawn and Her Dawn Patrol Orchestra, then by Guy Lombardo, Kay Kyser, and Benny Goodman (Weiner). The following year Carmen Lombardo and Loeb wrote a sequel touching on price controls in "There's No Ceiling On Love" (Melrose Music, 1943). The Office of Price Administration may "regulate the prices that we pay," but love is absolutely priceless: "I called the O. P. A. / And THERE'S NO CEILING ON LOVE."

It was 1943 before songs devoted mostly to food product rationing appeared, which makes sense because only gradually did more and more items appear on the ration lists. About mid-year Vick Knight wrote "I Love Coffee (I Love Tea)" (Hollywood: Carmichael Music, 1943)—not to be confused with Milton Drake and Ben Oakland's 1941 hit for the Ink Spots, "Java Jive," which begins with the same two phrases. According to a full-page ad in the sheet music, the song was featured on the NBC Tuesday-night program *Johnny Presents,* starring Sgt. Ginny Simms (the popular vocalist was now a WAC). Knight "assigned all his royalties to **The Ginny Simms Birthday Fund** to provide birthday parties and cakes for servicemen away from home." The gist of the clever but serious song is that suffering through rationing is a lot better than the prospect of losing the war: "I LOVE COFFEE I LOVE TEA, / But not as much as I love liberty! / Miss my butter, miss my ham / But not as much as I'd miss Uncle Sam!"

The uncontested hit among songs about rationing, Louis Jordan, Anthonio Cosey, and Collenane Clark's "Ration Blues" (Leeds, 1943), was one of a number of songs that commiserated with people over shortages and rationing by presenting a singer who is equally, though comically, miserable himself. In a blues idiom—and with some pretty heavy sexual innuendoes for those times—the number is a lament over rationing guaranteed to make people smile: "Baby, Baby, Baby, what's wrong with Uncle Sam? / He's cut down on my sugar, now he's messin' with my ham, / . . . Gotta cut down on my jelly, / It takes sugar to make it sweet, / Gonna steal all your jelly baby, and rob you of your meat." Jordan's record first is a *Hot Charts* Extra in December 1943, ranks 21st in both January and February 1944 and 24th in March, the returns to the Extras list for April and May.

Some songs had fun with the scarcity of clothing materials for civilians. The huge demand for military uniforms and such field gear as tents, blankets, bandages, and combat boots created shortages of leather and fabric materials like cotton and wool. Civilian shoe rationing took effect in 1943, limiting each person to three pair a year (Lingeman 243). Natural fiber fabrics were never rationed, but Washington issued directives aimed at reducing their civilian use. One ordered "a 10-per-cent reduction in the amount of cloth in a woman's bathing suit, an objective reached by banishing the billowing bathing skirts of the 1930's and concentrating on two- rather than one-piece outfits" (Blum 95). This led the *Wall Street Journal* to remark, "The two-piece bathing suit is now tied in with the war as closely as the zipperless dress and the pleatless skirt" (qtd. in Blum 95). So was the man's vestless, cuffless, pleatless suit, tailors' and suit makers' solutions to cutting down on civilian wool consumption. This fashion change led to Sammy Cahn and Sy Oliver's deliciously silly jump tune "Can't Get Stuff In Your Cuff" (Dorsey Brothers Music, 1943), featured by both Tommy's and Jimmy's bands. The number showed fashion-conscious guys why the back-to-basics suits were practical: "CAN'T GET STUFF IN YOUR CUFF, 'cause you got no cuff to get the stuff in!" and, similarly, "Can't get a crease in your pleats, 'cause you got no pleats to get a crease in!" In 1943 the MWC published Florence Tarr, Oscar Catsiff, and Al Goodhart's pseudo-Gospel number "Patch and Pray." The premise is that with enough prayer and mending, maybe people's clothes will last through the war: "Stitch away on your old shirts, stitch away on your old skirts / Stitch away until it hurts— / Glory Hallelujah to that vict'ry day!"

Essential for making parachutes, the man-made fabric nylon was unobtainable to civilians except on the black market. This nylon deprivation was, to put it mildly, a source of great consternation to home front women. As George Marion Jr. and Fats Waller's "When The Nylons Bloom Again" (Advanced Music, 1943) put it, the ladies had to deal with "woolens which itch! Rayons that spread!" or simulate nylons with leg make-up, some going to "excruciating lengths in painting on a seamline" with an eyebrow pencil; other "more practical, less vain sorts simply went barelegged" (Lingeman 122). Marion and Waller's comic song is a woman's lament about her diminished sex appeal without nylons: "Cotton is monotonous to men, / Only way to keep affection fresh, / Get some mesh fo' yo' flesh." Though he never recorded it, this was one of Waller's happiest compositions. It was also one of his last. The prolific composer and prodigiously gifted musician died of bronchial pneumonia on December 16, 1943, at the age of only thirty-nine (Waller and Calabrese 177).

Two numbers humorously chastised complainers about rationing and shortages as unpatriotic and obstructing the war effort. For six long verses, Walter G. Samuels and Saul Chaplin told people who beefed about the rubber shortage, "meatless Tuesdays," and gas and coffee rationing just where they could go in "Take The Door At The Left" (Mills, 1943). Dick Mack, Mac Murada, and Robert Armbruster comically urged people to accept philosophically the changes in place for the duration in "Don't Forget There's A War Going On" (Hollywood: Boris Morros, 1944): "If you find a western saddle on your juicy sirloin steak DON'T FORGET THERE'S A WAR ON," alluding to butchers who passed off horsemeat for beef. With his laid-back humor, Louis Jordan, along with Sam Theard, replied to gripes about how the war was causing shortages of everything from groceries to desirable dates by telling folks "You Can't Get That No More" (Leeds, 1944): "Fellas, you can't jive these girls like you used to do, / 'cause some of them is makin' more money than you. / So you can't do that no more / . . . Girls, you can't be particular, you gotta take what's left. / Either those worn out 3A's or those beat up 4F's." Jordan scored another hit with "You Can't Get That No More," a *Hot Charts* Extra for February 1945, 33rd in March, 40th in April, and then an Extra again in May and June.

Finally, Frank Loesser and Arthur Schwartz wrote two rationing songs, both romantic, one comically, and both for the 1943 Warner Bros. musical *Thank Your Lucky Stars*. Dinah Shore sang the title song (Remick, 1943) and Eddie Cantor the unpublished "We're Staying Home Tonight (My Baby And Me)," their rationale for the latter being things like "I've

# 10:

# *"Arm In Arm"*

## Wartime Romance

Tin Pan Alley usually approached casual boy-girl relationships in war-related songs with a breezy lightheartedness, saving its more serious treatments for songs about and for people in committed relationships who were separated by the war (see chapter 11). The OWI and trade-paper cranks incessantly carped that Tin Pan Alley merely slipped incidental war references into standard boy-girl songs as window-dressing and to boost the songs' chances for success. But boy-girl songs would have been popular anyway (they always were); romantic ballads constituted the bulk of wartime popular songs, and most didn't touch on the war at all. Still, the majority of professional songwriters understood that the conditions of war had an impact on affairs of the heart, and that romantic relationships could anchor men and women at home or apart. In most of the nearly 120 Tin Pan Alley and hillbilly songs about love during wartime, the war was an organic part of the songs' points of view on wartime romance.

### *"Wacky For Khaki": What Is It About a Uniform?*

Rumor—and some theatrical evidence—has it that women love men in uniform. The Miles Gloriosus figure in ancient Roman comedy and the *commedia dell'arte* Il Capitano character in the Italian Renaissance were both magnets for impressionable maidens until they were exposed as puffed-up phonies. Closer to the present, but still sixty years before Pearl Harbor, Gilbert and Sullivan in their comic opera *Patience* featured a chorus of young women whose affections vacillated between a regiment of Dragoon Guards in scarlet tunics with gold braid and a couple of drably dressed, emaciated poets. The Colonel of the Dragoons is acutely and astutely aware of the effect his uniform and those of his picturesque troops has on the young ladies: "I said when I first put it on, / 'It is plain to the veriest dunce / That every beauty / Will feel it her duty / To yield to its glamour at once'" (Gilbert 167).

In World War II there was an epidemic of this behavior on the home front. The press labeled it going "khaki wacky." Tens of thousands of teenage girls, mostly white and middle or working class, became infatuated with the image of men in uniform. Although most girls' infatuation was probably innocent, widespread delinquency, primarily sexual delinquency, is also a matter of record (see Perrett 348; Lingeman 88; Bailey 148; the sources of the data following). All khaki-wacky numbers ceased abruptly after 1942, the music biz perhaps reluctant to release any more songs that might be construed as encouraging teenage girls to pick up soldiers and sailors for casual sexual encounters. To the press and public they were the Cuddle Bunnies, Round-Heels, Patriotutes, or, most often, Victory Girls—teens and pre-teens "as young as twelve years old" who ranged from those just out for a good time to amateur streetwalkers offering sex for cash, a movie, or a meal. A social worker in San Antonio remarked in *Time* on March 29, 1943, that the city's professional prostitutes were "sore as all get out. They say the young chippies who work for a beer and a sandwich are cramping their style." An unnamed observer quoted by Ronald Bailey maintained that the V-Girl behaved as she did because out of "a misguided sense of patriotism [she] believes she is contributing to the war effort by giving herself to the man in uniform." Heavily made-up to appear older but usually dressed like bobbysoxers, these girls hung around bus depots, train stations, drugstores, and any other places frequented by servicemen on leave. The V-Girl epidemic was nationwide: in 1943, the city of San Diego reported an increase in delinquency among teenage girls of 355 percent (and only 55 percent among boys); "In Detroit the Navy had to build a fence around its armory, located in the city, to keep out not the enemy, but the bobbysoxers"; in Chicago sailors said it was "worth one's life" not to be accosted walking from Navy Pier to State Street, "where the V-girls swarmed like flies"; in Mobile it was reported that "the girls themselves bought contraceptives for their dates"; and in New York City social workers recorded that more than 60 percent "of the cases of venereal disease among soldiers had been contracted from girls under 21." In 1942, the first full year of the war, the national rate of female juvenile delinquency, largely by V-Girls, rose 31 percent.

Songs about girls enamored of guys in uniform didn't deal explicitly with teenage sexual exploits, but a loosening of sexual strictures was im-

plied if not directly stated in some of them. The songs all treated such behavior, by the way, as amusing and inconsequential. In 1941, hillbilly
tunesmiths Jimmie Kerr, Claude Heritier, and Russ Hull wrote "They Go
Goo-Goo, Gaga, Goofy Over Gobs," published by Chicago's Bell Music,
a major country publisher. A mere two lines sum up the entire lyric: "Girls
in ev'ry port / All love a sailor sport." The later "Gobs of Love" (Paramount Music, 1942) was by Redd Evans, who wrote much differently of
women in "Rosie The Riveter." The number was something of a hit for
the King Sisters; their record is a *Hot Charts* Extra from October 1942
through February 1943 and ranks 35th for March of that year; Teddy
Powell's orchestra with Peggy Mann on vocal also had a successful recording of "Gobs." This song is about as explicit as they get, the verse declaring, "I'm just wild about soldiers, daffy over Marines / But I'm savin'
my love for sailors especially in their teens." Throughout the song's two
choruses, the girl describes in various ways how she's "got GOBS OF LOVE
for the Navy / . . . Tho' my heart skips a beat when a soldier I meet / What
it won't do when I see a man in blue." Mickey Stoner was a lyricist and
occasional composer who wrote, among other things, two of the loveliest
wartime ballads in no way related to the war, "You Rhyme With Everything That's Beautiful" and "I Guess I'll Have To Dream The Rest," but
in 1942 Stoner jumped on the khaki-wacky song-wagon with Alex M.
Kramer to write "I Took My Girl To An Army Dance" (Nationwide Song
1942), the sad-funny tale of a poor civilian guy who makes the mistake
of taking his girlfriend to a dancehall filled with men in uniform: "First
she danced with all of the engineers and then the signal corps, / And it
broke my heart to see her take the boys around the floor." The final line
in that sequence is a stroke of genius; Stoner and Kramer might have written "to see the boys take her around the floor," but in fact khaki-wacky
girls were most often the aggressors in their dealings with servicemen.
Well, the poor civilian shlep tries to cut in to dance with his girl, only to
get beat up by the sergeant dancing with her. As the boy and girl leave the
dance in the final verse, "She confessed the boys in uniform have always
made her fall," prompting the boy to enlist: "I'll join up, and I'll win my
true love back." Frank Loesser wrote just about the best khaki-wacky
number, but the song wasn't published or recorded. The only public exposure "Wacky For Khaki" got was Judy Canova singing it in the Paramount
film *True To The Army,* released in June 1942. Its content isn't much different from other songs about soldier-infatuated girls, but Loesser's wit
and verbal facility make the number stand out from the crowd: "I'm
wacky for khaki, I'll say that twice. / It scratches a little, but it scratches
so nice. / . . . Not tweed, not serge. / It's khaki by cracky that gives me the
urge. / The stripes on the shoulders they set me aflame. / Why, sure I'll
marry you, Lieutenant—oh, what's your name" (Kimball and Nelson 84).

Not all girls and women were attracted to just *any* man in the service; some were a little more choosy, as suggested by the titles of Ira Schuster, Paul Cunningham, and Leonard Whitcup's "I Wanna Dance With A Sailor" (Paull-Pioneer, 1942) and Mack David and Leonard Whitcup's totally silly "I Wanna Marry A Bombardier" (Leeds, 1942), in which a girl tells her mother that she's narrowed down the field: "I went out with a sailor but he left me all at sea, / I went out with a soldier, but he made me do K. P. / And I've been seen with a marine who'd really make you cheer, / I like 'em all but when I fall, / I'll fall for a bombardier." Carmen Lombardo and Pat Innisfree sang of a girl who thought one particular guy was "just a joke in my neighborhood" when he dressed as a "Killer-diller fashion plate," but "Since He Traded His Zoot Suit For A Uniform" (Irving Berlin Inc., 1942), "He certainly looks good to me now." And reinforcing the notion that the clothes *do* make the man was Jack Yellen and Sammy Fain's hilarious "The Mamas With The Moo-Lah" (Leo Feist, 1942), sung by a guy who's become a catch in high society since he enlisted: "It took a uniform to show the dames my charms, / You oughta see the babes I'm holdin' in my arms! / . . . I chauffeured for a guy for thirty bucks a week, / And now I'm waltzin' with his daughter, cheek to cheek!" The only serious number about attachments to military garb was John Jacob Loeb and Edgar Leslie's "Wait Till She Sees You In Your Uniform" (Loeb-Lissauer, 1940), which came out around the time the Draft Act went into effect late in 1940. To be sung to any young man with a sweetheart, the lyric says that she'll adore him even more now that he's in uniform.

Lest it seem that going khaki-wacky was gender-tied, a few songs had men attracted to women in uniform. By Pvt. Charley Murray, Pvt. Kurt Kasznar, and Tin Pan Alley's Al Stillman, "Bars On Her Shoulders And Stars In Her Eyes" (Chappell, 1942) describes how a young woman is getting more male attention as a WAAC than when she was a civilian: "She's got bars on her shoulders, and stars in her eyes / And she's giving heartaches to hundreds of guys / She used to pose as a model at Saks / But now she goes as the pride of the Waacs." Similarly, Charlie McCord, Franklin Rockwell, and Tommy Jordan's "Wait Till You See Nellie In A Soldier's Uniform" (Shermack Publishing, 1942) recounts how guys who didn't pay much attention to Nellie before are taking notice of her since she joined the WAAC. And the one such number by a woman, "Sally WAAC" (Leeds, 1943) by Lt. Ruby Jane Douglass, 2nd Officer, WAAC, doesn't vary much from the others in its content or tone: "When she passes, soldiers whistle and shout, / 'Look who's comin', face right about'!" These songs' common denominator is that while sex appeal certainly plays a role in men noticing women in uniform, there is also a stated or implied attraction based on an admiration for their choice to serve in the armed forces.

Then there were those civilian girls, in song at least, who were terrifically popular with throngs of servicemen not because they offered sexual favors wholesale like the V-Girls but because they were cute, personable, and made guys feel good just by being there, like the girl in Lou Shelley, Bobby Kroll, and Bette Cannon's "Pretty Sal, What A Gal For Morale" (Crown Music, 1943) who makes "even generals sigh." Or because they knit, as in Jack Meskill and Ernie Burnett's "Since Kitten's Knittin' Mittens (For The Army)" (Shapiro, Bernstein, 1941), the song's title hinting at the swarms of soldiers clamoring for Kitten's knit goods. Both soldiers and sailors were enamored of the "cute and sweet . . . builder-upper of morale" in Irving Taylor and Vic Mizzy's "The Corporal Told The Private" (Santly-Joy-Select, 1942). Taylor's lyric devotes a separate verse to her effect on members of each service, in descending order of rank: "The General told the Colonel, / The Colonel told the Major, The Major told the Captain her name and address," all the way down to the private, and similarly for the navy from the admiral to the sailor. Milton Drake, Al Hoffman, and Jerry Livingston's "Lalapaluza Lu" (World Music, 1942) makes it very clear that some of her charms were physical: "Every time she puts a sweater on / They love to pin a medal on / Lalapaluza Lu." A song about another popular young lady focused more on her admirers than on "the Colonel's daughter Genevieve" in "Ten Little Soldiers (On A Ten Day Leave)" (Lincoln Music, 1942). With words by the Werner twins, Sue and Kay, and music by Abner Silver, this comic tale has its title characters frantically rushing to the colonel's house to get a date with his much sought-after daughter, until "The TEN LITTLE SOLDIERS went from bad to worse, 'cause ten little sailor boys had got there first, / They crowded her door like a pack of sardines / When out walked Genevieve with ten marines." Of all the "miss popularity" songs, this was the popular one. Plugged often on the radio starting in late September 1942, by mid-October *Variety* listed its sheet music as the 12th best-selling. Strong record sales came a bit later, with recordings by the English orchestra of Peter Piper and the Four Vagabonds, which were both *Hot Charts* Extras from December 1942 through May 1943.

### "He Loved Me Till The All Clear Came": Flirtation, Seduction, Dating, and Flings

There's a fine, often blurry line between flirtation, seduction, dating, and flings, and wartime songs about casual romance (and casual sex) didn't always demarcate with strict rigidity among them, though all treated the subject in ways as offhand and sometimes hilarious as these impermanent involvements were themselves. Of roughly thirty-three songs, it's most striking that eleven of the seventeen by established Tin Pan Alley writers had their widest audiences in Hollywood musicals and two in Broadway shows. The reason is obvious. Broadway had no formal self-censorship, and in Hollywood the Production Code's parameters for the permissible in movies were still wider than those for radio and the recording industry. This meant that songs in Hollywood films and Broadway shows could get away with even transparently risqué innuendoes—and they did, as did sheet music publishers. So integral were such lyrics to these Hollywood and Broadway songs that few were recorded, and those few only after numerous cuts and alterations. None was successful enough to be even a *Hot Charts* Extra. These songs' exposure depended largely on the popularity of the movies they were in.

With one blockbuster of an exception, wartime songs about casual dating *not* from the stage or screen got little national attention, though some were cute, clever, and innocent enough for the radio networks. Describing soldiers' wholesome flirtations with a comely desert miss in North Africa, Lt. William L. Russell and Sgt. Paul Reif's "Flirty Gertie From Bizerte (Tune From Tunis)" (Edward B. Marks, 1943) was a revision of Reif's own notoriously ribald soldier-song "Dirty Gertie From Bizerte," sanitized almost beyond recognition for the home front. Similarly, three sequels of sorts to World War I's "Mademoiselle From Armentieres" stressed innocent flirtations more than sexual encounters: George Graff and George Wiest's "Who'll Take The Place Of Mademoiselle From Armentieres" (Mills, 1942), Henry Russell, Irving Gordon, and Frankie Carle's "We're Going Across (To See The Mademoiselle From Armentieres)" (Allied Music, 1943), and Herman Ruby and Lew Pollack's "The Daughter Of Mademoiselle From Armentieres" (Hollywood: Pyramid Music, 1944), whose "picture has set the sergeant on his ears, / It is signed 'My love belongs to you,' / But all his buddies have one too." Innocent flirting is about as far as things ever get in songs about how it makes a stateside soldier feel good just to dance or talk with a USO hostess or other local girl, as in Nelson Cogane, Edgar Battle, and Ira Schuster's "Jumpin' With A G. I. Gal" (Paull-Pioneer, 1943). Allie Wrubel went global with this local thought in "Best of All!" (Irving Berlin Inc., 1943), a list song about a GI's flirtations with girls from Australia to Kiska to Bengal, but "It's the gal he left back home / That he loves the best of all."

But there was nothing innocent about "Rum and Coca-Cola" (Leo Feist, 1944), with words by comedian Morey Amsterdam and music by Jeri Sullivan and Paul Baron. Nothing innocent, that is, except for the altered, abbreviated, and revised lyrics for the hit record by the Andrews Sisters and the other big sellers by Vaughn Monroe and Abe Lyman's orchestra with Rose Blane's vocal. But in the sheet music, the fourteen unexpurgated verses of this calypso-style number show just how naughty parts of Amsterdam's lyrics were, as they describe Trinidad as an island paradise for both GIs and the native girls. Two sections of the song, one altered, the other retained intact on the Andrews Sisters' record, are both instructive and puzzling in determining just what was acceptable to the music industry (and, presumably, its critics) in wartime America. On the record, one verse is "From Chica-chi-carry to Mona's Isle / Native girls all dance and smile / Help soldier celebrate his leave, / Make every day like New Year's Eve." In the sheet music, the last two lines come from a different verse, replacing two that would have been clearly unacceptable: "They wear grass skirts, but that's okay / Yankee likes to 'hit the hay.'" Yet, mysteriously, the following verse remains unaltered between the sheet music and the recording: "You will see on Manzinella Beach, / G. I. romance with native 'peach' / The whole night long make tropic love, / Next day sit in hot sun to cool off." Granted, "making love" in 1940s' parlance referred as often to a verbal encounter as to a physical one, but considering the last line of this verse it doesn't sound as if the soldier and the girl were just chatting on the beach all night long. To confuse matters even more, the chorus to every verse on both the record and in print ends with "Both mother and daughter / Workin' for the Yankee dollar"; these Trinidadian ladies may therefore have been plying a professional trade. Either way, in the early months of 1945 the Andrews Sisters' recording made lots of "Yankee dollar," between January and March jockeying for the top spot with "Don't Fence Me In," another of their own efforts in tandem with Bing Crosby, and Johnny Mercer's "Ac-Cent-Tchu-Ate The Positive." Even against such stiff competition, in *Hot Charts* the Andrews Sisters' "Rum And Coca-Cola" is 3rd in January and 1st in both February and March and was also a top jukebox play during most of that time on both the *Billboard* and *Variety* charts. While the song never hit number one in sheet music sales, for most of February and March it hovered around the 3rd or 4th spot. I wonder how people reacted to what some of the "real" lyrics looked like (or maybe that's what they bought the sheet music for). Most singular about the meteoric rise of "Rum And Coca-Cola" is the demonstrable fact that it received no network radio plugs whatsoever to familiarize the public with the song, nor, as big a smash as it was, did it ever appear on *Your Hit Parade*. The most likely reason for its absence from the airwaves is not that the networks' stringent standards found even the sanitized lyrics unacceptable, since such lyrics could have been sterilized even more for the live bands and singers on radio shows. Nor was the reason the mention of an alcoholic beverage in the song, which had been a problem for "Pistol Packin' Mama" some time before. Rather, in all probability what kept "Rum and Coca-Cola" off the radio wasn't the rum but the Coke. Broadcast executives (and, most likely, the FCC) would have seen the repeated mentions of

Coca-Cola as a product endorsement. Without radio plugs, it was mostly jukebox plays (often instigated by the malt shop or tavern proprietors themselves) that caught the public's ear, helping make "Rum and Coca-Cola" one of the fastest-rising and biggest-selling hits of the war years.

Predictably, of the two Broadway songs about casual wartime encounters, the suggestive one was by Cole Porter, who wrote titillating prewar songs like "My Heart Belongs To Daddy" and postwar ones like "Always True To You In My Fashion." "Something For The Boys" (Chappell, 1942) doesn't come close to those Porter classics in length or cleverness, but it holds its own against them in innuendo. Before the war a gold-digging gal used to live "Beyond several gentlemen's means," but now her "life's completely cluttered with soldiers, sailors, not to speak of those big marines." She shelves her sugar daddies for the duration and instead does her patriotic duty by "always doing something for the boys, / 'Cause they're doing something for me." The other Broadway excursion into casual wartime romance was as innocent as Porter's was borderline salacious. In home front America, even platonic encounters with girls were thought to keep up soldiers' spirits, as expressed in "You're Good For My Morale" (Mills, 1943) from the musical revue *The New Meet The People.* The music is by Jay Gorney, the lyrics by his usually off-the-wall lyricists Henry Myers and Edward Eliscu, here writing in a sweetly mellow yet still inventive mood. A rather shy soldier is trying to strike up a conversation with a girl: "Don't know if you'd like a soldier, just know that I need a pal. / So won't you please let a soldier hold yer, you're good for my morale. / Don't care what movie they're showing, just want the moon and a gal; / Don't need to go U-S-O-ing / Knowing YOU'RE GOOD FOR MY MORALE."

Of all the songs about casual wartime relationships, those from movies are the cleverest and most varied. Overall, the movie tunes cover the spectrum of casual wartime encounters from wholesome innocence to outright seduction. From the United Artists film *Stage Door Canteen,* released in June 1943, Al Dubin and James V. Monaco's "A Rookie And His Rhythm" (Edwin H. Morris, 1943) is innocence itself: "Gals prefer a private who can jive it, / He'll surpass a colonel making a pass. / . . . He improves the morale of a gal." And for the 1942 20th Century-Fox musical *Iceland,* "You Can't Say No To A Soldier" (Twentieth Century Music, 1942), by Mack Gordon and Harry Warren, tells girls that a little innocent romancing with servicemen is patriotically obligatory: "If he's gonna fight he's got a right to romance . . . So, get out your lipstick and powder, / Be beautiful and dutiful too, / If he's not your type, / Then it's still okay, / You can always kiss him in a sisterly way."

The much less innocent excursion of sailors and marines known as shore leave was the subject of no fewer than four songs for films. Fairly innocuous was the title song for the 1945 Paramount musical *Bring On The Girls* (Famous, 1945), by Harold Adamson and Jimmy McHugh; for guys who've been at sea, "if you want morale, let me tell you pal, / Better dress it up in curls." "We Hate To Leave" (Leo Feist, 1944), by Sammy Cahn and Jule Styne, from the 1945 M-G-M musical *Anchors Aweigh* is similar. Gene Kelly and Frank Sinatra taunt their shipmates who have to stay onboard, claiming that they really hate to go ashore but promising "we'll be back, before we're even missed / And tell you guys about the countless dames that we have kissed." In Mort Greene and Harry Revel's title song for the 1942 RKO film *Call Out The Marines* (Greene-Revel Inc., 1942), things get a bit more aggressive with the advertising of marines on leave as the answer to girls' romantic inclinations: "When a park bench looks inviting, / You'll know what it means. / If you've got some extra love to make, / CALL OUT THE MARINES."

But it was Johnny Mercer who ran up the red flag about sailors on shore leave in "The Fleet's In" (Famous Music, 1942). In fact, Mercer wrote the lyrics for five of the eleven Hollywood songs about casual wartime romance, all of them deliciously wicked. "The Fleet's In" is one of several numbers for the 1942 Paramount musical of the same name that Mercer wrote with gifted composer and musician Victor Schertzinger in 1941, before Schertzinger's untimely death at fifty-one on October 26. Mercer's lyric is explicit, from its opening "Hey there, Mister!—You'd better hide your sister, 'cause the fleet's in" to its closing "So if you love her, keep her under cover / The fleet's in town." His versatility is fully on display in Mercer's other four casual fling songs for the movies. He wrote each one to be sung by a woman, and each expresses a different attitude about such brief encounters, from the one who lays down limits right away to the one who's disappointed things didn't go farther than they did. Among their songs for Paramount's 1942 *Star Spangled Rhythm,* Mercer and his frequent collaborator Harold Arlen wrote "I'm Doin' It For Defense" (Famous, 1943), in which a girl who has agreed to a date with a serviceman spells out the ground rules in no uncertain terms: "If this is gonna be romance / I'm gonna be the one who wears the pants"—and that's just in the verse. In the choruses she gets down to specifics: "I'm your date for tonight / But when I hold you tight / I'm doin' it for defense. / If you kiss my lips and you feel me respond, / It's just because I can't afford a bond, / . . . I'm a pal nothing more / This isn't love, this is war." A more aggressive girl is out with a sailor in Mercer and Schertzinger's "Uncle Sammy" (Famous, 1942): "Oh, tomorrow you may belong to Uncle Sammy but tonight you belong to me / You may never get your chevrons walkin' me in the park, But I can guarantee you'll get a black and blue mark." Not just aggressive but also fickle *and* an officer in the WAVES is the singer of Mercer and Arlen's "There's a Fella Waitin' in Poughkeepsie" (Edwin H. Morris, 1944), who tells a mere enlisted man, "Forget my rank, you beautiful Yank! [and] pretend we're both on leave" in Paramount's 1945 film *Here Come The Waves*. She lets the sailor know there isn't just a fella waiting in Poughkeepsie, but one in Pomona and another in Daytona, "But if you held my hand / I suppose they would all understand." She wraps up her argument with a declaration of her romantic or sexual independence: she may have guys in far-flung locales, "But I'm strictly on my own tonight." Finally, also for *Star Spangled Rhythm* Mercer and Arlen wrote a hilarious song for a woman on her own, but not by choice. "He Loved Me Till The All Clear Came" is the only casual encounter song about two civilians. A guy and gal take advantage of a blackout: "He had the strongest yen in the dark and then suddenly the all clear came / . . . I looked around and he was gone." The ending is about as explicit a sexual innuendo as Hollywood could possibly allow: "Isn't that an awful shame and to think he really loved / He nearly *really* loved me till the all clear came."

### *"I'm Red, White And Blue Over You": All's Not So Fair in Love and War*

At first blush it might seem that a home front that endorsed romantic involvements from casual dating to marriage as morale-builders for servicemen and civilians alike would have been unresponsive or even hostile to songs that treated shaky or unstable relationships comically. But that wasn't the case at all. Six of the eleven such songs by major Tin Pan Alley or hillbilly songwriters reached millions of people in popular Hollywood films. Rather than demoralizing them, comic songs crabbing about lousy relationships had a therapeutic effect. Subject aside, humor and laughter are good morale-boosters, and laughing about some other guy or gal's rotten love life could make people feel better about their own.

During the war Tin Pan Alley looked with a wry eye on all manner of fractured relationships, from awful first dates to terrible marriages. Some songs linked wartime conditions to rocky romances; others just playfully used military or patriotic jargon to describe involvements that would have likely fizzled even in peacetime. In Johnny Bond's "She Was A Washout In The Blackout" (Southern Music, 1942), a guy out for a drive on his first date with "the sweetest little blonde" tries to take advantage of a blackout and the girl but doesn't get what he bargained for: "When I put my arm around her just to steal a little kiss, / She socked me in the kisser, / And Boy! She didn't miss." The girl gets out, walks home, and leaves him with his "bloody nose" and bruised ego, contemplating, "I think I'll join the army today" to avoid similar humiliation and a bruised nose from future dates.

Romantic partners whose affection was cooling off, perhaps because it was heating up for someone else, gave headaches to lovers of both sexes. The singer could be of either gender in "I'm Red, White And Blue Over You" (Santly-Joy-Select, 1942), with Sam H. Stept's music and Eddie De Lange's self-explanatory lyric: "I see red when I see you in somebody's arms; I get white with jealousy over you. / And the color blue is nothing new, the way you make me feel / I'm a sentimental soul, but you treat me like a heel." The words of lyricist Mack Gordon and composer Harry Warren's "That's Sabotage" (Twentieth Century Music, 1942) aren't gender-specific either, but the number sounds like a girl's complaint about a guy because Marion Hutton with Glenn Miller's orchestra introduced it in the 1942 20th Century-Fox film *Orchestra Wives* and also recorded it. In the verse, the girl tells the guy she's been noticing "When it comes to romance, you're never in the mood." In the chorus she catalogues her specific complaints: "If you don't kiss me like you used to kiss me, that's sabotage," concluding with "I can't sleep, I've got to keep my F. B. I. on you / 'Cause if you've been untrue, that's sabotage." From the Warner Bros. 1943 musical *Thank Your Lucky Stars,* the problem with Katy in Frank Loesser and Arthur Schwartz's "Ice Cold Katy" (Witmark, 1943) is more cold feet than the cold shoulder she's been giving the GI camped out on her doorstep for a week: "ICE COLD KATY, he's a-dyin' to hold ya, / Keep that date he came a-hurryin' for, / ICE COLD KATY, won't you marry the soldier? / Soon he's off to war." In the sheet music for popular home consumption, the question is never answered, but in the movie the song is an elaborate production number. After several choruses, three dance breaks, and the arrival of a preacher, Katy Brown finally marries Private Jones.

Some girls in long-term relationships were as intractable as Katy— or worse. The Nat King Cole Trio record of Louis Jordan and Timmie Rodgers's "If You Can't Smile And Say Yes, Please Don't Cry And Say No" (Leeds, 1944) is a *Hot Charts* Extra from April through June 1945. A GI's girlfriend is so willful that she won't even give him a little affection before he's shipped out: "When I ask for a date, the answer is 'no,' . . . / Baby let bygones be bygones, / 'Cause men are as scarce as nylons." In *Stage Door Canteen,* Ray Bolger sang a song hilariously detailing why one GI's girlfriend was "The Girl I Love To Leave Behind." Richard Rodgers wrote the music of this unpublished piece, and the caustic, clever lyrics were the work of Lorenz Hart. Other than their new and equally brilliant pieces for the revival of *A Connecticut Yankee,* this was one of Rodgers and Hart's last songs together. Hart died five months later, on November 22, 1943, at the age of forty-eight. The verse sets the stage for the soldier's harangue in the choruses: "I met her on a Friday in November twenty-nine; / That's how depression started for me." What follows is a barrage of sharp one-liners, like "She is known to her daddy as Mother's mistake," "If I live through this big romance, then the Japs haven't got a chance," and the truly wicked "Her deportment at parties would cause you to weep; Lou Costello is slightly more refined."

Sometimes the problem isn't dealing with a romantic partner but with finding one, an especially difficult task for home front girls, since—in the estimation of some in songs, at least—the most desirable guys had been shipped overseas. Such is the lament of the girl in Jerry Seelen and Lester Lee's "Nothing Can Replace A Man" from the 1944 Paramount comedy *You Can't Ration Love,* who says it's easier to cope with shortages and rationing than with the one irreplaceable commodity—men: "I can walk, who needs gas? / If it's tough to get beef, I eat bass or mackerel / [but] . . . When the moon shines above, / It's a cinch that you can't ration love like porterhouse, / Oh nothing, nothing can replace a man." Sometimes the shortage of manpower, romantically speaking, meant one poor civilian guy was stuck with too many girls, like Horace in Hughie Prince and Sonny Burke's "He's Got A WAVE In His Hair (And A WAAC On His Hands)" (Mutual Music Society, 1943), another song with a perfectly self-explanatory title, but with lyrics that cleverly play on the acronyms of the women's services: "He's so awfully nervous, his appetite is gone, / 'Cause a WAVE's got him wacky / And a WAAC keeps wavin' him on." Horace enlists to cut back on too much female attention, but his plan backfires—now the WAAC and the WAVE, joined by a WAF and even a British WREN, are all in hot pursuit of him.

Was not even marriage sacred in the eyes and minds of songwriters playfully toying with relationships made more in hell than in heaven? Apparently not, according to one song by two prominent Alleymen and another by an equally well-respected and successful hillbilly songwriter and singer. For the 1943 Paramount musical *Salute For Three,* lyricist Kim Gannon and composer Jule Styne wrote "My Wife's A W.A.A.C." (Paramount, 1943), looking comically at how the war disrupted marriages in which both the husband and the wife remained on the home front: "I wash the dishes, I cook the fishes, / I peel potatoes by the sack, / I'm mindin' the baby and I don't mean maybe, / This business is breaking my back, / My wife's a WAAC!" The most outrageous comic complaint about strained wartime relationships came from country songwriter Dave McEnery (a.k.a. Red River Dave), writer of the sentimental "I'm A Convict With Old Glory In My Heart" and "I'd Like To Give My Dog To Uncle Sam." McEnery wrote "I'd Rather Die For My Country (Than Live With My Wife)" (Noble Music, 1943) with Sam Martin, and it's anything but sentimental. The soldier singing this song considers war a welcome respite from his wife: "I'd rather dodge, dodge, dodge, from a bullet / Than duck, duck, duck, all my life," and "I'd rather creep, creep, creep in a shell-hole / Than sleep, sleep, sleep by her side," because when his wife snores, "Folks think it's an air raid / And they flop right on the floor."

That the comic mode prevailed during the war in songs about unsuccessful home front romances says a lot about the mindset of wartime America. People could laugh at these songs' funny, cartoon-like pictures of fouled-up relationships. But they wouldn't have accepted serious treatments of friction between more real, believable lovers, since in wartime few cared to think about love going awry. Real romance was to be cherished in those difficult days. Many people regarded—and some relied on—a freely chosen compatible romantic relationship not only as something to help them get through the war but as one of those American values like home, mother, and apple pie that our boys were fighting to preserve.

### *"In Times Like These"*: Boy Meets Girl—And Sings About It

Not all songs about true love on the home front (and occasionally overseas) were serious or sentimental slush. In fact, of the thirty-nine such songs by established Tin Pan Alley writers, twenty-six were playful, the other thirteen sentimental to some degree, a two-to-one majority in favor of playfulness. Songwriters usually saved their heavier sentimental artillery for songs whose subjects most closely touched the emotions of the wartime public: servicemen saying goodbye to their girls, their separation from them while overseas, and the loneliness of the girls back home, as well as some songs featuring the mothers or children of GIs, all the stuff of chapter 11. Though most songs about home front romance were playful, the public mostly bought the sentimental ones, which isn't surprising given Americans' penchant for sentimental love songs since at least the nineteenth century.

There were two kinds of songs about home front romance: one told stories about boys and girls falling in love, the other extolled the virtues or charms of the singer's boyfriend, girlfriend, or, occasionally, spouse. The narrative songs were more popular than pure outpourings of emotion, and there are, I think, good reasons for this. First, the songs about falling in love were more active or dramatic. The average popular song in the 1940s was under three minutes long—but still long enough for lyricists, if they chose, to tell a story or dramatize a situation that the listener could get caught up in. Straightforward love songs are generally more "passive" in their praise of the singer's beloved and, without a tale to tell, must rely almost entirely on exceptional writing and a memorable melody to capture the listener's attention. Some lyricists have been true poets and a few tunesmiths truly great composers, but overall it was easier to succeed with narrative or dramatic songs than strictly lyrical ones. The second reason songs about *falling* in love edged out those about *being* in love during the war is that most of the latter, both sentimental and playful, were pretty inconsequential as songwriting compared to the higher-quality narrative/dramatic numbers.

The earliest war-related love song actually had fun being sentimental. Yet lyricist Leo Robin and composer Ralph Rainger's "Another Little Dream Won't Do Us Any Harm" (Robbins, 1941) had little commercial success with the public. Most people just heard Betty Grable and some chorus girls sing it in the 20th Century-Fox film *A Yank in the R. A. F.,* released prior to Pearl Harbor in late September 1941. The song's fun comes in its pairing of romantic lyrics with a frothy, even silly, upbeat tune. It's one of several songs saying that being in love makes war, or the prospect of war, much more bearable: "though some gloomy people view things with alarm / . . . Let's have another little dream / Another Little Dream Won't Do Us Any Harm." The only other sentimental love song of note confronted the war as directly as Robin and Rainger's piece did allusively. By 1944 lyricist Howard Dietz and composer (and at the time Lieutenant Commander, U.S. Coast Guard) Vernon Duke each had numerous Broadway and Hollywood songwriting credits, usually with other collaborators, but that year they teamed up to write the revue *Tars and Spars* to assist the coast guard in recruiting both men and women. In the midst of a lot of clever and gung-ho service-oriented numbers was the quite lovely ballad "Arm In Arm" (Carl Fischer, 1944). The verse explained that a young man and woman enlisted together, the chorus then echoing "Another Little Dream" in saying that their mutual love makes their wartime tasks, and the war itself, easier to bear: "We'll weather the wind and the rain, / Arm in arm, like a hand in a glove, / War's alarm seems a myth, / Keep your chin up and pin up the one you go with— / . . . We're a tar and a spar in love"—the "chin up" / "pin up" rhyme, incidentally, demonstrates how a fine craftsmen like Dietz successfully incorporated playful elements into a romantic love lyric.

Love songs in a lighter vein ranged from outrageously silly to cute yet sincere, but, like the sentimental ones, none caught the public's attention for very long. Most outrageous was a number that affirmed that the way to a man's heart is through his stomach. Mack Gussow and Thomas Hearon suggested the way for girls to keep romance alive in their GIs away would be to "Send A Great Big Salami To Your Boyfriend In The Army" (Broadcast Music, 1943): "That garlicky aroma might soon put him in a coma, but when he's coming to he'll be thinking of you. / His Uncle Sam feeds him ham, turkey mean with dressin', / But I'll bet he won't get such sweet delicatessen." Gussow and Hearon undoubtedly based the song's title and concept on a wartime sign in the legendary Katz's Delicatessen on New York's Lower East Side—"Send a salami to your boy in the army." The sign is still there! Almost as silly, and by two more prominent songwriters, was a piece that in *Hot Charts* is 32nd for March 1945 in the recording by Guy Lombardo's orchestra with vocal by Jimmy Brown. Overall, it's a soldier's love song to his girl with waltz-time music by Lombardo's brother Carmen and lyrics by Charlie Tobias. Most of the humor comes from the guy's accent, as he yells to his girlfriend's window above in "Oh! Moytle" (Tobias and Lewis, 1945): "OH! MOYTLE my toitle, / When ya kiss me the woild is all right / . . . Tho I ain't much at grammer, I'll loin about glammor, / When I'm with my MOYTLE tonight."

Twice in fifteen months Cole Porter jumped into the wartime love song field and twice landed with a disappointing thud. *Let's Face It* opened on Broadway on October 29, 1941. Numbers like "Farming" and "Let's Not Talk About Love" displayed classic Porter wit, but "Jerry, My Soldier Boy" (Chappell, 1942) was not in their league. The singer says that people told her, "Never let yourself get too warm, / And go loony for a uniform!" She evidently didn't listen, since for the rest of the song she raves about "My rookie, / My sweet cookie" and how he makes her feel. Porter's usually brittle wit failed him also in "I'm In Love With A Soldier Boy" (Chappell, 1943) from *Something For The Boys*—considered one of Porter's weakest scores—which opened on January 1, 1943. The song is pretty clever, but the way Porter's lyric gets to the punchline is all but uninspired. Again a young woman is singing about her fabulous relationship with a soldier; after taking her home from a dinner date, "often he stays for days and days and days and days." The song's kicker legitimizes that seemingly naughty behavior: "He's the greatest event in my life, / . . . After all, I happen to be his wife." Compared to Porter's breezy best, the number is leaden. But genuinely breezy, indeed a breath of fresh air, was Kim Gannon and Jule Styne's "Wha D'Ya Do When It Rains" (Paramount, 1943). Dona Drake and Her Girl Band performed it in the 1943 Paramount musical *Salute For Three,* to which Gannon and Styne also contributed the unromantic "My Wife's a W. A. A. C." Though it sounds like hit material, the song's popularity was mostly determined by the film's. Gannon's lyric in the sheet music provides pronouns for either a man or a woman to sing the song. In either case, the verses simply catalogue various things a stateside GI and his girl can do during a rainstorm, culminating with "Never be blue when it rains, / Here's what to do when it rains, Ya get the one that you adore, / Ya kiss 'n' kiss 'n' kiss some more, / . . . That's what I do, What d' you do when it rains?" The rain in this number is just rain, by the way, and not, as it often is, a metaphor for the war; in this song the young lovers don't want it to stop.

Towering above all other lighthearted home front love songs was a rare number from an army camp show that became popular with the general public. It may not have been popularity of *Hit Parade* or even *Hot*

*Charts* proportions, but Perry Como's recording of Pfc. Frank Loesser's "First Class Private Mary Brown" (Frank Music, 1944) found a considerable civilian audience after it appeared in *About Face!* at Camp Shanks, New York, in 1944 and again in the WAC musical revue *P. F. C. Mary Brown.* It's sung by a soldier fairly bursting with simultaneous love and pride for his girl, all couched playfully but romantically in military metaphors. He says she wears "that uniform like a million dollar gown," and "How my heart would leap, when she drove her jeep with the one big stripe on her arm, / And it seemed to me that a P. F. C. stood for 'Perfectly Feminine Charm.'" Loesser's true genius shows in a tiny detail. Many, if not most, lyricists would probably have the soldier's girl cry at least a few tears when he's sent overseas, even though she herself is in the military. But Pfc. Loesser knew better and wrote, "Oh, how she smiled good-bye when they shipped me out of town." Mary doesn't smile because she's glad to be rid of him, but to express a WAC's love and pride in her GI guy— and maybe offer a little morale boost for him too. She surely wouldn't want him to see her cry.

Among the home front love songs are a half dozen or so about servicemen on furlough (or "foilough," if we include "Oh! Moytle"), all but one going home to see their girls. While these are sincere love songs to or about a longstanding girlfriend, some typical titles show that they all express romantic desire in playful, lighthearted ways: "Say Sarge (I Wanna See Marge)," "I Can't Wait Until Tomorrow ('Cause Tomorrow I Go Home On Leave)," "I Got Ten Bucks And Twenty-Four Hours Leave," and "Ten Days With Baby." All were pretty inconsequential in the larger scheme of wartime songs, only one furlough number really making the public sit up and take notice. The song was unusual for those about servicemen on leave because it's about a lonely GI on furlough without a girl. Amidst all of the lighthearted furlough tunes, only Bobby Worth's "A Fellow On A Furlough" (Hollywood: West'rn Music, 1943) is a mellow, sentimental song. The title character is looking for the "one who's in his dreams every night." That he's "A lonesome FELLOW ON A FURLOUGH in search of company, / Somebody who will be his guiding light" is another manifestation of the wartime belief that romantic involvements made getting through the war more bearable for servicemen and civilians alike. Though "Beautiful lady / Are you going my way?" sounds like a pick-up line, in context it's clear that the soldier wants a real romance, not a one-night stand. This is perhaps one reason why the number had widespread appeal. Bob Crosby introduced it in the 1944 Columbia musical *Meet Miss Bobby Socks,* and Louis Prima and Al Sack's bands recorded "A Fellow On A Furlough," as did vocalist Phil Hanna with Leonard Joy's Decca studio orchestra. Prima's and Sack's records are *Hot Charts* Extras during the summer of 1944, and in August Hanna's ranks 40th, then rising to 31st in September, when it is joined by Sack's disk at 29th. Trade paper charts show sheet music sales and jukebox plays were also strong during August and September. While "A Fellow On A Furlough" never made the top three on "Your Hit Parade," it was 8th when it first showed up, according to the announcer introducing Mark Warnow and the Hit Parade Orchestra and Chorus performing it, as reissued on several CDs of wartime songs.

As a sentimental piece about someone searching for a girl, not already in love with one, "A Fellow On A Furlough" links to the "boy meets girl in wartime" songs, both in its subject and its sentimental mood; that mood prevailed in this kind of song about home front romance and generated some genuine hits during the war years. There were also a few playful and even comic boy-meets-girl numbers that had some success, starting with the earliest, and easily the funniest: Jerry Bowne and Frank De Vol's "Little Bo-Peep Has Lost Her Jeep" (Southern Music, 1942) is the saga of a girl whose new soldier boyfriend calls her Bo-Peep. Without a car, the GI "borrows" a jeep to take her out on a date. Bo-Peep is thoroughly enjoying the scenic if bumpy ride in the jeep that "didn't drive like a Cadillac; / She wondered who designed it." Suddenly the GI recalls, "this jeep's gotta be in camp by eleven," so now "LITTLE BO-PEEP HAS LOST HER JEEP and doesn't know where to find it; / Her soldier boy drove it back to camp and left Bo-peep behind it." She can only wait and hope he will return someday (assuming he isn't court-martialed for absconding with government property). The song's melody is as silly as its lyrics, and it had some vogue in 1942 in an equally silly recording by that silliest of bands, with its oddball instruments and goofy noises, Spike Jones and His City Slickers. Also, according to *Hot Charts,* Horace Heidt's recording with vocals by Donna and the Don Juans ranks 29th in May. Though funny, "Bo-Peep" is thematically identical to most of the sentimental boy meets girl numbers in which the GI and the young woman fall in love, only to be parted by the serviceman departing for duty, each song ending with the promise and hope that the two will meet again.

The only other playful boy-meets-girl numbers of interest had boy meeting girl but not losing her because of the war—songs like Redd Evans and Earl Bostic's "The Major And The Minor" (Famous, 1942) and Henry Myers, Edward Eliscu, and Jay Gorney's "The Streamlined Sheik" (Mills, 1944) from the 1944 Columbia musical *Hey Rookie*. The best and most popular of these came out so late in 1945 that it had most of its success after the war in 1946. Still, once the war was over, servicemen kept meeting girls and falling in love, in life as in Hollywood films and Tin Pan Alley songs, the way Van Johnson and English actress Pat Kirkwood did in the 1946 M-G-M musical *No Leave, No Love*. One of the film's highlights is Kirkwood's performance of Ralph Blane, Kay Thompson, and

George Stoll's bubbly and bouncy romantic vehicular excursion, "Love On A Greyhound Bus" (Robbins, 1945), which is exactly what the number is about: "Stopped for hot dogs and soda pop—Asked the driver, 'How long till we make another stop?' / Soon the sun disappeared from view, / The stars came out like they always do, / And then I snuggled up close to you, / And we both fell in love on a trip on a Greyhound Bus, / That's us, in love on a Greyhound Bus." Beyond the film, the trip was pretty successful for records by Vaughn Monroe, Guy Lombardo and, especially, Kay Kyser's orchestra with vocal by Lucy Ann Polk.

Despite all of the fun in the best of the funny or playful boy-meets-girl songs, romantic and sentimental ones gained most of the public's favor until late 1943. After that, songwriters' attention was drawn more and more to songs about servicemen away and girls back home. Axel Remark, Frank Stanton, and Del Sharbutt's "Nickel Serenade" (Nationwide Songs, 1941) is sentimental and playful simultaneously—sentimental in the lyric, playful in the music. The number tells the simple, familiar tale of a soldier and a girl who met, danced, and fell in love to a jukebox's "nickel serenade"; the soldier promised "he would always stay," but of course he had to return to his brigade, "So the lonely little maid is left all alone and blue, / Cries while she listens to the Nickel Serenade." Despite the melancholy ending, it does not seem that the girl's new boyfriend will be lost to her forever—he just had to go back to camp—and the song's joyful music, not its words, reinforces that feeling. Even though the romantic lyric ends on a blue note, all feelings of sadness are swept away by the song's happy, up-tempo melody, with its roots in the exuberant, lively klezmer music of Eastern European Jews, immediately apparent in Les Brown's killer klezmer-style clarinet solo, which opens his band's record of the number, with Betty Bonney's vocal. Brown's is one of four recordings of "Nickel Serenade" on the *Hot Charts* Extra lists for September through November 1941; the others are by Sonny Dunham, Art Jarrett, and the Andrews Sisters. The Andrews Sisters' record ranks 40th in September. Curiously, neither trade paper's chart reported significant jukebox plays for "Nickel Serenade."

Not long after American troops began to be deployed around the globe, songs about GIs finding romance overseas started to follow. The title, words, and music of Kay Twomey and Al Goodhart's "Johnny Doughboy Found A Rose In Ireland" (Crawford Music, 1942) are so saccharine they sound like a throwback to World War I—and it was a major hit! Just "Doughboy" in the title lends an old-fashioned World War I aura to the song. Though still used, "doughboy" was far less common than "Yank" or "GI" for an American serviceman in World War II. But Twomey and Goodhart were savvy Tin Pan Alley professionals who probably knew exactly what they were doing. The title is a harbinger of the song's almost excessive sentimentality, both in Twomey's words and Goodhart's music, recalling the soldier-boy songs of World War I and, with the strong pull nostalgia always has, evoking what seemed by 1942 to be the more romantic days of the previous war. The fictional Johnny is shipped out to Ireland, as were many actual American troops in preparation for the North African and, later, European invasions. There he falls in love with "the fairest flow'r that Erin ever grew" because "the Blarney in her talk, / Took him back to old New York, / Where his mother spoke the sweetest blarney too." Irish-American Twomey managed, in good Irish tradition, to get romantic love and sentimental attachment to Mother into one song. Anticipating orders to move out, Johnny promises his fair colleen he'll return when it's all over, seeing it as his duty "To make an American beauty, / Of a sweet Irish rose like you." Other than the slight pun on a variety of rose in the final lines, Twomey and Goodhart opted entirely for sentiment over their more usual playfulness, and they struck pay dirt doing it. On the *Variety* sheet music charts, it was number one for all but five weeks between May 20 and August 5, and in those five weeks it was 2nd. The leading recordings were those by vocalist Kenny Baker and the orchestras of Kay Kyser, Guy Lombardo, Tommy Tucker, Freddy Martin, and Sammy Kaye. Kenny Baker was a genuine Irish tenor who worked the number's sentiment for all it was worth. His record ranks in *Hot Charts* the highest for any for a single month at 12th in July. "Johnny Doughboy" is hardly a dance tune, unless for *really* slow dancing, but according to both *Billboard* and *Variety*, Kay Kyser, Guy Lombardo, and Tommy Tucker's disks were popular jukebox plays from late April through late August. The song stayed on *Your Hit Parade* for sixteen weeks, in 2nd place for one of them.

Of all the songs in Irving Berlin's all-soldier show *This Is The Army*, which opened on Broadway on July 4, 1942, and toured both stateside and internationally throughout the war, the most popular number was "I Left My Heart At The Stage Door Canteen" (This Is the Army, Inc., 1942), outstripping even "This Is The Army, Mr. Jones." A soldier falls in love with a hostess named Eileen (was she Irish too?) at the American Theatre Wing's Stage Door Canteen in midtown Manhattan. It's mostly a charming little song, with the soldier so enamored of the girl that he "kept her serving doughnuts, 'til all she had were gone / I sat there dunking doughnuts 'til she caught on." The number never says if his attraction was love or infatuation, or whether the hostess reciprocated the soldier's affection. But in any case, like the GI in "Nickel Serenade," this one has to return to "the Army routine." In its last two lines the song takes a darkly portentous turn, when the GI sings, "A soldier boy without a heart has two strikes on him from the start / And my heart's at the Stage Door Canteen." Is he actually foreseeing himself with no will to fight, perhaps as a battle casualty? If so, or if that's how people interpreted those lines, small wonder "Stage Door Canteen" never became as popular as "Johnny Doughboy" that same year, with only twelve weeks on the *Hit Parade* and lower overall rankings for fewer months than "Johnny Doughboy" in the trade paper charts and *Hot Charts.*

Two other romantic boy-meets-girl numbers that achieved some popularity in the war years followed the prototypical pattern of "Johnny Doughboy Found A Rose In Ireland" but without its heavy dose of sentimentality. Yet their similarly floral titles make one wonder if the writers were attempting to ride the coattails of the earlier song's success. Lyricist Kermit Goell and composer Mabel Wayne's "Rose Ann Of Charing Cross" (Shapiro, Bernstein, 1942) is essentially "Johnny Doughboy" transplanted to London's Charing Cross Hospital, where a wounded American soldier falls in love with a nurse when she gently says to him—in the song's best moment—"That's only thunder overhead." She apparently also falls for him, since in the final stanza he says, "one day you'll be my bride / And . . . I know our paths will cross at Charing Cross again, Rose Ann." Though it was an American song, the top recording of it here was by Peter Piper's English orchestra, which ranked 34th and 28th for January and February 1943 in *Hot Charts,* followed by the Four Vagabonds' disk at 35th in March and as an Extra for April and May.

Just reading the lyrics or hearing a record of Marty Symes and Joe Burke's "By The River Of The Roses" (Shapiro, Bernstein, 1943), one would be hard put to find even a hint of the war in Symes's lyric. A boy sings of meeting the "sweetest girl this side of the Alamo," who, later in the song, "With tear dimmed eyes whispered 'I'll miss you so'" when he had to leave. He concludes with "some day by THE RIVER OF THE ROSES / I don't know when, but we'll meet again I know." Nothing indicates where he is going or why. Only the "I don't know when" could be construed as a veiled reference to the war, but it doesn't have to be. What confirms that the number was intended to touch on the war by association isn't verbal or even musical, but visual—the sheet music cover art. Framed by a river in the background and roses in the foreground is a soldier with a girl. Shapiro, Bernstein was noted for releasing potential hits late every year and marketing them with great skill. So even if Symes and Burke didn't intended "Roses" to be war-related, the publishers chose to associate the song with the war through the sheet music cover. Either way, singer Phil Hanna and the big bands of Abe Lyman, Phil Brito, and Woody Herman all recorded "By The River Of The Roses," and their versions were all *Hot Charts* Extras between two and four times from January through May 1944, with Woody Herman's rendition ranked 34th, 37th, and 32nd in March, April, and May—not a major hit, but a big seller for some big bands.

One boy-girl-in-wartime song achieved true greatness artistically, but not much success commercially outside of the movie it was in. E. Y. Harburg and Sammy Fain's "In Times Like These" (Leo Feist, 1943) is as nearly forgotten today as it was largely unnoticed in its own day, except for appearing in the 1944 M-G-M musical *Meet The People,* in which Dick Powell sang it to, and briefly with, a young and drop-dead gorgeous Lucille Ball, Ball's singing voice dubbed by Gloria Grafton. Usually thought of for his witty lyrics and wacky rhymes—and perhaps most of all for his songs with Harold Arlen for *The Wizard of Oz*—Harburg was also a songwriter of great thought, depth, and lyricism, all of which can be seen in this song, which refers to the war only allusively. Yet the war is unquestionably the context for Harburg's core idea, an idea found in no other popular song about wartime romance—that it was more than a minor miracle that home front civilians or service personnel could still meet and fall in love "In Times Like These." The verse, not in the sheet music, dramatically makes the point that "all the world has slammed the door on spring," leading into the verse that begins "In times like these, who would think that love could find a way / With all the lights dimmed out, with darkness all about." The singer includes himself with everyone else preoccupied with thoughts of the war: "Like all the rest, I was adrift, my heart was all at sea / Just when the world needed a lift you came and smiled at me." Set to Fain's stunningly gorgeous music, Harburg's skillfully structured lyric concludes by bringing the end back to the imagery at the beginning, "And there was spring . . . / telling the dawn that love goes on / In times like these."

# 11:

# *"A Boy In Khaki, A Girl In Lace"*

## The Servicemen Away, Their Girls Back Home

During World War II, America's professional songwriters wrote more than 370 songs about servicemen saying goodbye, GIs away, or their sweethearts, wives, mothers, or children back home. This constitutes more songs than there were on any other topic, including all of those about home front conditions and support for the war, which, at about 262 songs, is a pretty distant second. The reason for this enormous outpouring of songs about people parted by the war is easy to understand. In the war years nothing touched American adults and children more directly and deeply than how the war affected personal relationships: "the physical and social upheavals of the War imposed severe strains on . . . marriage and the family, which endured conflicting and often intolerable stresses" (Bailey 147). Separations imposed by the war also strained romantic relationships between boys and girls not yet married, and even relationships between parents and children. Since over thirteen million men served at one time or another during the war, it stands to reason that most were attached to women back home. Between the GIs overseas and the women on the home front, Tin Pan Alley had a ready market for quality songs about these relationships. And Tin Pan Alley delivered. Of all the songs inspired by World War II, more hits then and classics ever since came from the ranks of those touching on the emotions of GIs abroad, the girls they left behind, or servicemen coming home (see chapter 12). The proliferation and popularity of such songs defied the OWI's warnings that such slush sapped the will of our soldiers and depressed home front girls, thus dangerously weakening American morale. To the contrary, these songs, by personalizing the war, inspired greater determination to win it.

Once again the nation's songwriters and music listeners were proved right and Washington wrong.

### *"Something To Remember You By": Saying Goodbye in Wartime*

How many ways can you say goodbye? Musically, Tin Pan Alley and country songs during World War II said it with infinite variety, but the lyrics that verbalized those goodbyes were much more monochromatic. Still, a number of lyricists found innovative ways to express the thoughts and feelings that were endlessly repeated in such songs. Prominent Alley or hillbilly songwriters wrote about seventy of these leave-taking songs, and while some numbers fell short of their usual writing, over twenty of the seventy achieved contemporary popularity or are of historical interest.

It was the British, already in the thick of the European conflict, who prepared prewar American ears and emotions for songs of servicemen bidding farewell to their sweethearts or wives. English songs of parting began to arrive here in 1939—songs like Tommie Connor and Eddie Pola's "Till The Lights of London Shine Again" (London: B. Feldman, 1939; New York: Crawford Music, 1939), with the leading disk in the states recorded by Bob Chester's orchestra on November 26, 1940. Also late in 1940 came Ross Parker and Hughie Charles's timeless "We'll Meet Again," which only caught fire after Pearl Harbor (see chapter 4). The steady flow of servicemen saying goodbye in song began with the draft in 1940 and continued unabated right to the end of the war and even beyond, with the late 1945 Andrews Sisters' hit "The Blond Sailor" (Mills Music, 1937, 1945). While the number of such songs was naturally highest in 1942, they tapered off but slightly in '43 and '44, since more American troops were continually being sent overseas. Even in 1945, as the war gradually concluded, American troops were sent abroad as occupation forces or to staff the growing network of American military bases around the globe. What's interesting about the hundred or more songs of servicemen's goodbyes throughout the war years is their consistency. Except for a cluster of numbers in 1941 and '42 whose immediate impetus was the draft, the songs written later in the war look and sound just about the same as those at the beginning, suggesting that saying goodbye in wartime is pretty much a painful constant. What separates the great and near-great leave-taking numbers from the pedestrian ones isn't so much their content as the skill, taste, and artistry of those writers who found fresh, original ways to say goodbye.

When conscription went into effect on October 29, 1940, draftees were committed to just twelve months of military service. This triggered a number of songs, mostly hillbilly and mostly interrelated, predicated on an absence of just a year. First to gain national attention was Ben Shelhamer Jr., Claude Heritier, and Russ Hull's "I'll Be Back In A Year Little Darlin'" (Chicago: Bell Music, 1941), which is a *Hot Charts* Extra as early as January 1941 in the recording by Texas Jim Robertson and remains so through May, except for ranking 52nd in April. The song, like so many to follow, has the soldier telling his girl not to worry or cry but instead to "be proud of your soldier boy," and ends with the inevitable promise that he'll return. Toward the end of that number's popularity came along Mack Kay's "Good Bye Dear, I'll Be Back In A Year" (Coast to Coast Music, 1940), which is more faux than genuine hillbilly but sounds very country even in the hit recording by Horace Heidt's orchestra with vocals by Ronnie Kemper and Donna and the Don Juans. *Hot Charts* first ranks it 28th in June, and it rises as high as 10th in July, staying on the charts in the twenties and thirties through September. The lyric has a certain elementary charm in the way the departing serviceman makes a typical promise for the future—another recurring leitmotif in songs of parting and separation: "I'll save ev'ry bit of my dollar a day / For we'll have some wedding expenses to pay." The first reciprocal song, "I'll Be Waiting For You Darlin' (Answer To 'I'll Be Back In A Year')" (Bell Music, 1941), was by Russ Hull, one of the triumvirate responsible for the first one. Sung by the girlfriend of the departing serviceman "with a sigh and a tear," she promises to "be brave and true," and, in another major motif mostly in songs about the girls back home, also promises she'll "pray night and day" for her GI away. These few early numbers reveal certain recurring formulaic patterns developing in the songs of goodbye, yet some numbers achieved greatness by skillfully manipulating such material. Once the handwriting was on the wall at the end of 1941, the outlook of the remaining interrelated songs shifted considerably. Country songwriters Bradley Kincaid and Buck Nation contributed a kind of footnote to "I'll Be Back In a Year" with their brief and direct "I Won't Be Back In A Year Little Darling" (Southern Music, 1941), in which the soldier tells his girl that he can't keep his earlier promise because now Uncle Sam needs him to fight a real war and "Tho' it may be for long, you must be brave and strong." Then, early in 1942, Russ Hull—again—returned with new collaborators, Nicola and Rose Fantetti, to have a GI tell his girl realistically, "It's Not A Year, Dear Nor Two" (Country Music, 1942), not even daring to project how long he'll be away. A few minor songs promising a year or two's absence came out just before or after Pearl Harbor, but that theme quickly evaporated as the home front began to acknowledge the gravity of the conflict.

Since the remaining songs of servicemen's farewells display no discernable pattern or progression during the course of the war, their types, tones, and points of view are clearest seen not chronologically but through clusters of representative songs of each variety that had some success or are of special historical significance. As in the early hillbilly numbers inspired by the draft, the most prevalent motifs in Tin Pan Alley songs were those in which the GI encourages his wife or sweetheart not to cry, to be as brave as he must learn to be, and to stay focused on the day they will be together again. Hy Zaret was a skillful lyricist who could pack a lot into very few words, as in "My Sister And I," and he managed to compress all three of those themes into the last two lines of "Be Brave, Beloved" (Leeds, 1942), with music by Arthur Altman: "Till then, BELOVED, BE BRAVE, no tears, no sighs, / Next time we meet there'll be no more good-byes." Vaughn Monroe recorded the song on March 11, 1942. Two songs with almost identical titles expressed similar sentiments: Sunny Skylar's "Don't Cry" (National Music, 1942) and Remus Harris, Irving Melsher, and Russ Morgan's "Don't Cry Sweetheart" (Chicago: Glenmore Music, 1942); Morgan's own recording of the latter is a *Hot Charts* Extra during the summer of 1942 and ranks 52nd in October. The number emphasized, as did many of them, that the lovers' parting was only temporary: "So DON'T CRY, SWEETHEART, just kiss me now and smile. / It's not good-bye forever, it's only for a while." One wonders if such thoughts weren't as much to reassure GIs of their own safe return as they were to console their girls about their enforced absence from one other.

Of the many songs about a GI's leave-taking, just one dared address the possibility that he might not return. True to form, that was a hillbilly song—and by one of the greatest of all country singer/songwriters, Roy Acuff. Acuff ventured into territory that Tin Pan Alley left unexplored. His "I'd Die For The Red, White and Blue" (Nashville: Acuff-Rose Publications, 1944) is a model of the "don't cry / be strong" song of goodbye, except for the grimly realistic picture the departing soldier paints for his girl: "Dry those teardrops and smile for me, little darlin' / . . . let's kneel down and pray that someday I'll come back. / If I die over there never more to see you, keep your chin up and be brave for me, little darlin'"; in the third verse he even says, "if after the war you are one dressed in black / Don't let it make you bitter . . . / Just be glad in your heart for the ones that come back." With no reliable hillbilly charts, there's no way to know if Acuff's frank approach to a soldier's departure found an audience.

Only six Alley or hillbilly songs of farewell find GIs saying goodbye to anyone other than sweethearts or wives, yet none is addressed to a mother—rather remarkable considering the "mother songs" written about soldiers who were already away. In half of the six a serviceman and his child say goodbye. Marriage wasn't grounds for deferment from military service, but early in the war children were often referred to as "draft insurance." Indeed "by mid-1943, eight million fathers were deferred." But as more and more men were needed for combat duty, deferments for parenthood decreased until by "the end of 1944, only 80,000 men still held deferments as fathers" (Bailey 44, 45). Not remarkably, two of the songs of this type came later in the war. Only Irving Caesar, Al Koppell, and Gerald Marks's "Be A Good Soldier (While Your Daddy's Away)" (Irving Caesar, 1942) came early, displaying an obvious kinship with the "don't cry / be brave" songs to sweethearts and wives: "Smile for me, buddy, you know soldiers don't cry, / . . . So pray for me, soldier, and promise each day, / You'll Be A Good Soldier while your daddy's away." The later songs were hillbilly numbers. Russ Hull, the seemingly ubiquitous writer of parting songs, and Ida De Millo Lammers wrote one from the standpoint of the child, which, while sentimental, has some charm, as a three-year-old boy tells his soldier-father "I'll Take Good Care Of Mommy While You're Gone" (Chicago: Country Music, 1943): "Don't worry, daddy dear, / . . . It won't be awful hard / 'cause my soldiers will stand guard / And I'll kiss away the teardrops if she cries." Roger Riddle's "Little Soldier Man" (Southern Music, 1944) uses similar metaphors from the father's point of view: "You're not even three, / But you'll have to be the captain of the home artillery, / So keep your chin up, don't you cry, / My little soldier man, good-bye."

Two of the "be brave / don't cry" songs are of importance because they were genuine hits, and another near-miss stands out because of its unusual way of writing about the subject. Phil Moore's "Shoo-Shoo Baby" (Leeds, 1943) had the rare distinction of appearing in four Hollywood films in the single year of 1944: Columbia Pictures' *Beautiful but Broke*, Republic's *Trocadero*, and two films from Universal Studios. In *South of Dixie*, Ella Mae Morse sang the number, and in *Follow the Boys* the Andrews Sisters cut loose with the rendition that had already rocketed their record of "Shoo-Shoo" to hitdom, with Morse's never far behind. African American Moore was a very hip songwriter and jazzman and "Shoo-Shoo" is arguably the hippest musical goodbye of the war. It stayed for seventeen weeks on *Your Hit Parade*, hitting the top spot for two, and on *Variety*'s sheet music charts it rose rapidly from 12th in mid-December 1943 to 4th by the end of the month, then either 2nd or 3rd each week till early March 1944. On the *Billboard* charts from late December 1943 though mid-April '44 the records by the Andrews Sisters and Ella Mae Morse look like a horserace between two top thoroughbreds, neither ever quite reaching the winner's circle but at least jockeying with each other for 3rd or 4th place every week. And on the *Hot Charts* tally for January through March 1944, the Andrews Sisters place 3rd, 3rd, and 4th, with Morse close behind at 5th, 4th, and 9th. In a word, "Shoo-Shoo" was uncommonly popular for a song of goodbye, most likely because it's an upbeat, groovy number, not just in Moore's swingtime music but in his lyric as well: "Bye, bye, bye, baby, / Don't cry baby, / SHOO-SHOO, SHOO

BABY, / Your papa's off to the seven seas." With Ella Mae Morse's success singing "Cow Cow Boogie" a year and a half earlier, she was adept at numbers treading a fine line between jazz and pop, and the Andrews Sisters' styling of Moore's song is about as close to improvisational as three singers working together in close harmony can get. Between Moore's writing and the performances by Morse and the Andrews Sisters, "Shoo-Shoo" qualifies as a triumph of wartime popular song—and a five-month hit!

The other hit "please don't cry" song wasn't quite so big, but again the Andrews Sisters were responsible for its success, and mostly after the Japanese surrender. The song's origins are similar to those of "Lili Marlene" but without the intrigues. It was originally a German song by Jacob Pfeil. Mitchell "Stardust" Parish and Bell Leib wrote English lyrics, and "The Blond Sailor" was copyrighted and published by Mills Music in 1937 and again in 1945. The lyric is fairly sentimental and the music pretty syrupy, as a sailor asks his girl to "send me off with a kiss and a smile, dear," as she brushes away a tear. Whatever the song's intrinsic merits, the extrinsic reason for its popularity had to have been the Andrews Sisters recording alone, because the song made no waves in the sheet music market. But *Hot Charts* ranks the sisters' disk 28th in September, 21st in October, and 26th in November 1945.

But hit or not, among all the "don't cry" songs Charles Newman and Allie Wrubel's "A Boy In Khaki, A Girl In Lace" is the most striking for all it leaves unsaid. This minimalist, shorthand account of a boy and girl saying goodbye speaks volumes in elegant understatement. Wrubel's melody is eminently hummable, and Newman's spare lyric sometimes even eschews complete sentences: "The same old sweethearts, the same old place / A BOY IN KHAKI A GIRL IN LACE." Meaningful actions replace words between the GI and the girl: "He bends to kiss her / She lifts her face." All that's spoken is his promise to return and her reply of "please do"—and that's it. The song simply ends with "And so we leave them in fond embrace" and a repetition of the title line. Reducing a moment of parting to just its essential elements is the core of the emotional clout of "A Boy In Khaki," making it one of the most effective of such numbers during the war. Apparently some of America's most popular singers thought so too, since Bing Crosby, Kate Smith, and Dinah Shore rushed to record it, as did the orchestras of Guy Lombardo, Horace Heidt, and Tommy Dorsey with Jo Stafford's vocal. The public spread its enthusiasm among all six records, all of them appearing as *Hot Charts* Extras for November 1942 and only then, and not at all in the trade papers, except for *Variety*'s charts of jukebox plays for four weeks between September 16 and October 7, which list the Crosby and Dorsey disks under "Other Favorites."

Closely related to the "don't cry" leave-taking numbers were the "think of me" and, sometimes, "wait for me" ones; like the other songs of parting, they also spanned all the years of the war. Typical of the type is Benny Davis, Russ Morgan, and Ted Murry's "Please Think of Me" (Witmark, 1942), with its redundant, repetitive lyric of "PLEASE THINK OF ME whenever you're lonely / Whenever you're lonely PLEASE THINK OF ME," set to an oddly pleasing up-tempo tune for a song packed with such thoughts. Though it was played by the orchestras of Harry James, Hal McIntyre, Teddy Powell, and the song's own co-author Russ Morgan, the disk by Shep Fields with vocal by Ralph Young became the biggest seller, a *Hot Charts* Extra from December 1942 through May 1943, except for March, when it shot up to 17th. Expressing similar sentiments later were Ned Washington and Max Steiner's "Someday, I'll Meet You Again" (Witmark, 1944) from the 1944 Warner Bros. war drama *Passage to Marseille,* and, from country music, Ernest Tubb's "Keep My Mem'ry In Your Heart" (Hollywood: American Music, 1945). But the biggest "think of me / wait for me" song from the departing soldier's point of view was Eddie Seiler, Sol Marcus, and Guy Wood's "Till Then" (Sun Music, 1944), thanks to the Mills Brothers' hit record that leaps from 38th in June 1944 to 11th in October in *Hot Charts.* Each stanza basically repeats the song's central thought of "Please wait TILL THEN," but the image of the war evoked in the release is quite stunning: "Although there are oceans we must cross, and mountains that we must climb, / I know ev'ry gain must have a loss, so pray that our loss is nothing but time."

A group of similar songs expressed thoughts of parting from the girl's point of view, and three of them achieved some popularity early in the war. Not only does the girl promise her departing GI "I'll Pray For You" (Harms 1942), with words by Kim Gannon and music by Arthur Altman, she also tells him what servicemen in such songs usually tell their girls: "So let me see you smile before we say goodbye," even as she candidly admits that "this moment's breaking my heart." Gannon's typically concise, honest lyric and Altman's melodic setting paid off, with the Andrews Sisters' record ranking 46th in March 1942 and remaining a *Hot Charts* Extra through May, along with records by Lanny Ross and the orchestras of Hal McIntyre, Tony Pastor, and Tommy Tucker. Harry Tobias, Nick Kenny, and Harold Levey's "I'll Keep The Lovelight Burning" (Remick, 1942) was introduced by Kate Smith and had moderately successful records by the orchestras of Bob Crosby, Freddy Martin, Hal McIntyre, Ray McKinley, and Dick Jurgens in spring and early summer 1942. The girl in the song assures her GI guy that she and her love for him will still be there when he returns, a common motif also in songs about girls back home. One truly great song from the girl's point of view surfaced in 1943. Except for the verse, which wasn't recorded anyway, the number looks like it was tailor-made for the situation of a girl sending her sweetheart off to war. Yet Arthur Schwartz and Howard Dietz wrote "Something To

Remember You By" (Harms, 1930) thirteen years before Dinah Shore's moving record made the song a quiet little hit for a time in 1943. Whoever recalled the song to revive it must have had a keen eye for timing, since everything in it resonates with the war years, from its opening "Oh, give me something to remember you by, / When you are far away from me" to the girl's thoughts in the bridge, "Though I'll pray for you, / Night and day for you; It will see me through like a charm, / Till your returning"— all this set to the kind of gorgeously legato melody composer Schwartz excelled in.

A number of songs took unusual approaches to saying goodbye and had some success doing it. Once in the army, Pfc. Harold Rome wrote a song for his Fort Hamilton All Soldier Show *Stars and Gripes* that offered a realistic and pragmatic view of sweethearts separated by the war. "Love Sometimes Has To Wait" (Leeds, 1943) cleverly describes how a romance has to be put on hold during wartime: "If these were normal times we'd be in clover, / Hunting two rooms and a kitchenette," but "For two hearts in rhyme, there's no depending, / The happy ending isn't running on time," and these days "Sometimes lovers part at the start of the song." That same year Nat Burton, Al Sherman, and Arthur Altman said much the same thing, though more romantically and metaphorically, in "There's A Harbor Of Dream Boats (Anchored On Moonlight Bay)" (Shapiro, Bernstein, 1943). Right from the opening lines of the verse, the songwriters took the unusual approach of having the departing serviceman generalize from his situation with his girl to that of millions of other couples parted by the war: "Darling you and I are not the only ones / Whose dreams are halted temporarily." The chorus picks up the metaphor of the "dream boats" lying at anchor "because their skippers went away [and] / There are millions of sweethearts / Waiting along the shore." The number received considerable airplay by Kate Smith, Jimmy Dorsey, Russ Morgan, and Kay Kyser, but its success on phonograph records in the spring of 1943 came largely from the English orchestra of Peter Piper. Most likely this was because Petrillo's recording ban precluded any name bands from recording the piece on any labels hit by the strike. Piper's disk is a *Hot Charts* Extra for April and May 1943. That the public took "Harbor Of Dream Boats" to heart is also evident from its sheet music sales; according to *Variety*'s weekly charts, it averaged in the 10th place between mid-April and late June 1943.

A few songs of parting, including two that involved some very prominent songwriters, fused romantic love and love of country in a single number. For the M-G-M musical *Ship Ahoy*, released in May 1942, E. Y. Harburg and Burton Lane (later responsible for the great musical theatre score of *Finian's Rainbow* in 1947), together with one Margery Cumming, wrote "The Last Call For Love" (Leo Feist, 1942). Sung in the film by

Frank Sinatra and the Pied Pipers with Tommy Dorsey's orchestra, it is reprised at the end as numerous sailors are being shipped out. With his usual ingenuity Harburg manages to virtually *equate* romantic love and patriotic love of country in two lines: "With your eyes in the stars of Old Glory, / Can I help but be faithful to you?" The Sinatra/Dorsey recording makes it to 31st in *Hot Charts* for June, the month after the film came out, with other records by Bob Crosby, Freddy Martin, and Tommy Tucker as Extras in the summer months. More direct was "My Heart Belongs To America" (Robbins, 1942), the original idea and lyric of which, according to the sheet music, were by one Mrs. William G. Foley. The revised published lyric is by Alleyman Paul Cunningham and the music by Sam H. Stept, who is best known for "Don't Sit Under The Apple Tree," to be discussed later in this chapter. The departing serviceman tells his girl that he has "two sweethearts" but she needn't fear he'll be unfaithful since "My Heart Belongs To America, / And my love belongs to you."

Cautionary songs were most commonly addressed to girls back home from GIs already away, but in a few playful ones departing servicemen fire a warning shot to let the girl know she better be on her best behavior while her guy's away. Late in 1942, and in a fashion typical of their accustomed playfulness, Kay Twomey and Al Goodhart wrote "Better Not Roll Those Blue, Blue Eyes (At Somebody Else)" (Crawford, 1942); the rest of the departing GI's lyric is a list of more cute "better nots" for his girl. The girl's verse goes beyond cute to funny but wasn't printed in the commercial sheet music, and just a few lines of it, like "don't rehearse with some cute nurse," were recorded in this country by the Dinning Sisters. But when Anne Shelton recorded the song in England, she included the whole girl's verse, culminating in the wonderfully self-referential "don't let my sigh say you're the guy found the Rose across the sea," alluding to Twomey and Goodhart's uncharacteristically sentimental hit "Johnny Doughboy Found A Rose In Ireland" earlier that year. Collaborating with Cee Pee Johnson and Lou Victor, the versatile Hoagy Carmichael was in equally rare form in "Don't Forget To Say 'No' Baby" (Southern Music, 1942), in which a GI going off to basic training cautions his girl, "Don't be thrillin' while I'm drillin'," his list of don'ts reaching a comic crescendo with "While I'm out to train, don't you entertain, / Remember you're not the 'U. S. O.' / Till I return, baby, DON'T FORGET TO SAY 'NO.'"

Playful approaches to the serious business of saying goodbye in wartime were understandably rare, but of the few others one became an enormous hit and another had fun with the conventions of the serious and sentimental songs on the subject. It was almost inevitable that someone would eventually parody such sentimentality, and composer/lyricist Vick Knight became that someone in his "Bye Bye Bessie" (Hollywood: Variety Music, 1943). It begins seriously in the verse with a "country boy . . .

khaki from head to toe" preparing to say goodbye to his best girl with her "big brown eyes a-grievin'." In the chorus, the soldier begins his plaintive farewell: "BYE BYE BESSIE, don't cry / Dry that tear in your eye / Gotta save this world from ruin', still, I'll miss your mooin'"—he's been singing to his cow! Which he does throughout the rest of song, giving his bovine pal some words of encouragement: "While I carry out my mission keep your tail a-swishin'."

Typically offbeat, Frank Loesser wrote a song in which a GI laments that he doesn't have a girl to say goodbye to. Loesser did double-duty in the ingenuity department, first by coming up with that new angle for a song of farewell, and second by doing so in a manner not at all lugubrious but happily playful. Musically "In My Arms" is a bright breezy waltz, even as the boy keeps wailing, "Ain't I ever gonna get a girl in my arms?" When he addresses his relatives sending him off with gifts and other kindnesses, he does so with Loesser's usual wit: "You can wine and dine and cigarette me, / But if you really wanna get me, / Gimme a girl in my arms tonight." Still, for all its fun, the number underscores how much it meant to GIs to have a girl back home—someone to be fighting for. We'll never know whether the public sensed that in the song, but they bought enough sheet music for it to rank between 3rd and 5th nearly every week on *Variety*'s chart between July 7 and October 27, 1943, just when Dick Haymes and the Song Spinners' recording rose in *Hot Charts* from 13th in July to 9th in August and 10th in September.

### "There Are Such Things": Love Transcendent

Beyond the newly minted songs about boys away or girls back home, World War II occasioned the revival or writing of a tiny but significant group of seven songs that eloquently express the constant and eternal nature of love or of parted lovers' feelings for one another. These songs are equally meaningful sung by a man or a woman, and, in fact, most were sung by vocalists of both sexes. All seven became hits to one degree or another during the war, and five have remained standards ever since.

Many people like myself who lived through the war years later grew to appreciate a terrible irony about them: for the home front it was one of the best, even happiest, times to be living in America during the twentieth century, and yet the backdrop to this was a devastating global conflict. The war engendered not just new prosperity and years of national unity so tangible you could feel it but also the tremendous enrichment of our popular arts, especially movies and popular music. The war was also responsible for the success of revivals of a few songs that otherwise would remain as forgotten today as they were unnoticed originally. Their relevance to wartime situations led to their resuscitation during the war, bringing them contemporary popularity then and lasting fame ever since. Of the seven songs about love transcending time and distance, four were revivals.

In the order of their wartime revivals, the first song's origin wasn't even American, except in the Latin sense. In the 1930s Cuban composer Gonzalo Roig and lyricist Augustin Rodriguez wrote "Quiermo Mucho"; with Jack Sherr's English lyrics it became "Yours" (Edward B. Marks, 1932, 1937), but it met with little success despite Dinah Shore's 1939 recording. Only in 1941, before Pearl Harbor but with the draft in full swing and war seemingly imminent, did this ballad really take off, pledging, as it does, undying love in lines like "YOURS in the gray of December / Here or on far distant shores!"—lyrics resonating with wartime imagery and sentiments written nearly ten years before the United States entered the war. Seventeen weeks on the *Hit Parade,* in 2nd place for four, and twelve weeks ranked between 10th and 2nd on *Variety's* sheet music charts indicate how strongly the public embraced "Yours" just for the song itself. But it was the now-classic bilingual recording by Jimmy Dorsey's orchestra with English vocal by Bob Eberly and Spanish by Helen O'Connell that really caught fire; high in *Hot Charts'* rankings from May through October, it peaks at 3rd in August.

On October 13, 1931, an unremarkable musical called *Everybody's Welcome* with Sammy Fain's undistinguished score opened on Broadway for a modest 139 performances (Bordman 471). In it, Frances Williams sang an interpolated song by Herman Hupfeld, and its subsequent radio performances and recordings by Rudy Vallee and Jacques Renard were given little more than a cordial reception at the time. But twelve years later "As Time Goes By" was revived in the 1943 Warner Bros. drama *Casablanca*—a film that couldn't have been made were it not for World War II. If the war hadn't prompted its revival, what has become a timeless standard among American songs might have been completely forgotten. As Sam the piano player at Rick's Place in the Humphrey Bogart/Ingrid Bergman classic film, African-American baritone Dooley Wilson sang and played "As Time Goes By," launching a revival of staggering proportions. *Your Hit Parade* featured the song for twenty-one weeks, four times in 1st, and the sheet music, its cover splashed with photos of Bergman and Bogart and billing the song as "From the Warner Bros. Picture *Casablanca,*" was 1st or 2nd for fourteen weeks on *Variety's* charts. Not only that, but the film, the war, and the musicians' union recording ban combined to revive not just the song but Rudy Vallee's original 1931 Victor recording of "As Time Goes By" and the Brunswick disk by Jacques Renard. Both Vallee's and Renard's renditions do well in *Hot Charts* between March and July 1943, each reaching as high as 7th, Vallee's in May and Renard's in June. From its familiar opening of "You must remember this, a kiss is still a kiss" to its equally familiar conclusion that "The world will always welcome lovers," "As Time Goes By" goes beyond the wartime survival of two people's love for each other to say that love itself will always transcend even the worst of times.

In 1944 two songs on this theme were revived: "I'll Be Seeing You," even more spectacularly than "As Time Goes By" in 1943, and "The Very Thought Of You," a more gentle reminder of how the war gave a song that was once fairly popular a new and heightened meaning. The genesis of "I'll Be Seeing You" (Williamson Music, 1938) is similar to that of "As Time Goes By." Irving Kahal and Sammy Fain wrote it for the musical *Right This Way*, which opened on January 4, 1938, and closed fifteen performances later. Since it had no discernable recognition on radio or records at the time, that lovely song would have died unnoticed if someone in 1944 hadn't seen its lyric's relevance to the plight of lovers separated by the war and revived it. Kathleen E. R. Smith's claim that the chorus is filled with "images of small-town life" (37) is belied by the lines of the verse "Was it the spell of Paris / Or the April dawn?" The song's separated lovers clearly fell in love in the French capital, and Kahal's references in the chorus to a "small café," "children's carousel," and "chestnut trees" are certainly more Parisian than smalltown American. Of course most singers omitted the verse from records and radio performances, though it was printed for all to see in the published sheet music, with its cover drawing of a very French sidewalk café. The number contains not the vaguest allusion to the war, but listeners could and did see its overarching theme of a couple's love transcending time and distance as having special relevance to a man and woman parted by the war: "I'll be looking at the moon / But I'll be seeing you." The song was on *Your Hit Parade* for twenty-four weeks (nearly half a year!), in 1st for ten. On *Billboard*'s charts the records by Bing Crosby and Tommy Dorsey with Frank Sinatra's vocal vied for top honors or close to it every week between June 3 and October 7, the sheet music ranking either 1st or 2nd every week from May 24 through August 16. And enough home front Americans, GIs in Europe, and Frenchmen *did* grasp the song's Parisian relevance since "I'll Be Seeing You" was "spontaneously taken up as the anthem of liberation" when the Allies' liberated Paris on August 25 (Perrett 278).

In 1934 English bandleader and songwriter Ray Noble wrote "The Very Thought Of You" (London: Campbell Connelly, 1934; Witmark, sole U.S. selling agent). That year Noble's own orchestra had the hit recording in Britain, while in the United States it was Bing Crosby. The song became Noble's theme song even before he came to the United States in 1936 to continue his musical career. By the war years the song was no longer on most Americans' lips, but in 1944 it was revived in the Warner Bros. film of the same name, some studio exec probably realizing the wartime relevance of Noble's lyric: "I see your face in ev'ry flower Your eyes in stars above, / It's just the thought of you, / The very thought of you, my love." Unlike the other revivals in this group, "The Very Thought Of You" never reached the top of the *Hit Parade*, but Kitty Carlisle, Guy Lombardo, and Louis Prima's disks are *Hot Charts* Extras for October and November 1944, and Vaughn Monroe's is ranked 33rd in December.

The three new songs of love's constancy and transcendence that appeared in the war years were written with the war very much in mind. Though never making it to any of the trade papers' charts, Al Dubin and James V. Monaco's "We Mustn't Say Goodbye" (Edwin H. Morris, 1943) was nominated for an Academy Award for its appearance in the 1943 United Artists musical *Stage Door Canteen* and found most of its audience in movie theatres. Set to Monaco's rich but simple melody, Dubin's clean, lyrical words say that not even a global war can separate two people in love, so saying goodbye is never necessary: "In dreams, we'll always be together, / Beneath a moonlit sky, / WE MUSTN'T SAY GOOD-BYE." Though the song was recorded by top vocalists like Jo Stafford, only Allen Miller's recording makes even the *Hot Charts* Extras list, and then just for May 1943. The other two songs had a happier fate with the public. Roc Hillman and Johnny Napton scored a major hit with "My Devotion" (Santly-Joy-Select, 1942). It spent four of its sixteen *Hit Parade* weeks in 1st place, and between August 19 and November 18 *Variety* charted its sheet music sales in the single digits, and in 1st or 2nd for seven weeks. Records by the King Sisters, Vaughn Monroe, Jimmy Dorsey with Bob Eberly's vocal, and Charlie Spivak with vocal by Garry Stevens all did well, with Spivak's skyrocketing in *Hot Charts* from 62nd in August to 2nd in September, 5th in October, and still holding strong at 11th in November, and Vaughn Monroe's reaching a high of 7th in October. The theme of the song isn't so much the everlasting nature of love per se as of the love between the singer and his or her absent beloved: "MY DEVOTION is endless and deep as the ocean / And like a star shining from afar / Remains the same."

The last of this group, Stanley Adams, Abel Baer, and George W. Meyer's "There Are Such Things" (Yankee Music, 1942) was about as big a hit as the revivals of "As Time Goes By" and "I'll Be Seeing You," with eighteen weeks on *Your Hit Parade*, six in 1st place. But this remarkably lovely song apparently didn't have what it took to become an enduring classic after the war. Frank Sinatra with Tommy Dorsey's orchestra had the hit record; in *Hot Charts* every month from October 1942 through April '43, it ranks 1st in January, 2nd in February, and 4th in March of the latter year. When "There Are Such Things" first hit *Variety*'s sheet music chart on January 13, 1943, it was already in 1st place, where it stayed four more weeks, only slowly descending to 3rd, 4th, and lower, but staying on the chart through March 31. The idea of the song is that some eternal verities do exist among all that is transitory in the troubled time of war. The off-beat verse begins startlingly with "You may laugh about Thanksgiving, you may think that life is wrong," the chorus then pointing out the positives in a world of so many negatives: "A heart that's true, THERE ARE SUCH THINGS . . . / A peaceful sky, THERE ARE SUCH THINGS." For me the centerpiece of the lyric is its stating with a candor unusual for Tin Pan Alley that someone loves you, "Not caring what you own but just what you are." What unites these seven songs about love transcending the vicissitudes of war is the uncommon artistry in the music and lyrics of each, all of which transcend the mundane and ordinary in so much American popular song.

### "Heaven Is A Place Called Home": Homesickness, Holidays, and the Absent GI

The millions of GIs overseas naturally missed the familiar things of home. This did not go unnoticed by Tin Pan Alley and hillbilly songwriters, though only a few of the many songs of homesickness achieved anything like popularity, let alone greatness as songwriting. One of the few truly great ones is one of the earliest—Bernie Grossman and Walter Jurmann's "Beneath The Lights Of Home" (Remick, 1941), sung by Deanna Durbin in the Universal film *Nice Girl?* released in February 1941. At that time virtually all American servicemen away were in training camps. Grossman's lyric is a bit sentimental in its images of longing to return to a small town, home, and "somebody there, / Loving eyes and silver hair," but the long soaring lines of Jurmann's hauntingly beautiful melody more than make up for any such excesses. Prewar Americans couldn't connect to its emotions, but when the film reached Britain, the English warmly embraced "Beneath The Lights Of Home," relating it to British troops fighting abroad—a classic instance of a song's association with the war coming from its listeners.

Only one other notable homesickness song came early in the war, the majority appearing in 1944 and '45, as the boys were away longer and longer. But in 1942 Bill Crago and Grace Shannon wrote the hillbilly tune "I Wanna Go Back To West Virginia" (Hollywood: Vanguard Songs, 1942). On paper the number expresses a lonesome soldier's longing for his home state, "Where the friends I knew were so kind and true" and "Where the flowers bloom all over / Till they make you wanna cry." But the song's success came in an upbeat but not totally outlandish arrangement by Spike Jones and His City Slickers that is a *Hot Charts* Extra from February through April 1943. The singer's earnestness actually survives—or is enhanced by—all the wacky instruments and goofy sounds in the "orchestral" accompaniment.

Later Tin Pan Alley nostalgia and homesickness songs included Ben Raleigh and Bernie Wayne's "The Things That Mean So Much To Me" (Broadcast Music, 1943), the first of several pieces that were mainly lists, this one starting "The drug store on the corner, the schoolhouse farther down." In Dick Moffitt, Albert M. Hague, and Esther Van Sciver's country tune "In My Home Town" (Bob Miller, 1944), a similar list begins "I'd like to have an ice cream cone, / And put a nickel in the phone." Perhaps not an especially familiar name, Herb Magidson was nevertheless a clever, perceptive lyricist who wrote with nearly all of the great Tin Pan Alley composers of his day. With Allie Wrubel's music, Magidson wrote "Heaven Is A Place Called Home" (Burke and Van Heusen, 1945), a list song that layers in surprising juxtapositions and cute diction after its conventional opening of "Ice cream sodas and apple pies": "It's the chug, chug, chug—of a choo-choo train / . . . It's Aladdin's lamp wrapped in cellophane / . . . Beans and baseball, and jive and swing / Land of liberty of thee I sing." Without the wit but with a lot of heart, bandleader and composer Gordon Jenkins wrote both the words and music of "Homesick—That's All" (Mayfair Music, 1945). It was popularized in the fall of 1945 by Frank Sinatra's recording with Axel Stordahl's orchestra. Jenkins's absent GI openly prefaces each item with "I miss": "I miss the midnight services on Christmas Eve / And the joy when Christmas morning came. / I miss the scramble for the wishbone ev'ry Sunday / And the big Thanksgiving football game."

Nothing infects Americans away from home as much as homesickness and nostalgia for holidays, especially Christmas. A whole book could be written about Irving Berlin's "White Christmas." As a matter of fact, a whole book *was*—Jody Rosen's *White Christmas: The Story of an American Song* (New York: Scribner, 2002). Despite some factual errors and an occasional tendency to stretch or distort the truth to strengthen his case for the song's importance and popularity, Rosen, a staffer with the *New York Times,* wrote an entertaining, informative, and uncommonly well-written account of Berlin's Christmas song from its inception to its reception, both in the war years and through the rest of the twentieth century. When Berlin first wrote "White Christmas," in either 1938 or 1939, for a revue he was thinking of producing, the war and the song's possible connection to it were the farthest things from his mind. He copyrighted the first unpublished version on December 4, 1940, more than a year before Pearl Harbor (see Kimball and Emmet, 350–51). When Bing Crosby premiered the song in the Paramount musical *Holiday Inn,* released on August 4, 1942, he sang the rarely heard verse beginning, "There's never been such a day / In Beverly Hills, L. A.," since "White Christmas" was a number for a guy stuck in Southern California and wishing he were home in New England for the holidays. But the war changed all that. Music historian David Ewen well expressed what virtually everyone writing about the song's history has said: "American soldiers fighting in the swamps and jungles of the Pacific islands seized upon 'White Christmas' as a nostalgic recollection of home and Yuletide and peace and goodwill to cherish when the going was the roughest" (430). An anecdote Rosen gleaned from the Irving Berlin Collection at the Library of Congress illustrates the impact the song had on American troops overseas. Later in the war, Crosby was entertaining paratroopers in France when a "gruff, square-jawed sergeant" asked him, "You gonna sing 'White Christmas'?" When Bing said he would, the sergeant replied, "I guess I'll duck out," explaining, "I like the song all right, but . . . it's no good for the men's morale to see their sergeant cry" (149, 150).

Wartime conditions also made the home front nostalgic for more tranquil days, and it responded to the description of such a past in "White Christmas" by propelling the song to unprecedented popularity through the fall and winter of 1942. It spent an astounding thirty-six weeks on the *Hit Parade*, in 1st place for ten. In *Hot Charts* the Crosby recording ranks 1st from October through December 1942 and 12th in January 1943, then reappears around holiday time every year of the war after that. Lest one think Crosby had a monopoly on "White Christmas," Charlie Spivak, Gordon Jenkins, and Freddy Martin's records also did reasonably well. Sheet music sales were astronomical, *Variety* ranking "White Christmas" number one weekly from October 7 through December 30, 1942. Like Bing's recording, the sheet music resurfaced on the charts every year of the war and through December 1945.

But "White Christmas" wasn't the only Christmas song to appeal to the home front and GIs overseas; two others did as well, for much the same reasons. One of Rosen's overstatements is his assertion that Berlin's song—and much of its appeal—was because it is "the darkest, bluest tune ever to masquerade as a Christmas carol" (13). My quibble with "carol" aside ("White Christmas" is just a Christmas *song;* a carol is quite a different animal), I agree that longing and melancholy do pervade the number. Still, I'm not sure how to measure whether it's darker or bluer than Kim Gannon, Walter Kent, and Buck Ram's "I'll Be Home For Christmas" (Hollywood: Charles Warren, 1943) or Hugh Martin and Ralph Blane's "Have Yourself A Merry Little Christmas" (Leo Feist, 1944) from the 1944 M-G-M musical *Meet Me In St. Louis*. Granted, "I'll Be Home For Christmas," which Crosby also popularized a year after "White Christmas," saves its dark, melancholy note for the ending: "I'LL BE HOME FOR CHRISTMAS / If only in my dreams." Still, after all the warm fuzzy images earlier, this kicker packs an emotional punch by consolidating the absent GI's loneliness and homesickness into a single line. Martin and Blane's "Have Yourself A Merry Little Christmas" seems to keep saying "in spite of everything" throughout a lyric that resonates with images of the war years, even though the song was written for a movie musical set in 1903. After its title line opens the chorus, the second already says "Next year all our troubles will be out of sight." The song longs for a Christmas like bygone ones when "friends who were dear to us will be near to us once more" and openly acknowledges the world's present uncertainties: "Someday soon we all will be together if the fates allow, / Until then, we'll have to muddle through somehow." With its dark tone pervading the lyric, my vote goes to Blane and Martin's number as the darkest Christmas wish of the war years. Which may explain why, of the three big Christmas songs during the war (and as moving as it is), "Have Yourself A Merry Little Christmas" was the least popular at the time; Judy Garland's record ranks 47th in *Hot Charts* only for December 1944, and sheet music sales were never high enough to make *Variety*'s top ten.

### *"Ma, I Miss Your Apple Pie"*: Of Mothers, Children, and Dogs

There's always something to be thankful for. The torrent of shamelessly sentimental Tin Pan Alley "mother songs" that gushed forth from World War I slowed to a trickle during World War II. Including both songs about Blue Star Mothers at home praying for their sons overseas and numbers about GIs missing their moms, there are only seventeen mother songs among the roughly 135 songs in my files that deal with servicemen away. My sampling of amateur songwriting suggests that amateurs wrote both a higher number and higher percentage of these.

Sentimental as they are, Tin Pan Alley's more popular mother songs during World War II were written with a lighter touch than the failed saccharine members of the species, both professional and amateur. It also didn't hurt the four most successful that they were recorded by some of the most popular recording artists of the war years. Well before Pearl Harbor, when the boys away were still in training camp, Guy Lombardo's record of brother Carmen and John Jacob Loeb's "Ma, I Miss Your Apple Pie" (Loeb-Lissauer, 1941) is an Extra in July and rises in *Hot Charts* to 37th and 48th for August and September 1941. The most lighthearted and musically most up-tempo of the mother songs, "Ma" depicts a rookie writing or phoning from camp to tell his mother, "Ma they're treating me alright / But they can't cook like you." The only sentimental moment is nicely offhand and underplayed in the final lines, "Oh! MA, I MISS YOUR APPLE PIE / And, by the way, I miss you too." Almost as easy to take without an insulin shot is Maury Coleman Harris's "Dear Mom" (Republic Music, 1941), with leading records between February and May 1942 by Sammy Kaye, Glenn Miller, Charlie Spivak, Orrin Tucker, and Kate Smith.

The melody is more syrupy than "Ma, I Miss Your Apple Pie," and while the lyric is generally melancholy it takes time out to be playful too: "And oh how I wish they'd make this army co-ed." The soldier also asks his mom to give a message to "a certain 'You know who'" and to "Tell her to write me nightly." As with the earlier song, the major moment of sentiment comes at the end: "I like it here but I'm kinda homesick for you, for I love you / DEAR MOM." Between March and May 1942 the orchestras of Glenn Miller, Hal McIntyre, and Dick Jurgens, and singers Kate Smith and Dinah Shore shared in the moderate success of the yet more syrupy "She'll Always Remember" (Witmark, 1942), by Eddie Pola and Johnny Marks. The song reminds a soldier of the things his mother will always remember about him from the time "when you were only four, / Your fav'rite game was playing with your soldiers on the floor" to "Did you ever notice that teardrop in her eye / The first time she discovered there was lipstick on your tie," finally telling the GI that no matter how grown-up he becomes, "you are still her baby, / SHE'LL ALWAYS REMEMBER / So don't you ever forget."

Even Pfc. Frank Loesser wrote a mother song, but he tempered sentimentality with some fun in "Hello, Mom," written with co-lyricist Capt. Arthur V. Jones and composer Capt. Eddie Dunstedter for the Warner Bros. concert-film short *Army Show*. Bing Crosby recorded it with Dunstedter conducting the West Coast Army Air Force Training Center Orchestra, and the disk is a *Hot Charts* Extra in November. In a phone call to Mom, a pilot in training ("I made my solo flight") tells her about the good food, a pay raise, and other chatty news while asking his mother to spy on the girl next door to "Find out exactly who / She's really waiting for." The song is upbeat even while projecting a wistful longing for life before the war, all concluding with what had to be one of Loesser's contributions to the lyric: "I hope that Dad won't mind I called collect / But I just had to say HELLO MOM."

Besides a few songs about babies born after their fathers went overseas, twenty or so other Tin Pan Alley and hillbilly songs about children (or dogs) vis-à-vis absent servicemen have a unique place among numbers about GIs away from home: all but one are written not from the point of view of a GI away but from that of the child (or dog) at home who is missing him. While there were more of these than mother songs, all by established professional songwriters, only one had anything like commercial success, though the content or approach of a few others makes them interesting too. These songs are sentimental almost by definition, but since they're written from the standpoint of a child, most have enough cute in them to temper some of the sentimentality. Very early, typically cute, and written by the team that would give the world "My Sister And I" the following year was Hy Zaret, Joan Whitney, and Alex Kramer's "Got A Letter From My Kid Today" (Broadcast Music, 1940). A rookie in training camp gets a letter from his kid, gender not specified, that begins "I lost my teddy bear. / I can't remember where. / Daddy, is he there with you?" and then asks if he/she can keep a stray puppy, saying "We could be so happy, / Only, without you it's lonely." That epitomizes the sweet, wistful tone of all the songs of children missing their GI fathers. A few titles and their writers reveal the narrow range of these songs, yet all are by recognized Tin Pan Alley types: Tot Seymour and Vee Lawnhurst's "Daddy's Letter" (Irving Berlin Inc., 1942); Jack Meskill, Larry Stock, and Vincent Rose's "I Sent A Letter To Santa (To Watch Over Daddy For Me)" (Bregman, Vocco, and Conn, 1942); Bernie Grossman and Larry Shay's "Please Take A Kiss To Daddy" (Southern Music, 1943); and Kay Twomey, Allan Roberts, and Fred Spielman's "A Tiny Little Voice (In A Tiny Little Prayer)" (Sun Music, 1944).

The one briefly successful song dealing with the child of a GI overseas, Sam M. Lewis and Fred E. Ahlert's "Goodnight Captain Curlyhead," is singular on two counts: the singer is the little boy's mother, and the number is a lullaby as much to comfort herself as her child: "Be brave little soldier man / Let him know we're not afraid, / GOODNIGHT CAPTAIN CURLYHEAD of the high chair brigade." Dinah Shore's recording found an audience in early 1942 and ranked 43rd in *Hot Charts* for April. Lewis had also been the lyricist for one of the best of such songs in terms of its craft—a revival from 1935. When Lewis and Peter De Rose originally wrote "Santa, Bring My Daddy Back to Me" (Shapiro, Bernstein, 1935, 1943), the lyric could only have referred to a child's wishing for the return of a divorced or deceased parent. With no changes to its text, during the war it became an eight-year-old girl's cute yet affecting plea for her father to return from overseas: "Some kids wanna sailboat, and some kids wanna sled / They always want most anything they see / But if you want me to be gooder than good / Santa, Bring My Daddy Back To Me." One song sung by a child isn't just sentimental but an out and out tearjerker, and of course it was a hillbilly song. For grownups, the title of Bill Boyd and Bill Nettles's "I Wonder Why Daddy Don't Write" (Peer International, 1944) answers its own question. But from the viewpoint of a little girl, presumably singing sometime between her father falling in action and her mother receiving notification of his death, for four long stanzas the child raises childlike questions about why she hasn't heard from her daddy: "I can't understand it, dear mother, / Why Daddy can't write just one line, / For all of my playmates, they tell me / That their daddy writes, why can't mine." "I Wonder Why Daddy Don't Write" has tremendous emotional power and is another example of hillbilly songwriters being unafraid to face some head-on wartime subjects that the Alley steered clear of.

A happier wartime subject a few Alleymen did tackle was the "'goodbye babies,' those conceived just before their GI fathers went overseas," a situation so widespread that "in 1943, after declining since the 1920s, the birth rate reached its highest level in two decades" (Bailey 147). Other than their subject, the one thing these songs have in common is their inconsequentiality despite the prominence of some of their writers. Sung by a father who's never seen his son, and just about the most banal and inconsequential of them all, is Irving Berlin's "What Does He Look Like" (This Is The Army Inc., 1943) written for the Warner Bros. film version of *This Is the Army*. About the best Berlin can do is have the soldier ponder, "Does he resemble his homely dad? / Does he look like the girl I left behind?" The talented Lew Brown and John Jacob Loeb didn't fare much better with "Send Me A Picture Of The Baby" (Bob Miller, 1944), a song whose title says all there is to say about it.

If babies couldn't articulate how they felt about Dad being overseas, neither could dogs. So a small number of songwriters helped them articulate their feelings. I have no idea if any of these lyricists were dog owners themselves, but even if not, they understood how dogs manifest their feelings about the protracted absence of a human who lives with them and is their friend and companion. I've encountered only three such songs, all with some merit though not much public success. Jack Peters and Matt Farrell's "A Soldier And His Dog" (Excelsior Music, 1943) is a hillbilly number about how a dog called Blackie behaves now that his human is in the army: "His tail wags no more, he don't play as before." Long-time Alleymen brothers Nick and Charles Kenny, along with Abner Silver, wrote the brief "Old Rover" (Lincoln Music, 1944), which similarly describes a listless dog as well as someone else back home, seemingly a wife. But easily the best and most vivid dog song is "Old Sad Eyes" (Hollywood: Variety Music, 1943), by Irving Kahal and Sammy Fain (yes, the "I'll Be Seeing You" team). Like "Old Rover," this song includes the wife of the absent GI but focuses on the mopey dog, "Snoopin' round the old garage and up at Perkin's store / Wond'ring where his buddy's gone" and "Showin' less ambition than the neighbor's lazy cat / Old sad eyes ain't much company." The wife shares center stage with the dog only in the song's bittersweet ending: "Monday when your letter came, you would have laughed to see / A pair of sentimental fools as lonesome as could be / Old sad eyes and me."

### *"I'm Getting Tired So I Can Sleep": Thinking and Dreaming of the Girl Back Home*

Of all the songs concerning servicemen away, around seventy—all by major Tin Pan Alley or hillbilly writers—dealt with GIs thinking about their girls back home. Of those only about twenty generated any real public interest. Curiously, the two biggest hits were revivals of songs written decades before the war, and not hitherto obscure songs but songs popular when they were written. The older of the two, Neville Fleeson and Albert von Tilzer's "I'll Be With You In Apple Blossom Time" (Broadway Music, 1920), was originally featured by then-popular Broadway and singing star Nora Bayes. The song lacks any references to war; a young man away from home in September says he'll return in May "to change your name to mine" and say, "Happy the bride the sun shines on today." In the months before Pearl Harbor, when military matters still meant just the draft, training camps, and the prospect of boys being away for only a year, this lovely old song breathed with new life when it was reprised by the Andrews Sisters in the Universal comedy *Buck Privates,* released in January 1941, and on their Decca recording, which *Hot Charts* never ranks lower than 15th between April and August, and once, appropriately in May, as high as 4th. The success of Roy Turk and Fred E. Ahlert's "I'll Get By" (Irving Berlin Inc., 1928) had gone in waves in past decades, only to be given an enormous boost into popularity and even immortality by the circumstances of the war. In 1928 records by Aileen Stanley, Nick Lucas, and Gus Arnheim's orchestra first popularized the number, and in 1930 Harry Richman sang it in the United Artists musical *Puttin' on the Ritz* (Lissauer 361). Irene Dunne also performed it in the 1943 M-G-M film *A Guy Named Joe,* but "I'll Get By" really took off in 1944, when it remained for twenty-two weeks on *Your Hit Parade,* four of them in 2nd place. Dick Haymes with Harry James's orchestra had the top-selling record, with the Ink Spots' disk a not too distant runner-up between April and October of that year. Sheet music sales held between 5th and 3rd every week from April 19 through August 23, despite stiff competition from "I'll Be Seeing You." Another case of a song's relationship to the war purely by association, Turk's lyric, old as it was, had immediacy in 1943 and '44 in voicing the prevalent romantic idea that thoughts of a faithful girl back home get a soldier through the war: "I'LL GET BY as long as I have you. / Tho' there be rain and darkness too, / I'll not complain, I'll see it through."

That having the love of a girl back home was morale building and spiritually uplifting to American servicemen overseas is dramatically illustrated by its opposite in a single song in which a girl lets a GI abroad know she's left him. And once again this tough subject matter is in a hillbilly song. By two prominent country songwriters, (then Sgt.) Gene Autry and Fred Rose, "At Mail Call Today" (Hollywood: West'rn Music, 1945) depicts the deepening desolation of a GI reading a "Dear John" letter from a girl who had promised everlasting love. In the second verse he says getting the letter was "worse than all [the] Hell" of sleeping in fox holes

"Amid shot and shell." His words crash to the pit of demoralized despair at the end: "Good luck and God bless you / Wherever you stray / The world for me ended / At Mail Call To-day." Autry's own recording was a *Hot Charts* Extra from April through November 1945, suggesting that the song had reasonably good sales over eight months. It's easy enough to see why Tin Pan Alley never picked up on this lachrymose and potentially demoralizing theme. The Alley had enough problems with the OWI already; writing such stuff would just be asking for trouble.

Typical of letter songs with much more salubrious content was "Just A Letter From Home" (Atlas Music, 1942), by Nick and Charles Kenny and Harry Tobias. It's a sweet little song in which a GI is reading a letter that is at first filled with many hometown images, making it seem that it will be a nostalgia piece. But then the lyric takes a turn for the personal, and the personally reassuring, in its final lines: "Just a letter from home, / And it makes life complete, when it ends with the words, 'I love you.'" Letters from GIs to their girls either ask them to wait for them or reassure them that they'll be back someday. The popularity of Charlie Tobias, Nat Simon, and Harry Tobias's "Wait For Me Mary" (Remick, 1942) was accelerated by the happy circumstance of its being the flip side of Dick Haymes and the Song Spinners' smash recording of "You'll Never Know," one of the most popular of all the girl-back-home songs (see the next section). Recorded on May 27, 1943, at the height of the recording ban, the song's folksy melody, reminiscent of "Down By The Riverside," stands up well to the a capella treatment by the Song Spinners and Haymes, as does Tobias, Simon, and Tobias's literate lyric, with lines like "WAIT FOR ME MARY till the world will smile again, / Till a smile's in style again / And a dream's worthwhile again." Their record of "Wait For Me Mary" ranks in *Hot Charts* from July through October 1943, reaching 16th in August. *Variety*'s sheet music charts listed it between 11th and 5th for twenty weeks.

The letters from GIs abroad reassuring their girls back home are well represented by Nat Burton and Walter Kent's "When The Roses Bloom Again" (Shapiro, Bernstein, 1942) and Nelson Cogane, Dick Robertson, and Lee Davis's "Send This Purple Heart To My Sweetheart" (RYTVOC Inc., 1944). Everything about Burton's words and Kent's music suggests that they were trying to equal or surpass the success of their earlier "The White Cliffs Of Dover" by writing a more American-oriented counterpart. They didn't make it. The melody is pretty enough and the images of being reunited once the war is over are lushly romantic, but lines like "WHEN THE ROSES BLOOM AGAIN / And the fields feel the plow / We will meet again, sweetheart, somehow" lack the fresh originality and immediacy of those in Burton and Kent's masterpiece. The highest *Hot Charts* ever charts it is 44th for the Jimmy Dorsey and Bob Eberly recording in the single month of April 1944; other records by the King Sisters, Benny Goodman, Kay Kyser, Vincent Lopez, Glenn Miller, and Kate Smith are Extras for March, April, or both. "Send This Purple Heart To My Sweetheart" was written by three mainstream Tin Pan Alley songsmiths but recorded by popular "singing cowboy" and songwriter Dick Thomas, born Richard Thomas Goldhahn in Philadelphia and best known for writing and recording "Sioux City Sue" in 1946. Everything about "Purple Heart" smacks of country songwriting, which is likely why it attracted not just Thomas's attention but also country singer Denver Darling's. To the best of my knowledge, it's the only professional song during the war in which a wounded GI is sending a message to his girl that he'll be coming home. He's dictating a letter to a nurse, telling his girl "to keep right on smiling," adding, to the nurse, "And mention that she's always on my mind." The song's best if sweetly sentimental moment is at the end, when the GI asks the nurse to "SEND THIS PURPLE HEART TO MY SWEETHEART, / To keep beside the heart I left behind." Thomas's record was, to put it mildly, a slow but steady seller, remaining a *Hot Charts* Extra for fourteen months from November 1944 through December 1945; Darling's makes the list only from September through December '45.

Of all the songs about an absent GI simply longing for his girl back home, the earliest was the shortest, the most elemental, and the most successful for the largest number of recording artists. The simple melody of Stanley Cowan and Bobby Worth's "'Til Reveille" (Hollywood: Melody Lane, 1941) spins off of the notes of the "Taps" bugle call, the substance of the merely six-line lyric nothing more or less than "From 'Taps' 'til Reveille / I dream of you, Sweetheart." The song caught on for quite a long time in the months prior to Pearl Harbor, making the *Hit Parade* for fifteen weeks, twice in 2nd place. Recordings by Freddy Martin and Clyde Rogers, Kay Kyser and Harry Babbitt, Wayne King, and Bing Crosby are all ranked in *Hot Charts,* with Kyser's and Crosby's ranking 8th and 10th, respectively, in August. On *Billboard*'s chart of weekly record sales, the Kyser and Crosby disks came in between 10th and 6th from July 26 to October 4, and on *Variety*'s sheet music charts "'Til Reveille" quickly rose from 15th on July 9 to 2nd on September 3 and held strong at 3rd or 4th every week through October.

Dreams and daydreams were a prevalent motif in songs about servicemen missing their sweethearts. In Irving Berlin's 1942 *This Is The Army,* one soldier still in training rationalizes that from all of the hiking "I'm Getting Tired So I Can Sleep" (This Is The Army Inc., 1942), and "I want to sleep so I can dream / I want to dream so I can be with you." Records by Tony Pastor and Claude Thornhill are *Hot Charts* Extras from November 1942 through February 1943, with another recording by Jimmy Dorsey and Bob Eberly joining them in January and moving up to rank

30th in February. Far more vivid and emotionally intense was Al Dubin and Cliff Friend's "A Soldier Dreams (Of You Tonight)" (Witmark, 1942), which was introduced by Kate Smith on her radio program on March 20, 1942; her recording is a *Hot Charts* Extra only for June. The number begins with a rather harrowing question: "What does a soldier dream of in the middle of the night? / When bombs come down a-bursting and the battle's at its height." The answer ranges from dreams of "peace on earth" to "dreams of fond embraces and someone's goodnight kiss," ultimately linking the global war with personal happiness back home: "'Mid the strife for the life of a nation / A SOLDIER DREAMS of you tonight." It can only be hoped that the title's hilariously Freudian implications were unintentional when Allie Wrubel wrote "Cleanin' My Rifle and Dreamin' Of You" (Southern Music, 1943), in which a soldier daydreams while cleaning his weapon: "That goodbye kiss you left on my lips is still just like new, / And the dream you left in my heart will someday come true." Lawrence Welk's disk is 52nd in *Hot Charts* for January 1944.

Two short songs featured GIs thinking about their girls while wide awake—good thing, since both were pilots flying: Irving Berlin's undistinguished "With My Head in the Clouds" (This Is The Army Inc., 1942) and Johnny Mercer and Harold Arlen's brief but unforgettably melodic "My Shining Hour" (Edwin H. Morris, 1943) from the 1943 RKO war drama/musical *The Sky's The Limit*. The singer of the latter is an Air Force pilot on what seems to be a critical mission. He powerfully equates thoughts of his girl with all else that helps guide and protect him: "Like the lights of home before me, / Or an angel watching o'er me, / This will be MY SHINING HOUR, / Till I'm with you again." Glen Gray with Eugenie Baird's vocal had the lead recording, which *Hot Charts* ranks 7th in January and 18th in February 1944. The sheet music climbed to 7th place on *Variety*'s charts during the same seven weeks.

Finally, bucking what would appear to be the rigidly gender-specific basis of songs about a GI away, Sammy Cahn and Jule Styne's "The Boy I Left Behind" is a girl's charming explanation of how she decided to do her part and enlist in the WACS because her boyfriend was 4-F and couldn't do his. Copyrighted unpublished on December 2, 1944, the number appeared in the 1945 Columbia war drama *Tonight And Every Night,* starring Rita Hayworth. The song's popularity was limited by the film's since it apparently wasn't recorded or published. Cahn's lyric cleverly keeps things romantic even as it turns upside down some previously gender-based conventions in songs of parting and GIs missing their girls. This time it's the girl onboard and the boy on the platform: "As he waved goodbye at the train / I started to cry, he yelled chin up, one of us has to remain." Like male GIs in songs, this WAC says "I'm saving most of what they pay me / For the boy I left behind," and she even worries whether her guy can resist the home front girls: "Oh they should have told me I'd get nervous / For the boy I left behind."

### *"I Wish That I Could Hide Inside This Letter"*: The Feelings of the Girls Back Home

Only two themes run through the numerous songs about the girl back home: her loneliness and her fidelity to her serviceman away. In a sense, it's more a matter of emphasis than of separate themes, because the girl's loneliness was an inevitable consequence of her fidelity. Songs in which GIs worry over their girls' faithfulness are just one spin on the constancy theme, and invariably a playful one, which is indicative of a major difference between boy-away and girl-back-home songs. The latter display a richer variety of tone, mood, and even content, in contrast to the almost uniform melancholy that pervades the songs of servicemen missing their sweethearts.

Well before we were in the war, a huge hit that combined a woman's constancy with her loneliness, and that listeners construed to be war-related, preceded any actual wartime song on these themes. Canadian Ruth Lowe was a pianist for the CBC and with Ina Rae Hutton's all-girl orchestra between 1937 and 1939. She wrote a few songs but will always be remembered as a "one-song writer" for "I'll Never Smile Again" (Sun Music, 1939). Canadians first heard it on a CBC broadcast in 1939, but it didn't take the United States by storm until the following year. Recently married to Chicago music publisher Harold Cohen, whom she met while touring with Hutton's band, Lowe wrote the plaintive number in June 1939 after her husband died unexpectedly of kidney failure during routine surgery. Lowe turned her emotional devastation into a song that was "the perfect encapsulation of the sentiments of those separated from loved ones by World War II." An outstanding piece of songwriting, "I'll Never Smile Again" had its popularity heightened immeasurably by the widespread but erroneous story that Lowe's husband had been a Canadian flier killed on a mission with the RAF (*Encyclopedia*). Throughout the economical lyric, the singer expresses both her feeling of desolate loneliness and her intent to remain true to the man she lost: "I'll never thrill again to somebody new / Within my heart I know I will never start / To smile again until I smile at you." Recorded with some success by Tony Martin, Gene Autry, and the bands of Glenn Miller, Gene Krupa, and Ray Noble, the number only rocketed to hitdom with Tommy Dorsey's record with vocal by a skinny Jersey kid on the way up named Frank Sinatra. In *Hot Charts* from June through November 1940, the Dorsey/Sinatra "I'll Never Smile Again" places 1st in July, August, and September. It was one of Dorsey's all-time hits and the number that jumpstarted Sinatra's career. Sheet music sales were equally strong, and the *Hit Parade* featured the song for sixteen weeks, in 1st place for seven. Equally effective sung by a man or a woman, Lowe's song had meaning for both GIs away, even those in training, and for the girls back home.

It wasn't until late 1941 and, especially, 1942 that constancy or loneliness songs intentionally related to the war started showing up, which makes historical sense because it wasn't until very late in 1941 that American servicemen were being shipped overseas. Aside from "I Don't Want To Walk Without You" early in 1942, a song never intended to be war-related in the first place (see chapter 1), the more romantic and wistful songs about lonely and faithful girls generally began appearing later that year, growing in number and intensity as the war went on. But far from melancholy, some of the earliest and best girl-back-home numbers were actually playful. This playfulness resonates not only in numbers where an absent GI appeals for his girl's constancy but even in some songs about a girl feeling lonely or promising her fidelity to her guy overseas. On occasion, this playfulness cropped up in songs later in the war, though generally the mood then became more serious. The predominance of playfulness in early numbers of this type may be attributed to their songwriters' wanting to make as light as possible of a bad situation and relieve some of the home front girls' stress and sadness through humor.

Before Pearl Harbor, the Glenn Miller Orchestra with vocals by Tex Beneke and Marion Hutton had some success with the first playful girl-back-home number, Stanley Joseloff and Sidney Lippman's "Dear Arabella" (Mutual Music Society, 1941), the record a *Hot Charts* Extra for November 1941. A rookie at training camp writes a cautionary letter to his girl: "While I'm paradin' and reducin' fore and aft, / I hope your love won't get cold in the draft." Arabella replies sweetly, letting "Private Johnny" know she's "As faithful as can be" and even keeps a picture of him "by the sofa near the fire / For me and my boy friends to sit and admire. / They may want kisses but I am always true, / I close my eyes and make believe it's you." Arabella is the most unfaithful of the girls back home, but the tone of Joseloff's lyric and Lippman's music makes it plain that the song is just having some fun.

If Glenn Miller had a minor success with "Arabella" in 1941, he had a blockbuster in '42 with Lew Brown, Charlie Tobias, and Sam H. Stept's now classic "Don't Sit Under The Apple Tree (With Anyone Else But Me)" (Robbins, 1942). The lyric is the familiar list of "don'ts" from a rookie at camp to his girl back home, but this guy's getting a little paranoid: "I just got word from a guy who heard from the guy next door to me, / The girl he met just loves to pet and it fits you to a 'T'"; worse yet, in the rarely heard second chorus that's printed in the sheet music, "I told the gang the whole shebang that you were sweet and true, / They ran right in and came right out with a photograph of you." Beneath its frothy façade the song's underlying advocacy of wartime fidelity held special meaning for GIs away from home. Most people in later years have tended to associate the song with the Andrews Sisters' exceptional recording, but it was the Miller orchestra, again with vocals by Tex Beneke, Marion Hutton, and the Modernaires that was the chart-buster for months, summed up in *Hot Charts* as 9th, 3rd, 3rd, and 9th again from April through July 1942. The Andrews Sisters performed it in *Private Buckaroo,* but their disk got to only a high of 37th in July. The sheet music entered *Variety*'s chart on April 8 at 12th but then averaged between 2nd and 5th through July 15. "Apple Tree" sat around the *Hit Parade* for twelve weeks, in first place for five. In an obvious word, it was hugely popular.

The superb craft of "Apple Tree" and its place in American home front culture were paid a high tribute by its writers' peers, other prominent Alleymen. If imitation is in fact the sincerest form of flattery, Brown, Tobias, and Stept must have been very flattered indeed to watch three clever imitations or spin-offs of their hit (plus another by Stept himself) appear in the movies or roll off sheet music and record presses later in the war and even after it was over. The first two came in 1943. For the RKO musical *Around The World,* featuring Kay Kyser and his orchestra, lyricist Harold Adamson and composer Jimmy McHugh wrote the deliriously silly "They Just Chopped Down The Old Apple Tree." Kyser's V-Disc recording is incomplete, but in the commercial pressing by the Dinning Sisters, the girl tells us in the verse that she "got a ten page letter from my boyfriend and he wants an answer right away" about her fidelity. The letter then repeats verbatim "Don't sit under the apple tree till I come marching home" from the original song. So she writes a ten-page letter back assuring him that there won't be a problem because "They Just Chopped Down The Old Apple Tree," so she simply *can't* sit under it—alone or with anyone else. Adamson's off-the-wall lyric and McHugh's appropriately goofy tune are a perfect match as the girl tells her GI, "they walked right by the cherry tree, the chestnut tree, the walnut tree," and only felled the by now notorious apple tree, whereupon "The woodchuck chuckled and jumped with glee and mumbled to the bumblebee, 'They chopped down the old apple tree where you said you'd marry me.'" The piece is inspired nonsense, but its life was mostly limited to the movie it was in.

The other 1943 "Apple Tree" spin-off was Frank Loesser and Arthur Schwartz's hit "They're Either Too Young Or Too Old," sung by Bette Davis (hard to believe—even after you've heard it!) in the Warner Bros. musical *Thank Your Lucky Stars.* Loesser's lyric is the apple tree girl's reply to her GI to let him know he has nothing to worry about: "I can't sit under the apple tree with anyone else but *me,*" since the male population stateside is "either too gray or too grassy green": "Tomorrow I'll go hiking with that Eagle Scout unless / I get a call from grandpa for a snappy game of chess." As he did so often and so well, Loesser imbued a richly comic lyric with genuine feelings, in this case the girl's pledge of constancy to her man away. And it paid off: an Academy Award nomination, twelve weeks on the *Hit Parade,* twice in 2nd, its sheet music in *Variety's* top fifteen sellers for thirteen weeks, over half of those weeks 5th to 3rd, and the leading recording by Jimmy Dorsey's orchestra with Kitty Kallen's vocal in *Hot Charts* for four months, reaching a high of 7th in December 1943. In 1945 Sam H. Stept wrote the words and music for a spin-off of his hit collaboration with Brown and Tobias. The chorus of "I Was Here When You Left Me (I'll Be Here When You Get Back)" (Irving Berlin Music, 1945) is a cute, upbeat take on the girl promising to be waiting faithfully when her sweetheart returns from overseas: "Let others do what they wanna do, / But as for me I'm gonna be goody-good-good for you." In the verse Stept is self-referential: "Remember when you wrote me not to sit 'neath the apple tree / Well, you can count on me / I've been good as good can be." Happily, this is a rare verse that got recorded, thanks to the disk by Louis Prima's band and his girl singer with the three first names, Lily Ann Carol. Hal McIntyre and Frankie Carle also recorded it; all three disks are *Hot Charts* Extras between May and July. Finally, the spin-off containing what is arguably the single funniest line was by two big names in the business, Sammy Cahn and Jule Styne, and it wasn't copyrighted or published until June 1947—a real salute to the staying power of the original "Apple Tree." Called "I'm Still Sitting Under The Apple Tree," it's a comic lament by a girl who's *still* sitting there "With nobody else but me," waiting for her GI guy to come home and frankly wondering what he's up to: "I just got a letter from Paris; It said just a few weeks more. / I'm thinking of going to Paris / Just to tell him we won the war."

In one unusual cautionary song, the GI away addresses not his girl but a guy trying to steal her from him. There's certainly a worried undertone to Frank Loesser and Jimmy McHugh's "Please Won't You Leave My Girl Alone" (Southern Music, 1942), from the 1942 RKO musical *Seven Days Leave,* yet Loesser finds wry ways of expressing the absent GI's fear of the guy's mere proximity to his girl: "I'm far away in the army and you're Johnny on the spot!" While the soldier directs most of the song to the would-be Don Juan trying to steal his girl, he also has some misgivings about her fortitude: "She wrote she misses my kisses, / On lonely summer nights, / She might be giving her kisses to hungry parasites."

Beyond playful cautionary songs and spin-offs of "Don't Sit Under The Apple Tree," a few skilled writers actually wrote playful numbers on the central themes of loneliness and fidelity. The earliest about constancy with no cautionary note came in 1942. "Cute" is the operative word for the substantial hit "Three Little Sisters" (Santly-Joy-Select, 1942), with words by Irving Taylor and music by Vic Mizzy. In this upbeat and up-tempo song of eternal fidelity (well, maybe), the sisters, "each one only in her teens," are in love, respectively, with a soldier, a sailor, and a marine. When the boys shipped out, the girls promised they'd be true, so now they "Stay home and read their magazines, / You can tell it to the soldiers, / Tell it to the sailors / And tell it to the Marines," the last line implying what it had implied at least since 1830—"If you believe that, I'll tell you another one!" Whether the sisters were true or not, record buyers were definitely loyal to the Andrews Sisters' disk, charted by *Hot Charts* in the thirties between May and September, with Vaughn Monroe's recording performing equally well and Dinah Shore's trailing only a bit in the forties. On October 26, 1943, Monroe's orchestra with the Murphy Sisters' vocal recorded the equally cute "I Saw My Sweetie In The Newsreel" (copyright unpublished, September 16, 1943), with words by Eddie De Lange and music by John Benson Brooks. In just an eight-line lyric, a girl makes a spectacle of herself in a movie theatre, thanks to her faithfulness and a lot of pride: "I saw my sweetie in the Newsreel / I stood right up in my chair / I said hello hello my darlin' / And ev'rybody turned to stare," even as she fancied seeing her marching "sweetie" turn to smile at her. Mann Curtis and Vic Mizzy's "Pretty Kitty Blue Eyes" (Santly-Joy, 1944) is another cute song combining the themes of loneliness and constancy. The Merry Macs had good luck with their disk, which *Hot Charts* ranks in the twenties or thirties between July and October. When Kitty walks down the street, the boys shout, "Here, pretty Kitty, / Here PRETTY KITTY BLUE EYES," but she ignores them though "she's lonely in New York / 'Cause she loves a doughboy, named Johnny O'Rourke" and can't wait till she hears *him* shout, "I'm here, pretty Kitty, / Here PRETTY KITTY BLUE EYES."

Cuter yet was a much bigger hit late in the war, Moe Jaffe's "Bell Bottom Trousers" (Santly-Joy, 1944). In spring 1945 the song was twelve weeks on *Your Hit Parade*, three times in 1st. "Trousers" entered *Variety*'s sheet music chart on May 9 in 2nd place, stayed on the chart for twenty weeks, and was the nation's number-one bestseller for ten of those, from May 30 through August 1. The three leading records, by Tony Pastor, Guy Lombardo, and Kay Kyser, remained on *Billboard*'s weekly charts between May 19 and September 15, and the big picture via *Hot Charts* puts Pastor's record on top—an especially hip rendition with Ruth McCullough and himself on vocal—at 3rd for May and June and 5th for July, although Kyser's also hit 5th and Lombardo's 7th in June. When I was a four-year-old kid growing up with the tune, I thought it sounded like a folk song or a sea chanty. It wasn't one, of course, but the melody's seeming familiarity may have helped drive the song's success.

Jaffe's saga tells of a girl's longstanding fidelity to her sailor boy, *very* longstanding: "Once there was a little girl who lived next door to me / And she loved a sailor boy; he was only three." Now, with the war on, "he's on a battleship in his sailor suit, / Just a great big sailor man but he's just as cute." And so goes the song for five verses, though none of the top records included every one—or even the same ones—except the first. Each band picked different verses to record, but any way they did it, they all playfully spun the yarn of the girl's constancy until and after her sailor comes home, "So they can get married, and raise a family / Dress up all their kiddies in sailor's dungarees." A war-weary nation entering the fourth year of a seemingly endless war welcomed it as simple, fun, and singable.

One playful number about a girl's loneliness can't be called comic but is a splendid example of the whimsical and idiosyncratic style of the three-man team of composer Jay Gorney and lyricists Henry Myers and Edward Eliscu. Much of their work was for stylish revues and musicals and generally too sophisticated, quirky, and "out there" to gain much public acceptance or commercial popularity, but it was appreciated by other Tin Pan Alley and Broadway types. Accordingly, the audience their "It's No Fun Eating Alone" (Mills, 1941) reached was mostly that of *The New Meet the People,* the Broadway revue in which it appeared. The original *Meet the People* had opened in 1940, and the show went through several editions and title changes, but just when *The New* edition began is unclear. But a line in the lyric, most likely revised specifically for the show, suggests that it was sometime in the latter half of 1943. The woman says that her "love is flying . . . / Above Calais and Cologne." If her guy was an RAF pilot rather than an American, that would place the song's appearance in *The New Meet the People* sometime after May 30, 1943, when the RAF carried out a successful thousand-plane bombing raid on Cologne. The U.S. Air Force had not yet made significant aerial assaults on Germany. The song is the melancholy complaint of a solitary woman dining in an upscale restaurant and wishing her absent serviceman were there, but Myers and Eliscu punctuate her melancholy with offbeat, amusing imagery: "What's underneath that silver cover? / Don't tell me (sniff), minestrone. / But what is soup without my lover. / It's no fun eating alone." In reply to the waiter's concern that she's not eating much, she says, "No, thank you, waiter, it's not the food. / It's only me dying of solitude." She almost accepts the waiter's suggestion of hearing some music from the orchestra (common enough in 1940s restaurants) to help her mood, but thinks better of it: "Oh, no, not Tristan and Isolde, / At least not on the saxophone, / . . . I'll keep my chin up, I'll be his pin-up / Until his lips meet my own, / Then no more eating alone." Not a run-of-the-mill song of loneliness, with the lyric's playfulness counterpointing and underlining the woman's unhappiness, but despite its extraordinary craftsmanship not the stuff of commercial success either.

In contrast to the urbane but uncommercial "It's No Fun Eating Alone," Leo Robin and Harry Warren injected into a basically serious number a few moments of earthy and borderline risqué playfulness that make extremely vivid a girl's feelings about being alone, faithful, and frustrated. They wrote "No Love, No Nothin'" (Twentieth Century, 1943) for the 20th Century-Fox musical *The Gang's All Here,* released in December 1943. In January 1944, Ella Mae Morse's record is 10th in *Hot Charts* and remains there through April, along with another strong disk by Johnny Long with Patti Dugan's vocal. A girl promised her guy she wouldn't fool around while he's away, and she's keeping her promise: "NO LOVE, NO NOTHIN' / Until my baby comes home." One can sense her frustration in "I'm lonesome, Heaven knows, / But what I said still goes," and "No fun with no one. / I'm getting plenty of sleep." *Your Hit Parade* kept "No Nothin'" around for ten weeks, twice in 3rd, and after an initial week at 14th on *Variety*'s sheet music chart, it averaged 6th over the next nine weeks.

Commercially successful romantic or sentimental songs about the girls left behind greatly outnumbered those with a playful streak, probably because those girls comprised much of the record-buying public for such songs, and they didn't find being apart from their sweethearts very amusing. It was easier for them to relate to lyrical or even melancholy numbers. More songs about loneliness became popular than those focusing on constancy, but both types produced a few songs for the ages. Each variety first appeared in 1942 and continued throughout the war, with few changes in mood or method.

To start with loneliness, short-term success came to four such songs in 1942, suggesting the girls back home began missing their GIs away as soon as we entered the war. Hy Zaret and Arthur Altman's "You Can't Hold A Memory In Your Arms" (Leeds, 1942) appeared in the Universal musical *What's Cookin',* released in February, and Woody Herman's recording is a *Hot Charts* Extra in April. Though not one of Zaret's top-flight lyrics, it still has some well-crafted moments; the girl says that memories are nice, but "in a love scene, they don't follow through," and, at the end, she implores her guy, "please come back to me / Darling let me hold the memory in my arms." Starting in May, Johnny Burke and Jimmy van Heusen's "Just Plain Lonesome" (Mayfair, 1942) remained popular longer than "You Can't Hold A Memory," even though, like Zaret's, Burke's lyric isn't close to one of his best, mostly just reiterating what the title says. Still, Freddy Martin's record with Clyde Rogers's vocal is 43rd in the May *Hot Charts* and in June and July is an Extra along with Kay Kyser and Harry Babbitt's disk.

The title of Kermit Goell and Arthur Kent's "Wonder When My Baby's Coming Home" (Crawford, 1942) sounds like it's about an anticipated GI homecoming, yet its words are strictly those of loneliness. Kent's melody is memorable and Goell's thoroughly professional lyric succinctly captures the feelings of a girl back home: "Haven't slept a week at night, / Worryin' if he's all right," and "Oh! I really can't help cryin', I'm so hungry for his caress, / Though I promised I wouldn't be cryin' / I'm not brave enough I guess." Between danceable music and singable, emotional lyrics, "Wonder When" appealed to name bands and singers and was recorded by Kay Kyser with Dorothy Dunn's vocal, Jimmy Dorsey with Helen O'Connell, Sammy Kaye with Nancy Norman, Shep Fields, and Kate Smith. In *Hot Charts,* the two most popular disks are Dorsey's and Kaye's, the first ranked 47th in June, the second 46th in July, and all but Kay Kyser's remain Extras through October 1942. The last loneliness song to arouse any interest in 1942 shows that traditional sentimentality still had appeal. By Buddy Kaye and David Saxon, "Do You Miss Your Sweetheart? (Like Your Sweetheart Misses You)" (Paramount, 1942) is a song with language as syrupy as the music, save for one truly unfortunate image—"so I dip my pen in my heart"—and one other rather nice one—"In your arms I found love so exciting, / Darling put your arms around me if only in writing." But something about it appealed to the wartime public, because records by Johnny Long, Hal McIntyre, and Alvino Rey are *Hot Charts* Extras from June through August. While all four songs found a listening audience in 1942, they presumably had less appeal for home musicians; none appeared for even a single week on *Variety*'s sheet music chart.

The big loneliness hit of 1943 was Bob Russell and Duke Ellington's "Don't Get Around Much Any More" (Robbins, 1942), which had nothing to do with the war. The loneliness in it, as in "I Don't Want To Walk Without You," is the aftermath of a break-up, not a wartime separation. No doubt some people heard or read into it a connection to the war anyway, perhaps helping to account for its tremendous sales of sheet music and records by the Ink Spots, Glen Gray, and Duke Ellington. The other loneliness number of 1943 was never the hit that "Don't Get Around" was, or the standard it became, but at least it had an intentionally war-related theme that brought it considerable popularity at the time. "I Never Mention Your Name (Oh, No!)" (Irving Berlin Inc., 1943), with words by Mack Davis and Don George and music by Walter Kent, is the only wartime ballad I have run across to employ irony as a major device in the lyric. Through two choruses and the release, a girl trying to make her separation from her absent lover easier claims such things as "I NEVER MENTION YOUR NAME, Oh, No! / . . . I never go where we used to go / To hear the echo of your sighs" and "I never feel the slightest desire / To hold you when it's night again." The final chorus a is wonderful reversal of all this: "I never know you're away / Except for ev'ry minute, / Of ev'ry hour, / Of ev'ry day." While the song is written from the standpoint of a girl back home, the three biggest recordings were by "boy singers"—Dick Haymes with the Song Spinners, Jack Leonard, and Allen Miller. Teenaged and twentysomething girls made up a large part of the wartime music-buying public and tended to buy records by male vocalists. The song's success may then be attributed in part to lyrics the girls could relate to, sung by a boy singer whose vocal style or charisma they enjoyed. The records by Haymes, Leonard, and Miller are all ranked from August through November in *Hot Charts*, Haymes's top-seller peaking at 16th in September.

In 1944, two loneliness songs caught on, a modest success and a hit of mammoth proportions. True, there's a bit of the playful in the title and a few lines of Charlie Tobias and Nat Simon's "I Wish That I Could Hide Inside This Letter" (Shapiro, Bernstein, 1943), but the playful always serves the romantic, as when the girl sings that she'd like to "seal me up and send me out to you." The recording by Lawrence Welk's orchestra with Jayne Walton's vocal is 48th in the January *Hot Charts* and remains an Extra through the next two months. According to variant sheet music covers, the song was also featured (which could mean just on radio) by Nancy Norman, Joan Brooks, and Kay Kyser. In late April one of the giants of American popular music debuted with the release of the Universal film *Follow The Boys,* in which Dinah Shore introduced what quickly became the archetypal anthem of girls' wartime loneliness, Sammy Cahn and Jule Styne's "I'll Walk Alone" (Mayfair Music, 1944). Cahn's words reverberate with the thoughts and feelings associated with separation forced by the war, and underneath the girl's expression of loneliness lies the tacit assumption of her constancy as well: "I don't mind being lonely / When I know that you are lonely too," "If you call I'll hear you, no matter how far; / Just close your eyes and I'll be there," and, at the end, anticipating her GI's safe return, "Till you're walking beside me, / I'LL WALK ALONE." Cahn and Styne's megahit garnered an Academy Award nomination, twenty weeks on the *Hit Parade,* (eight in 1st), sheet music sales that just wouldn't quit for twenty weeks on *Variety*'s weekly charts (number one for ten of them), and hit records by Dinah Shore and Martha Tilton trading places for weekly top honors, or close to it, on *Billboard*'s charts from July through November.

With the war going into a fourth year, loneliness was settling in and deepening for more home front girls than ever, which is perhaps why the first loneliness song to become popular in 1945 tried to lift the weight of such feelings a bit as the girl claims she's "A Little On The Lonely Side" (Advanced, 1944). Dick Robertson, James Cavanaugh, and Frank Weldon's lilting melody is anything but lugubrious, as the girl writes to her guy overseas of her loneliness and constancy: "So if I'm seen with some-one else / It's just someone to dance with," the rest of the lyric making it clear that she means this and isn't just handing the absent GI a line. The photos and captions on the variant sheet music covers reveal that "A Little On The Lonely Side" was "Featured" by at least eight singers and bands great (Guy Lombardo) and small (Lee Castle). The leading records were Lombardo's with Jimmy Brown's vocal and Frankie Carle's with Paul Allen's, again male vocalists making popular a song expressing the thoughts of a girl back home. Between January and April in *Hot Charts* Carle's hits 7th in February, Lombardo's 13th in March. Sheet music sales were even stronger, averaging between 4th and 2nd from January 24 through April 18 on *Variety*'s weekly charts, which is especially impres-sive since it was bucking a new entry that was soon to become the hands-down 1945 winner in the loneliness department.

Similar to "Don't Get Around Much Anymore," which wasn't war-related, Sammy Cahn and Jule Styne's "Saturday Night Is The Loneliest Night Of The Week" (Producers Music, 1944) arguably did connect to the war, if only obliquely. No break-up is implied; in fact, a projected reunion occurs in the final stanza—"Until I hear you at the door / Until you're in my arms once more / Saturday night is the loneliest night of the week." Never as big as Cahn and Styne's "I'll Walk Alone," "Satur-day Night" still sold well between January and April 1945, Frank Sina-tra's record being the most memorable (and remembered). Other popular disks were Frankie Carle's with Phyllis Lynne's vocal, Sammy Kaye's with Nancy Norman, Woody Herman's with Frances Wayne, and the King Sisters. On *Variety*'s charts, the sheet music shunted between 4th and 2nd with "A Little On The Lonely Side" from March 7 to April 11, and it held on for ten weeks on the *Hit Parade,* twice in 2nd place.

Not everything Cahn and Styne wrote was a hit, but in the war years an inordinate number of their collaborations found an audience, if only briefly. One such song was "Can't You Read Between The Lines" (Shapiro, Bernstein, 1945). Cahn's premise is a girl explaining the brave face she puts on in her letters: "When I write to you and say / 'Ev'rything is okay' / CAN'T YOU READ BETWEEN THE LINES? / . . . It might worry you if I told you I cried ev'ry night / You'll tell me it won't but why take a chance that it might." *Hot Charts* for June and July 1945 ranks in the thirties the records by Jimmy Dorsey with Jean Cromwell's vocal, Kay Kyser with Dolly Mitchell, and Charlie Spivak. The last loneliness number of the war years big enough to make *Hot Charts* had a bigger audience because of its place in the 1945 M-G-M musical/drama *Weekend At The Waldorf,* which is based loosely on Vicky Baum's *Grand Hotel.* Throughout a long career writing with many top composers, Ted Koehler was a sensitive, skillful lyricist who put feeling into carefully crafted images, a trait evident in "And There You Are" (Leo Feist, 1945), with music by Sammy Fain. In this straightforward song of loneliness, Koehler's verbal ingenuity (here playing off lines in other songs) is never showy but instead lets the girl's feelings come through: "There in the dawn's early light, there in the still of the night, / I look behind a star, AND THERE YOU ARE." Kate Smith, Freddy Martin, Andy Russell, and the Three Suns' records are *Hot Charts* Extras from September through November. If these twelve songs spotlight the girl's loneliness, her constancy seems always to be waiting in the wings; in a smaller group of numbers it takes center stage.

Written and published early enough to be reprinted in *Song Hits* for January 1942—virtually coincident with America's entry into the war— a song of a girl's steadfastness that sounded like a hillbilly tune became a low-lying success for months on end as performed, by a "singing cowboy." Freddy Martin, Bobby Worth, and Stanley Cowan's "I'll Wait For You" (Southern Music, 1941) employs images of impossibility for a girl telling her GI how long she'll wait for him: "I'll wait for you till grass grows red, / Till the moon overhead turns blue / . . . And I'll be true till you're not you." The sales of Gene Autry's record were protracted; it appeared as a *Hot Charts* Extra from February 1942 through January 1943. Later in '42 a genuine hillbilly number was revived with slightly revised lyrics that sharpened its relevance to the war, one recording by an authentic country performer, another by about as mainstream a male vocalist as there was. In A. P. Carter and Don Marcotte's "I'm Thinking Tonight Of My Blue Eyes" (Peer International, 1930; Southern Music, 1942), a girl declares fidelity to her sweetheart "far over the sea": "Quiet moon up above shining down on my love, / Tell him I'll wait 'till he comes home to stay." Another disk with tremendous longevity as a *Hot Charts* Extra, country singer Montana Slim's record is first listed from August through December 1942 and again, after a four-month hiatus, between May and December 1943; it is joined in August by Bing Crosby's disk with Woody Herman's band in a rather upbeat Dixieland treatment that stays an Extra through the end of the year.

About midyear in 1942, Eddie De Lange and John Benson Brooks's "Just As Though You Were Here" (Yankee Music, 1942) was gaining a good bit of public attention, especially via Frank Sinatra's recording with Tommy Dorsey's orchestra (augmented in spots by some perfectly dreadful strings), another instance of a song thematically about a girl back home finding success through a boy singer. The girl promises her serviceman that in his absence she'll try to carry on, as the title says, "Just As Though You Were Here": "I'll wake each morning and I'll promise to laugh, / I'll say good morning to your old photograph." The song's nicest expression of constancy is in the release: "The farther you go, the longer you stay, / The deeper you grow in my heart." *Hot Charts* ranks the Sinatra/Dorsey record for July through October 1942, reaching 6th in July and going only as low as 15th in October. Just at the end of 1942 came along "That Soldier Of Mine" (Hollywood: National Music, 1942), a song in the venerable tradition of torch songs that goes back at least to "Bill" in *Show Boat,* in which a girl tries to explain why she's devoted to a seemingly ordinary, average kind of guy. Composer Matt Dennis always attracted especially urbane and sophisticated lyricists, most frequently and notably Tom Adair, and Paul Herrick, the writer of "This Soldier Of Mine," was another of that sort. His technique in the first two stanzas is to contrast the girl's personal description of the guy with his role as a soldier: "He's not so handsome, he's not very tall / And in the smart set he's nothing at all / He was the first one to answer the call / THAT SOLDIER OF MINE." With Dennis's sultry music, perhaps the song was too "torchy," or too sophisticated, to successfully sink into the war mentality of a nation, since it's a *Hot Charts* Extra only from November 1942 through January '43 in the record by Harry James with a killer vocal by Helen Forrest—or perhaps the disk's chance for popularity was killed by some more really awful strings.

Aside from decent sheet music sales between March and May 1943, Mack David and Harry Warren's "I Just Kissed Your Picture Goodnight" (Crawford, 1942) was scarcely a footnote in the history of wartime popular song, but a little later that spring Warren and another Mack, Mack Gordon, hit it very big with "You'll Never Know" (Twentieth Century Music, 1943). Written for the 1943 20th Century-Fox period musical *Hello, Frisco, Hello,* which had nothing to do with the war, Gordon and Warren's skillfully crafted song made the association of "You'll Never Know" with faithful though parted lovers in wartime hard to miss: "You went away and my heart went with you, / I speak your name in my ev'ry prayer. / If there is some other way to prove that I love you, / I swear I don't know how, / YOU'LL NEVER KNOW if you don't know now." Again the biggest-selling records about a girl's constancy were by male vocalists, headed by the a capella rendition of Dick Haymes and the Song Spinners, whose disk ranks in *Hot Charts* from June through November 1943, 1st in June and 2nd in July. Sinatra's record performed well for four out of five months and ranks 4th in August and September. The sheet music made *Variety*'s weekly charts for twenty-six weeks between April 28 and November 3 and was the top-selling sheet for ten of them. *Your Hit Parade* acknowledged the tremendous success of "You'll Never Know" by airing it for twenty-four weeks, nine times in 1st place.

While successful romantic songs about loneliness continued well into 1945, the last sentimental depiction of a home front girl's constancy came in the spring of 1944, with its popularity increasing and then peaking during the summer months. Dick Robertson, Al Hoffman, and Frank Weldon's melodious and moving "Good Night, Wherever You Are" (Shapiro, Bernstein, 1944) reserves most of its direct expression of faithfulness for the verses, which were often not recorded, but Mary Martin, backed by a more than usually lush (and competent) studio string orchestra, included the first one: "The moment you walked away, darling, / You walked away with my heart / And now ev'ry night when I turn down the light, / I whisper while we're apart," the last line a segue into the song's title as the first line of each chorus expressing her fidelity: "I'll be with you, dear, no matter how far." The recording by Blue Barron's orchestra is a *Hot Charts* Extra for March, with those of Will Osborne and Russ Morgan joining it in April and Mary Martin in May. Morgan's disk pulled away to join the ranked listings from May through August, at a high of 12th in June and July. The sheet music averaged 6th place on *Variety*'s charts for sixteen weeks, from April 26 through August 16.

Thanks to some especially gifted composers and lyricists, it's easy to see why more songs about girls back home, including those in chapter 12 whose guys come back, generated more mass enthusiasm and commercial success than songs on any other topics during the war.

# 12:

# *"It's Been A Long, Long Time"*

## Victory, Homecomings, the World after the War

Along with its morbid fear that romantic slush would sap the strength of America's fighting forces and the home front's will to support the war, the Office of War Information lived in dread of songs with a simplistic Pollyanna attitude that downplayed the strength of the Axis Powers or the length of time it would take to win the war. But the OWI's paranoia was unfounded for the simple reason that among professional songs virtually no such numbers were ever written that reached the ears of large segments of the population. The closest Tin Pan Alley and hillbilly writers came was in songs about projected victory that started to appear early in the war, and the related so-called "peace-and-ease" songs about how wonderful the world will be once the fighting is over. The OWI utterly failed to see the positive role such songs played in giving the nation a dream of something, no matter how remote, to be fighting for. *Variety's* editorial "Tactless War Songs" on July 15, 1942, shows that the OWI's fears began a mere six months after the United States entered the war: "Uncle Sam, probably through the Office of War Information, is expected shortly to urge songwriters and publishers to give heed . . . to the question of 'tactfulness' in song titles and lyrics." The editorial points out that the government is particularly concerned about songs "belittling the size and power of the enemy" and "peace-and-ease songs of the future" (3). If in that summer of 1942 the OWI could have looked ahead to the songs about victory and the postwar world, it would have seen there was nothing to fear but its own fear itself. As it turned out, Tin Pan Alley and hillbilly writers together wrote only thirty or so songs about projected victory and another thirty or so "peace-and-ease" songs looking forward to life after the war, and none of them promulgated the sort of unrealistic optimism the OWI considered virtually treasonous. As in Tin Pan Alley's other kinds of war-related songs, more pieces about people's personal life after the war found an audience than the victory and peace-and-ease numbers. These were, of course, the songs about returning American servicemen. Tin Pan Alley and country songwriters wrote just under seventy of these, and over a dozen became contemporary hits. In fact, looked at overall, GIs' homecomings, along with the girls back home, inspired some of the best popular songwriting of the war years.

### *"Swing Out To Victory": Celebrating the End of the War—Mostly in Advance*

The content of the lyrics aside, the mere fact that songwriters were writing and publishers publishing numbers about victory already in 1942 argues for some premature optimism among the Tin Pan Alley crowd. But while the songs may have jumped the gun, rarely did any of them say that the victory would come soon or easily. Opening for a long run on July 2, 1942, *Stars on Ice,* the same Broadway ice skating revue that gave the world Al Stillman and Paul McGrane's fun and non-war-related "Juke Box Saturday Night," also included their "Big Broad Smile" (Mutual Music Society, 1942), most likely the first victory song to reach a fairly wide public for a long time, albeit in an ice show. Without using the word "victory" once, Stillman's typically tight, professional lyric conveys the idea without cliché or contrivance: "There'll be a big broad smile / On the big broad map of the world again / When we've won our way to glory and to fame, / . . . When the army's only foe is Notre Dame."

On July 13 the great but too shortlived Fats Waller recorded in his inimitable piano and vocal styling his "Swing Out To Victory," with lyrics by Ed Kirkeby. The number is the only celebration of projected victory in a jazz idiom with lyrics in a correspondingly appropriate jive idiom: "With a riff, and a break and a flair; trumpets blasting thru the air; / With a rap and a tap on the drum; yeah, man, solid, here we come. / . . . Let's get going, buddy, come on, spank the plank"—the last phrase being the '40s jive equivalent of the later "gimme five," "gimme some skin," or later yet "high five." It's a splendidly entertaining piece and has been reissued on CD collections of World War II songs, but there's no evidence that the wartime public took much notice of it. The recording by Fats Waller and His Rhythm was issued by Victor's subsidiary label Bluebird, but the song appears on none of the trade journal charts, including those for network radio plugs, or in *Hot Charts.*

The next major victory song found an audience both in a theatre—a movie theatre—and, briefly, among record buyers. In *Stage Door Can-*

*teen,* released in June 1943, Ethel Merman sang the shouting, secular spiritual "We'll Be Singing Hallelujah Marching Thru Berlin" (Music Products, 1942), with words by Bob Reed and music by Harry Miller. Prior to the film's opening and during the musicians' union recording ban, on December 8, 1942, Merman recorded an a capella version backed by the Andy Love Vocal Group (Talbot). That record was released before the film, *Hot Charts* listing it as an Extra for January and February 1943. Frankly, it's not a great song, mostly just repetitions of its long title phrase alternating with lines like "We'll put that old devil back in his place," but it's of more than usual historical interest. The second verse in the sheet music, not sung by Merman, begins "Gonna open up the concentration camps / Give those people another chance," very likely the only reference to the camps in wartime English-language popular songs in the United States, although some of the Yiddish war-related numbers include such references. Even though Americans understood concentration camps to be just detention camps long before they learned of the death camps, people didn't talk about them much, especially in popular songs. And, though it was written about a year after Pearl Harbor and the flood of Axis-bashing songs venting outrage against the Japanese, "Marching Thru Berlin" focused solely on Germany and Hitler as the devil incarnate, revealing how quickly American thinking (and feeling) reverted to its predominant pre-Pearl hatred of all Hitler's Germany stood for. In the song victory is synonymous strictly with the defeat of the Nazis and the end of the war in Europe.

One of the few other victory numbers of any consequence in 1943 also had its day mostly in movie houses, and it's a rare instance of an exception proving a rule—here, the rule that songs projecting victory were never unrealistically sanguine about those projections. The film was the R-K-O musical *Around the World,* starring Kay Kyser and his orchestra and released in November 1943, and the song was Harold Adamson and Jimmy McHugh's "Great News Is In The Making" (Robbins, 1943). In the opening section, Adamson, often exuberant but usually judicious, threw all proverbial caution to the winds (just slightly hedging his bets with the "seem" in the first line): "Reports from ev'ry quarter would seem to indicate / We've taken the offensive, / We won't have long to wait."

Also in 1943 three victory songs, an American rewrite of an English import and two numbers by prominent Alleymen, took a playful approach. Actually, throughout the war almost all Tin Pan Alley songs about victory were playful to some degree, while the solemn ones were strictly the products of amateur songwriters. To give it its American title, the British song was "I'm Gonna Get Lit Up (When The Lights Go Up On Broadway)" (London: Peter Maurice, 1943; Shapiro, Bernstein, 1943); John Klenner adapted the American version from the English original with words and music by Hubert Gregg. In no uncertain terms, the singer says he's going to celebrate victory by getting unapologetically, shamelessly inebriated: "I'M GONNA GET LIT-UP when the lights go up on Broadway / I'm gonna get lit-up like I've never been before / I'll be all dressed up in smiles, Oh! I'll roll 'em in the aisles / I'm gonna get so lit-up I'll be visible for miles." Irving Caesar and Al Koppell's plans for celebrating were more subdued but still included imbibing German wine and lager in their comic "I Always Wanted To Waltz In Berlin (Under The Linden Tree)" (Irving Caesar, 1943). Five mock schmaltzy-waltzy choruses catalogue all the things "I WANTED TO" do in Germany and will do when the war is over. Each chorus at one point slips in some silly bilingual word games: " Ein—Zwei—Drei—One—Two—Three—Ach! Du Lieber Victory," and later "Ach! Du Lieber Lager Beer." The song didn't attract much attention, but it's another one that's historically interesting for equating victory with defeating Hitler's Germany. The second homegrown victory number late in 1943 and early '44 was the only one to become a genuine hit. The sheet music for "Vict'ry Polka" (Chappell, 1943) gives credit for the lyrics oddly and formally to "Samuel Cahn" and the music to Jule (mercifully not "Julius") Styne. The number averaged 8th on *Variety*'s sheet music charts for seventeen weeks, and Bing Crosby and the Andrews Sisters had a hit record that *Hot Charts* ranks 12th in November and 28th in December 1943 and 39th in January 1944. A minor effort compared to Cahn and Styne's other great war-related songs, "Vict'ry Polka" still found a sizable audience, thanks to its upbeat, patriotic sentiments and a tune that is definitely a polka. Today we are so enamored of what we call 1940s "swing dancing" that we tend to forget the polka was just as popular among some large segments of the home front population as the jitterbug was among others. To its credit, Cahn's lyric packs a lot into a small space: inspiring sentiments like "When a man can proudly say 'I'm free' / We'll be dancing the Vict'ry Polka"; playful moments like "And we'll give a mighty cheer / When a ration book is just a souvenir"; and even a romantic one in "And we'll heave a mighty sigh / When each gal can kiss the boy she kissed goodbye."

The hillbilly voice was relatively quiet on the subject of projected victory, and the few songs by major country songwriters that did emerge attracted so little attention that none became even a *Hot Charts* Extra. Of the few, three were of the "hallelujah, jubilee, great day comin'" species of victory song, the faux hillbilly/spiritual: "There'll Be Jubilation Bye And Bye" (Hollywood: West'rn Music, 1943), by Alleymen Jack Meskill and Ernie Burnett; Zeb Carver, Billy Hayes, and Jack Rollins's "The Red, White And Blue Jamboree" (Peer International, 1944); and "Swing That Liberty Bell" (Peer International, 1944), by Billy Hayes, Hart Jones, and Bob Hilliard. The remaining hillbilly song was another equating victory with the defeat of Nazi Germany—Graham Prince, Fats Ryan, and Esther Van Sciver's "When The U. S. Band Plays Dixie In Berlin" (Bob Miller, 1943).

Also written in 1943, but not making a popular impact until the fall of 1944, was Sgt. Joe Bushkin and Pvt. John De Vries's rousing "(There'll Be A) Hot Time In The Town of Berlin (When The Yanks Go Marchin' In)" (Barton Music, 1943), which also focuses entirely on victory over Germany, "When the Brooklyn boys begin / To take the joint apart and tear it down / When they take Berlin." The whole lyric flaunts this kind of cocky Yankee self-confidence, and the melody and orchestration are in Dixieland style, combining to create the sort of upbeat, happy stuff that was music to the home front's ears late in 1944. The sheet music stayed on *Variety*'s weekly charts throughout October and part of November, and the recording by Bing Crosby and the Andrews Sisters ranks in *Hot Charts* for September through December with highs of 15th in October and 16th in November.

It's intriguing and inexplicable that of all the Tin Pan Alley and hillbilly songs celebrating a projected victory, none—literally not *one*—was written, published, and recorded to celebrate the *actual* victory over Japan or the final, complete end of the war in the summer of 1945. The closest any songs came were two that applauded partial victories, one of them while still acknowledging that there was yet more to be done. An advertisement on page 32 of the July 5, 1944, issue of *Variety* suggests that Jack Rosenberg, Paul Cunningham, and Ira Schuster wrote and Paull-Pioneer published the original "Paris Will Be Paris Once Again" sometime after D-Day, when the Allied armies were advancing toward the French capital. Shortly after British and American troops actually liberated Paris on August 25, the writers and publishers came out with their revised "Victory Version," reflecting the actuality, rather than the prospect, of the event: "Ev'ry ma'mo'zelle was gay / As the kids from Ioway / Taught them how to boogie woogie / On the Rue de la Paix." Of considerably more interest but no more commercial success was Cliff Friend and Charlie Tobias's sequel to their briefly triumphant rouser from the very outbreak of the war, "We Did It Before And We Can Do It Again." The 1944 copyright date indicates that Friend and Tobias were ready with "We Did It Before And Now We've Done It Again (Victory Version)" (Witmark, 1944) well in advance of Germany's surrender on May 7, 1945. Historically inaccurate as part of the lyric may be, it seems somehow fitting that the writers of the first great American militant number of the war revised it to write the only song celebrating the actual victory over one of the Axis powers. The historical inaccuracy comes in the song's lines that make it appear that the entry into Berlin was an American effort: "The day we started we knew we'd win / We said we would and we took Berlin." In fact, the Soviet forces entered the German capital first, on August 23, a week after Russian troops had begun an all-out attack on the city. The song is laced, as might be expected, with American bravado like "And now they know what a G. I. Joe / Can do to supermen." Yet while basking in the Allied victory over Germany, Friend and Tobias made it plain at the song's end that there was more to do (getting in a Japan-bashing slur along the way): "And now we'll go into Tokio / And show those monkey men / WE DID IT BEFORE — WE'VE DONE IT AGAIN." Of course, despite all of the songs that mentioned American troops marching through Tokyo, they never did. Perhaps the way the war with Japan ended with the dropping of the two atomic bombs was so overwhelming that it effectively squelched the writing of any victory songs celebrating such an event.

### *"Waitin' For The Train To Come In"*: The Boys Come Home

Songs about returning GIs can be divided broadly into two types: those anticipating their arrival, and those about them being home again. Romantic songs from the standpoint of the girl back home dominate both types; others express the thoughts of family, friends, or even larger groups of people, though few of these had much commercial viability. A few of both types were also written from the perspective of the returning or just-returned serviceman; a couple of these from the folk tradition are significant because they were atypically dark and negative. But, as might be expected, most homecoming songs were upbeat and celebratory, even while some were simultaneously lush, sentimental, and romantic. The anticipatory songs began early and continued through the war's end and beyond since many boys didn't return home till long after the war was over, while, generally speaking, those about GIs already home began to appear rather late in the war and also continued into 1946.

The year 1942 saw the writing and publishing of a few generic, premature, and unexceptional returning GI songs, such as George Miles and Bobby Gregory's hillbilly tune "Till The Boys Come Home" (American Music, 1942) and Alleyman Buck Ram's "When The Gang Gets Together Once Again" (Noble Music, 1942). And 1943 produced the only one of seventy-some homecoming songs that was a mother song—and it was a hillbilly number. Dave "Red River Dave" McEnery, a songwriter who was never embarrassed to wear his sentiment on his sleeve, did so this time in "We'll Be Coming Back This Year" (Southern Music, 1943), one of the few songs expressing undue optimism about the war's duration. Just the diction in the first line of the verse, "I saw a sweet lonesome mother" reading a letter, lets listeners know where McEnery's song is headed, and he doesn't disappoint them: "We'll be back this coming year and gray skies will disappear, / When fathers, sons and brothers all come home . . . so keep praying Mother dear, / Till I kiss away each tear this coming year." Only in 1944 did songs of real merit anticipating or celebrating a GI's return start to get popular. The earliest anticipatory one that gained the public's notice was "When My Man Comes Home" (no publishing information available), by black bandleader Buddy Johnson and J. Mayo Williams. Written in something close to traditional blues form, the singer declares she "won't start nuthin'" till her soldier boyfriend is back. Johnson, with his twenty-year-old sister Ella on vocal, scored a modest hit with their Decca disk, ranked 42nd in *Hot Charts* for March 1944 and remaining an Extra through July.

Phil Moore's "There'll Be A Jubilee" (Leeds, 1943) was also published in 1943 but not recorded until late in 1944, most likely because of the recording ban, and then for only a limited audience. The number sounds like a spiritual, shouting hallelujah on behalf of the home front girls for the day their guys come back: "Your man and my man too, Your man and my man too, Your man and my man too, / Will be comin' home to stay." Moore's melody is infectious, and the rendition by Mildred Bailey with Benny Goodman and His V-Disc All-Stars, recorded on July 31, 1944, is an irresistible hand-clapper and foot-stomper, but apparently the only people clapping and stomping during the war were the GIs who heard the V-Disc, whether at home or overseas; there's no evidence that this far-better-than-average song was ever blessed with a commercial recording of any magnitude. Phil Moore's other GI homecoming number from 1944 found a substantial home front listening public. "I'm Gonna See My Baby" (Santly-Joy, 1944) is one of the rare songs in which the singer is a GI anticipating his return to the states and, most particularly, to his girl: "V mail's all right when you have something to say, / But V mail's not like when your arm's around your honey and you're home to stay." Recorded by Kay Kyser's orchestra, Johnny Mercer, and Moore's own combo, the Phil Moore Four, it was Mercer's record that is charted in *Hot Charts* at 39th in February and 28th in March 1945, the other recordings paving its way as Extras and remaining so through March. The only other 1944 number looking forward to a soldier's return was Frank Loesser's sole entry into this field of popular song, "When He Comes Home" (Words and Music, 1944). In Loesser's original lyric, the verse had a girl singing about a faithful "guy from New Orleans" (Kimball and Nelson 116); without altering so much as a word of the chorus, for the published sheet music Loesser merely wrote a new war-related verse beginning "I'm the girl the soldier left behind." She's also the girl of a man who's "been gone before" but always comes back, so she's not a bit worried about him being away at war, because "When he comes home, he comes right straight home to me, / Right straight home to me, not to Mabel or Marie." A typically well-crafted Frank Loesser song, its bouncy rhythm and melody perfectly match the girl's confident faith in her GI's safe—and faithful—homecoming. It isn't clear when Loesser wrote the revised verse, but it was available for Ginny Simms to perform on her weekly radio show late in 1944, possibly on December 5.

Since contingents of American troops returned home periodically throughout the war and long afterward, it isn't as curious as it first seems to be that more songs still anticipating a GI's return were written or made popular in 1945—mostly in the latter half of the year—than in 1944, including the three biggest hits among such songs. Bob Russell and Carmen Lombardo's "Back Home For Keeps" (Irving Berlin Music, 1945) wasn't one of those but is of real sociological interest in light of a phenomenon that began as servicemen returned. The number is another song in which a GI still overseas reflects on coming home, and his reflection includes a rather astonishing admission: "You'll sweetly kiss the angry years away / Some things will have changed, that much we knew from the start. / We wanted them changed, after all that's why we're apart." While the last line implies the global changes effected by the defeat of the Axis Powers, the line just previous is a personal admission that long separations have the power to change things between two people in a relationship. The rest of the song suggests that this couple will withstand the changes, but too often that wasn't the case for returning GIs and their girls—especially their wives—once the men were back. Indeed, "the burden of long separation between servicemen and their wives" took a real toll on American marriages; in 1945 over half a million "were dissolved—almost double the prewar figure" (Bailey 147). Russell and Lombardo's song appears to be the only one that glances at the war's role in America's increasing number of divorces and annulments. Even hillbilly songwriting, frequently adventurous and often dark, opted not to go there.

In 1945, four Tin Pan Alley songs anticipating a GI's return found a substantial listening audience. The earliest one began to attract the public's notice in spring. Mentioned briefly in chapter 1 for its serious playfulness with meanings of the verb "to count," "Counting The Days" is a song, at least in my estimation, that deserved better than it got, with Hy Zaret's warm, intelligent lyric perfectly complemented by Alex Kramer's richly melodious music. Though the girl is lonely and longing for her absent GI, throughout the lyric she is steadfastly confident he'll return: "No need to worry, I tell my heart, / . . . It's just a matter of time, / Till I'm counting the days with you." The recordings by Dinah Shore and Frankie Carle with Paul Allen's vocal both had some short-lived success, each a *Hot Charts* Extra for May and June, with Carle's ranked 38th in July. While Ruth Lowe in fact wrote a few moderately successful songs other than her runaway hit "I'll Never Smile Again," for all intents and purposes

Frances Ash was absolutely a one-song woman, scoring big in the summer of 1945 with "I'm Gonna Love That Guy (Like He's Never Been Loved Before)" (Bourne Music, 1945). With its singable, breezy swingtime music and a lyric that, while not brilliant, candidly conveys a girl's intense desire to be with her absent GI again ("I'm gonna kiss that guy like he's never been kissed before"), it's hard to comprehend why no reasonably accessible records indicate that Ms. Ash ever wrote another song. Photos and captions on variant issues of the sheet music show that "I'm Gonna Love That Guy" was performed, perhaps even recorded, by Eddie Stone, Kay Armen, Monica Lewis on radio's *Chesterfield Program,* and Freddy Martin, but it was Perry Como's record, with the title altered to "I'm Gonna Love That Gal" and appropriate lyric changes, that made the song a hit. First in *Hot Charts* for July 1945 in 22nd place, it moves up to 14th in August, 11th in September, and back down only slightly to 16th in October, when Benny Goodman's record with Dottie Reid's vocal joins it in 31st place. By the week of October 17, the sheet music was the 7th best-selling nationally according to *Variety,* and the song stayed nine weeks on the *Hit Parade,* in 3rd place for one.

In midsummer, as "I'm Gonna Love That Guy" was moving up the charts, Buddy Kaye and Sam Medoff ambled onto the soon-to-be-returning soldier scene with "I'll Be Walkin' With My Honey Soon, Soon, Soon" (Republic, 1945). The song became a strong seller for Sammy Kaye with Nancy Norman's vocal from August 1945 all the way through February 1946, an Extra in *Hot Charts* for most of those months but ranked 24th in October and 28th in November 1945. Like so many anticipatory songs, the mood of the girl back home is bright and positive in the verse: "But until the day I can show him the way, / I'll keep an optimistic view." But with lines like "I'LL BE WALKIN' WITH MY HONEY down honeymoon lane soon, soon, soon," the lyrics of the chorus are nothing to write home about. Still, they work well with Medoff's music, a foxtrot clearly intended for dancing, which probably helped the song's success. Also in August, Irving Berlin made a contribution to songs about GIs coming home. Shortly after Japan surrendered on August 14, Berlin's publishing house took out a full-page ad on page 56 of *Variety* for August 22, heralding his "Just A Blue Serge Suit" (Irving Berlin Music, 1945) as "*THE FIRST POSTWAR SONG!*" Whether the hype was accurate or not, the song is another from a serviceman's perspective but unusual in that it's written not in the first person but in the third, briefly listing a GI's desiderata for his return home: "JUST A BLUE SERGE SUIT and a bright new necktie, / A room of his own with a door," concluding with "All that he wants to do is go out walking / IN A BLUE SERGE SUIT and a peaceful mind / With the girl he left behind." With its uncomplicated lyric and melody in typical Berlin fashion, "Just A Blue Serge Suit" attracted enough interest for *Hot Charts* to rank Vaughn Monroe's recording of it with the Norton Sisters at 41st in October.

By the time the last successful number looking forward to a GI's return came along, it was so late in 1945 that nearly all the songs about servicemen's actual homecomings had been published and recorded, with a few already, or about to become, hits of considerable magnitude. That an anticipatory piece like Sunny Skylar and Martin Block's "Waitin' For The Train To Come In" (Martin Block Music, 1945) could still find a large audience among such company was due in part simply to its being an uncommonly good song with strong jazz and blues idioms in it. In addition, as of fall 1945 many American troops still had yet to arrive home. While the girl's loneliness is present ("I've counted ev'ry minute of each livelong day, / Been so melancholy since he went away"), her diction also exudes a kind of giddy elation as she awaits what is clearly the imminent, not distant, return of her GI guy: "I'm waitin' in the depot by the railroad track, / Lookin' for the choo-choo train that brings him back." The sheet music didn't generate much interest until December, but well before then three recordings of "Waitin' For The Train To Come In" are charted in *Hot Charts*. While none ever ranks in the single digits, all three perform well in the teens and twenties for months, indicating that the song sold well throughout the waning months of 1945 and early 1946. Peggy Lee's smoky voice and the jazz styling of the small band that is uncredited on her Capitol record made it the top-selling of the three, on the charts from October 1945 through February 1946 and peaking at 11th in November. The high for the Harry James/Kitty Kallen record is 18th in November, and Johnny Long's with vocal by Dick Robertson lags well behind, in the twenties.

Like the songs looking forward to GIs returning, the majority about their actual homecomings came in 1944 and '45. Most of those— including all that became hits of any magnitude—were of the boy-girl variety since that sort of song touched the listening public most personally. But a few numbers weren't about renewing a romantic relationship, and while only one of these had even short-term success, all four are interesting for their different, and in some cases off-center, perspectives on GIs coming home. One faux hillbilly number was wholly serious, two from the folk movement were darkly sardonic and ironic, and the last, the successful one, was anything but in its upbeat, zany tone. Fred Meadows, George B. McConnell, and Charles J. McCarthy's "I'm All That's Left Of That Old Quartette" (Triangle Music, 1945), recorded by country singer Elton Britt, wasn't afraid to face the grim realities of war and its aftermath for a returning GI. A cowboy sings of how returning home to Texas "was a treat for my two eyes" but "when I passed the Bunkhouse I began to realize / How things can change in just a year or so." He discovers that of the three buddies he used to sing with, one is "still over there, some-place," another is a sailor still at sea, and, as for the third, "A gold star lights the window that was once the Tenor's home." So, rather than elated, the returning GI is despondent and "sitting all alone tonight."

While the faux hillbilly number reflects a returning soldier's unsettling emotional response to coming home, the two folk numbers look with dark humor at how veterans were affected in more material ways by their return to civilian life. Written by Pete Seeger and recorded by him at an uncertain date during the war but not released (Logsdon), the more benign of the two numbers focuses on former soldiers having to adjust to life without the glamour of being in a uniform—or at least a military uniform. The overall theme of "Now That It's All Over (He'll Go Back To Selling Shoes)" is encapsulated in the song's repeated refrain of "Many a man who struts aroun', he'll have to be taken down," which applied equally to enlisted men and top brass. The remainder of the brief song illustrates its general thesis with such examples as "Be kind to workin' people wherever you may go, / The waiter at the table may be your old C. O. [commanding officer]." While many of its tag lines are equally comic, the overall thrust of Bernie Asbell's "I'm Lookin' For A Home," with music adapted from the traditional "Boll Weevil," is so bitter about how the United States treated its discharged veterans that it looks more like a product of the post-Vietnam era than of World War II. But, of course, what had been a seriously pinched housing shortage during the war was made even worse by the return of millions of men with no wife or parent to welcome them back, many of them effectively homeless and, since their discharge, jobless as well. Humor reigns in the early verses, as when the singer goes out for a beer after finally finding a room to rent with just a bed and a chair and comes back to find "five guys sleepin' there." But, progressively, the lyrics get darker and darker. In each of the last verses, the singer (Pete Seeger again, incidentally) says that if people ask him who's singing this song, he first replies, "I'm a homeless veteran and I ain't slept all week long," and then, "I'm a discharged soldier waiting on the housing bill." It would be difficult for a postwar song to be more direct—or disillusioned—than that.

But songs of this ilk were obviously not the stuff of Tin Pan Alley, which more often ran to the joyous, even ecstatic, emotions of friends, family, and loved ones over the return of a son, husband, father, or boy-friend. The joy even to the point of hilarity in Spike Jones, Milton Berle, and Gene Doyle's "Leave The Dishes In The Sink, Ma" (Pyramid Music, 1945) was so infectious with the public that it caused a quite unexpected if shortlived hit for Spike Jones's recording of this silly yet sincere welcome home to Sergeant Joey. The title is part of Pa's directive to Ma to drop everything since an airmail letter came saying Joey is on his way home. The rest of the song (all in mock hillbilly fashion) turns into combination block party and barn dance as friends and neighbors wait for Joe to arrive, which he does in the final verse. The lyrics alone barely hint at the number's spirit of spontaneous celebration, but a bit of it is seen in Pa's preparations for the party: "I'm goin' to the cellar, there's cider in the keg. / Bologna's in the icebox, and there's cheese and pickles too, / We'll call in all the neighbors, tonight's our night, Ya! Hoo!" The song's overall effect of barely controlled mayhem is created by the exuberant lyric sung to a melody and musical arrangement perhaps best described as hayseed-Dixieland and played by Jones's ensemble with its accustomed manic enthusiasm on instruments both conventional and highly improbable. Still, no GI could possibly have asked for a happier homecoming. The public liked it enough for Jones's recording to rank 37th in *Hot Charts* for February 1945.

What the public liked even more were romantic ballads about soldiers arriving home, liking none better than the first one of 1944, with its twenty consecutive weeks on *Your Hit Parade,* holding down 1st place for six. Without meaning to put down popular musical tastes more generally, that the home front had a six-month love affair with Ira Gershwin and Jerome Kern's "Long Ago (And Far Away)" (Crawford, 1944) confirms that in this case America's music listeners showed their proper appreciation for a truly great song. As well it should be, with words by one of the most literate lyricists of the twentieth century and music by arguably its single greatest melodist for Broadway, Hollywood, and Tin Pan Alley. With songs to his credit like "They Didn't Believe Me," "I've Told Every Little Star," "The Way You Look Tonight," and "All The Things You Are," the lyricism of Kern's melodies matches and often exceeds the lyricism of the words. Such was certainly the case when he wrote with Gershwin this simple, moving expression of a woman's ecstasy over her lover's return: "Chills run up and down my spine, / Alladin's lamp is mine, / The dream I dreamed was not denied me. / Just one look and then I knew / That all I longed for, long ago, was you." Gene Kelly and Rita Hayworth (dubbed by Nan Wynn) introduced "Long Ago (And Far Away)" in the Columbia musical *Cover Girl,* released in March 1944, and the song received an Academy Award nomination. By April *Hot Charts* already ranks the Helen Forrest and Dick Haymes recording at 14th, Perry Como's at 20th, and Jo Stafford with Paul Weston's orchestra at 33rd; records by Bing Crosby, the Three Suns, and Guy Lombardo also had some success. But over the long haul the Helen Forrest/Dick Haymes and Jo Stafford disks emerged as the big winners, especially in May, June, and July, when Stafford's ranks 8th, 7th, and 8th, and Forrest and Haymes's 3rd, 5th, and 9th. Between April 26 and July 26, "Long Ago (And Far Away)" never fell below 3rd on *Variety*'s weekly charts of sheet music sales, was in 2nd place for six, and the bestseller for three. Only one other GI homecoming song became a hit of comparable proportions, and it did so after the war was over, yet a few others during the course of 1944 and '45 are still worth looking at.

But first, a conjecture and a caveat. There's no arguing with the fact that Bud Green, Les Brown, and Ben Homer's "Sentimental Journey" (Edwin H. Morris, 1944) was one of the biggest hits of the war years, especially the recording by Brown's own band with Doris Day's vocal, which rode high on all the charts from February through September 1945 and was in 1st place for four of its sixteen weeks on *Your Hit Parade*. It's more than clear from the song's lyrics, however, that it has nothing to do with the war, though people probably thought it did. The timing of the song's release early in 1945, combined with its lyric about someone eager to return home, may have created in the minds of listeners an association with soldiers returning from the war, possibly helping to account for the song's tremendous commercial success. But it is patently clear from the lyric of "Sentimental Journey" that it is about someone who regrets the choice he/she made to leave the old hometown and looks forward to returning to his/her roots. This is visible from the opening lines of its arcane verse, "Ev'ry rolling stone gets to feel alone / When home, sweet home is far away," to the singer's direct question in the final stanza, "Why did I decide to roam?" Any association with the war came from listeners ignoring what the song really said. In any event, its tremendous popularity may have been partly responsible for precluding any significant success for the majority of actual GI homecoming songs while "Sentimental Journey" was popular. (Incidentally, the song contains one of the worst stretched rhymes in professional American songwriting, one so bad that the writers or publisher felt compelled to put the dubious word in quotation marks in the sheet music; desperate for a rhyme with "journey" in the final stanza, they came up with "Never thought my heart could be so 'yearn-y.'" Ye gods!)

To get back to numbers in fact about servicemen coming home, Bob Russell and David Saxon's "Wish You Were Waiting For Me" (Hollywood: Saunders, 1944) is intriguing for raising more questions than it answers. For people buying the sheet music, the cover art provided the setting for the song's unusual scenario. The drawing depicts civilian and military men and women in a train station, one girl in the foreground looking longingly but hopelessly at a handsome GI. The verse, not on either of the leading recordings, verbalizes that setting as "Happy faces, anxious faces; / The laughter and tears of a crowd." But the chorus survives beautifully on its own, as the girl looking around at the crowd sings in the first stanza, "There you stand alone at the station / Staring at everyone you see. / Gee! Somebody is lucky, / WISH YOU WERE WAITING FOR ME." The rest of the brief song develops and intensifies the girl's infatuation at first sight with a military man just arrived home. There have been plenty of songs about infatuation written down through the decades, but "Wish You Were Waiting For Me" is particularly poignant and perplexing for its unanswered questions. First, and most simply, the questions about the girl: Since she is clearly not waiting for a GI or anyone else, what is she doing at the station? Does she work there? Is she about to board a train to go somewhere? Or does she just like watching and cheering for trainload after trainload of returning servicemen, as many people did during the war? Whatever the case, she is clearly unattached and lonely, something nicely reinforced by David Saxon's music. But then there's the more baffling object of her infatuation. In the second stanza, the girl notices he's "Walking back and forth kinda worried / Wondering where someone can be." Is the GI's own girl just late meeting him or has she walked out on him without so much as a word? If the latter is so, and assuming he even notices the girl, the song sets up a wonderful tension as to whether the two might possibly connect or, most likely, pass like two trains in the night. Recorded by both Ginny Simms and Georgia Gibbs, Simms's recording is a *Hot Charts* Extra from October through December 1944, with Gibbs's disk joining it for the last of those three months. Very likely the number's unresolved drama and slightly melancholy tone kept it from doing any better as the boys were coming home.

Richard Nelson and Pvt. Cecil Gant's "Put Another Chair At The Table" (Leeds, 1944) found a much larger audience for a much longer time than "Wish You Were Waiting For Me." This argues that the home front preferred more comfortable, even if inferior, songs about returning GIs. The melody is as numbingly predictable as it is lugubriously slow, especially for a song sung by a GI announcing he's on his way home. (The Mills Brothers recording kicks it up slightly the second time through.) The song's title sounds like it will be about a GI coming home to Mother, but the lyric makes it clear he's returning to his wife: "I know that you've been blue, / I know you've missed me too, / But now I'm coming home to you, my dear." The song was first recorded on the Gilt-Edge label by its co-writer, black songsmith, pianist, and singer Cecil Gant, whose best-known number is his wartime hit "I Wonder." Gant's disk is a *Hot Charts* Extra from December 1944 through June 1945, but it was the Mills Brothers' Decca record that sold best, at 29th for May and 35th for June 1945. Allan Roberts and Doris Fisher's "Gee, It's Good To Hold You" (Criterion Music, 1945) has perhaps less to recommend it as songwriting than "Put Another Chair At The Table." Its appeal may have lay in its generic sentiments as a girl repeatedly asks her returned GI to "hold me, hug me, kiss me once more, / Hold me, hug me, kiss me like you did it before [sic]." Or perhaps the public just found the renditions by Jo Stafford and Woody Herman and His Herd musically appealing. In any case,

Stafford's record is a *Hot Charts* Extra from August through December 1945, and Herman's from October through December.

But then again, as we saw with "Long Ago And Far Away," sometimes the public also recognizes and rewards quality songwriting, and they did so in the autumn of 1945, a few months after the war was over, by making hits, one moderate, one major, of two songs splendidly expressing a girl's reaction to her GI guy being home. For a drummer, singer, and bandleader, Ray McKinley was a darned good lyricist on the few occasions he chose to be one. One of those was when he collaborated with composer Mel Powell to write the unequivocally hip and groovy "My Guy's Come Back" (Peter Maurice, 1945). Benny Goodman's recording with Liza Morrow's vocal is as much a jazz classic as a Tin Pan Alley popular song; and Dinah Shore's rendition isn't half bad either. Shore's first is a *Hot Charts* Extra in October 1945, then ranks 32nd and 49th for November and December; in those same two months the Goodman/Morrow disk ranks 45th and 37th, almost exactly trading places with Shore's. Short as the song is, its structure is intricate. The two verses are integral to the two choruses and in fact segue into them so they become an organic part of the whole, and, unlike many verses of popular songs, can't be cut in performance. McKinley's skill as a lyricist appears, among other places, in his clever images and quadruple rhymes in the first of those verses, which sets up the rest of the song: "Somethin's cookin' that rates an ovation, / Note that I'm in a state of elation, / Call the press in, I've got a quotation, / Tell the Nation MY GUY'S COME BACK," the last line sliding seamlessly into the chorus. The number is so good it could have become *the* homecoming song for the months just after the end of the war, if an even greater song hadn't hit the charts almost simultaneously and skyrocketed right to the top.

Sammy Cahn and Jule Styne's "It's Been A Long, Long Time" (Edwin H. Morris, 1945) lacks the verbal and musical complexity of "My Guy's Come Back," but that may be one reason it was the far bigger hit of the two. For the average music listener its tune would have been easier to sing and remember, and its succinctly stated sentiments easier to relate to, than the jive and jazz idioms of the other number. By contrast, Cahn's lyric and Styne's music are squarely in the mode of the Tin Pan Alley romantic swing ballads of the war years, easily accessible to popular music listeners of virtually any age or taste. In the familiar opening phrase of the chorus, "Kiss me once, then kiss me twice, / Then kiss me once again," Cahn's lyric seems to exhibit a bit of the repetitiveness of its contemporary "Gee, It's Good To Hold You," but it rises above that song's static redundancy in the buildup of the mathematical progression of how many kisses the girl is asking for. The popularity of "It's Been A Long, Long Time" thrust it onto *Your Hit Parade* for fourteen weeks, in the number one spot for five, and on the *Variety* sheet music charts it ranked as number one for six of the eleven weeks between October 17 and December 26, 1945, its popularity continuing into 1946. But its recordings mostly made the piece a hit in its own day, one of them immortalizing it forever. The three runner-up disks were by Stan Kenton with Julie Christy's vocal, Charlie Spivak with Irene Daye's, and Bing Crosby. All these records performed well—especially Crosby's—but the one by Harry James's orchestra with Kitty Kallen's vocal was leagues ahead of the rest, ranked in *Hot Charts* at 4th for October, 1st for November, and 3rd for December 1945, and then 17th for January 1946. And with good reason. Before Kallen sings even a note, the record begins with Harry James playing arguably the most thrillingly expressive trumpet solo in all of American popular music (not jazz). And when Kallen does sing, she begins with the verse, very much an emotional setup for the chorus, and sings the whole number like she really means it. This is a rare and classic instance of everything from a song's writing to its interpretation in performance working in favor of its success.

GIs were still returning in 1946, and songwriters were still writing songs about them. In fact, Sammy Cahn and Jule Styne wrote two. "Kiss Me Hello" and "I'm Glad I Waited For You" (Shapiro, Bernstein, 1945) both appeared in the Columbia musical *Tars and Spars,* released in January 1946, and both also repeat verbatim the theme and some language of their enormously successful "It's Been A Long, Long Time." These two numbers were not. But two songs—one American, the other English—that celebrate a serviceman's return in especially welcoming ways had their moment in the sun around the same time. Carmen Lombardo and John Jacob Loeb's "Seems Like Old Times" (Leo Feist, 1946) is best remembered (by any of us who remember it at all) as Arthur Godfrey's theme song on both radio and television years after the war. But the winter and spring of 1946 saw the moderate success of three recordings by major artists Kate Smith, Vaughn Monroe, and (naturally) Carmen's brother Guy Lombardo. In the *Hot Charts* rankings, Lombardo's is 24th in February, 23rd in March, and 33rd in April. Monroe's and Smith's disks rank only in April, at 25th and 45th, respectively. The melody is warmly romantic, and the sentimental lyric sounds sincere, combining remembrances of things past with plans for the future now that the GI is home again: "Seems Like Old Times, dinner dates and flowers, / Just like old times, staying up for hours, / Making dreams come true, doing things we used to do." The focus is on the present and future in the equally lovely English song, Ivor Novello's "We'll Gather Lilacs (Now That You're Home Once More)" (Chappell, 1945): "We'll gather lilacs in the spring again, / And walk together down a shady lane / Until our hearts have learned to sing again, / Now that you're home once more." Significant interest began in March 1946, manifested by the fact that records by

Tommy Dorsey, Gene Krupa, and Alvino Rey are all listed as *Hot Charts* Extras, Dorsey's moving up to 51st in April. Overall, Tin Pan Alley produced more returning GI songs of real quality than any other kinds of war-related songs.

### *"When The Lights Go On Again": The World After The War*

The two biggest hits about life after the war came not near the end but at the very beginning of the United States' involvement in World War II, one even starting its rise to success before Pearl Harbor. These two songs were also most often cited by the OWI as the sort of flagrant "peace-and-ease" numbers that weakened the country's morale and softened its resolve, which of course as we now know—and as was felt even then—was utter nonsense. Nat Burton and Walter Kent initially intended the earlier of the two, "The White Cliffs Of Dover"—already discussed in chapter 4—as a tribute to the fortitude of the English and a hope for restored tranquility in the British Isles once the war was over. But with the Japanese attack on Pearl Harbor coming almost immediately after the song was published and first recorded, it took on a meaning that hit home for the United States as well, helping to account for the enormous contemporary popularity of what went on to become an enduring classic of popular song.

The other big number looking forward to a better world after the war came later in 1942, by which time American forces were fully engaged in the conflict. It's fair to call Eddie Seiler, Sol Marcus, and Bennie Benjamin's "When The Lights Go On Again (All Over The World)" sentimental, but its sentimentality is couched in such original, concrete, and vivid images that it can be forgiven. Essentially, the song's two choruses are a list of things that will happen "when the lights go on" and "the boys are home again / All over the world": "And rain or snow is all / That may fall from the skies above, / A kiss won't mean 'Good-bye,' / But 'Hello' to love," and "Then we'll have time for things like wedding rings." Other images allude to freedom, peace, and commerce restored among nations. This combination of the global and the personal consequences of the return of peace is extremely effective and may have been one reason for the song's success. Other than "The White Cliffs of Dover," "When The Lights Go On Again" was the only peace-and-ease song to score big on *The Hit Parade,* "Dover" staying on the program for seventeen weeks, with six in first place, and "Lights" also for seventeen weeks, in second place for one of them. *Variety* first ranked its sheet music sales at 8th on September 16, 1942, the song then staying on its charts for twenty-three more weeks, usually the 4th to 2nd top seller. But the true popularity of "When The Lights Go On Again" came in its record sales, especially considering the competition. Dick Todd and Shep Fields's recordings had some success for a couple of months each, and Lucky Millinder's with Trevor Bacon's vocal is on the *Hot Charts* rankings from November 1942 through February 1943, peaking at 18th in January; Millinder's disk also made an unusual one-month comeback in December 1943 in 33rd place.

But the song is most associated with Vaughn Monroe, and rightly so. Monroe's record first appeared on *Billboard*'s chart of record sales at 10th on October 31, 1942. On the same date Bing Crosby's "White Christmas" was in the number one spot, and Kay Kyser's "Praise The Lord And Pass The Ammunition" was number two. Overall, "White Christmas" stayed on the chart for fifteen weeks, fading just after the holiday season, and "Praise The Lord" for fifteen also, with "When The Lights Go On Again" passing both by a week for a total of sixteen. Granted, Monroe's recording never competed in the weekly battle between "White Christmas" and "Praise the Lord" for first and second place. Well, hardly ever: though its usual rank was between 5th and 3rd, in the week before Christmas Monroe's disk hit 2nd place, clearly because of the song's message of peace in the world of tomorrow. Viewed from the monthly perspective of *Hot Charts,* in November and December, when "White Christmas" was 1st both months and "Praise The Lord" 2nd and then 3rd, "When The Lights Go On" was 5th each month; by January 1943, when "White Christmas" dropped down to 12th and "Praise The Lord" to 23rd, Monroe's recording of "When The Lights Go On" was still riding high in 6th place, with Lucky Millinder's holding its own at 18th. If this song is less remembered today than the others, it's most likely because the lyric's topicality was tied even more to its time than "Praise The Lord," but that topicality, painting a picture of a world worth fighting for, was something the home front very much wanted, or needed, to hear late in 1942.

Unlike "When The Lights Go On Again," most of the thirty-some "after the war" songs were comparative to absolute failures, probably because their music was less than memorable and their lyrics fell into the trap of repeating clichéd conventions about the "gray skies" and "storm clouds" of the war replaced by "sunshine, rainbows, blue skies, bluebirds" and the other happy trappings of songwriters' brighter tomorrows. But a few songs used stock material in ways original or creative enough to make it interesting. Two of these reached an audience by appearing in a film, even if they didn't make moviegoers rush out to buy the records and sheet music. Partly responsible for both was the ingenious E. Y. Harburg, a lyricist who avoided clichés at all costs, or if he had to use them found new ways of employing them in a song. This is what he did when he co-authored with Ralph Freed "Hanging Out A Rainbow Over The U. S. A." (copyrighted unpublished, May 10, 1943), with music by Sammy Fain, for the M-G-M musical *Meet the People,* and then teamed with Ira

Gershwin on the lyrics of "Make Way For Tomorrow" (Crawford, 1944), with Jerome Kern's music, for the Columbia musical *Cover Girl,* both films released in April 1944. Not exactly vintage Harburg, and each also the product of working with a co-lyricist (although in Gershwin a very fine one), the two songs still show how Yip could take some pretty shopworn phrases and spiff them up a bit for optimistic songs about life after the war. Typical of "Hanging Out A Rainbow" are such lines as "We've had a lot of stormy weather / But there soon will come a day / We'll be hanging out a rainbow over the U. S. A. / . . . And when the skies begin to clear up / And those sunbeams are unfurled / We will look up at a rainbow over the wide, wide world"—appropriate sentiments from the man who wrote the immortal "Over The Rainbow" in *The Wizard Of Oz.* In "Make Way For Tomorrow," Ira Gershwin's hand is very visible in the opening reference to a musical he wrote with his late brother George, but the felicitous phrases and internal rhyming in the rest were characteristic of both Ira and Yip: "Strike up the band for a brand new tomorrow. / . . . Night is through and a new dawn is breaking / We're on the beam with a dream in the making."

After Vaughn Monroe's triumph with "When The Lights Go On Again" in late 1942 and early 1943, only three other songs of the same kind had anything resembling a public life outside of the country's movie theatres, one of them becoming a short-term hit. Nat Burton came nowhere close to matching the quality and emotional power of his lyrics for "The White Cliffs Of Dover" when he wrote the words for "My Dream Of Tomorrow," with music by Vic Mizzy and Irving Taylor (Santly-Joy, 1943). Like the two similar numbers to follow, this one is a lyrical ballad of a slightly sentimental stamp in which Burton nicely embeds a personal vision within a global one: "In MY DREAM OF TOMORROW / You are so close to me, / In a home full of laughter, / In a world that is free." His vision of that tomorrow also should have precluded any cavils from the OWI, since the song has no illusions about it coming unrealistically soon: "So, my darling, chin up: We'll see it thru, / Till MY DREAM OF TOMORROW comes true." Perry Como sang the number on May 3, 1943, on his weekly CBS radio show, but, probably because the recording ban precluded most American name bands from recording it, the leading record of "My Dream of Tomorrow" was by the English orchestra of Peter Piper. Also, later in 1943 Perry Como had brief success with a curious little after-the-war song the lyric of which is entirely allusive, rather nicely taking the conventional images of rain, rainbows, the sun, and so forth and creating from them an extended metaphor that runs through the entire chorus. These rather clever words for "There'll Soon Be A Rainbow" (Santly-Joy, 1943) were by Henry Nemo, whose best-known song is "Don't Take Your Love From Me," and the music is by David Saxon. The interlocking images begin at the top of the chorus and continue to the end: "THERE'LL SOON BE A RAINBOW I heard a raindrop say; / He sang of the warm glow as he pitter pattered away." Como's recording is a *Hot Charts* Extra for September and October and ranks 34th for November 1943.

Closer to what would prove to be the end of the war, cautious optimism was again expressed in the opening lines of Charlie Tobias and David Kapp's "Just A Prayer Away" (Shapiro, Berstein, 1944), written and published in 1944 but making a mark for itself during six months in 1945. The first verse wisely begins, "A brighter day is on the way / But who can say how soon," but, typically, the major recordings by Bing Crosby, Sammy Kaye, and Kate Smith omitted both verses. Still, it's easy to see why "Just A Prayer Away" became a minor hit. David Kapp created a throat-catching melody that's hard to get out of your mind—vaguely folksy, patriotic, and like something you've heard before, though it's altogether original. And Charlie Tobias, an uncommonly good Tin Pan Alley lyricist, supplied words that are sentimental in a good way and touchingly personal. Following the song's repeated statement that there's a happy land somewhere, just a prayer away, the release continues, "Where the skies look down on a friendly town filled with laughing children at play / Where my heart will sing for it means one thing—I'll be home at the close of each day." George Olsen's recording came first to the public's attention and is a *Hot Charts* Extra in January 1945, remaining one through May. In February and March Sammy Kaye's disk with Billy Williams's vocal joins Olsen in the Extras and in April moves up to the ranked listings at 21st and in May at 33rd. Kate Smith then joins the Extras from March through May, but it was the late-coming record by Bing Crosby that really took off, ranked 6th in April, 16th in May, and outlasting all the others by ranking 26th in June. The song's sheet music was on *Variety*'s chart of top sellers for fifteen weeks from March 28 through July 4, generally in 4th or 5th place but hitting the top spot once on May 16.

The final number envisioning the world after the war broke the lyrical ballad mold of the rest by being a jivey, groovy, and utterly hilarious look at the United States reconverting from a wartime to a peacetime mode. With lyrics by Steve Graham and music by Fleecie Moore, "Reconversion Blues" (Chicago: PIC Music, 1946) was recorded first by Ivory Joe Hunter, whose record is a *Hot Charts* Extra from December 1945 through March 1946; Louis Jordan's disk joins the Extras in February and March. Typical of the song's four funny choruses is "I can walk right by my draft board, / Without gettin' no dirty looks, / I can go down to the grocer, / Without takin' no ration books. . . . / I got those RECONVERSION BLUES / Gonna buy myself a radio that cannot get the latest news."

It's perhaps coincidental but altogether appropriate that the cycle of songs about life after the war began with wistful longing for the future in a sentimental vein in "The White Cliffs of Dover" and "When The Lights Go On Again" and ended with the outrageous humor of "Reconversion Blues," which is not about some distant and uncertain future but about a here-and-now getting back to normal. Maybe, after all, this is what comic relief really means—taking a big, deep breath and letting it out as a big, long laugh in thankful relief that the war was finally over.

# Bibliography

Allen, Frederick Lewis. *Only Yesterday: An Informal History of the 1920's.* New York: Harper & Row, 1931; rpt. New York: John Wiley, 1997.

———. *Since Yesterday: The Nineteen-Thirties in America, September 3, 1929–September 3, 1939.* New York: Harper, 1940. [cited as Allen, *Since*]

Ambrose, Stephen E. "Eisenhower, Dwight David." *American National Biography.* Ed. John A. Garraty and Mark C. Carnes. Vol. 7. New York: Oxford UP, 1999. 374–79.

American Jewish Historical Society. *American Jewish Desk Reference.* New York: Random House, 1999.

"Anchors Aweigh." http://www.chinfo.navy.mil/navpalib/traditions/music/anchor1.html#History.

Anderson, Maxwell. Music by Kurt Weill. *Knickerbocker Holiday.* New York: Anderson House, 1938.

"Army Goes Rolling Along, The." http://lcweb2.loc.gov/cocoon/ihas/loc.natlib.ihas.200000019/default/html. ["Army Goes"]

*Army Hit Kit of Popular Songs.* Issued monthly by Special Service Division, Army Service Forces, United States Army. Random issues from July 1943 through October 1944.

Bailey, Ronald H. *The Home Front: U.S.A.* Chicago: Time-Life Books, 1978.

Barfield, Ray. *Listening to Radio, 1920–1950.* Westport, Conn.: Praeger, 1996.

*Biographical Directory of the United States Congress, 1774–Present.* http://bioguide.congress.gov/scripts/bidisplay.pl?index=T000175. [bioguide. congress]

Birchfield, Marilee. "Robison, Carson J." *American National Biography.* Ed. John A. Garraty and Mark C. Carnes. Vol. 18. New York: Oxford UP, 1999. 682–83.

Bloom, Ken. *Hollywood Song: The Complete Film and Musical Companion.* 3 vols. New York: Facts on File, 1995.

———. *American Song: The Complete Companion to Tin Pan Alley Song.* 2 vols. New York: Schirmer, 2001.

Blum, John Morton. *V Was for Victory: Politics and American Culture during World War II.* New York: Harcourt Brace Jovanovich, 1976.

Bordman, Gerald. *American Musical Theatre: A Chronicle.* 2nd ed. New York: Oxford UP, 1992.

Boyes, Roger. "Lili Marlene waits again in Balkans." http://www.timesonline.co.uk/article/0,,343-102873,00.html.

Brock, Gordon. "The Official Lili Marleen Page." http://ingeb.org/lmarleen.html.

Burroughs, Todd Steven. "The Double V (Pt. 1)." *BlackPressUSA.com.* http://www.blackpressusa.com/history/Timeline.Essay.asp?NewsID=104.

Calvocoressi, Peter, and Guy Wint. *Total War: Causes and Courses of the Second World War.* London: Penguin, 1972.

Citron, Stephen. *The Wordsmiths: Oscar Hammerstein 2nd and Alan Jay Lerner.* New York: Oxford UP, 1995.

Cohen, Aaron I. *International Encyclopedia of Women Composers.* 2 vols. New York: Books & Music (U.S.A.), 1987.

"Collecting British War Relief Memorabilia." http://ww2homefront.com/junkie5. html.

Day, Barry, ed. *Noël Coward: The Complete Lyrics.* Woodstock, N.Y.: 1998.

"Disney Song 'Der Fuehrer's Face' Razzes Nazis with a German Band." *Life,* 2 November 1942: 44. ["Disney Song"]

Doherty, Thomas. *Projections of War: Hollywood, American Culture, and World War II.* Rev. ed. New York: Columbia UP, 1999.

*Encyclopedia of Music in Canada.* http://www.thecanadianencyclopedia.com/ index.cfm?PgNm=TCE&Params=U1ARTU0001689. [*Encyclopedia*]

Ewen, David. *All the Years of American Popular Music.* Englewood Cliffs, N.J.: Prentice-Hall, 1977.

Flanagan, Hallie. *Arena.* New York: Duell, Sloan, and Pearce, 1940.

Gale, Robert A. "Pyle, Ernie." *American National Biography.* Ed. John A. Garraty and Mark C. Carnes. Vol. 18. New York: Oxford UP, 1999. 18–19.

Gilbert, W. S. *The Complete Plays of Gilbert and Sullivan.* New York: Norton, 1976.

Goldberg, Marv. *More Than Words Can Say: The Ink Spots and Their Music.* Lanham, Md.: Scarecrow, 1998.

Goldstein, Malcolm. *The Political Stage: American Drama and Theater of the Great Depression.* New York: Oxford UP, 1974.

Green, Col. Murray, USAF, Retired. "Off We Go . . . : The Story of the Air Force Song." http://public.amc.af.mil/band/history/afsong.htm.

Harrison, Nigel. *Songwriters: A Biographical Dictionary with Discographies.* Jefferson, N.C.: McFarland, 1998.

Hayes, Joanne Lamb. *Grandma's Wartime Kitchen: World War II and the Way We Cooked.* New York: St. Martin's, 2000. [Hayes, *Cooked*]

———. *Grandma's Wartime Baking: World War II and the Way We Baked.* New York: St. Martin's, 2003. [Hayes, *Baked*]

Heskes, Irene. *Yiddish American Popular Songs, 1895 to 1950: A Catalog Based on the Lawrence Marwick Roster of Copyright Entries.* Washington, D.C.: Library of Congress, 1992.

Hitchcock, H. Wiley, and Stanley Sadie. *The New Grove Dictionary of American Music.* 4 vols. London: Macmillan, 1986.

Hoehling, A. A. *Home Front, U.S.A.* New York: Crowell, 1966.

House, Son. *Delta Blues: Son House.* CD. Biograph Records, 1991.

Huizinga, J. *Homo Ludens: A Study of the Play Element in Culture.* London: Routledge & Kegan Paul, 1949.

Jasen, David A. *Tin Pan Alley: An Encyclopedia of the Golden Age of American Song.* New York: Routledge, 2003.

Jonas, Manfred. *Isolationism in America, 1935–1941.* Ithaca: Cornell UP, 1966.

Jones, John Bush. *Our Musicals, Ourselves: A Social History of the American Musical Theatre*. Hanover, N.H.: Brandeis UP, 2003.

Kimball, Robert, ed. *The Complete Lyrics of Ira Gershwin*. New York: Knopf, 1993.

Kimball, Robert, and Linda Emmet, eds. *The Complete Lyrics of Irving Berlin*. New York: Knopf, 2001.

Kimball, Robert, and Steve Nelson, eds. *The Complete Lyrics of Frank Loesser*. New York: Knopf, 2003.

Kiner, Larry F. *The Al Jolson Discography*. Westport, Conn.: Greenwood, 1983.

Kinkle, Roger D. *The Complete Encyclopedia of Popular Music and Jazz, 1900–1950*. 3 vols. New Rochelle: Arlington House, 1974.

Klein, Joe. *Woody Guthrie: A Life*. New York: Knopf, 1980.

Larkin, Colin, ed. *The Guinness Encyclopedia of Popular Music*. 4 vols. Enfield, Middlesex, England: Guinness Publishing, 1992.

Lax, Roger, and Frederick Smith. *The Great Song Thesaurus*. 2nd ed. New York: Oxford, 1989.

Leuchtenburg, William E. *The Perils of Prosperity, 1914–32*. Chicago: U of Chicago P, 1958.

*Life's Picture History of World War II*. New York: Time, Inc., and Simon and Schuster,1950. [*Life's*]

Lindsay, Cynthia. Textual notes. *The Frank Loesser Songbook*. New York: Simon and Schuster, 1971.

Lingeman, Richard R. *Don't You Know There's a War On*. New York: Putnam's, 1970.

Lissauer, Robert. *Lissauer's Encyclopedia of Popular Music in America*. New York: Paragon House, 1991.

Livingston, Jeffrey C. "'Still Boy-Meets-Girl-Stuff': Popular Music and War." *America's Musical Pulse: Popular Music in Twentieth Century Society*. Ed. Kenneth J. Bindas. Contributions to the Study of Popular Culture 33. Westport, Conn.: Greenwood Press, 1992.

Logsdon, Guy, and Jeff Place. Booklet. *That's Why We're Marching: World War II and the American Folk Song Movement*. CD. Smithsonian/Folkways, 1996.

Lotz, Rainer E. Booklet. *Charlie and His Orchestra: German Propaganda Swing, 1941–1944. Vol. 2: I Got Rhythm*. CD. Harlequin HQCD9, 1991.

Malone, Bill C. *Country Music, U.S.A.* 2nd rev. ed. Austin: U of Texas P, 2002.

Marine Corps League—Westchester County Detachment #254. "The History of the Marines' Hymn." http://www.mclwestchester.org/USMC/Hymn_History .asp.

McKuen, Rod. "A Salute to the Songs and Songwriters of WWII." Booklet. *Songs That Won the War: Something to Remember You By*. CD. Delta Music: n.d.

Meyerson, Harold, and Ernie Harburg. *Who Put the Rainbow in* The Wizard of Oz?: *Yip Harburg, Lyricist*. Ann Arbor: U of Michigan P, 1995. [Meyerson]

Millett, John D. *The Organization and Role of the Army Service Forces*. Washington, D.C.: Office of the Chief of Military History, Department of the Army, 1954.

Mohrmann, G. P., and F. Eugene Scott. "Popular Music and World War II: The Rhetoric of Continuation." *Quarterly Journal of Speech* 62 (1976): 145–56.

Morgereth, Timothy A. *Bing Crosby: A Discography, Radio Program List, and Filmography.* Foreword by Kathryn Crosby. Jefferson, N.C.: McFarland, 1987.

"Newsletter No. 24: Marlene Dietrich Collection." Filmmuseum Berlin. http://www.marlene/news-views/news24.pdf. ["Newsletter"]

"Norbert Schultze." http://jazzzprofessional.com/report/Norbert%20Schultze.htm. ["Norbert"]

"Nordyke Publishing Company." *American Song-Poem Music Archives.* Ed. Phil X. Milstein. http://www.aspma.com/labels/nordyke.htm. ["Nordyke"]

Osterholm, J. Roger. *Bing Crosby: A Bio-Bibliography.* Westport, Conn.: Greenwood, 1994.

Panse, Sonal. "Lili Marlene." http://www.buzzle.com/editorials/text4-23-2004-53290.asp.

Perrett, Geoffrey. *Days of Sadness, Years of Triumph: The American People, 1939–1945.* New York: Coward, McCann & Geoghegan, 1973.

Rosen, Jody. *White Christmas: The Story of an American Song.* New York: Scribner, 2002.

Sanjek, Russell. *Pennies from Heaven: The American Popular Music Business in the Twentieth Century.* Rev. ed. updated by David Sanjek. New York: De Capo, 1996.

Schubart, Mark. "New Music Council Seeks Songs for World War II." *PM,* 7 July 1943: 26.

Sears, Richard S. *V-Discs: A History and Discography.* Westport, Conn.: Greenwood, 1980.

Sforza, John. *Swing It!: The Andrews Sisters Story.* Lexington: UP of Kentucky, 2000.

Shull, Michael S., and David Edward Wilt. *Hollywood War Films, 1937–1945: An Exhaustive Filmography of American Feature-Length Motion Pictures Relating to World War II.* Jefferson, N.C.: McFarland, 1996.

Smith, Kathleen E. R. *God Bless America: Tin Pan Alley Goes to War.* Lexington: UP of Kentucky, 2003.

"Songs for John Doe." http://www.geocities.com/Nashville/3448/doe/html.

Stillman, Edmund. Narrative sections. *The American Heritage History of the 20's & 30's.* New York: American Heritage, 1970.

*The Story of Lili Marlene,* a.k.a. *The True Story of Lilli Marlene.* Dir. Humphrey Jennings. 1943 or 1944. Videocassette. International Historic Films, n.d.

Talbot, Bruce. Booklet. *The Victory Collection: The Smithsonian Remembers When America Went to War.* CD. Smithsonian, 1995.

Taylor, A. Marjorie, comp. *The Language of World War II: Abbreviations, Captions, Quotations, Slogans, Titles and Other Terms and Phrases.* New York: H. W. Wilson, 1948.

Teubig, Klaus, comp. *Straighten Up and Fly Right: A Chronology and Discography of Nat "King" Cole.* Westport, Conn.: Greenwood, 1994.

Van Der Hiede, Dirk (pseud.). *My Sister and I.* Trans. Mrs. Antoon Deventer. New York: Harcourt, Brace, 1941.

Visser, Joop. Booklet. *Spike Jones and His City Slickers: Strictly for Music Lovers.* CD. Proper Records, Ltd., n.d.

Waller, Maurice, and Anthony Calabrese. *Fats Waller.* New York: Schirmer, 1977.

Weatherford, Doris. *American Women and World War II*. New York: Facts on File, 1990.

Wecter, Dixon. *The Age of the Great Depression, 1929–1941*. Rev. and enl. ed. New York: Macmillan, 1948.

Weiner, David J. Booklet. *Something for the Boys: The Songs of World War II*. CD. Vintage Jazz Classics, Ltd., 1992.

Wentworth, Harold, and Stuart Berg Flexner. *Dictionary of American Slang*. Supplemented edition. New York: Crowell, 1967.

Wilder, Alec. *American Popular Song: The Great Innovators, 1900–1950*. Ed. and with intro. by James T. Maher. New York: Oxford UP, 1972.

Woll, Allen L. *The Hollywood Musical Goes to War*. Chicago: Nelson-Hall, 1983.

*WWII: Time-Life Books History of the Second World War*. New York: Prentice Hall, 1989.

"YOUR HIT PARADE"—THE LUCKY STRIKE HIT PARADE. http://nfo.net/hits.

# Index of Song Titles

# General Index

Bernay, Eric, 61–62
Betzner, Jack, 40
big bands, 2, 6
*Billboard,* xi, 20–24; "folk music"
   catchall chart, 50; popularity polls,
   26–27, 28
Bishop, Walter, 96, 208
black songwriters, 44–46, 67–68, 129–31
Blake, Eubie, 45
Blanchfield, Florence A., 169
Blane, Ralph, 127; army-life songs,
   102–3; homesickness songs, 251–52;
   love songs, 231–32
Blane, Rose, 220
Bledsoe, Jules, 67–68
Blitzstein, Marc, 91
Bloch, Ray, 129
Block, Hal, 152–53
Block, Martin, 135, 282
blues music, 44–45, 130, 212
Blue Star Mothers, 252
Bogart, Humphrey, 246
Bolger, Ray, 225
bombing songs, 152–53
Bond, Johnny, 224
Bonney, Betty, 232
boogie woogie, 101
boot camp, 28
Bostic, Earl, 231
Boswell, Connie, 81, 83
Botkin, Perry, 174
*Bound For Glory,* 152
Bowne, Jerry, 231
Boyd, Bill, 131
Boyer, Charles, 86
Boy Scouts, 202
Brady, Leo, 195
Bratton, John W., 61, 70
Braverman, Sam, 47–48
Breen, May Singhi, 194
Brewster, Kingman, Jr., 56
Bridges, Ethel, 103
*Bring On The Girls,* 223
Bristol, Margaret, 171, 172
British-American Ambulance Corps,
   Inc., 177
British songs, 9, 10, 14; Axis-bashing
   songs, 136–37; goodbye songs, 237;
   homecoming songs, 288–89; love

songs, 247–48; patriotic songs,
   72–74; romantic/sentimental songs,
   74–77; soldier salutes, 174; victory
   songs, 275–76; working-women
   songs, 194–95
Brito, Phil, 234
Britt, Elton, 122, 123, 282–83
Broadcast Music, Inc. (BMI), 3, 35–36
Brookhouse, Win, 47–48
Brooks, Joan, 268, 270–71
Brooks, John Benson, 38, 264
Brown, Jimmy, 229, 269
Brown, Les, 97, 232, 285
Brown, Lew: allies-support songs, 85;
   girls-left-behind songs, 261–62;
   homesickness songs, 255; isolationist
   songs, 59; service songs, 164; War
   Bond songs, 200
Brown, Nacio Herb, 151
Bryan, Al, 59, 150
Bryer, Ruthe, 208
Buck, Gene, 8–9
*Buck Privates,* 101–2, 110–11, 256
Bundles for Britain, 86, 91, 177
Bureau of Motion Pictures (BMP), 26
Burke, Joe, 90–91, 234, 266
Burke, Johnny: patriotic songs, 69; ser-
   vice songs, 167; Victory Garden
   songs, 205; War Bond songs, 200
Burke, Sonny, 226
Burke-Wadsworth Bill, 94–96
Burnett, Ernie, 219, 276–77
Burnette, Smiley, 191
Burton, Nat, 9; allies-support songs,
   87–88; celebrity songs, 144; goodbye
   songs, 243; peace-and-ease songs,
   289, 291; separation songs, 257
Bush, Prescott S., 178
Bushallow, Jon, Jr., 174
Bushkin, Joe, 277
Butler, Ralph, 73
Byron, Bob, 107

*Cadet Girl,* 69
Caesar, Irving, 276; civil-defense songs,
   207; defense-industry songs, 190,
   192; goodbye songs, 240; national-
   unity songs, 184; victory songs, 276
Cagney, James, 111, 164